PERSPECTIVES ON PASTORAL CARE

Heinemann Organization in Schools Series

General Editor: Michael Marland

Perspectives on Pastoral Care

edited by

RON BEST, COLIN JARVIS
and PETER RIBBINS

HEINEMANN EDUCATIONAL BOOKS

LONDON

Heinemann Educational Books Ltd
22 Bedford Square, London WC1B 3HH

LONDON EDINBURGH MELBOURNE AUCKLAND
HONG KONG SINGAPORE KUALA LUMPUR NEW DELHI
IBADAN NAIROBI JOHANNESBURG
EXETER (NH) KINGSTON PORT OF SPAIN

First published 1980

British Library Cataloguing in Publication Data

Perspectives on pastoral care. — (Organization in
schools).
1. Personnel service in secondary education
— Great Britain
I. Best, Ron   II. Jarvis, Colin
III. Ribbins, Peter   IV. Series
373.1'4'0941   LB1620.5

ISBN 0-435-80066-3

Typeset by The Castlefield Press of High Wycombe
in 11/12pt Journal Roman, and printed in Great Britain
by Biddles of Guildford

Contents

Acknowledgements

The editors would like to thank Michael Marland for his advice and encouragement in the preparation of this volume, and Dorothy Smith for typing parts of the manuscript.

Articles previously published are acknowledged as they occur in this book.

Bibliographical Note

Bibliographical and other references are given as endnotes to each individual chapter, under the heading *References*. Where appropriate, they are indicated by superior figures in the text, which correspond to numbered entries at the end of the chapter. Some authors have preferred to list sources alphabetically, in which case the authors' names (and where appropriate the publication dates) are given in the text.

Foreword

The *Heinemann Organization in Schools Series* is devoted to a methodical study of the different aspects of school organization in the belief that the quality of educational experience for the pupil can be significantly affected by the quality of the organization of the school, and that in the devolved British system of educational administration the opportunities offered to individual schools are very great indeed.

The phrase 'pastoral care' has featured from the first in the series: one of the earliest volumes was devoted entirely to its organizational background (my own *Pastoral Care*), and a later volume studied the role of *The Tutor* (Keith Blackburn). The present volume is important in that the editors have specialized in a study of the whole concept, indeed have directed the only 'Pastoral Care Research Unit' in the country. They have been able to bring together a very wide range of detailed studies, which between them consider the problems of the subject and produce a new synthesis of approaches, in a way that is most useful for the profession. The Contents list shows the breadth of their collection, and the fact that almost all those who have given time to a professional study of any aspect of the subject are represented. The especial achievement of the editors, it seems to me, is that they have not merely 'collected' (indeed many of the pieces are specially commissioned), but have created a dynamic relationship between the contributions, so that the reader is constantly aware of the tension implicit in the concept of pastoral care, and is led to create her or his own resolution of it.

Michael Marland

General Introduction

For many educationalists the 'seventies will be remembered as the 'decade of problems' when long-standing doubts and gathering uncertainties about the role and function of the school were expressed in one event. This event was the 'Great Debate' on the British educational system; and the occasion marked a confrontation between the ideologies of progressivism and traditionalism.

In the political arena of the Debate, the problems of the secondary school were perceived to be largely practical ones relating to the raising of standards and the provision of a curriculum more closely linked to the needs of industry. James Callaghan, then Prime Minister (revealing a hitherto undeclared interest in education), initiated the public discussion in his speech at Ruskin College in October 1976, arguing that the school was neither equipping pupils with the necessary knowledge and skills for today nor instilling in them a sense of vocationalism. His own words were well qualified, and in terms of their implications for practice less certain, but nevertheless they were widely interpreted as a call both for a return to 'basics' embodied in a core curriculum, and for the gearing of the school to the needs of a society moving into an age of unprecedented technological development.

Commenting upon Callaghan's speech at the time, one observer, Harry Judge[1] wrote that it was made to defuse growing criticisms from the CBI and TUC 'that industry was sagging because the schools were not producing the right chaps to create wealth — conveniently ignoring the awkward fact that there were no jobs'. It can also be argued that this oversight was no accident, since the speech was itself a tactical event intended, in part at least, to apportion blame to the school system for economic setbacks and therefore to identify schooling as a contributory factor to high rates of unemployment. Be that as it may, when Callaghan's speech was given in the public arena it was received as a criticism of the relative autonomy of the school, argued on broad educational and vocational grounds rather than strictly economic ones — largely, one suspects, because there were growing fears among many politicians and their administrators that the control of education now rested too largely in the hands of the school. Callaghan's statement thus was taken to be representative of widely-held views which questioned the degree to which earlier policy and organizational changes like the establishment of the Schools Council and the introduction of a broad-based 'liberal' examination system (CSE) had given teachers too large a measure of control over all aspects of the curriculum and of the personal development of pupils.

But the Debate was also a questioning of the nature of the teaching and learning process, fuelled in no small part by direct and veiled references to research being undertaken in schools. The findings of studies about courses for the ROSLA pupil were coupled with others about 'standards of reading' (Bullock) and grouping practices[2], and collectively seen to point to wide-ranging 'problems' about standards and evaluation procedures generally, which the comprehensive school had so far failed to resolve. Selective readings of Bennett's work contrasting different teaching methods[3], and to a lesser extent of the accounts of others like Sharp and Green[4] and Judge[5] were used to express doubts and criticisms of progressive approaches and of contemporary philosophies of social development at both primary and secondary stages.

So it was that when Callaghan and others remarked that 'the methods and aims of informal instruction are a cause for concern', their statements were taken to be a 'considered' indictment of new teaching styles on the one hand and as a call for more centralized control over schools and their practices on the other. The event was a signal for the questioning of teaching approaches which appeared to separate out, and leave out, training from education. It provided an occasion for the questioning of teaching approaches which, seemingly, were not compatible with any proposals supporting the introduction of a core curriculum. But more than this, the event can be seen as a political performance through which the public at large could be informed and satisfied that a vocational shot was being fired across the bows of the school; while at the same time educationalists and teachers were admonished for abdicating their duty to control as well as care for children. And an uncontrolled generation has no place in a programmed technological society.

Today, as we move into the 'eighties, the Great Debate has been shelved in the political arena; but its significance and implications for policy-making cannot be denied or ignored. Its effects can already be seen in the growing confidence of policy statements by Her Majesty's Inspectorate, in the prominence given to the activities of the Assessment of Performance Unit, and in the development of Social Education and World-of-Work schemes which are held to be relevant and purposeful for all pupils. Changes in the organizational arrangements of the school can also be noted which, in part, have been prompted by the Debate. The appointment of Vocational Guidance tutors to schools and the linking of academic with pastoral posts, even in large comprehensives, can arguably be seen as a response to a felt pressure to redefine roles with a view to meeting some of the problems highlighted earlier.

Yet it needs to be remembered that many of the statements made in the Great Debate were polemical and ideologically charged. And certainly some of the reforms proposed were contentious. The calls for a core curriculum and for a much more closely controlled system of education were made on political grounds, and in narrow vocational terms. As strategies for change they were not held to be educationally or organizationally problematic. Polemics masked epistemological questions about what a 'relevant' curriculum should properly consist of; and similarly masked sociological questions about changing individual role definitions, and the wider implications of having a central body control curriculum planning.

At the same time, however, the polemical statements of the Great Debate have had at least one salutary effect — that of calling into question established educational texts (the conventional wisdom), and of emphasizing the need for much more purposeful in-depth research into curriculum design, teacher–pupil relationships, the organization of schooling and guidance. Towards this end the Open University teams had already pointed the way, and others like Reeves[6], Willis[7], Wankowski[8], Davies and Cave[9] and Rutter[10] have followed. This book is offered as a further response.

Our book is intended to present a more considered and critical view of pastoral care both as an organizational arrangement and as an integral part of teaching and learning and of the teaching–learning relationship. Criticisms of pastoral care were implicit in the Great Debate in discussions about the vocational role of the school. But what was not called into question, yet on reflection needed to be, was the fact that over the last decade — accompanying the growth in the size of schools — elaborate and often complicated systems of pastoral care have been established in which academic affairs were separated from welfare and guidance. Formal hierarchies of pastoral positions were created with administrative, care, and control aspects of the teacher's role distinguished from the academic. Even a range of specialists in care were appointed to support the staff. However, in accounts, recognized to be the conventional wisdom, these structural changes were given approval through the issue of optimistic statements like 'these arrangements help to overcome many of the disadvantages of the large school and help the pupil to develop a sense of belonging' or 'these arrangements provide a framework through which individual identities can be preserved'. In all, emphasis was placed on the provision of a new form of positive 'support'. Seldom were questions raised about the way the structure would define roles, decide 'good' or 'bad' teachers, influence communication patterns among staff, or determine individual expectation and role identity in the eyes of others. Nor were pupils' understandings of the relationship between staff like the Head of House, the Year tutor, and the Counsellor, ever considered worthy of more than a passing reference; nor, either, was 'working the structure' a topic for consideration in accounts of pastoral care. Indeed, the addition of specialists to established structures had only to be justified in terms of perceived individual competences and the extent to which pupils availed themselves of the expert's services.

In the Great Debate the relative autonomy of the school was seen to be a problem and something to be challenged. But again what was not illuminated was the event to which schools, as relatively independent organizations, were and still are subject to fashion. Various systems of pastoral care — vertical, horizontal, school, house, and mixtures of two or more — were established and modified both to meet particular 'growing needs' (like the addition of a 'sanctuary' which had to be supervised), and as a response to the fashionable educational commonsense thinking of the time. Justifications for changes or modifications or additions were explained and legitimated in terms of superficial explanations like 'the new structure affords greater opportunities for staff to get to know their pupils' or in statements like 'it allows for a greater delegation of responsibility among members of the staff'.

Yet now what also seems so disturbing is that the schools were not fully to blame for the latest 'in' model of pastoral care being employed. Little published material was available which critically assessed the fashions or offered informed guidance for those planning changes. As Hamblin so perceptively points out[11], it was simply taken for granted that 'when any pastoral care arrangement is institutionalized — pastoral care happens (and solves problems)'. Or put another way, because pastoral care was perceived in additive terms — as the provision of emotional and behavioural first aid — its actual organization mattered little providing it could be justified in terms of enabling teachers to care more effectively.

That teachers may have thought otherwise or raised doubts about the recorded 'merits' of fashionable arrangements was not a topic for concern; although pointers to the problems facing the teacher were given by Marland[12], Moore[13], Bennett[14], and others concerned with the management of schooling. Only more recently has greater attention been given to the critical analysis of pastoral care as a concept, structure, and process, and serious attention given to the need to view it as an integral part of the general learning process of the school.

If lessons are to be learned from the Great Debate then the 'problems of the decade' need themselves (in Young's terms[15]) to be made problematic. This means that any informed debate about a future 'closer relationship between the school and industry' or on 'the establishment of a core curriculum' or about 'the raising of standards' cannot properly proceed without the discussion of the 'conventional wisdom' for informing change. Further, questions need to be posed about the sort of organizational structure which is appropriate for the provision of effective social education in both its narrow and broad sense; about the relationship between social education, guidance, pastoral care, and the curriculum; and about the distinction between generalist and specialist teaching roles, and the sorts of reactions that can be expected from implementing organizational change.

Historical, philosophical, and sociological analyses of welfare roles and practices must be undertaken. For it is not sufficient for strategies-for-change to be introduced on the basis of 'fashionable' considerations;

this, as we have all experienced through the Debate, only leaves the school open to ideological attack.

What is required is informed theory and practice — from a variety of perspectives on pastoral care — from which prescriptions can be drawn. In short, what is wanted is a 'new wisdom', and to achieve this educationalists, teachers and social analysts must be brought together to provide different insights and experiences from which all can benefit. This book of readings is offered as one contribution towards realizing this end.

References

1 H. Judge, *New Society*, 21 October 1976.
2 C. Lacey, 'Destreaming in a pressured academic environment' in Eggleston (ed.) *Contemporary Research in the Sociology of Education* (Methuen, London, 1974).
3 N. Bennett, *Teaching Styles and Pupil Progress* (Open Books, London, 1976).
4 R. Sharp and A. Green, *Education and Social Control* (Routledge & Kegan Paul, London, 1975).
5 H. Judge, *School is Not Yet Dead* (Longman, Harlow, 1974).
6 F. Reeves, 'Alienation and the Secondary-School Student' in *Educational Review*, Vol. 30 No. 2, 1978.
7 P. Willis, *Learning to Labour* (Saxon House, Farnborough, 1977).
8 J. Wankowski, 'Educational Counselling and learning-through-teaching' in *British Journal of Guidance and Counselling*, Vol. 7 No. 1, January 1979.
9 B. Davies and R. Cave, *Mixed-ability Teaching in the Secondary School*, (Ward Lock, London, 1977).
10 M. Rutter, *Fifteen Thousand Hours — Secondary Schools and Their Effects on Children* (Open Books, London, 1979).
11 D. Hamblin, *The Teacher and Pastoral Care* (Blackwell, Oxford, 1978).
12 M. Marland, *Pastoral Care* (Heinemann, London, 1974).
13 B. Moore, *Guidance in Comprehensive Schools* (NFER, Slough, 1970).
14 S. J. Bennett, *The School: An Organizational Analysis* (Blackie, London, 1974).
15 M. F. D. Young, *Knowledge and Control* (Collier-Macmillan, London, 1971).

SECTION A

Dimensions of the Problem

Introduction

Some time ago we published a paper which was designed to present a challenge to the 'conventional wisdom' that has grown up around the concept of 'pastoral care'.[1] At the same time we aimed in a modest way to make good some of the deficiencies of existing publications in this area. We argued for rigorous philosophical, historical and sociological analyses of pastoral care as a concept and of the institutionalized structures and processes with which it is associated in schools. Regrettably, the response to our challenge has been disappointing to date. The occasional accusations of 'cynicism' and 'negative thinking' which have been directed at our paper have not as yet been accompanied by the publication of any systematic and coherent discussion of the issues we raised. The challenge stands, and is reprinted as the first chapter in this section.

However, some of the themes we dealt with are developed in a number of places in this book. In this section, the chapters by Dooley and Hughes take up the idea that the concept of 'pastoral care' itself richly deserves close scrutiny. Dooley investigates the relationship between 'pastoral care' and 'authority', and argues that the intentional aspect of 'pastoral care' is compatible with the aim of personal autonomy only if its meaning is rather different from that which its etymological and theological roots suggest. On any reasoned understanding of 'education', the overtones of dependence and paternalism which 'pastoral care' evokes make it a singularly inappropriate description of what teachers *ought* to be doing.

Hughes argues that it is also curiously out of phase with the general trend of developments in educational thought and practice in the last few decades. The development of a child-centred progressive ideology, its translation into practice in many primary schools, and the growth of an enlightened Psychological Service are all seen as contributing to an education which aims at freedom and self-determination. Other developments (for example the Youth Employment Service) can also be identified with such objectives. It is therefore surprising that we should employ words which carry 'the aura of nineteenth-century unction and righteousness'[2] to describe an aspect of teaching which ought rightly to be about 'self-understanding, self-confidence and some measure of self-fulfilment'.[3]

It might be argued that it matters little what a thing is *called*, and that what is important is what it *is*. Such an argument is misguided. There is ample evidence from the Sociology of Education that the labels

we attach to activities and to those who engage in them are very significant for how they are perceived by the actors concerned. If we want
schools to function in a particular way, and teachers to behave appropriately, we ought at least to use words which convey adequately what
it is we are asking of them. There is a real danger here of a 'tyranny of
language' in which the objectives of education are distorted, and their
realization thwarted, by the use of inappropriate concepts.

The historical development of the welfare aspect of schooling is also
a theme in Craft's chapter. Developing ideas with which he has been concerned for some time,[4] he shows how the tradition of piecemeal and
incremental change in the social services generally has led to a loose
network of welfare agencies with considerable regional variation and
less than adequate channels of referral and communication. His is a
timely reminder that a consideration of pastoral care in schools which
does not take account of broader social structures will be partial and
limited. Such developments as the growth of vocational guidance, and
the appointment of School Counsellors and Teacher/Social workers are
important, but how these innovations relate to each other is not always
clear. The key problems are those of the co-ordination of the various
teams that exist within the school, and the creation of clear lines of
communication with outside agencies. One possibility here is that the
Counsellor could both act as internal co-ordinator and be an important
medium through which contacts with the outside world are established.
Both the role of the Counsellor and the concept of 'team' are issues
which are further considered in later chapters of this book.

Taken together, the chapters in this section sketch out some of the
broad dimensions of the problem of 'pastoral care' and argue for a
tightening-up both of our thinking in this area and of the structural
arrangements we make to cater for the welfare of our children.

References

1   R. E. Best, C. B. Jarvis, and P. M. Ribbins, 'Pastoral Care: Concept and Process'
    in *British Journal of Educational Studies*, Vol. XXV, No. 2, June 1977.
2   P. M. Hughes, Chapter 3 of this volume, page 30.
3   Ibid, page 30.
4   See M. Craft, J. M. Raynor, and L. Cohen, (eds.), *Linking Home and School*
    (Longman, 2nd Edn, 1972).

1   Pastoral Care: Concept and Process*

Ron Best, Colin Jarvis and Peter Ribbins

Introduction

Whatever the merits of the various innovations the British education system has seen over the last thirty years — comprehensive secondary reorganization, child-centred informal–progressive methods, the raising of the school-leaving age, open-plan school designs amongst others — a number of generalizations may be made with some confidence about them.

Firstly, it is apparent that these innovations have tended to be introduced as 'acts of faith',[1] or as manifestations of particular social philosophies or of political ideologies, rather than as a result of systematic and comprehensive empirical evidence of the educational and social advantages to be expected. Secondly, the debates surrounding such innovations have been more than a little confused by lack of clear and shared definitions of the key concepts involved. Thirdly, it may be asserted that the actual functioning and effects of these innovations are rarely exactly what their advocates expected and are apparently as likely to defeat the stated purpose as they are to achieve it.

While such innovations as comprehensive reorganization and informal–progressive methods are only now receiving their share of analysis and criticism[2] other developments of similar magnitude have gone more-or-less unnoticed. We have in mind especially the rapid development of the concept of *'pastoral care'*, the mushrooming of 'pastoral care structures', and of 'pastoral posts of responsibility', especially in secondary schools, in the last two decades. During this time 'pastoral care' has certainly 'arrived' as a fashionable category in the vocabularies of teachers, academics, educational journalists and administrators, and in the organizational strategies and structures of educational institutions at all levels. These structures have attendant upon them a growing commitment of economic resources for their creation and maintenance.

It is the purpose of this paper to make a preliminary statement about 'pastoral care' as concept, structure and process in order to open the way for a critical theoretical and empirical appraisal of this phenomenon. In so doing, we shall be adopting the critical perspective of social phenomenology which has now established itself as a (partial) alternative to conventional 'normative' sociologies of education.[3] Indeed, the phenomenological dictum: 'render problematic the taken-for-granted

*Reprinted from *British Journal of Educational Studies*, Vol XXV No. 2, June 1977.

assumptions of actors in their social contexts', informs our position in this paper, for we want to suggest that, in terms of the everyday practices of actors in education, 'pastoral care' is not (or at least not *necessarily*) what it seems. However, we do not wish to restrict our comments to the micro-situation of actors in specific contexts. Rather, we seek also to raise a number of broader issues which we believe need elaboration and investigation, and which derive as much from our study of the sociological and organizational theories of education and society as from our own commonsense understandings of 'pastoral care' as practising teachers and lecturers. These are issues which can perhaps only ultimately be dealt with at the macro-theoretical level within the debate about the relationship between educational structures and society at large; this in turn raises the problem of the relativity of knowledge in relation to competing 'paradigms' of society.

The present paper is concerned to expose these and other problems which surround the study of 'pastoral care', and as a preliminary to an empirical investigation it must be expected to pose problems rather than solve them, to formulate tentative theories rather than to test them. Nonetheless, we shall be sketching the plans of a particular theory about the blossoming of pastoral care in secondary schools, a theory which we believe is susceptible to empirical investigation and worthy of serious consideration.

The Concept of Pastoral Care

The general neglect of this concept amongst educationalists and social scientists is clearly demonstrated by the paucity of literature which deals explicitly with 'pastoral care' as its central concern. Most often it is discussed as one facet of the 'teacher's role',[4] or as a concept implied by students of 'guidance and counselling' in education,[5] or as a structural dimension in the formal organizational or bureaucratic structure of educational institutions.[6] Moreover, within the context of such discussion, 'pastoral care' is seldom defined with any great precision, and when it is, it is usually accepted as unproblematic in itself.

Thus, the NFER study of *The Teacher's Day* includes 'Pastoral' as one of the six categories of teacher activity measured, and tells us the percentage of the teacher's day which is spent in 'pastoral activities'. But what these activities are is very loosely described in the text:

> There are many moments during a school day when teachers are concerned with the personal welfare of an individual child: it may be that the pupil has lost his spectacles or dinner money, or is not feeling well; the teacher may talk to a boy or girl about his or her hobbies, a family outing or a brother's success at the secondary school. In a few cases, the child may have some serious problem that needs attention. Any of these events may be called pastoral. Added to these personal contacts, there are the broader activities such as Sports Day or Open Day, clubs and societies, which can often create an important opportunity for pastoral work.[7]

Similarly, Moore[8] contents himself with a description of pastoral care as 'personal responsibility for a specified group of pupils' before launching into a descriptive analysis of the organizational structures concerned with guidance in five comprehensive schools. Nor have official definitions of pastoral care been any more enlightening. For example, in 1968 the Scottish Education Department issued a document entitled *Guidance in Scottish Secondary Schools*, where 'guidance' was taken to mean 'the taking of that personal interest in pupils as individuals which makes it possible to assist them in making choices or decisions'.[9] Such vague conceptions as this are capable of very different interpretations, and according to one researcher (Bennett), the guidance systems which were subsequently established in Scotland were often characterized by serious disagreements about the organization, function and purpose of pastoral care within the schools.[10] There seems a strong possibility that similar disagreements exist in England.

It may be argued that such statements reflect the 'true nature' of pastoral care as an educational concept; i.e. that it *is* vague and nonspecific, that 'pastoral care' just does stand for 'multifarious kinds of personalized service'[11] and that it is unreasonable to expect more precise definitions. However, we repeat that educational innovations ought to be based on more clearly defined and shared understandings of the categories being used, and that this has hardly been the case in regard to 'pastoral care'.

Part of the problem lies in the failure of much of the literature to make careful distinctions between 'pastoral care' and such associated concepts as 'guidance' and 'counselling'. On occasions such words appear to be used as synonyms for 'that part of the teacher's role which is not concerned directly with the imparting of knowledge', whilst on others 'pastoral care' is used to describe the activities of 'ordinary' teachers with 'guidance' and 'counselling' seen as separate categories reserved for specialist roles within an institution' the Counsellor, Careers Adviser, etc. These alternative vocabularies present us with at least three possibilities:[12]

(a) that 'pastoral care' refers to the non-instructional aspects of the roles of teachers and others in schools, and thus includes 'guidance and counselling'; i.e. 'pastoral care' is the umbrella word under which the activities of the school counsellor, careers adviser, house tutor, etc., are subsumed. 'Guidance' and 'counselling' then become specific aspects of pastoral care rather than separate activities.

(b) that 'pastoral care' is related to, but constitutes a category distinct from 'guidance' and 'counselling' in so far as the latter refer to situations of personalized service, including advice and discussion of personal problems requiring a degree of specialist expertise and training outside the province of the 'ordinary' teacher. Thus, the class teacher gives 'pastoral care', but the specialist counsellor, careers adviser, educational psychologist, etc., 'guide' and 'counsel'.

(c) that 'guidance and counselling' is the umbrella concept under which 'pastoral care' falls as merely one form: i.e. the form guidance and counselling takes when it is provided by school-teachers within a particular institutional setting.

No doubt good arguments can be advanced in favour of each of these alternatives, but in the absence of an agreed usage some initiative is necessary. From our reading of Cicourel and Kitsuse[13] it seems to us that the interrelation of teachers' pastoral activities on the one hand, and the activities of specialist counsellors through referral, reporting, and the compilation and consultation of records on the other, is so fundamental and has such profound implications for the careers of the children involved, that we ought to be concerned with the activities of both. We therefore intend adopting the first of the above alternatives, with 'pastoral care' as a general or umbrella category under which guidance and counselling are subsumed. Caution will need to be exercised when referring to the non-specialist caring activities of 'ordinary teachers': 'pastoral care' may imply more than it ought and perhaps here should be replaced by an analytic category like 'teacher-care' for the exercise of pastoral care by the teacher in day-to-day routine.

In suggesting a distinction between specialist guidance, counselling, and 'teacher-care' we have provided what might amount to one dimension along which different orders of pastoral care might be identified: i.e. in terms of the status and expectations of the person providing the care. Such an internal classification of pastoral-care activities certainly seems desirable, given its multifarious character, and when combined with the conventional classification (used by Hughes, Moore and others) in terms of the *types* of service rendered, leads to the typology shown below.

However, we would suggest that conceptually these areas are not always distinct, nor can we assume they have substance in reality. The accuracy and heuristic value of such a typology can be established only by empirical study of what actually constitutes 'pastoral care' for the actors involved.

Typology of Pastoral Care

(With some conjectured roles which seem to be implied)

| | | Status of Provider | |
		Specialist (Guidance, Counselling)	Non-specialist (Teacher-care)
Type of Service Rendered	Educational	Academic counsellor Director of studies	Class teacher Year master Heads of subject departments
	Vocational	Careers adviser Youth employment officer	Careers master
	Personal	School counsellor Educational psychologist	Form tutor Class teacher Housemaster

The Growth of Pastoral Care

In the 'conventional wisdom', pastoral care is viewed as an essential
aspect of educational provision, facilitated by 'pastoral care structures'
which take the form of intra-school divisions (e.g. Houses), with such
roles as school-counsellor, careers adviser, year-master and form-tutor
built into them. These structures are support-giving, reassuring, convivial institutions whose functioning makes possible the fullest and
happiest development of the individual pupil's school career(s). The
growth of these structures is explained as a response on the part of
those who organize and administer education to a growing awareness
of the non-academic needs of children on the one hand, and the proliferation of choices and potential problems confronting children in
large, modern schools on the other.

This 'conventional wisdom' is informed by the 'second-order theorizing' of educationalists and other academics (e.g. Craft,[14] Hughes,[15]
Marland[16]), who have evolved a functionalist account of the growth
of pastoral care. Craft, for instance, sees three possible related explanations of this phenomenon:

(a) The post-war years have been characterized by the growth of an
egalitarian political ideology which emphasizes the right of each individual to social security, health services, housing, employment and
education, and thus to the possibility of social mobility. This, together
with the problems created by other egalitarian reforms in education
(e.g. the postponement of selection, non-streaming, and proliferation of
alternative subjects), has led to a shared belief in the necessity of
guiding and supporting individuals through the system.

(b) The anxiety-prone nature of advanced urban-industrial societies
with 'their rapid rate of social change, their cultural pluralism . . . the
decline of the large, extended family, the influence of the mass media,
and so on . . .' creates an 'acute social need' to which pastoral care is
a 'psychotherapeutic response'.[17]

(c) The demands of a technological society for specialization together
with flexibility and adaptability in its workforce have led to an education system with an unprecedented diversity of courses, and a daunting
array of choices to be made by those within it.[18] Pastoral care structures
are necessary to guide individuals in these choices and, in the process,
to ensure a supply of appropriately qualified labour.

Craft depicts the growth of pastoral-care structures as the evolution of a
device to meet the functional imperatives of a society in transition. Thus,
pastoral-care structures emerge both to manage the tensions and alleviate
the anomic effects of rapid industrialization and urbanization, and to
maximize society's utilization of human talent. In short, Craft's account
is couched in the vocabulary of grand theories of social order deriving
from Durkheim and exemplified by the modern systems approach of
Talcott Parsons.[19]

We suggest that such accounts as Craft's can be criticized from the point of view of an alternative macro-perspective on the one hand (that of the Conflict–Action paradigm) and from the micro-perspective of social phenomenology on the other. It is to this critique we now turn.

Critique of the Conventional Wisdom

Our first point is that discussions like that of Craft fail to treat as problematic either the first-person accounts of the actors in particular situations, or the 'second-order' accounts of educationalists and sociologists like Craft himself. We believe that a gulf may exist between what theorists and students of education *assume* about pastoral care, and what it actually means to those for whom it is part of the taken-for-granted routine of daily life (i.e. pupils, teachers, counsellors, and so forth). There may also be a disparity between the accounts actors give when playing different roles (see the typology above), and marked differences between the descriptions they produce in different contexts of accountability. For example, teachers' accounts when they speak or write as *educationalists* may be very different from those they give as practising *teachers* negotiating reality on a day-to-day basis.[20] At the same time, the possibility cannot be discounted that *none* of these accounts corresponds to that which would be offered by an unattached observer.

Our reasons for posing these possibilities lie ultimately in our experience as teachers and lecturers involved with pastoral care. This experience leads us to the view that there exists amongst teachers and others an 'unofficial' version of pastoral care which stands in stark contrast to the 'official' version of the conventional wisdom discussed above.

'Pastoral care' in this alternative version is a nuisance, a 'crashing bore', an impossible, impractical, and largely unnecessary diversion from the real jobs of teaching.[21] So-called 'pastoral-care structures' have more to do with providing the school with a workable division into teams for sports and other competitions than they have to do with genuine concern for the welfare of pupils. Similarly, so-called 'pastoral-care periods' are actually provided to facilitate petty administrative functions such as marking the register, reading the school notices, and collecting the dinner money. It is unusual, in our experience, for these periods to be used in conscious attempts to 'guide' and 'counsel' pupils: more frequently the time is passed in idle chatter or glum silence, or in administrative and disciplinary activities. Indeed, 'pastoral care' has on occasion been used as a euphemism for corporal punishment, and the connections in the literature between 'pastoral-care structures' and the control of deviance in schools, and the disciplinary–control function of many of those playing 'pastoral care' roles in our own experience, suggest that this apparently jaundiced view is not without foundation.

This raises a second major point which is the doubtful assumption made in the conventional wisdom that pastoral-care structures behave in the way their designers expect them to. We would argue that 'pastoral care' has been reified in the process of designing formalized institutional machinery with the result that the nature of pastoral care as a *human action* has been lost. Much effort is put into creating pastoral-care structures whilst the activities it is supposed to facilitate go largely unanalysed. Structure has been mistaken for process and the actual functioning of those within the structure has been neglected.[22] Of course, this phenomenon has been exposed in some of the literature; e.g. Burton Clark's exposition of the 'cooling-out function' of high-school counsellors in the USA[23] and in the similar work of Cicourel and Kitsuse.[24] But such work has been limited mainly to the role of *specialist* counsellors, and the role of the 'ordinary' teacher in pastoral care ('teacher-care' as we have suggested it might be termed), has been largely ignored.

In voicing these criticisms, it will be noted, we have slipped out of the vocabulary of the 'conventional wisdom' about pastoral care and into the vocabularies of phenomenology and the conflict model of society. In adopting the 'conflict vocabulary'[25] we may highlight the question of whether educational structures generally, and pastoral-care structures in particular, are necessarily the positive, functional, convivial institutions so readily assumed. We want to suggest that perhaps they are structures facilitating social *control*, rather than 'order', in which *alienation* rather than 'anomie' is the operative concept, and where 'deviance' may be seen not as the result of 'inadequate socialization' but as an understandable response for the individual in terms of the way he defines his situation. The emphasis here on the individual making sense of his world ('defining his reality') in what is essentially a context of *conflict*[26] has already borne fruit in recent sociology of education drawing on phenomenological and symbolic interactionist perspectives. Thus a good deal of the work on counselling in the United States[27] and on streaming and the growth of 'anti-school' or 'delinquescent' sub-cultures in this country[28] has demonstrated the necessity of focusing on the individual's definition of the situation. These accounts highlight the dangers of reifying human actions to the level of the 'functioning' of 'structures'. It seems to us that the conventional wisdom about pastoral care is lagging well behind such accounts and that the empirical study of the actions and vocabularies of motive of teachers and others involved in pastoral care is well overdue.

Empirical investigation might well find that for the individual teacher 'pastoral care' does mean something like the 'unofficial version' sketched earlier, and that in fact pastoral care is a consciously evolved device for managing a potentially explosive situation which enables the teacher to remain in control. Consistent with this would be a reinterpretation of the relationship between the growth of pastoral care and comprehensive re-organization, the increasing size of schools, mixed-ability teaching, ROSLA, and the proliferation of public examinations. Such developments amplify existing problems of organization, administration and control, and create a host of new ones. As a consequence of such development, 'pastoral care' may well be a mechanism for the imposition of tighter discipline on recalcitrant pupils now that they are perhaps a feature of most secondary schools (and not just 'modern' schools), of most teaching groups (and not just the 'D' stream). 'Pastoral-care periods' may well become a euphemism for 'administration periods' to enable a school of 1,500 plus to be run smoothly and efficiently. Similarly the 'Housemaster' may well become the last resort 'chopping block' when the establishment of firm and deep pupil—teacher relationships is greatly impeded by a proliferation of subjects and the exigencies of the timetable.

Of course, teachers and head-teachers are not the only actors whose definitions and motives in the area of pastoral-care provision would have to be investigated: policy-makers at national and local level and their professional advisers and administrators may play key roles in the setting up of pastoral-care structures. And of course there are other interest groups (teachers' and parents' associations, for instance) who have expressed opinions and brought pressure to bear on school organization.

We wish to draw attention to three related events which seem to us to have important implications for an explanation of the proliferation of pastoral-care posts in schools. These are (i) the creation of comprehensive schools by the merging of existing grammar and modern schools; (ii) the raising of the school-leaving age to sixteen; and (iii) the development of a stratified 'career structure' of 'scaled posts' in secondary education. We would submit that the first two confronted grammar-school teachers and head-teachers with unprecedented problems of discipline and control. At the same time LEAs found themselves faced with the poblem of locating, within the structure of the new comprehensives, largely non-graduate teachers who held posts of academic responsibility in modern schools. Agreements between the teachers' unions, the DES and the LEAs ensured that teachers would be offered where possible 'comparable posts' in new institutions formed by merging existing ones, but of course there were never enough 'comparable posts' to go around. In any case, non-graduates were frequently considered unsuitable to head departments teaching subjects to 'A' level. This coincided with a vociferous campaign from some teachers' associations for a more stratified career-structure generally.

We would suggest that the creation of 'pastoral-care structures' (Heads of Upper/Middle/Lower School, Heads of House, Heads of Year, etc.) to stand beside the traditional structure of subject departments in comprehensive schools, might have been a convenient solution to these problems. Such an innovation would provide an alternative career structure for non-graduate teachers, satisfy the unions, and at the same time provide a whole new structure of 'pigeon holes' to receive secondary-modern Heads of Department displaced through comprehensive reorganization.

If these conjectures are correct, we might expect that what passes for 'pastoral care' will, in the eyes of the pupils also, be very different from its characterization in the conventional wisdom. To them it may well mean interminable and boring House meetings with 'pastoral-care periods' in the morning, setting the key for the (equally boring) lessons which are to follow. It may mean a regular 'dressing down' of 'trouble makers' by the Housemaster for 'letting the Team down', and perhaps the ritual exercise of the 'ultimate deterrent'. Goffman,[29] Becker[30] and their followers have demonstrated the capacity for institutional structures to *confirm* 'deviants' in their 'deviant identities', and we would suggest that such confirmation of the 'bad pupil' role may well be an unintended consequence of the creation of pastoral-care structures and the playing of pastoral-care roles. Rather than alleviate the distress of *anomie*, 'pastoral care' may actually contribute to the *alienation* of sections of the school population.

Finally, it is important to remember the wealth of evidence suggesting that structural changes often fail to alter fundamental attitudes, leaving certain regularities in the education system unchanged. For instance, streaming was supposed to facilitate the fuller development of each child's abilities yet was subsequently shown to discriminate in favour of middle-class children and against working-class children.[31] The same was true of selection at eleven-plus for a tripartite system of secondary schools.[32] It may also be true of comprehensive organiza-tion[33] and of the binary system of examinations (GCE and CSE). In each case the general pattern of inequality of opportunity in education as between social strata remains substantially unchanged.

The question this raises for us is on what grounds it is assumed that the results of pouring resources into the creation of pastoral-care structures are going to be any different? We would like to know whether the pattern of differentiation between social classes in terms of selec-tion, streaming, etc., is being repeated in the provision of 'pastoral care'. For example, do middle-class children receive more/less/different 'pas-torial care' when compared with working-class children? The value of adopting a critical perspective on pastoral care must be assessed to some extent in terms of its contribution to our understanding of the relation-ship between education and society as a whole. If it is, after all, merely a disciplinary necessity and an administrative convenience, one is forced to wonder whether the so-called 'functions of education' in society are not also euphemisms for social control and administrative expedience.

Summary

The growth of pastoral-care structures in secondary schools, and the popularity of the concept of 'pastoral-care' in the vocabularies of a variety of people involved in education, have occurred in the absence of both a clear and shared understanding of the concept itself and a systematic and comprehensive investigation of these phenomena. We have attempted to correct this situation to some extent by discussing the concept itself, and preparing the ground for a concerted theoretical and empirical analysis of both the structure and the process of pastoral care.

We have suggested that the growth of pastoral care has been legitimated by relevant actors in terms of a 'conventional wisdom' about pastoral care as a positive and convivial institution within education on the one hand, and by theorists' accounts of 'the functions' of pastoral care on the other. We have argued that these have taken for granted a great deal more than they ought, and that empirical investigation which renders problematic both the actors' first-order accounts and academics' second-order theorizing about pastoral care is long overdue.

Finally, we have pointed to an alternative explanation in which pastoral care is conceived in terms of the meanings which teachers and others in education actually give it. We have conjectured that an empirical investigation may show 'pastoral care' to be less concerned with the problems of pupil-welfare than with the problems of *social control* and *administrative convenience* following substantial changes in the provision and organization of secondary education.

References

1 See, for example, Crosland's statement in M. Kogan (ed.), *The Politics of Education* (Penguin, Harmondsworth, 1971), p. 190.

2 Bennett's much-publicized research on informal-progressive methods and Benn and Simon's monitoring of comprehensive reorganization are cases in point. See N. Bennett, *Teaching Styles and Pupil Progress* (Open Books, London, 1976), and C. Benn and B. Simon, *Halfway There* (Penguin, Harmondsworth, 2nd Edn, 1972).

3 D. Gorbutt, 'The New Sociology of Education' in *Education for Teaching*, 89, 1972.

4 See, for example, S. Hilsum and B. S. Cane, *The Teacher's Day* (NFER, Slough, 1971), and D. Hargreaves, *Interpersonal Relations and Education* (Routledge & Kegan Paul, London, 1972).

5 Either as parallel to, subsumed by, or subsuming the role of school counsellor.

6 See, for example, B. M. Moore, *Guidance in Comprehensive Schools* (NFER, Slough, 1970).

7 S. Hilsum and B. S. Cane, op. cit., pp. 27-9.

8 Op. cit., p. x.

9 S. J. Bennett, *The School: An Organizational Analysis* (Blackie, London, 1974).

10 Ibid., pp. 112-27.

11 P. Hughes, *Guidance and Counselling in Schools* (Pergamon, London, 1971), p.156.

12 There is, of course, also the possibility that pastoral care is not so distinguish-

able from the learning/academic aspect of education.
13 A. V. Cicourel and I. J. Kitsuse, *The Educational Decision-Makers* (Bobbs-Merrill, Indianapolis, 1963).
14 In M. Craft and H. Lytton (eds.), *Guidance and Counselling in British Schools* (Arnold, London, 1969).
15 P. Hughes, op. cit.
16 M. Marland, *Pastoral Care* (Heinemann, London, 1974).
17 M. Craft, op. cit., p. 11.
18 Bernstein has given a similar account of the development of 'integrated knowledge codes' as a feature of contemporary curricula. See B. Bernstein, 'On the Classification and Framing of Educational Knowledge', in M. F. D. Young (ed.), *Knowledge and Control* (Collier-Macmillan, London, 1971).
19 T. Parsons, *The Social System* (Routledge & Kegan Paul, London, 1951).
20 Such a disparity between teachers' accounts in a related area is described by N. Keddie, 'Classroom Knowledge', in M. F. D. Young, op. cit.
21 For example, 'Another principal teacher said that the schools ran well enough without the house staff. He thought the way things were going education would be up the spout. They ought to get back to the three Rs.' S. J. Bennett, op. cit., p. 118.
22 E. Richardson, *The Teacher, the School and the Task of Management* (Heinemann, London, 1973), p. 146.
23 B. Clark, 'The Cooling-out Function in Higher Education', *American Journal of Sociology*, LXV, May, 1960.
24 Op. cit. (note 13).
25 These competing vocabularies are spelled out in J. Horton, 'Order and Conflict Theories of Social Problems as Competing Ideologies', in *American Journal of Sociology*, Vol. 71, 1965-6.
26 For a discussion of conflict and negotiation in the educational context, see B. Greer, 'Teaching', in *International Encyclopaedia of the Social Sciences* (Collier-Macmillan, London, 1972), p. 560.
27 For example, A. V. Cicourel and J. I. Kitsuse, op. cit. (note 13).
28 For example, C. Lacey, *Hightown Grammar* (Manchester University Press, 1970); D. Hargreaves, *Social Relations in a Secondary School* (Routledge & Kegan Paul, London, 1967).
29 E. Goffmann, *Asylums* (Penguin, Harmondsworth, 1968).
30 H. S. Becker, *Outsiders* (Free Press, New York, 1963).
31 B. Jackson, *Streaming: an Education System in Miniature* (Routledge & Kegan Paul, London, 1964); J. C. Barker-Lunn, *Streaming in the Primary School* (NFER, Slough, 1970).
32 J. W. B. Douglas, *The Home and the School* (MacGibbon and Kee, St Albans, 1964).
33 J. Ford, *Social Class and the Comprehensive School* (Routledge & Kegan Paul, London, 1969).

2 The Relationship between the Concepts of 'Pastoral Care' and 'Authority'*

S. K. Dooley

Abstract

The term 'pastor' clearly has a religious origin and is thought of in connection with providing spiritual sustenance. Such provision must be seen in relation to some concept of authority since the pastor's job could otherwise not be done.

It is likely that the connotation of a pastor in the religious sense has been carried over to the schools, especially when it is considered that schools are traditionally structures of authority.

What is necessary is to insist upon the conceptual link between 'pastoral care' and 'authority' explicitly, so as to judge the final appropriateness of 'pastoral care' in schools.

Introduction

As an idea 'pastoral care' is comparatively new in schools whereas the idea of authority goes back a long way. What may be true, though, is that both ideas are very much related; and it is the particular relationship which I would like to investigate.

At a basic level, for example, the idea of a father can be easily assimilated to pastor (as would be the case in the usage of padre); and at the same level, it can be assimilated to authority (as it so often is not only at home but in the august terminology of 'father-figure' which has achieved some status in psychological theory).

From the start, then, the biological aspect of fatherhood is not really being considered. What are being considered are the aspects of various expectations of a father: and here, the area of discussion is directed not at descriptive but at evaluative points. So 'fatherly' or 'like a father' are concerned with what values are placed upon the activities of a particular father.

When this evaluative idea is looked at, we may find that there is some analogy between the expectations of a concept of father and that of a pastor. What is worrying, though, at this stage is that some people

*I would like to express my thanks to R. E. Best, C. B. Jarvis, and P. M. Ribbins for their suggestion that this article should be written, and for their criticism of the original draft. Thanks are also due to the *Journal of Moral Education* for permission to reprint this paper, which first appeared in Vol. 7, No. 3, May 1978.

would expect a father to be operating much more in the area of command, than in the area of patience, kindness and concern. Would the same people have similar expectations when they considered what a pastor should be?

The idea of a pastor is importantly grounded in religious experience. 'Pastor' itself refers to a minister of a congregation; and this relates directly to the New Testament story of the Good Shepherd. Here the Good Shepherd, the *pastor bonus*, is the one who tends the sheep, who checks that they don't stray, who recognizes each one and who in turn is recognized and acknowledged as the pastor. Much is made of the lost sheep and the rejoicing when it is finally restored by the shepherd to the flock. The whole idea of this concern is in fact used by way of metaphor and allegory to illustrate an important point of Christian teaching.

So the idea of a pastor in a congregation can be thought of very easily with the kind of background that it has. At first sight, though, the adjectival form relating to the pastor is a little removed from its other usage in 'pastoral' poems but the actual connection can be found in its root word, and this may well be the clue in attempting to discover some relationship between authority and pastoral care.

The root word is *pascere* which means 'to feed', and it looks as if the other words as well as pastor itself which are derived from it, have scarcely moved away from their origin. As examples, the word 'pasture' refers immediately to the basic need of animals to eat; again, because of images of animals grazing in green fields which can be conjured up when the countryside is suggested, we have talked of pastoral poems. So, the arranging, organizing and carrying out of programmes with the specific intention of enabling others to eat, and further to eat what is beneficial and sustaining, is the job of the pastor. When, therefore, the notion of feeding others is applied to human beings, what is of central concern, as is seen in the story of the Good Shepherd, is that allegorically, food is conceived of in a spiritual way. It is in this sense, at least, that the concept of pastor brings with it a concept of caring, and for that reason, the mere addition of 'care' to 'pastoral' may not be necessary.

However, what has probably happened in the school set-up is that other kinds of care related to medical, mental, athletic and intellectual needs have not catered for the specific concern generated by the idea of a pastor.

It is very likely that this specific concern became an important consideration within the context of large schools, because here especially, teachers began to detect that pupils frequently lacked a sense of 'belonging'. These pupils looked as if they had needs which demanded some fatherly (or motherly) attention. Further, if the context had been small, as say in a home for maladjusted children, the term 'father' or 'house father' might well have been chosen. Because of the wider context of a school and its comparison with a parish, the term 'pastor' would have been more appropriate.

Now, in introducing the idea of pastoral care there seem to be two possibilities of interpretation concerning meaning. Both are underpinned by the idea of catering for needs: and it is at this point that the evaluative function of 'pastor' can be seen quite clearly. The first possibility is that simply because pupils had needs then these needs had to be catered for in terms of compassion. This looks to be a primarily moral but equally it may be seen as generated by a religious motive. Here, the pastor is to be seen principally, if not entirely, in a fatherly role of patience, kindness and concern. On the other hand, because schools have been traditionally associated with a structure of authority, and in so far as the primary aim of a school is to engender learning, then all else may have been subordinated to this structure and to this aim. This, then, would render the fatherly virtues of patience and kindness suspect since they would merely have an outward manifestation but would really be instrumental to the fatherly role of commanding and showing the way. Because of the instrumentality of the 'concern', the evaluative aspects of the father in his authoritative role would then be paramount.

In whichever role the father or the pastor operates, he is seen as the one who must decide. Now, in the school when it was agreed that pupils sometimes lacked a sense of 'belonging', this was not because pupils were consulted about the matter. They clearly had needs but while in themselves the pupils might merely have felt wretched, they were not able to be aware of their particular needs, or what is more, not able to identify any means of catering for them. A similar position exists within the idea of interests when these are thought of normatively. For example, when we speak of a baby's needs for affection and nourishment we are thinking on very similar lines when we hear that a doctor has advised a patient that a visit to the hospital would be in his interests (*cf.* Peters, 1966). In both cases there is no requirement that those in need have any genuine awareness of these needs.

What is crucial to the concept of a pastor is that he is the one who must determine what the needs of individual members of the flock are. He may, just like the shepherd, look for signs of ailments; and, like the *pastor bonus* in reference to humans, may ask questions very much as a doctor would do. His questioning, though, is not aimed at eliciting a viewpoint but at generating points of specificity concerning anxiety, pain or waywardness.

Now it may seem that because of the etymological and religious points which I have suggested, I am imposing upon the concept of 'pastoral care' a meaning which those engaging upon the task do not employ. Some of those actually engaged may look upon their work as essentially related to the personal development of their pupils, possibly in the sense of having an aim towards their autonomy. If this

is true, however, I would wonder why they lighted upon a term which
has a clear etymology, and following this, an extremely strong religious,
and indeed authoritative background. That this term was chosen to
be used in connection with a structure which was itself authoritative
may indicate that it was deliberately chosen.

What, of course, is possible is that because there has been developed
a general counselling function in some schools, 'pastoral care' has sometimes been seen to be synonymous with counselling. What is just as
possible is that because of the strong religious and authoritative background of pastoral care, some teachers have deliberately turned to the
idea of counselling as answering some of their particular objectives,
which in fact do not presuppose feeding.

It is therefore against this background that I want to argue that the
concept of 'pastoral care' is essentially related to authority. Here,
there would be points of comparison with teaching, but unlike teaching,
its final aim would not be autonomy.

First of all, the concept of authority, as Peters (Peters, 1966, p. 238)
has argued, is essentially related to the following of rules. This rule-
following applies throughout the various aspects of authority; and this
is highlighted especially when someone is in authority *de facto*, because
here, unless people obey the commands or the decisions of this person,
there is nothing at all in the concept. What is necessary even with an
appointment of someone in authority *de jure*, is that there is an expectation of rule-following, for otherwise the appointment would lack
meaning.

Clearly Professor Peters (Benn and Peters, 1959, p. 22) has in mind
a context in which rules are to be formulated and executed since he
makes a special point of maintaining that in certain areas, namely
those of science and morality, the idea of having someone to appeal
to who should pronounce on these matters, is to move away from
what it would mean to act scientifically or morally.

While this notion of having a context is clear, it is one that I think
ought to be emphasized, as once we look at the context of pastoral care
it will be seen that not all aspects of the concept of authority can be
applied to it.

The force of this notion of a context can be seen more clearly
by pursuing the implications of the various usages of authority. First,
a person who is in authority *de facto* does get obedience from others
but this is normally for the sake of a particular end which is related
to the exercise of that authority. If there is nothing to be done, then
authority does not arise; and the implication of this is that if it were
to arise, it would do so only in relation to its particular end.

Concerning a person who is appointed to be in authority *de jure*,
he is so appointed because of an expectation on the part of those
appointing that there will be a general submission to the legal system
in which his authority manifests itself. Here again, the submission

to rules is for the end of maintaining that form of activity which is sanctioned by the legal system.

Further, if an individual is an authority on a particular subject or way of looking at the world, then his expertise lies merely in such areas.

In all these exemplifications of authority it is clear that there is always a supposed or intentional end, and that end is related to the implicit or explicit end of the exercise of that authority. This is its context.

Now this context is one that is really apart from the person who is in authority or who is an authority. The actual context could be a cricket match or a jumble sale or an accident on the road; and anyone who is in authority *de facto* or *de jure* would be the one to listen to or to approach in the case of determining what should be done. Again, if someone is in authority, then the context could be horse racing or twentieth-century poetry, but in every instance the context looks to be independent of any particular authority. In none of these examples is there any idea that authority is being employed simply for the sake of authority.

However, there is one other usage which seems to be an exception. This is charismatic authority. Certainly here, Professor Peters (Peters, 1966, pp. 245-6) was right in drawing attention to a conceptual distinction that could be applied within this notion because a charismatic figure could be, but need not be, an authority on a particular subject or way of looking at the world; and, therefore, in looking to him for some kind of insight or guidance, we could easily be led astray, merely because we think that we are going somewhere or we are about to achieve some end.

Now, if a charismatic individual is of such a striking appearance, he may 'look the part', and what he indicates as good or true will be seen as good or true by others. Concealment or some other form of pretence may be practised by such an individual but equally he may be plainly ignorant or misguided. Here, there is frequently a context that can be seen independently of the charismatic figure. The context could well be the organizing of a state or of religious festivals or teaching. Clearly, in these situations it is assumed by those who follow that there is a point in what is being commanded or organized or prohibited.

There is, though, one aspect of charismatic authority which looks as if it exacts obedience for no end that lies outside of itself. Nothing at all hangs upon the outcome of the obedience to the commands of the charismatic figure: it is merely a matter of commands being issued for the sake of self-aggrandisement, and this is internal to the charismatic individual. To accompany this, it must also be admitted that some people do enjoy being commanded, and the charisma of a particular person is simply perfect for them.

It may be claimed that when this happens, authority is being abused and yet it looks like a legitimate usage of authority. When, on the other hand, an appointed or accepted person employs authority for his own end rather than for the appointed or accepted end, this looks to be an illegitimate usage, because the context in which his authority should be wielded is ignored. However, with this charismatic figure he is not claiming that there is any context outside of himself where something needs to be done. There is no special problem to be solved, no organizing of an event. It is simply that he gives orders, makes up pronouncements which he can countermand at will: and yet others willingly follow. These followers also have nothing in mind other than following. They do not even have to be convinced that all these rules are in their final interest since this is not even at stake. All that has to be done is to adhere to the dictates of the charismatic figure. The context in which he operates requires only himself and obeying people.

The force of looking at authority in this way is that it emphasizes a context; and as soon as we examine any context, like teaching or medicine or plastering, then the idea of employing this charismatic authority which exacts obedience for the sake of nothing beyond itself is inappropriate. Even in a context like teaching where there is a premium on authority, if the charismatic authority operates within his narrow context of himself and obeying ones, then he does not approach the context of intentionally enabling others to learn, which is the context of teaching.

In the same way, within the context of pastoral care, the function of authority will be necessarily limited to that context; and if, as a matter of fact, an individual employs authority for his own benefit or for any reason which lies outside of the meaning of pastoral care, then in no sense is he engaged in the activity of pastoral care.

Because of the connotation of pastor, it is clear that those coming under his charge are presupposed to have no vision of what contributes to their general advantage. Their goals are immediate. As a minister of a congregation, the pastor is likened to, and derived from the good shepherd: and both are seen to have been initiated into their proper vocations. Just as a shepherd cannot correctly be termed a shepherd if he is unfamiliar with the idiosyncrasies of his sheep, so a pastor cannot make a correct claim to the title unless he is familiar with the idiosyncrasies of his flock.

In the first instance, then, the obeying ones may not specifically look to the pastor to check that he is an authority, an expert in the requirements of the vocation. but this is certainly their expectation. There is, of course, always a difficulty here, and it is this. The whole point of looking to an authority is that he is held to have more knowledge than the others. However, this can only ever be comparative. An authority in biology may be merely very slightly ahead of many others in the field; and some of these others may well surpass him in a few years. Yet, for countless others, unversed in biology or who are beginning to study the subject, he will also be held to have so much knowledge that they can simply listen and be shown the way through the apparent maze. Now, while it is true that an authority is not eternally an authority, to those unversed, there is no means of seeing a distinction between an eternal and a temporary authority. This is precisely the position of young children in reference to an authority. This also is the position of those under the aegis of a pastor, for he is the feeder, the provider, the one with vision: and, to whom, otherwise, could they turn?

Not only is this the expectation of the obeying ones. If a shepherd or a pastor is appointed, as it were *de jure*, the appointment is a farce unless the shepherd or pastor is an authority. In fact, the distinction between someone being an authority *de jure* and *de facto* becomes much less sharp when it is understood that an expectation of obedience exists in both, and that both are underpinned by an expectation of expertise and vision. If ever a pastor were appointed whose knowledge of the aim of his pastoral work was weak or whose understanding of the various needs and interests of the members of the flock was poor, then he should not have been appointed, since principally the expectation of the ones being guided would be shown to be as nothing.

There is, then, a threefold expectation centring on pastoral care. The flock expects that the pastoral knows his job, that in fact he is an authority with regard to the context; those appointing would have no grounds for making the appointment unless they had reason to believe that he could and would act pastorally; and finally, he himself could not logically be a pastor if he had no expertise and cared nothing for the job.

Now, because of a moral evaluation of the obligation of a father or mother, it is expected that they will allow that their children will develop, and most parents will welcome the idea of the children being able to run their own lives. Yet, there may still be aspects of their lives where the children look to parents for advice and guidance where, even in later life, they see the parents in authority, or as authorities. More often, however, it is parents who want to organize the lives of their offspring and who dislike the growing autonomy of the children simply because they are to be viewed as children and not as growing people.

Concerning the organizing of the lives of others there is an interesting and useful point which has a great deal of bearing upon how anyone should presume to engage in an authoritative role. In the giving of orders, even the most simple, there is presupposed a minimal understanding on the part of the one who is expected to obey. Even in crossing a road some understanding of the possible passing of traffic is required; and where it is clear that a child has not reached the necessary level of understanding, the parent needs to be with the child continuously during the crossing: and, by analogy, the same would apply to someone offering pastoral care. As a child develops the under-standing necessary for small tasks, then unless the parent or pastor allows that this is so, he is not taking full account of the needs and interests of his charge.

Yet, immediately this is said, there is a major worry. This is that a pastor must operate within the domain of authority. Certainly he can aim to increase the understanding of others by explanation and by a form of justification; but if his very authority is questioned, then that he is a pastor is also necessarily questioned. He is, of necessity, a feeder.

With some fathers the notion of being in charge is of first and last importance: but what we would say morally is that if a child has a point, he should be listened to; and to know that he has a point we should be prepared to listen. The very act of being willing to listen will indicate that we have an expectation of the possibility of his having a point. However, it certainly looks as if when a pastor listens he must do so in reference to his overall exercise of authority in the context of guidance in which he alone has vision.

So it looks as if one major aspect of morality is actually missing simply because autonomy cannot really be part of the concept of pastoral care: nor can it be any part of the aim of a pastor.

The status of a pastor, then, is very similar to the status of a par-ticular parent or of someone *in loco parentis*, who continually insists that the relationship of parent to child is not only eternal but is the most important. It would, if anything, reflect a traditional view of morality which would carry an authoritative structure with it.

So, as compared with teaching there is a parallel with pastoral care but there is also a sharp distinction. Unless, for example, one accepts the teacher, submits himself to his authority (Dearden, 1976, p. 68) then one cannot learn from him. A teacher's job is always concerned with teaching something, and whether this something is mathematics or chess, the teacher's job (Peters, 1966, Ch. 1, Scheffler, 1973, p. 62) is to initiate others into activities in which they will finally be competent: and so any authority will only be temporary. Obviously, in children's early years the authority will be quite constant but finally that someone is a teacher for someone else can be questioned: just as, in a rational scheme, it can be the case of the pastor.

Teaching, though, looks finally to the competence of the learner: the pastor's task is to presuppose continued feeding. The pastor, there-fore, cannot finally look to the competence of any member of his flock.

What, of course, should happen is that when people no longer need to be fed but can cope by themselves they should dispense with the pastor. However, in so far as the pastor is concerned, the very act of dispensing with him, especially religiously, will indicate even greater need for feeding.

While in the actual field of pastoral care, even though it is employed within the wider context of education, the pastor's brief is authoritative. What should happen, of course, is that because pastoral care is simply falling under an educational umbrella, its position should be seen in perspective. Therefore it should be admitted that although the pastor should go on feeding, not everyone will finally need to be fed. This point has not been made explicitly.

Conclusion

In particular schools 'pastoral care' may be seen as an overall term to cover the kind of work which is done to promote the personal development of pupils. This work, again, may be looked at by some people as leading to the autonomy of pupils.

However, I have indicated that both the etymological and religious origins of the concept of 'pastor' point directly to the idea of continued 'feeding' or nurturing of people. Thus there is a necesary connection between a pastor and being authoritative.

Since, moreover, schools have been traditionally thought of as structures of authority, it is possible that 'pastoral care' was deliberately chosen to direct attention to the task of looking after and guiding pupils.

In the light of the interpretation of 'pastor' as I have offered it, there is a reason why 'pastoral care' may not always be an appropriate title for the work which teachers claim, and should claim, they are doing.

References

Benn, S. I. and Peters, R. S., *Social Principles and the Democratic State* (George Allen and Unwin Ltd, London 1959).

Dearden, R. F., *Problems in Primary Education* (Routledge & Kegan Paul, London 1976).

Peters, R. S., *Ethics and Education* (George Allen and Unwin Ltd, London 1966).

Scheffler, I., *Reason and Teaching* (Routledge & Kegan Paul, London 1973).

3   Pastoral Care – the historical context

Patrick M. Hughes

The history of the concept of pastoral care is a subject that might tax the mind of an experienced professional historian. 'Facts' are hard to come by and those that are available are not very well related to each other. Reputable histories of education make no reference to the concept. Official publications on education before 1970 contain no specific references to it and a scrutiny of Educational Abstracts offers no help. It is only since the mid 'seventies that it has put in an appearance in official government publications, and then only in brief and very generalized form. *The Educational System of England and Wales* of 1973[1] makes no mention of the term, while the next issue covering the year 1974-75 has an entry entitled 'Pastoral care, careers education, and vocational guidance' which reads as follows:

> Schools in England and Wales have long considered it important to provide for oversight of the well-being and progress of individual pupils. The reorganisation of the secondary system and the development of larger comprehensive schools has, over recent years, made necessary a more structured approach to pastoral care, under which it is usual to find that the care and guidance of each pupil on both personal and educational matters is the formal responsibility of a nominated member of staff, usually a teacher but sometimes a counsellor appointed specifically for this purpose. At the same time, increasing attention is being given to careers education in the schools aimed at increasing boys' and girls' knowledge of opportunities in education, work and life generally, and helping them to make considered choices for their future.[2]

The next issue dealing with the year 1976-77 contains about the same amount of information but is now arranged under two separate headings: 'Pastoral care' and 'Careers education and guidance'. Someone with time and dedication may yet undertake the formidable task of exploration and interpretation required to produce a history of the development of a concept which has so suddenly acquired official respectability. This present chapter is concerned not with its evolution but with the wider historical context to which its emergent visibility seems most clearly related.

In examining the meaning of concepts of any kind, whether well used and articulated or not, the time-honoured practice of consulting the Oxford English Dictionary can make a useful contribution. In the absence of references in official documents and in less formal educational writings it will come as no surprise to find that 'pastoral care' does not appear under any entry or sub-entry. Under 'care' the meanings which seem most clearly related to the origins of our concept are 'to take thought for, provide for, look after' and 'oversight with a view to protection, preservation or guidance'. 'Pastoral' again contains no entry of direct relevance to the term as it is used in connection with the provision of personal and other help in schools, colleges, and so on. If one excludes rural simplicity and the natural charm attributed by poets and others to the activities associated with letting animals out to pasture, the remaining meanings are inescapably religious in connotation and tone. Apart from meanings which are clearly not related to the context which we are now examining the word 'pastoral' is used in the English language to refer to 'the spiritual care or guidance of a "flock" or body of Christians', a Pastoral, for example, being a book or letter relating to 'the cure of souls'. The word cure in this context is in fact the precursor of the contemporary word 'care'. All in all, then, unless one is to suggest that words are deployed fortuitously and without any reference to the common meanings embodied in their usage the words 'pastoral care' clearly refer to the exercise of responsibility for the spiritual welfare of others. Apart from the 'authority' implications in this shepherd and sheep conception which Dooley deals with in another part of this book, the emphasis is clearly a heavily paternalistic one, assuming without question, for example, that the 'pastor' knows what is best for his charges and is certain of the direction in which he is required to lead them. This conception is strikingly out of phase with current approaches and practices, not only in counselling but also in a number of areas of activity included under the heading of pastoral care in schools today. A key question, in fact, is why these particular terms have come to the fore at a time when an awareness and knowledge of radically different approaches and methods are steadily increasing among teachers in general, when for example a headmaster can advocate that a counselling philosophy should become a central part of a teacher's function,[3] or when a most stimulating and timely enquiry into the school's resources for furthering the personal development of pupils can be produced under the auspices of the British Association for Counselling.[4]

Where education is concerned, a conception of caring of this kind can be referred without too much difficulty to the public-school tradition written about and discussed at length in the latter part of the nineteenth century and the early nineteen hundreds, when voluntary and statutory provisions for education were being wedded and the new state secondary schools were in the process of being established. The moral earnestness of this tradition seems to have combined with the smug, condescending attitudes towards the lower orders represented in the activities of such people as Hannah Moore, who set out 'to train up the lower classes to habits of industry and virtue'. Her life-style, like that of some others of her contemporaries, has been described as 'compassionate, courageous and unselfseeking'.[5] With hindsight, it can also be as clearly identified as self-righteous and patronizing. Subordinates in both cases were presumably expected to respond with appropriate appreciation of what was being done for them and with due deference towards their benefactor. The 'counselling' techniques to which such attitudes led seem to have been much the same as those so devastatingly questioned by Carl Rogers working in a different country — threatening, remonstrating, exhorting, moralizing.[6] If then we accept the connotations with which the words were invested before the combined term 'pastoral care' came into common usage it would appear that they can now only have reference to a set of social attitudes and meanings of the kind referred to above.

This combination of attitudes is also out of alignment with the most authentic and enlightened attempts in education in this century to deal with the basic problems of which advocates of 'pastoral care' have apparently only now become aware. These movements in describing themselves used terms more in line with the ideas and action to which they were committed. I refer in particular to the development of two movements which can be identified under the headings of Child-centred Education and the Child Study Movement respectively.[7] Child-centred education basically began as a reaction against the crude and depersonalized atmosphere characterizing school methods in the initial years of universal education. Before the end of the century this movement of protest in the USA had generated the enthusiasm and momentum of a crusade. In Britain, as one might expect, reform moved at a much more leisurely pace, and in these early years was represented almost exclusively by the innovation of a small number of independent progressive schools opposed to the traditional type of education as enshrined in the major public schools of the day. It was only gradually and painfully that more humane and enlightened ideas came to influence state-supported schools and led among other changes to a shift of emphasis from mass teaching to individualized instruction and to a much less restrictive conception of the role of the school. Methods of teaching conceived originally in very narrow mechanical terms slowly acquired greater flexibility and variety. Accepted views of the aims of education were profoundly altered so that the phraseology of the Education Act drawn up during the Second World War had little in common with official pronouncements of the nineteenth century. Of the many changes which took place under the influence of these ideas none, I think, was more important than the shift from conceiving of children and young people in schools as passive recipients of facts, precepts and correct thinking to a recognition and acceptance of pupils as persons potentially capable of thinking for themselves and of making judgements and decisions in their own right. Not only was active participation in the learning process encouraged, but the pupil was thought of as being at the centre of this process. Freedom and self-determination came to be recognized as important educational objectives. This whole approach, which, in fact, gave priority to the welfare of the individual pupil, in essence seems a much more active and dynamic conception than that suggested by 'pastoral care'.

During the same period in which the ideas and practices briefly described above were bringing a new look and spirit into many schools, there was also developing a scientific attitude to children's education. The formal inauguration of this movement has been associated with the foundation of the Child Study Association in 1893. From these beginnings came eventually our School Psychological Service and subsequently our Child Guidance Clinics which from the start included all children in their brief and envisaged their role as fundamentally preventive and developmental. The slow development of understanding in the community in general, the difficulties involved in providing sufficient properly trained staff and the heavy overload of clients with severe problems, unfortunately, led to de-limitation of the service which they originally sought to offer. Nevertheless, they became a source of expertise and clinical experience unmatched by any other institutions in Britain, and in the inter-war years they introduced into the field of learning and development principles and methods which considerably influenced the changes taking place in school practice. This application of bio-psychological principles and research methods to the school scene was closely associated with real children and with the search for solutions to contemporary problems besetting teachers and other practising educators. Some of the problems for which urgent solutions were sought, for example, arose directly from the confusion experienced by teachers expected to deal with large numbers of unselected children in the state system. A case in point was the area of subnormality. At the turn of the century diagnosis and certification of mentally defective children were in the hands of medical officers who devoted most of their attention to physical symptoms. On the basis of the latter they happily proceeded to certify children referred to them as either feeble-minded or morally defective and to recommend that these children be excluded from school. Diagnoses of this kind were frequently so clearly at variance with the behaviour of the same children in school that teachers, parents, magistrates and others became disillusioned with such medical assessments and sought solutions elsewhere. Psychologists were able to demonstrate that many children labelled in this way could not, in fact, be said to suffer from inborn defects and that instead their backwardness was psychosocial in origin, deriving, for example, from emotional disturbance or unfavourable home backgrounds. The medical notion of generalizing from the abnormal or pathological to the normal was gradually replaced by the converse approach of the new evolutionary psychology which indicated 'that during childhood at least the vast majority of cases consist of deviations within the normal range rather than aberrations from the normal.'[8] From the outset the new psychology as applied to education stressed the importance of environmental, developmental education, and social factors in causation. It not only envisaged a comprehensive psychological service which would be available for all children, parents, teachers and schools, but also set out to raise the level of psychological knowledge and expertise in all areas within the school system, including the day-to-day work of the class-teacher.

These two enormously influential movements in education in this country have been responsible for much of what is most valuable in British education. In essence they can be summarized as a conviction that we must put the total emotional and intellectual development of the individual at the centre of educational theory and practice and that to enable each individual child to benefit to the maximum from his school experience, psychological and other behavioural sciences are indispensable sources from which educators must draw.

Other developments also had considerable influences on attitudes and approaches to the welfare of pupils in other than exclusively scholastic terms. Of these, the Youth Employment Service (now the Careers Service), with its emphasis on the provision of help with vocational information and decisions, is the most well documented. Without, however, taking such other influences into account it is clear from even a brief description of the two movements outlined above that the conception of pastoral care as described in the initial part of this paper is strikingly out of step with those most basic changes in attitude towards the welfare of children which have characterized the development of the education system in Britain. It also seems out of touch with many current approaches and practices, not only in counselling but also in a number of areas of activity not included under the heading of pastoral care in schools today. If one also takes into account the decline of the religious values and principles which apparently gave the conception its original meaning we are left with a historical and social mystery. Why have terms with such outmoded overtones been selected out in the contemporary educational scene in Britain to refer both to the process of helping pupils deal with non-academic aspects of their lives and to the provision of organizational arrangements in schools for providing such help?

In the absence of well-grounded information of a historical or investigative kind, explanations of this curious discrepancy must necessarily be tentative. Whatever opinions might be on this matter, however, it would seem highly desirable to direct attention to this anomalous state of affairs, as the implications for both theory and practice in this important field are considerable. Ultimately, the terms chosen to identify any particular area of intervention will influence the nature and quality of what actually takes place. This is particularly so in an area such as this where close attention is paid to the nature of the inter-changes between persons through which the bulk of the work is conducted. In terms of what knowledge we have of their past meaning and use the terms convey a confused and sentimental image of helping which does not fit well with either contemporary knowledge of human relations or the real problems facing modern youth. Unlike, for example, 'counselling' or 'guidance', 'pastoral care' could, without alteration, be used in association with the distribution of 'charity' to the poor and needy, an action of value still in itself but hardly likely to be accepted as a necessary part of the school's business. The aura of nineteenth-century unction and righteousness with which they are readily identified can evoke both misgivings and hostility from others within the school. Local-authority officials may think of them as associated with a sentimental do-gooder mentality or at best with the amateur though well-meaning and on the whole relatively harmless activities of a handful of teachers. Either way, attention is that much more distracted from the most pressing developmental needs of youth — living and growing in a world of change and uncertainty. Paternalistic intentions and the maintenance of control are poor substitutes for providing skilled help for all students with problem-solving, decision-making, study and other vital skills, with providing accurate and reliable information to pupils of immediate relevance to their particular needs and to help them, for example, work through their ideas and feelings towards greater self-understanding, self-confidence and some measure of self-fulfilment. They are singularly inappropriate in coping with difficult and distressed pupils whose problems not infrequently test a school's concern and competence to the limit.

The concept of counselling was first introduced in an articulated form in Britain fifteen years ago as an experimental attempt to raise the level of knowledge and skills thought necessary to provide more effective help with the personal as contrasted with the scholastic needs of young people. In the opinion of this author, at least, it was unfortunate that the movement did not firmly align itself from the very beginning with those endogenous traditions referred to above which subscribed, in fact, to the same fundamental principles. The influence of these first training courses, however, in the opinion of many, has been enormous. Paradoxically, the effects have been most striking in tertiary education (including the universities in which the first courses were established) and more recently in a variety of areas outside education; the immediate effect on the secondary schools at which they were initially directed cannot be said to have been great. In this respect, we have the curious and disheartening spectacle of what appears to be a widespread antipathy in many schools to such concepts as counselling, psychological growth, self-direction, personal freedom, while outside schools these ideas and goals are increasingly recognized and promoted by enthusiastic and committed people eager to become more informed and better equipped to help young people attain such goals. It is a curious paradox that some of the most informed and articulate representatives of the latter group apparently commit themselves wholeheartedly to the use of 'pastoral care' while writing authoritatively and usefully about concepts and methods to which its meaning seems alien. Best[9] et al., in Chapter 1, argue persuasively that a factual analysis of pastoral-care structures will show that in practice they represent not what conventional wisdom or academic theorizing conceive them to be, but a useful administrative means of coping with unprecedented problems of discipline and control facing teachers and school administrators in the period following reorganization. If this be an accurate assessment it supports the view that pastoral care as a term is out of phase with the spirit of those movements referred to above and more in line with a benign but conservative tradition which primarily stresses authority and obedience. Where the latter fails, exhortation, argument and persuasion are then invoked to induce the correct attitude of mind. Protecting others from their own mistakes takes precedence over encouraging them to take on responsibility for their own decisions. Assuming that such an analysis is correct and that teachers and administrators can be considered responsible for the choice of terms they use to describe their activities, it is difficult to avoid the conclusion that the traditions represented by pastoral care on the one hand and by counselling on the other are philosophically and historically quite different in origin. The attitudes conveyed by 'pastoral care' suggest that they are more in keeping with obsolescent ways of viewing relationships between teacher and pupil, approaches which from the standpoint of a counselling philosophy might be described as museum-pieces. It is to be hoped that some of the questions raised by other contributors in this book will hasten the day when 'pastoral care' will be perceived and felt as inappropriate by educators whose understanding and methodology will have rendered the gap between practice and nomenclature untenable.

References

1   *The Educational System of England and Wales*, DES (1973).
2   *The Educational System of England and Wales*, DES (1977).
3   A. Finch, in *Concepts of Counselling* ed. T. D. Vaughan, produced by the Standing Conference for the Advancement of Counselling, 26 Bedford Square, London WC1 (1976).
4   *Education for Personal Autonomy* ed. H. J. Blackham (British Association for Counselling, 1978).
5   M. G. Jones, *The Charity School Movement* (Cambridge University Press, 1938) pp. 159-60.
6   C. R. Rogers, *Counselling and Psychotherapy: newer concepts and practice* (Houghton-Mifflin, Boston, 1942).
7   Patrick M. Hughes, *Guidance and Counselling in Schools: a response to change* (Pergamon Press, Oxford, 1971), Chs 7 and 8.
8   W. D. Wall in *The Yearbook of Education* ed. R. K. Hall and J. A. Lauwerys, (Evans Bros Ltd, London, 1955).
9   R. E. Best, P. M. Ribbins, and C. B. Jarvis, 'Pastoral Care: Concept and Process', *British Journal of Educational Studies* Vol. XXV, No. 2 (June 1977): see Chapter 1 of this volume.

4   School Welfare Roles and Networks*

Maurice Craft

Over the past twenty-five years, a now well-known series of reports and researches have sketched the outlines of educational inequalities in modern Britain. This was not a new discovery, but a situation about which we have become increasingly concerned, with accelerating national needs for skill, and with changes in our political and moral beliefs about individual opportunity. Waste of talent and rigidities in the opportunity structure are no longer so easily accepted (Craft 1974). In more recent years, researches have tended to move away from large-scale studies of educational opportunity and have begun to focus more upon 'educability' or responsiveness to schooling, the analysis of the complex *mechanisms* of disadvantage, and the definition of disadvantage itself (Craft 1970, Young 1971).

An accompaniment of these changing patterns of concern has been the development of a steadily growing network of welfare specialists based in and around schools. The Newsom Report, for example, was in no doubt about '. . . the need for a good deal of social work in connection with the pupils . . .' in what it called 'schools in slum areas', and recommended the appointment of teacher/social workers (CACE 1963). Plowden expressed similar anxieties, recommending a co-ordinated programme of support, and observing that, 'In schools with special difficulties, social workers may spend so much time in the schools as, virtually, to be members of the school staff' (CACE 1967). The fabric of supporting services, however, has grown piecemeal, and is very much a product of national traditions of problem-solving: the preference for decentralized decision-making, for down-to-earth practical solutions to social dilemmas rather than for large-scale reform, for consensus by compromise between competing interests, rather than for decision by hierarchy, and, above all, for gradualism rather than cataclysmic change.

School welfare needs have therefore tended to be met very largely on a local and pragmatic basis by numerous separate agencies, and the range of provision is accordingly extremely varied. A further complication is that school welfare provision serves a diversity of functions ranging from the largely 'educational' to the largely 'therapeutic'. Home-visiting, for example, may be undertaken (by teachers) to sort out a problem relating to homework, or (by social workers) in respect

*This paper is reproduced from M. Craft, et al. (eds.), *Linking Home and School* (3rd Edn), Harper & Row (forthcoming).

of an aspect of family breakdown. Clearly there is a large area of overlap between the two extremes, and although an unreal distinction in many ways, the educational/therapeutic dichotomy will be utilized below in discussing the range of welfare tasks now recognized, and of welfare strategies now to be found in British schools.

Present Provision

The Education Welfare Service, which grew from the school attendance officers of the 1870s, is still probably the most widespread form of school welfare provision, and its function may range from a relatively limited concern with school attendance, clothing, school meals and transport, to a form of social casework (Macmillan 1977). The School Health Service emerged in the early years of this century, and the extent of its functions now varies a good deal from region to region. But the role of the school nurse may be very significant, for many are also qualified health visitors and knowledgeable about local families; and they have a competence in health-related social problems such as drug abuse or child neglect, and may also contribute to health education and to counselling. School psychological services developed after the 1944 Act, and educational psychologists may spend their time advising teachers about individual children with learning or behaviour problems, working with individual cases referred by teachers, or testing children. These activities may often involve devising remedial teaching programmes, liaising with parents, counselling teachers and offering inservice training. The educational psychologist may also spend some time in the local Child Guidance Clinic (part of the School Health Service), provision for which developed in the late 1950s; and which is staffed by an interdisciplinary team consisting of an educational psychologist, a psychiatric social worker and a consultant psychiatrist, and is concerned mainly with children designated as 'maladjusted'.

These are the major school welfare services located outside the school, to which others such as the Social Services Department (considered below), the Youth Employment Service, and perhaps the Probation Service might also be added (Stroud 1975). But in recent years, these area-based specialists have been supplemented by a growing number of school-based specialists, teachers often with additional training whose roles may range very widely indeed. Some may be appointed to foster links with parents, to bring them up to date with curriculum changes and to involve them more fully in the education of their children (McGeeney 1969, Cave 1970), and there have been numerous published accounts of experimental forms of parent-teacher co-operation (DES 1968a, Lang 1968, Haynes 1969, Midwinter 1972). In some cases, the 'home—school liaison officer' (or teacher/social worker) may have a particular interest in 'parent education', discussing with parents the value of conversation, reading, and particular kinds of toys and activities at home, and perhaps going on to deeper aspects of child-rearing (Pringle 1970). Another kind of specialist, the 'school counsellor', appointed to many LEAs in the past decade, may have an even more therapeutic function, requiring casework with individual children on personal problems and often involving their parents (Lytton and Craft 1974, Jones 1977). Usually an experienced teacher, having completed an advanced course of specialized training, the counsellor may often have a wide-ranging brief, as indicated later. All these kinds of welfare role can involve home-visiting.

Then there are welfare roles of a more instrumental sort which tend, on the whole, not to incorporate home visiting: careers teachers, for example, who may organize visits and work experience, provide careers information, and teach careers courses to ease the transition from school to work. Where a trained counsellor also undertakes work of this kind ('vocational guidance'), he may administer tests of ability, interest and aptitude, and be responsible for an elaborate record system covering the whole of a child's school life and not simply the final year. Educational and vocational guidance then merge. Form teachers and house tutors are the traditional specialists in these areas and will continue to outnumber counsellors and teacher/social workers in secondary education for many years to come. Most large comprehensive schools also have a remedial department, often staffed by specialists and making use of LEA advisers and of specialist remedial teachers based in the school psychological services and child guidance.

Some schools also have a *community* involvement through the appointment of a teacher/youth leader; or by designating themselves 'community schools' and creating a focus of cultural, recreational, or ameliorative activities (Poster 1971, Midwinter 1973). These links with the local community may generate much closer relationships with parents, social services and employers, and may create additional flows of local knowledge of great value to the school's welfare function — especially in its preventive dimension.

Area Variations

The total range of provision both within and outside the school is therefore quite extensive. But the pattern varies from LEA to LEA and from school to school, for traditionally, welfare services have depended not only upon the interests and abilities of individual heads, class teachers and education welfare officers, but also of Chief Education Officers and of their colleagues in other Departments. This is not to argue against variety *per se*, or to suggest that freedom to experiment should be curtailed. But where experimental roles tend to be laid alongside or are superimposed upon existing ones there is always the possibility of stress, duplication and inefficiency. As counsellors are appointed, for example, the precise role of the housemaster/mistress in a comprehensive school (or of the traditional pastoral function of the form teacher) will require some redefinition. Similarly with careers teachers, a fast-developing group of specialists whose role is being increasingly regarded as complementary to that of the area careers officer, and not in conflict with it (Ministry of Labour 1965, Roberts 1970). At the LEA level, there have been numerous experimental patterns of provision. Liverpool, for example, established five area-based 'social education' teams through which school referrals are channelled, with each team co-ordinated by an 'educational guidance officer' and linking the child guidance and school psychological service, remedial teaching teams and educational welfare officers (Birley 1972). Other LEAs, Southampton, for example, have experimented with less formalized co-ordinating mechanisms (Luckhurst 1969). The ILEA have traditionally made use of voluntary workers through a School Care Service, and this element has remained within a unified education welfare service.

However, the central issue to have emerged in policy discussions relating to school welfare provision in recent years arose from the deliberations of the Seebohm Committee (1968), and from their proposal for a unified social services department in each Local Authority, embracing all neighbourhood welfare provision and including school social workers based in individual schools or serving groups of schools. The proposal argued that this pattern would considerably clarify channels of referral from the school outwards; but there was sharp disagreement among LEAs as to whether the new school social workers, recruited from the existing EWOs, should become part of the social services department or remain with the education authorities (Clegg 1968, Cook 1968), and the Local Authorities Social Services Act 1970 left this question open and for local authorities to decide. In due course, a number of authorities proceeded to incorporate EWOs into their new social services departments, but as the British Association of Social Workers' discussion paper subsequently reported,

> Schools are generally unhappy with this development. They feel isolated and neglected and are resentful that their own welfare workers have been taken away from them. The social workers who have replaced them appear to them to place too low priority on this aspect of their work and in some respects even appear to collude with children and families against the school. (BASW 1974a).

The result was that the majority of local authorities reverted to the *status quo*, leaving only three — Cheshire, Coventry and Somerset — where the social services department provides a social-work service to schools. Even so, the powers of the EWO in relation to those of the new social services departments have diminished, and it is now more difficult to take families to court for non-attendance, a matter that has become a point of issue between the two professions. For social workers, poor attendance is merely a symptom of deeper unease; for teachers it represents the loss of a vital avenue to personal fulfilment and engenders the near certainty of more serious deviance.

The debate continues, and in their recent Report, the Association of Directors of Social Services notes the '. . . unnecessary and destructive professional competitiveness' which exists at departmental policy levels and calls for educational welfare to become the responsibility of qualified social workers – perhaps with additional specialized training (ADSS 1978). For their part, EWOs have endorsed the recommendation of the Ralphs Report that the Certificate of Qualification in Social Work should in future become the appropriate professional qualification for their Service (Local Government Training Board 1973). However, regardless of this inter-professional conflict about the future role of the EWO, schools frequently have need to consult area social-work teams, and on the evidence of Fitzherbert's recent account, accessibility is often a problem (Fitzherbert 1977).

The School's Welfare Tasks

It will be clear from this brief review of the present range of school welfare provision and of area variations, that even allowing for terminology (i.e. different titles describing essentially the same role, or 'modernized' titles describing long-established roles), there remains a wide range of tasks which fall into the welfare category. Indeed, it is perhaps worth including Milner's summary diagram in which she indicates her assessment of the extent of a 'planned guidance programme' for a comprehensive secondary school (Figure 1).

There can be little doubt that this extensive group of welfare tasks which is now being undertaken by schools has grown enormously since the 1950s, and the reasons for this expansion are possibly to be found in the structural and ideological changes referred to earlier: the need for skill and concern for the individual, changes which have been reflected in the growth of an affective dimension to many professional roles (particularly teaching) and in the normal corollary of this – a splitting off of new welfare roles. Thus, while the average teacher is now expected to possess an expertise that is psycho-social as well as academic, it is recognized that specialization must occur in this as in other fields, leading, for example, to the appointment of counsellors, as well as of academic team leaders.

When we come to review the range of welfare tasks it is evident that not all are alleviative. As suggested earlier, the distinction between 'educational' and 'therapeutic' roles is not always a clear one, but in the threefold classification suggested below this broad distinction is maintained for the purposes of argument. First, and perhaps foremost, school welfare provision seeks to offer effective systems for the identification of the *seriously disadvantaged*; and for their treatment or more skilled support, whether by referral to outside specialists, or as is more likely in many cases, given the general shortage of remedial and psychiatric facilities, by a supportive therapy within the school, perhaps in

Figure 1 *Planned guidance programme* [source: Milner 1974]

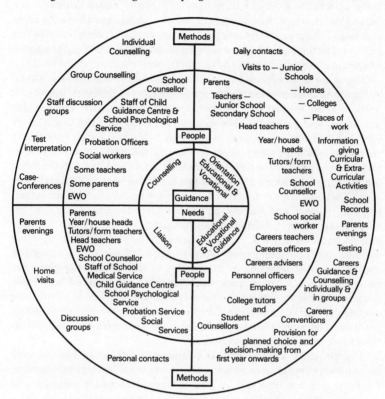

consultation with outside agencies. For this group, welfare provision may also involve a compensatory curriculum, particular techniques of educational and vocational guidance (terms which are considered below), medical measures, and relationships with parents of a 'therapeutic' as well as an 'informational' kind, often involving the social services. Whether this group of children 'at risk' comes from as large a proportion as 20 per cent of all families, as Pringle (1970) has suggested, it is impossible to say. But numerous reports and researches in education, housing, poverty, and nutrition, leave no scope for ambiguity about the existence of a seriously deprived minority whose children require special help within the schools.

Provision for these children immediately raises some sizeable issues, ethical and economic, which can only be touched upon here. For example, does the devising of more systematic school-welfare provision imply the more effective adjustment of children to what is generally regarded as an intolerable social environment? Can the provision of special salary allowances, ancillaries, playgroups, nursery-school and day-nursery places, reception and language centres, and new school buildings in 'educational priority areas' be extended to meet the need, by governments committed to reducing public expenditure? Is the urban land shortage, the preference for city living, and the consequent building of 'high-rise' flats going to provide new generations of problem children for the future? These wider policy issues are beyond the scope of a chapter concerned with the tactics of prevention at school level.

The second area of school welfare tasks is less obviously 'therapeutic', and concerns the needs not of a deprived minority but of the *overwhelming majority* of normal schoolchildren. Apart from health screenings, and perhaps some occasional remedial teaching, this consists very largely of the dual and interrelated category of educational and vocational guidance which seeks to identify abilities, interests and aptitudes, and to provide for their fulfilment in school and beyond. Probably the majority of parent–teacher programmes fall into this second category. They are largely concerned to provide information about school progress, courses and careers, and such 'parent education' as they involve is aimed at fostering supportive attitudes rather than at more basic matters of attitude change which may be entailed with deprived families. The comprehensive reorganization of secondary education and abolition of selection at eleven-plus in many LEAs has given rise to larger schools, more extensive curricula, and delayed and more flexible curriculum choice for an increasingly complex academic and commercial market, and these changes suggest the more obvious rationale for more elaborate systems of guidance to facilitate informed educational and vocational decision-making.

Thirdly, there are the normal stresses of *adolescence* and the need to provide personal counselling, a somewhat more 'therapeutic' service, for those children who seek it. This is a need which may sometimes be overstated by psychotherapists. None the less it is real enough for a number of children who could not be regarded as seriously deprived or disturbed, in a context of larger and more complex schools, smaller and more mobile families, and an accelerating rate of economic and social change which may foster an 'inter-generational gap'; and in an ideological setting in which the paradoxical commitments to individualism and to collective responsibility maximize freedom but set the adolescent a major learning problem. With this third group, home–school relations might be more casework-oriented.

Proposals for Team Functioning

So far this chapter has argued that the present pattern of school welfare provision is complex, first, because it has grown up piecemeal to meet the changing needs of a society which prefers local, gradual adjustments rather than large-scale, radical reform; and second, because it embraces a wide range of 'educational' and 'therapeutic' functions. It ought also to be added that the educational system of England and Wales, with its

33,000 schools, situated in regions of differing levels of economic development, and divisible into numerous categories by age of pupils, type of curriculum, and form of government, is hardly likely to produce a tidy pattern. None the less, this chapter has suggested that this range of school-welfare functions can be grouped according to three broad categories of need: the needs of a small minority, the seriously disadvantaged; the need of the great majority of school children for educational and vocational guidance; and the need of a minority of normal adolescents for personal counselling.

It will be obvious from this tentative grouping of welfare tasks that there are no neat divisions, either of clientele or of processes, in this field. 'Disadvantage' is a relative term and the size of this minority group fluctuates with time and place; and similarly with the proportion of young people who feel in need of help and advice as part of growing up. Secondly, the processes of guidance and counselling, themselves neither conceptually nor operationally distinct, can be applied to all three groups. None the less, this composite classification is felt to offer a workable basis for considering the shape of day-to-day machinery. This machinery, given the range of tasks, the growing size of secondary schools in particular, and rising standards of pastoral care, is increasingly being thought of in terms of a *team*, an idea that has been more widely implemented in the United States where the classroom teacher may be assisted, for example, by counsellors, a visiting teacher (or school social worker), a psychologist, and perhaps a psychiatrist, in a given school or school system (Arbuckle 1966, Strang 1968).

In Britain, the team notion is developing but slowly, and many of the proposals made so far relate more specifically to vocational guidance. The Albemarle Report on the Youth Employment Service, for example, advocated closer co-operation between the youth employment officer (now called 'careers officer') and the careers teacher:

> The future of careers counselling in schools will be best served through the development of a *team* approach. . . . Guidance given by the Y.E.O. [careers officer] without relevant information from and consultation with the school is likely to be based upon an inadequate knowledge of the young person. Guidance given by a teacher without the cooperation of the Y.E.O. is likely to be based on too narrow a knowledge of the field of employment and the requirements of occupations. (Ministry of Labour 1965.)

The CBI Report (1969) similarly recommended that each school should have a 'strong team of teachers' responsible for careers, working in conjunction with the careers officer, who should 'supplement the careers teachers' understanding of the individual's personality, interests, and attainments, with a detailed knowledge of careers in all areas of employment and the physical and psychological requirements of particular occupations'. Hoxter (1964) proposed a slightly more elaborate team structure for vocational guidance. He suggested that each school should appoint a counsellor responsible for educational and vocational guidance who would be assisted by an area-based 'vocational guidance counsellor' (the equivalent of the present careers officer but with more specialized training), and by an LEA-appointed 'vocational guidance adviser', who would plan and co-ordinate the work of the school counsellors. These different schemes place a varying emphasis upon the school-based and area-based elements in educational and vocational guidance. But although they argue for a *team* notion, the team they propose is to have fairly narrowly prescribed welfare functions. How are those needs which cannot be neatly classified as educational or vocational to be dealt with? With the Scottish Education Department's Report (1968) we have the recognition that even if counselling for personal problems is offered by a school, the counsellor would still need the assistance of other staff to cover careers work; and Daws (1967a) draws the important distinction between *therapeutic* counselling on the one hand and *educational and vocational* counselling on the other. He argues that together, both elements would comprise too demanding a role for a single welfare specialist and has elsewhere considered a three-man team: careers teacher, careers officer and counsellor, in which the counsellor would have a therapeutic concern (1967b). Clearly, this three-man team with its increased range would be likely to draw in form teachers, housemasters, and others on occasion (Daws 1968).

An additional dimension is added when the necessity to provide for home–school relations is taken into account. This adds yet a further role demand, a further caseload, and a further set of techniques to those of a counsellor who might already be trying to combine 'therapeutic' and 'educational/vocational' commitments; and it has led to the suggestion of a further specialization, that of the school social worker (Fuller and Juniper 1967, Juniper 1967) and to the proposal for a four-man team: careers teacher, careers officer, counsellor, and school social worker (Daws 1968, Vaughan 1970). Lytton's (1968, 1974) notion of a four-man team is very similar: he sees educational and vocational guidance being carried out by teachers (with some additional training) working in collaboration with the careers officer; home–school links would be maintained by welfare officers rather like the present EWOs; and personal counselling, diagnosis, and referral to outside specialists would be the function of a 'pupil personnel worker'.

All these schemes are an improvement on those considered earlier, for they recognize and seek to provide for a wider range of needs than those which are strictly vocational. But none makes specific provision for remedial education. 'Educational guidance' would probably embrace a compensatory curriculum in the educational priority area, but what of the average suburban school? Here, remedial education is often a largely self-contained area of work; but in any overall review of school welfare provision is it justifiable for it to remain so? There is certain to be a welfare dimension in the work of most remedial classes, and conversely, the work of welfare specialists will often have implications for remedial teaching. Secondly, none of these proposals for team functioning takes note of the contribution of outside specialists in the school health and psychological services, and in the neighbourhood welfare services. Nor do they speculate on the role of the EWO.

The Report of the National Association for Mental Health Working Party (1970), which also felt that school welfare is 'essentially a team function', put forward a more flexible team concept in which different members of staff and outside welfare specialists would be consulted by a school counsellor in particular cases. Thus, matters of 'educational choice' might involve consultations with departmental heads, parents, personal tutors or house tutors, and perhaps, the educational psychologist; 'vocational choice' would bring in tutors, parents, careers teacher, careers officer, and even employers; and 'critical developmental problems' would embrace the house tutor, form teacher, EWO, parents, and members of the Child Guidance team. Organizationally, the Report suggests, this pattern might be achieved by provision at two levels. At a senior level within each school, a counsellor would be responsible for co-ordinating an *overall programme*, including liaison with outside agencies, and he might be one of two key assistants to the headteacher (the other being a senior administrative colleague). At the second level, there would be a number of assistant counsellors who would undertake *specific tasks* in the educational, vocational and personal areas.

As the Report suggests, this kind of scheme has the merit of providing a career structure for school welfare specialists; and it makes the important proposal that a single, trained specialist at a senior level should be responsible for co-ordinating a rational welfare policy within each school. Jones (1977) has described a somewhat similar pattern in her own school where as Deputy Head (and a former counsellor) she co-ordinated a team of teacher/social workers, with close links with the remedial department and with year tutors, form teachers, the school's EWO, and outside welfare and psychological services.

Interprofessional Co-ordination

A major reason for the advocacy of a more coherent and co-ordinated pattern of welfare roles *within* the school arises from the still highly fragmented range of welfare services outside. The Plowden Report had drawn attention to this in relation to the needs of primary schools in deprived areas before the reorganization of neighbourhood welfare services had been undertaken, and Newsom had earlier recommended the appointment in secondary schools in difficult areas of '. . . additional members of staff who have special responsibilities for homevisiting, and who act as liaison officers with all the other medical, welfare and child care services in the district' (CACE, 1963, 1967). But even after the reorganization of local social services, co-ordination remains a serious problem, as was tragically illustrated in the case of Maria Colwell, who was battered to death shortly before her eighth birthday. Although several separate agencies had identified symptoms – teachers, EWO, social worker and others — they failed to effect any joint action, and as the subsequent Committee of Enquiry observed, the greatest and most obvious failure of the system in this case was '. . . the lack of, or ineffectiveness of, communication and liaison' (DHSS 1974).

The recent Report of the Association of Directors of Social Services (1978) states unequivocally: 'We think that it is only through the closest possible co-operation and co-ordination between the education service and the social services that the best results can be achieved in relation to the needs of those children who can be seen to be disadvantaged.' Their proposed solution is a unification of the Education Welfare Service and the social services department. Fitzherbert (1977), however, discusses a more functional and possibly more fundamental solution, originally proposed by a BASW Working Party (BASW 1974b). This is the regular screening of whole class groups of children, initially by an interdisciplinary team comprising teachers, EWO and social worker, in order to identify 'children at risk, not making normal progress or simply not thriving' (op. cit.), and then following this by further investigation and the involvement of other workers as required in individual cases. The BASW proposal claims that only in this way can genuinely shared decision-making — and its corollary, interprofessional co-operation — become possible.

Fitzherbert (op. cit.) comments that rather than wait until problems have become crises, *prevention* should be the objective, and regular multidisciplinary screening would seem to offer the best hope in this direction. She further notes: 'There is no question that the school with its knowledge of the child as a whole is the place where such an assessment should begin and where it should be co-ordinated', adding that parents ought also to be included in the assessment team when their own children are involved. The benefits to be derived when 'members of other professions visit the school regularly, make themselves at home in the staff-room and keep an eye on children with difficulties' include not only an enrichment of the school's capacity to cope with problems itself, but also a sharpening of teachers' perceptions of children's needs and of available strategies for meeting them (op. cit.). Lyons (1973) has made the same point in respect of her own experience as an education social worker as part of the London EPA action research project.

It is also worth noting that in their recent Report on the role of the school nurse, the Royal College of Nursing (1974) stress the importance of regarding this specialist as 'a member of the school team' who must maintain close liaison with all others responsible for the health of the school child.

Elements of Team Provision

The reorganization of primary and secondary education in the last decade has introduced an almost bizarre variety into the forms of British schooling, and it is clearer than ever that no single blueprint for school welfare provision could possibly meet the varied circumstances of more than a proportion of the schools. However, if the broad categories of need outlined earlier are accepted as valid; and if current trends in thinking (sketched in the previous sections) are any guide, it seems that three essentials in any future model must be, first, the establishment of a single, clear focus of welfare efforts, an *internal co-ordinator* or convenor, within each school; second, the elements, at least, of a *team* within each school; and third, the establishment of a *clear channel* out of the school to neighbourhood welfare services. Naturally, the interpretation of such a model would vary with local conditions. In some areas, the regular interdisciplinary preventive screening recommended by the BASW paper and by Fitzherbert would be a prime necessity; elsewhere it might be periodic. In one school the core team would always need to include the EWO and/or school social worker, in another it might be thought important to include staff concerned with careers.

In a large comprehensive school the internal co-ordinator or convenor might be a full-time (i.e. non-teaching) counsellor. Elsewhere, a part-teaching specialist might meet the need. Secondly, in large schools the range of welfare duties would obviously be too great and too conflicting for a single person to carry out alone, and the co-ordinator might therefore concentrate on the most demanding personal counselling while co-ordinating a *team* of part-teaching colleagues who were responsible for educational and vocational guidance, for home–school relations, and for remedial work; and responsible, above all, for acting in a consultant capacity to colleagues wherever required (Figure 2).

Figure 2 *The school welfare team — some basic roles*

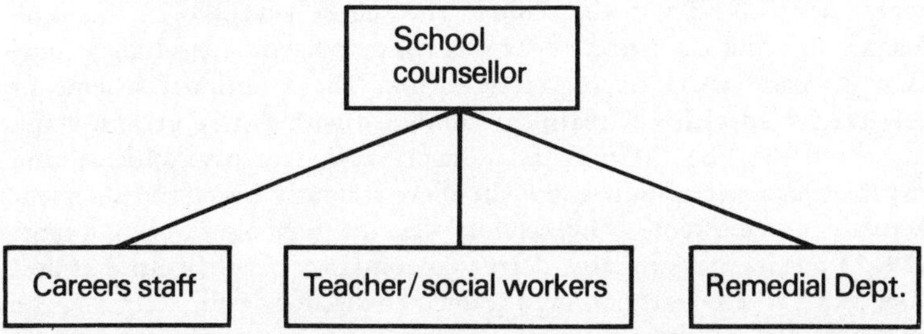

In this model, appropriately trained careers teachers would be capable of administering psychometric tests as part of their work in educational and vocational guidance; but if not, this could be done by the counsellor. Teacher/social workers (or 'home–school liaison officers' as they are sometimes called) would foster links with parents, mainly in connection with educational and vocational guidance, and they would have a timetable adjusted to allow for this. Home-visiting is so time-consuming that it is doubtful whether any of the other roles could be combined with it. In educational priority areas the teacher/social workers might also be involved in community work (Gulbenkian Foundation 1968), for this is a role which might lend itself to this line of development. In a small school, on the other hand, a teacher/social worker might have a less specialized role and might well be the internal co-ordinator. To these basic roles must be added the school's remedial teachers, and, of course, the outside specialists who would work with the team (Figure 3).

Figure 3   *The school welfare team — internal and external specialists*

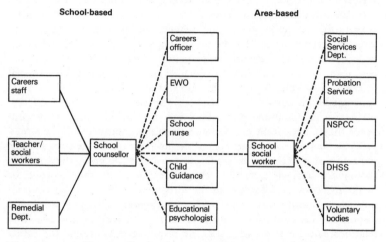

The careers officer, school nurse and EWO would each contribute a particular expertise, but as part of a co-ordinated team and not, as is so often the case at present, as visitors in isolation, occasionally granted a temporary foothold in the school. The school psychologist, like colleagues in Child Guidance, might well come to have a consultancy function in many areas, as suggested earlier. The traditional scheme of referral for specialized treatment combined with a supportive therapy in school may be the ideal relationship with area psychological and psychiatric services; but where these are seriously overstrained (if not actually non-existent), 'the schools' (as the Schools Council Report (1967) put it) 'have in large degree to contain their difficulties as best they can'. Where a school has a trained counsellor on the staff, and the rudiments of a welfare team, this containment could offer a constructive solution in many LEAs.

There would be much informal contact between members of the team, and regular consultation with housemasters and other colleagues. The role of housemaster/year tutor would probably centre upon traditional administrative and extra-curricular duties, facilitating the normative climate of a large school, and a pastoral concern at 'general practitioner' level with referral to the school welfare team wherever necessary. The co-ordinator would be responsible for calling regular case conferences/screenings which the outside specialists would attend as necessary.

The *internal co-ordinator* and the internal *team* are two essential elements in this model. The third is a *clear channel out of the school*. This might be thought to be the most ambiguous element, for Figures 2 and 3 have already indicated several channels: the relationship of the school-based members of the team with their area-based colleagues (i.e. careers officer, school nurse, EWO, psychologist, child guidance officer) will obviously be a flexible one and will embody clear and efficient channels as the occasion arises. Similarly, the teacher/social workers who will be involved in conveying information about courses and careers, discussing learning or behaviour problems, and in some areas, in aspects of parent education, will also maintain flexible 'channels' out of the school for these purposes. But when it comes to more serious cases of deprivation or disturbance involving family casework, probation, juvenile liaison, NSPCC, or other welfare services, this will be more appropriately a matter for the local social services department. The Seebohm Report recommended the establishment of a school social worker who would liaise between the schools and the department, and where such a role has been clearly designated this would provide the channel whereby referrals of this kind were made. The school social worker, school-based or area-based, would be responsible for convening case conferences of colleagues and might also be involved in casework with a child's family.

The need for a clear and effective channel in these more serious cases has often been stressed (for example in Wedge 1965), and some have argued that the *counsellor* (in our model, the internal co-ordinator) could provide it (Lytton 1974, DES 1968b). This would certainly seem to be a logical solution in smaller schools. But in larger ones, the co-ordinator of a large team who is also carrying a personal case-load would hardly have the time to undertake liaison with a variety of outside specialists, nor would it be right for *him* to decide which was the appropriate point of contact.

Roles, Networks and Welfare Policy

Figure 3, it must be stressed, presents a purely hypothetical model the purpose of which is to illustrate the range of functions involved in a modern conception of school-welfare provision. It is not argued that each school should have this particular blend of components; it will vary according to local needs and resources. But *co-ordination, team* functioning, and a *clear channel* for referral are felt to be basic concepts. The more rational and co-ordinated pattern of neighbourhood social services to which it is hoped we are moving will help little, if schools do nothing to rationalize *their* internal resources.

Secondly, it will be clear that this chapter has been mainly concerned with a tentative exploration of techniques. More basic organizational issues relating to role analysis, and a more theoretical concern

with the social functions of schools and the social process of education
have been largely left on one side. However, some theoretical assumptions have been made and these were referred to at the outset. Our
society's growing need for skill and its ideological commitment to
individual fulfilment have contributed, particularly since 1945, to the
greater emphasis placed upon developmental aspects of the educational
process. *All* teachers are being increasingly exhorted (and to some
extent trained) to take on a wider and more diffuse range of tasks,
including those of social welfare. But however desirable this may be
thought to be, it is functionally impossible given the increasingly
demanding pedagogic aspects of the teacher's role, and the wider
range of 'educational' and 'therapeutic' tasks now included under the
heading of school-welfare provision. Although all teachers may therefore be expected to be capable of identification and referral at 'general
practitioner' level, the emergence of school-welfare specialists of one
kind or another is inevitable, and in terms of functional efficiency,
highly desirable.

Not all would necessarily agree with this theoretical orientation.
Best, Jarvis and Ribbins (1977) have expressed the view that the development of pastoral-care structures may have more to do with social
control (the containment of disruptive behaviour associated with
the raising of the school-leaving age, for example), and with finding
appropriate alternative posts of responsibility for staff displaced from
senior departmental appointments in reorganized secondary schools.
This is a perspective which certainly has validity and might, indeed,
be applied to numerous other aspects of school-welfare provision,
inter-professional imperialism for example. But while quite rightly
calling attention to the latent functions of welfare roles and networks,
it seems doubtful that the manifest functions can all be so easily
explained.

There remain many issues for research, and for educational and
social policy. What the most functional team pattern should be for
schools of different types and in different localities is clearly a foremost
question, whether social workers should be school-based or area-based,
and whether the front-line workers should be responsible as a team to
the schools on the spot, or to a fragmented bureaucracy some way off.
The findings of Rose and Marshall's (1974) seven-year research into
counselling and social work in Lancashire tended to be pragmatic and to
suggest that there are no definitive answers, for the pattern of provision
will vary according to the case. Overseas experience may often suggest
helpful role models, but *co-ordination* also appears to be a central
problem in all the states of Australia, for example (Craft 1977).

In the realm of professional training, the proposal that teachers and
social workers should be trained alongside each other in an interprofessional setting has appeared in most major reports and commentaries
in this field for many years, and it again found widespread expression in
the recent reappraisal of teacher education (Craft 1971, Tibble 1972).

Such a development might well enhance the school's preventive function, and now that a part of teacher education is located in interdisciplinary Institutes of Higher Education and Polytechnics, it seems nearer than at any time in the past. But this is very much a long-term proposal and cannot be relied upon as the only strategy for future school-welfare provision.

Finally, this chapter has tended to assume that school-welfare provision is largely a secondary-school concern, and it would appear that the great majority of counsellors and other welfare specialists have been appointed to post-primary schools in recent years. But as Moseley (1968) has argued, there are obvious grounds for claiming that preventive measures should most logically be sited in the *primary* school. This, too, is something which needs close scrutiny at a national level.

References

Arbuckle, D. S., *Pupil Personnel Services in the Modern School* (Allyn & Bacon, Boston, 1966).

Association of Directors of Social Services, *Social Work Services for Children in School* (ADSS, 1978).

Best, R. E., Jarvis, C. B. and Ribbins, P. M., 'Pastoral Care: Concept and Process', *British Journal of Educational Studies*, Vol. XXV, No. 2, pp. 124-35 (1977) (see Chapter 1).

Birley, D., 'The social education team', in Craft, M. *et al.* (eds.), *Linking Home and School* (Longman, Harlow, 1972).

British Association of Social Workers, 'Social work in relation to schools', *BASW News*, 21 March, 1974a.

British Association of Social Workers, *Report of Working Party on Social Work in Relation to Schools* (BASW, Leeds and Mid-Yorks Region, 1974b).

Cave, R. G., *Partnership for Change: Parents and Schools* (Ward Lock, London, 1970).

Central Advisory Council for Education, *Half Our Future* ('Newsom Report', HMSO, 1963).

Central Advisory Council for Education, *Children and their Primary Schools* ('Plowden Report', HMSO, 1967).

Clegg, A., 'Seebohm' a sorry tale?', *Education*, 11 October, 1968.

Confederation of British Industry, *Careers Guidance* (CBI, 1969).

Cook, D., *Comment on Clegg*, in *Education*, 25 October, 1968.

Craft, M. (ed.), *Family, Class and Education: a Reader* (Longman, Harlow, 1970).

Craft, M., 'A broader role for colleges of education', in Tibble, J. W. (ed.), *The Future of Teacher Education* (Routledge & Kegan Paul, London, 1971).

Craft, M., 'Guidance, counselling and social needs', in Lytton, H. and Craft, M. (eds.), *Guidance and Counselling in British Schools* (2nd Edn, Arnold, London, 1974).

Craft, M., *School Welfare Provision in Australia* (Aust. Govt. Pub. Service, Canberra, 1977).

Daws, P. P., 'What will the school counsellor do?', *Educational Research*, Vol. 9, No. 2, 1967a.

Daws, P. P., 'The guidance team in the secondary school', *Abstracts of the Annual Conference of the British Psychological Society* (Education Section, 1967b).

Daws, P. P., *A Good Start in Life* (CRAC, 1968).

Department of Education and Science, *Parent—Teacher Relations in Primary Schools* (HMSO, 1968a).

Department of Education and Science, *Psychologists in Education Services* ('Summerfield Report', HMSO, 1968b).

Department of Health and Social Security, *Report of the Committee of Inquiry into the Care and Supervision Provided in Relation to Maria Colwell* (HMSO, 1974).

Fitzherbert, K., *Child Care Services and the Teacher* (Temple Smith, London, 1977).

Fuller, J. A. and Juniper, D. F., 'Guidance, counselling and school social work', in *Educational Research*, Vol. 9, No. 2., 1967.

Gulbenkian Foundation, *Community Work and Social Change* (Longman, Harlow, 1968).

Haynes, J., *Schools and the Community* (Kent County Council, 1969).

Hoxter, H. Z, 'Fresh thinking on guidance and counselling', in *Yearbook of Events, 1963-64* (Institute of Youth Employment Officers, London and S E Branch, 1964).

Jones, A., *Counseling Adolescents in Schools* (Kogan Page, London, 1977).

Juniper, D. F., 'School social work', in *Abstracts of the Annual Conference of the British Psychological Society* (Education Section, 1967).

Lang, P., 'A school with a department for home/school relationships', in *Parents and Schools*, Vol. 2, No. 4 (CASE, 1968).

Local Government Training Board, *The Role and Training of Education Welfare Officers* ('Ralphs Report', LGTB, 1973).

Luckhurst, C., 'Experiments in welfare', in *Trends in Education*, January, 1969.

Lyons, K. H., *Social Work and the School* (HMSO, 1973).

Lytton, H., *School Counselling and Counsellor Education in the United States* (NFER, 1968).

Lytton, H., 'An integrated approach to counselling and social work', in Lytton and Craft (1974).

Lytton, H. and Craft, M. (eds.), *Guidance and Counselling in British Schools* (2nd Edn, Arnold, London, 1974).

Macmillan, D., *Education Welfare' Strategy and Structure* (Longman, Harlow, 1977).

McGreeney, P. J., *Parents are Welcome* (Longman, Harlow, 1969).

Midwinter, E. C., *Projections' an Educational Priority Area at Work* (Ward Lock, London, 1972).

Midwinter, E. C., *Patterns of Community Education* (Ward Lock, London, 1973).

Milner, P., *Counselling in Education* (Dent, Dent 1974).

Ministry of Labour, *The Future Development of the Youth Employment Service* ('Albemarle Report', HMSO, 1965).

Moseley, L. G., 'The primary school and preventive social work', *Social Work*, Vol. 25, No. 2., 1968.

National Association for Mental Health, *School Counselling* (NAMH, 1970).

Poster, C., *The School and the Community* (Macmillan, London, 1971).

Pringle, M. L. Kellmer, 'Co-operation in child and family care', *Concern*, No. 5 (National Children's Bureau, 1970).

Roberts, K., 'The Youth Employment Service, the schools, and the preparation of school leavers for employment', *The Vocational Aspect of Education*, Vol. 22, No. 52, 1970.

Rose, G. and Marshall, T. F., *Counselling and School Social Work* (Wiley, New York, 1974).

Royal College of Nursing, *The Role of the School Nurse: Report of a Working Party* (RCN, cyclostyled, 1974).

Schools Council, *Counselling in Schools* (HMSO, 1967).

Scottish Education Department, *Guidance in Scottish Secondary Schools* (HMSO, 1968).

Seebohm Committee, *Report of the Committee on Local Authority and Allied Personal Social Services* ('Seebohm Report', HMSO, 1968).

Strang, R., 'Guidance and the classroom teacher', in Noll, V. H. and Noll, R. P. (eds.), *Readings in Educational Psychology* (Collier-Macmillan, London, 1968).

Stroud, J., *Where to get help: a Guide to the Support Services* (Ward Lock, London, 1975).

Tibble, J. W., 'Interprofessional Training', in Craft, M. *et al.* (eds.), *Linking Home and School* (Longman, Harlow, 1972).

Vaughan, T. D., *Educational and Vocational Guidance Today* (Routledge & Kegan Paul, London, 1970).

Wedge, P., *Preston Family Welfare Survey*, County Borough of Preston, 1965.

Young, M. F. D. (ed.), *Knowledge and Control* (Collier-Macmillan, London, 1971).

SECTION B

Strategies for Care: some aspects
of guidance and counselling

Introduction

The chapters in this section are concerned with specific aspects of guidance and counselling, and of the nature and activities of some of the roles associated with pastoral care. Together they provide some useful insights into the strategies which teachers and specialists might adopt in meeting the pastoral needs of their pupils.

Those who know Keith Blackburn's book *The Tutor*[1] will find his chapter on the developing role of the tutor an interesting extension of his thinking about this key position in the pastoral structure. They will also find many useful hints on how to convert tutorial aims into sound practice in the tutor room, and some of the strategies which teachers might adopt in helping the pupil to come to terms with himself and understand the various demands made upon him. Of particular significance is Blackburn's belief that the tutorial function must be seen as only one facet of the role of the member of staff as a *professional*, employed to bring about learning. Thus, although for analytical (and to some extent practical) purposes, the distinction between teaching and tutoring has to be made, the role of the tutor is developing into one of a support system for the child in all aspects of his school career. The thrust of the argument is therefore towards making the tutor's role more effective in achieving the broad aims of education, by recognizing the overall responsibility all teachers share for the welfare of their charges.

Conventional conceptions of the teacher's pastoral roles have been inadequate for other reasons. All too often the tutor has been expected to work either with a whole class (his form) or else on a one-to-one basis in individual counselling sessions. In either case, the tutor stands alone as a care-agent. At the same time, an emphasis on rather romantic conceptions of 'care' and 'support' for children has drawn attention away from the importance of order and discipline without which the fundamental aims of teaching — that is, bringing about occasions of learning — cannot be realized. A number of chapters in this section each, in their way, seek to correct these inadequacies.

Leslie Button demonstrates that an ability to work with and through groups of children is every bit as important for the tutor as the development of individual counselling techniques. This is particularly true if the social and affective aspects of the child are to be developed in the context of a meaningful programme of social education. In an important sense education is only 'social' if it is undertaken in the context of the group(s) which are significant for the child. In this respect, the casework model is inadequate, reducing the tutor's role (as Hamblin puts it[2]), to one of administering 'emotional first aid'. This does *not* mean that the individual child's development is not the central concern: what it means is that this can only be catered for adequately by a realistic appraisal of the group context in which such development takes place. It is therefore important that teachers develop expertise in group processes and strategies for handling them, and also that the pastoral programme of the school be thought out with group-tutoring in mind.

Douglas Hamblin takes up an aspect of pastoral care which, perhaps more than any other, is of pressing concern for many teachers. As we have ourselves suggested[3], pastoral-care structures and activities may have as much to do with resolving the problems of teachers as they have to do with the welfare of children, but it would be naive to think that the two are always mutually exclusive. In outlining a strategy for coping with difficult and disruptive classes, Hamblin reminds us that anti-social behaviour is indicative of mal-adaptation by either or both the child and the teacher. Where an entire class constitutes a control problem for several teachers, what is needed is a rational problem-solving approach by the teachers acting as a *team*. Although some readers may take issue with the concept of 'behaviour modification' with its overtones of 'conditioning', there can be no doubt that a careful analysis of situations of tension and disruption in the classroom is an essential step in planning teaching activities, whether pastoral *or* instructional.

The conventional distinction between different kinds of guidance — personal, vocational and academic — is no less artificial than the teacher—tutor dichotomy, but for purposes of analysis and organization it, too, has to be made. Tony Watts and Beryl Fawcett suggest that a softening of this distinction has helped to move the emphasis in vocational guidance away from the imparting of information and advice by outside specialists towards Careers Education and Counselling from within the school. The form tutor can play a part here, but if he is to play it adequately some sort of professional training is required. The Careers Department of the school will clearly play a key role in careers education, but it might also give leadership and direction to this aspect of the form tutor's role. How careers education is organized is a matter for those who organize the curriculum as a whole — a point which anticipates a number of papers in later sections.

The professionalization of guidance and counselling in schools is also the topic of Pat Milner's piece on changing patterns of care in schools. The piece-meal *ad hoc*-ism of the amateur tradition is simply inadequate, and she argues for a better planned and more systematic provision of guidance in education. In such a system the role of properly trained and professionally qualified counsellors would be pivotal.

However, the role of the school counsellor is not unproblematic. As Taylor's chapter shows, counselling itself may have to involve a good .

deal of *ad hoc*-ism in so far as there is no single, comprehensive and generally accepted theory of *either* counselling *or* the psychology which informs it. Counselling is more an art than a science, and in the last analysis it is perhaps an intelligent pragmatism which we ought to look for in both counsellor and tutor.

However that may be, some sort of division of labour is necessary, and there is no way in which all the guidance tasks of the school can be undertaken by tutors working in isolation. Certainly, as Blackburn, Watts and Fawcett, and Button amply demonstrate, the tutorial task is fundamental to any such endeavour, but it needs to be complemented, and to some extent advised and given direction by, skilled specialists in their fields. To improve pastoral-care provision, we need not only better, more professional, and more organized tutors; we need skilled experts to provide a specialized service as well. We also need to recognize that corporate goals are best achieved by collective means − thus the concept of *teams* of teachers and specialists in the areas of personal, academic and vocational guidance may be central to future developments in this field. Finally, such provision needs to be seen in the context of overall curriculum development, where group work in social and careers education is seen as an integral part of the educational enterprise. These concepts are among those developed in subsequent sections of this book.

References

1 Heinemann, London, 1975.
2 D. H. Hamblin, *The Teacher and Pastoral Care*, (Blackwell, Oxford, 1978).
3 See chapters 1 and 16.

5   The Tutor: a developing role

Keith Blackburn

In the 1950s, when the LCC began its programme of large purpose-built comprehensive schools, it was recognized that a new type of school would need new ways of working and new forms of organization. Such a school was Crown Woods in south-east London, which met this need in the following way:

> When the School was founded in 1957 it was decided to organise it on lines which are more familiar in boarding schools than in day schools. A dual system of organisation was devised. The social life of the school is channelled through *Houses and their constituent House Tutor Groups.* The work of the school is carried on in '*Ability Divisions', in Forms and sets.* From the beginning, a child thus forms relationships on two different levels. There are the 'working' relationships of the form in which he is placed, and in which he will find children of roughly similar ability to his own. And there are the 'family' relationships formed in the House Tutor Group, composed of children with all degrees of natural ability.[1]

The Head of House and the House Tutor were charged with 'the care and guidance of each pupil' and 'safeguarding the welfare of individual boys and girls throughout their school life'.[2]

At Crown Woods School the formation of mixed social groups was an important aspect of the school's philosophy. Devising a structure was a response to the problem of size. In the large boarding school — Eton was the model at Crown Woods — teachers *knew* the pupils they taught but it was the Housemaster and the House tutor who had an overall picture of particular pupils' progress and were able to offer guidance: so it would be in the large comprehensive school.

These developments at Crown Woods were paralleled in other schools. Robin Pedley reported in 1963 that the House system 'existed in ninety-five per cent of the comprehensive schools'.[3] He writes:

> The picture of a personal tutor watching over the interests of each child, in close touch with his parents, collecting and assimilating information about him from other members of staff, guiding his pupils in the choice of courses and the many personal problems of school life, is a fine idealistic one. There is no doubt that not only in schools of over 1,000 but in most schools of 500 or so, too, care of this kind is needed. It would transform the effectiveness of our education.[4]

In the mid-1950s it was seen that a new role was being created for teachers in secondary schools whose chief emphasis was *knowing individual pupils.* As far as I can discover it was in these years that the

terms 'tutor' and 'tutor group' came into use in maintained schools. /
    At the same time the Head of House and the tutors became the
focus for the school's discipline. 'In the day to day running of the
school the Heads of House take a very large share of responsibility
for discipline and the maintenance of good standards and their authority
is commensurate with the work they do.'[5] Heads of House and tutors
were expected to deal with problems of lateness, personal organization
and behaviour. Corporal punishment was delegated and the Heads of
House liaised with the supportive services. The focus was on dealing
with pupils who presented a problem to the institution of the school.
A *problem-solving model* was added to that of *knowing individual
pupils*.
    In the 1960s careers guidance became an issue of concern. 'Because
of poor advice (and no advice) thousands of young people at all levels
of education carry through their working lives feelings of aggrievement,
frustration and personal inadequacy.'[6] Writers were advocating a
programme of personal development within the schools.[7] Rita Howden
and Harry Dawson in *Practical Guidance for Schools*[8] spelt out the way
they saw the qualified careers teachers and tutors each taking part in
this work.
    The publication of *Cross'd with Adversity* and *Children in Distress*
focused attention on pupils who, while presenting no problem to the
institution, were themselves experiencing problems.[9] The role of the
school was to identify these pupils; some would be referred to external
agencies for help while others would need to be helped in school.
These developments coincided with the advent of counsellors, and
schools were led to think of their work with individual pupils in terms
of 'education, vocational and personal' guidance.[10] Some schools
appointed careers teachers and counsellors, but even where these roles
existed the tutor was seen to have an important part to play in these
developing responsibilities in the school.
    Patrick Hughes has described the development of guidance and
counselling as 'a response to change'.[11] He quotes Reuchlin' 'One
hears little of pupil guidance in periods of social and economic stability.'[12] In similar vein, Douglas Hamblin writes, 'As the rate of social
change accelerates, so does the work of the teacher and his contribution
to the pupil's search for identity and purpose in life becomes vital.'[13] It
is now being suggested that issues of personal growth and relationships
should form a principal focus of the school's learning programme.
Michael Marland has written about the 'pastoral curriculum', arguing
that a school needs to identify the concepts, attitudes, facts and skills
that it wants its pupils to learn.[14] Douglas Hamblin has put forward
ideas about the way that this might be worked out in practice.[15] Leslie
Button has described the techniques of 'developmental group work',[16]
and this thinking has found expression in a programme of 'Active
Tutorial Work' devised by the Lancashire Curriculum Development
Project.[17]

These developments coincide with the shift from subject learning to child-centred learning. R. S. Peters[18] has taught us to think of pupils becoming 'autonomous', but this has tended to be applied mainly to subject learning. The school is now seen also to have a role in helping pupils to become 'autonomous' as people, and this involves the pupils' understanding about themselves and their relationships with others. It can be argued that these issues have always been implicit in subject learning, but as a 'spin off' from learning in English or Biology or Games. Now the school is to engage in explicit learning activities in these areas.

Against the background of such developing expectations of what the tutor will achieve it is not surprising that there is a variety of understandings about what the role involves, not only from school to school, but within a school.

Tutorial Role and Aims

I want to argue that each member of staff is a professional, trained to bring about relationships in which learning can occur. This has tended to be thought of in terms of subject learning, with the tutor servicing the subject-learning needs of the school. But learning must be seen in a wider context which includes, in addition to learning the content and skills associated with subjects, learning about the individual and his relationships with others. Each member of staff contributes in various ways to the total learning experiences of the pupil and the way each contributes affects not only a pupil's success in subject learning but his understanding of himself, his relationship with others and his membership of the community. Each member of staff has to consider his contribution to all aspects of the school's work and measure it against the notion of learning and growth which leads to autonomy.

The division of roles between 'teacher' and 'tutor', while useful in sorting out ideas, leads to a false division in the role of a member of staff. 'In this context I am teaching. In this context I am tutoring.' Writ large this leads to an academic structure and a pastoral structure in the school which are seen as opposed to one another. The division is not a problem in the small one-teacher school. In the larger school staff must divide the work that they undertake between them and between groups of pupils. I should like to see included in the role of each member of staff responsibilities which for convenience, and in the absence of a better term, I will label *tutorial*.

Learning situations with particular groups will be distinguished by the principal focus of each occasion. 'In this context I am seeking to increase the pupil's understanding of himself and his relationships with others. In this context I am seeking to extend his understanding of the physical universe. In this context I am hoping to increase his

THE TUTOR: A DEVELOPING ROLE

skills in writing. In this context I am looking to increase his ability to cope with the demands that the school is making on him.' Each member of staff brings the demanding and caring aspects of his role, the teaching and tutoring aspects of his role, into every situation. Indeed on the shop floor person meets person.

The development of tutorial work has led to a perception of an additional role being added to that of the teacher. Since the pupil's role is of course made up of a variety of sub-roles — student, tutee, team member, actor, musician, monitor — so too is that of members of staff. In school adults as members of staff play roles which also involve a whole set of sub-roles, each brought to the fore in particular contexts. Staff and pupils alike bring to the task appropriate aspects of their role according to the demands of the situation. Pupils are more able than is often claimed to cope in their role as pupil with the varied aspects of the role of member of staff.

The tutorial aspects of the role of member of staff lead to the inclusion of the following aims among the others which he has already. He will seek to help the pupils —

to cope more successfully with their work in school and to monitor progress;

to understand and participate in the school community;

to understand themselves;

by contributing to their personal growth;

to make their own decisions;

to learn ways of coping with relationships and resolving conflicts;

to relate to others more effectively.

These aims are part of all aspects of a member of staff's work with pupils and inform every approach he makes. In some circumstances — in his dealings with members of his tutor group in tutorial time and in his one-to-one dealings with this group — they will form the principal focus of his work and he will seek to create learning situations in which these aims can be achieved. He will meet both groups and individuals in other contexts in which there are opportunities and sometimes the need to bring these aspects of the work to the fore. The group which arrives from a 'bad' experience in the previous period of time may need the opportunity to talk through their relationship in that context before there is any hope of the group tackling the tasks planned for the current lesson. Questioning a pupil about his missing homework in Mathematics will involve the member of staff in contributing to a pupil's work in school; handled appropriately, more successfully, handled insensitively the reverse is likely to be the case.

There is a confusion that recurs in discussion. At its extreme the picture is drawn of the member of staff who has so adopted a caring stance that he has become unable to make demands on a pupil. To extend the homework illustration: pupils need to have working standards set and to have the demands that this imposes firmly placed on them. To fail to work out the boundaries of what is expected and what is acceptable and to see that these boundaries are maintained is to leave the pupils in a state of confusion and gives rise to experiences of insecurity. John may need to be pushed to produce his homework and action taken if he fails. In this way he will be more successful. On the other hand John may be having difficulty with the work that is set, such that he cannot tackle what is asked of him. He may be experiencing difficulties beyond the immediate situation of the class which make it impossible to tackle the work at present. To increase demand in an unthinking way will certanly not lead to success but is likely to make success even more difficult to achieve. The good teacher is able to gauge this and to approach each situation in a way that will lead to success. To polarize demand and care and to institutionalize them into the demanding teacher and the caring tutor leads to total confusion. Every member of staff has to be both demanding and caring and to know in which situations, with which pupils, he needs to bring to the fore different approaches in order to help the pupil forward.

There may appear to be a conflict between the needs of the group and the needs of the individual. 'Can I allow John to get away with it, while others are having to do the work?' The answer to this goes beyond the particular teacher with a particular class. It depends on the ethos that exists in the school and the way pupils are being shown to relate to one another. In a situation where an understanding and acceptance of individual differences are encouraged in relationships, in which the variety of difficulties that are experienced can be acknowledged, in which, to use Leslie Button's phrase,[19] the group is 'encouraged to care for each other', pupils will be able to accept that some will need to be dealt with personally and therefore differently. This parallels the experience of the good family. The learning will be further helped if pupils are able to verbalize their experience of unjust treatment in a way that the reasons which lead to the difference in treatment can be discussed. The blanket statement 'no homework: detention', which imposes a right demand on some, increases the stress on others.

A further confusion arises in discussion of the various roles of a member of staff. We talk about the teacher and the class, focusing on the interaction as if this were the only teacher that the class met; the only class the teacher met. Similarly discussion of tutorial work tends to assume that tutorial aims will only be achieved by the tutor working with his group in tutorial time. In reality each school is a complex of relationships which make it impossible to tie down each situation in a way that precludes the possibility of learning about the topics designated to one period of teaching in other situations. Recent discussion about the false boundaries of subjects can be extended to say that the aims I have designated 'tutorial' will be furthered in many ways within the school.

Aims into Practice

Against this background I wish to discuss the possibilities for work with the tutor group and with its individual members, not making any exclusive claims that this is the only way in which tutorial aims will be furthered in a school, but exploring ways in which they can form the principal focus of work in part of the school's curriculum. Despite the difficulties of the concepts involved and because I have been unable to discover an alternative word, I shall for convenience continue to use 'the tutor' to refer to the role of members of staff in this work in school.

Each tutor has to pose the question, 'Where is this group now?' 'Where is each of the individual members of my group?' Each school is in some measure different from the next. These differences arise from the social context in which the school is placed, the ethos and aims, both explicit and implicit, that have been formulated over a period of years and the changes that are taking place both beyond the school and within it. I have argued elsewhere[20] that a member of staff when he joins the school joins a community that is in the process of change, and to take his part within that changing community he needs to 'size up' where the school is. His arrival is part of the process of change and his contribution to the school will be a contribution — perhaps great, perhaps small — to the change that is in process.

It is also true that each group of pupils is in the process of change. The tutor joins a group at a particular time and travels through a period of change to which he will contribute. In order to understand how he can fulfil his role he must discover where the group is — the hopes, the fears, the ethos, the style of relationship and the self-image that the group holds. The possibilities for a 'free hand' are greatest with a group of pupils who have just joined the school, but even here the members of the group bring from their homes and from their previous experiences assumptions which they contribute, usually unconsciously, to the group. The tutor who takes on a group that has already been formed and had a period of experience as a group will discover that parallel groups may be very different from each other in these terms. One group has always had difficulty in the personal relationships of its members in which conflict has led to rigid and hostile sub-groupings. The group has been experienced by teachers as difficult to handle and difficult to like. These reactions have led the group to believe that they are unlikeable and they have responded in a hostile manner to adults. It is with a curious pride that they declare 'We are unteachable' and this declaration may mask the underlying hope that someone will be able to help them to break out of this trap. The tutor alone may not be able to do much in the face of what the school keeps declaring to these pupils through other members. Another group may have jelled into a caring and co-operative group whose members have a basic liking of each other and have become accustomed to move from one successful experience to another. They need to be guided, and to look positively towards the tutor to contribute to their work. The variety is as great as the groups are many. 'Where is this group and what can I do next to take them effectively one step forward?' is the continuing question for the tutor. Week by week he poses this question in order to focus on the activities for the coming week. There are in each year matters that have to be tackled to forward the work of the institution, such as discussing choices of subjects for the fourth and fifth year, or organizing a letter to parents, which will provide part of the group's agenda. There are also likely to be issues in each year which are common to all groups such as the need of first-year pupils to find their way round the school or of fifth-year pupils to decide their next step. But the need of one group to talk through organizing homework or bullying or difficulties in relationships with adults does not mean that a parallel group needs to embark on that at the same time. The issue may arise at another point in the year; it may not arise at all. The tutor has part of the agenda for work with his group given by the institution; it is in part provided by the needs and issues expressed by the pupils, and it will be completed by the tutor's understanding of issues that are of concern to the group which they need help in to articulate. For a Head of second year to plan for all groups to discuss uniform in the first week in October and homework on 5th March is likely to give rise to tedious tutorial work, unless by curious chance the pupils happen to be particularly aware of these issues at these times.

Keeping a diary of what has taken place with the group during the week is a helpful way of focusing on where the group is and what might be the next step to take. The teacher who takes parallel groups in the same year knows that material has to be adapted and approaches modified from group to group. In tutorial work this difference is more marked.

What is true of the group is true of the individual members of the group. Each pupil is at a different point. The home is the chief source of this variation, and friendships give rise to further variation. From these sources each pupil is formulating a sense of his own image and identity. The school contributes to the formation of the pupil's understanding of who he is and how he is valued. The tutor has to understand the way each child pictures himself if he is to be able to contribute to his further understanding and insight. Mary is pressed hard by her family to be successful in school. Brian comes from a home which sees school in negative ways and he feels that he has to sit it out, perhaps actively expressing his protest, until the date of his 'final release'. John comes from a supportive home which has given him a right sense of freedom as he has grown up. He is basically confident in all that he does and has no difficulty in asking for help when he feels stuck. Jane has always been surrounded by fear — of colds, of accidents, of disapproval, of failing to do what was expected of her. Drawn in this way

it is easy to say that the competent teacher will respond appropriately
to these pupils, but this implies that steps have been taken to find
out where the pupil is. Further, the pupils in a school are subject to
change, and although the major factors affecting their response may
not change (they may), it is certain that their self-image will undergo
modification, their style of relating to others be adapted. In the long
view it is easy to see the way a particular pupil has developed. The
tutor works with pupils in the process of change and has to be aware
of the small changes in stances and image if he is going to be able to
work effectively with individual members of his group as one of the
agents contributing to that change.

It is sometimes asked if a teacher has a right to contribute to the
personal development of the pupil. In part, of course, schools exist to
bring about changes in those who come as pupils, and their *raison
d'être* is to affect the development of each pupil. More finely expressed,
the teacher is happy about changes which lead to mastery in Mathematics or French or on the games field. The question becomes whether
he should seek to influence the pupil in areas that are traditionally
defined as personal. This question is false. By being in group situations
with pupils and meeting them one by one each member of staff inevitably influences the pupils. The question is, in what ways will he
choose to present himself and to interact with pupils? Which of the
variety of ways of influencing them will he choose to adopt?

Tutorial planning has been seen as devising ways of occupying the
members of the group in a variety of activities which will enable the
tutor to get on with the 'real' work of one-to-one relationships. This
follows from the models of tutorial work that can be discerned in
schools. 'The predominance of the case work model through which
the teacher seeks to deal with one person at a time has involved a
neglect of the relationship between members of the pastoral group
and the urgency of creating a caring community within a class.'[21] In
practical terms this means that the tutor has to plan *both* what he
will do with the group as an integral part of his tutorial work *and*
what he will do with its individual members.

Classroom Strategies

How can tutorial aims be turned into practical classroom strategies?
Within the tutorial team there must be discussion of the needs of the
pupils and an exchange of experiences between tutors of ways that they
have found effective with particular groups. In the same way that resources have been built up for subject learning, each school needs to build
its tutorial resources so that tutors can draw from each other's ideas as
well as contributing their own. Tutors also need to become familiar
with the techniques of informal group work — leading an open discussion,
the use of 'buzz' groups and the ways pupils can find out for themselves

aspects of their relationships through 'action research'.

Traditionally, pupils are given their timetables for the year and, armed with a pen, a pencil, a ruler and a rubber, are launched into the deep. It is assumed that they will be able to cope with the problems of organizing their time to meet the demands that are placed on them. The opportunity to plan together how each can arrange his work in detail — what books to take home each evening and which to bring to school each day; when to bring shorts; how to deal with the problem of the games practice evening and the homework demands on that night — is likely to lead to a higher rate of successful coping with the work. A 'dead-lines' board helps pupils to focus on the forthcoming demands on their time. It is often assumed that pupils will know how to undertake tasks such as reading, note-taking, research, revision and learning. These were skills I stumbled on at school later rather than earlier! When asked to make notes the pupil is often confused about the extent to which he is expected to write. Is he to copy the whole section? Is he to reduce it to a few lines? Pupils are set to 'find out about'. Some parents provide their children with sources of reference and help; other pupils have no idea about the actions they must take in order to be successful in this activity. (It is sometimes sobering to ask a colleague what he expected the pupils to do and to discover that he was not sure — beyond them 'using their initiative'.) So with 're-vision' and 'learning'. What is the pupil expected to do when he leaves the class? Teachers will, of course, take responsibility for clarifying their expectations for pupils, but it is those pupils who find difficulty in coping with the work demands who are most likely not to 'hear' what is said. It is not until John actually starts to tackle the work task set that he discovers he does not know what to do. Mary may believe that she is doing what is expected of her because the possibility of other ways of tackling the work has simply not occurred to her.

In these situations the group can explore together how each of these tasks is undertaken so that pupils help each other by describing their own experiences and by seeing other possibilities. The tutor's role is not so much in providing the answers from his own experience but in creating a situation in which pupils learn from each other. Through the years of secondary education this provides a continuing area of work as the demands on pupils increase.

Douglas Hamblin has written of sixth-form students, but it applies to all pupils — 'instead of haphazardly urging higher achievement upon students, we provide them with an analysis of the factors influencing achievement which they can apply to themselves.'[22]

The tutor can contribute to this analysis and help pupils to discover the ways in which they must act in order to be successful in their learning. This will mean for the tutor that he will need to discover from his colleagues in disciplines other than his own how they approach their work with pupils so that he can have some insight into the problems that are posed for the members of his group.

Pupils joining a secondary school are often bewildered by the variety of expectations that each teacher has of them. In one class they must wait outside the room, in another they are expected to be in their places with their books out ready to start work. In one class they can discuss the work with their neighbour; indeed discussion may be an essential part of the teacher's plan for the lesson. In another class all communication must be through the teacher and pupils are not expected to talk with each other. The variety of expectations can be brought into tutorial discussion so that pupils contribute the differences that they experience and learn something of the variety of ways they have to approach people in relationships.

Induction into the school will involve giving pupils information about the routines and procedures that have been adopted. When Sally asks again about the procedure for lost property she may be asking for help in her approach to the adult who deals with this. 'I do not know how to ask a stranger for what I want.' Role-playing situations in which pupils approach adults will help her to see ways in which she can approach her problem.

Issues of relationship come to the fore when groups and individuals find themselves in trouble with a teacher. Sometimes the group is clear in their minds how they got into a particular difficulty; sometimes they are bewildered and are far from clear how they must act in future to avoid that problem. Exploring the factors that led to the situation, the way members of the group felt about their part in it, and the way the adult felt about his part may lead to an understanding of the relationships involved. A single discussion may effect change; there may be need for a continuing discussion if there is to be change. The same is true of the individual pupil who gets into trouble. Too often, perhaps, the tutor is seen as an additional sanction, rather than a way of helping the pupil to learn about himself through the difficulties he experiences.

Regular assessments and reports form an important part of a school's programme. Teachers write about their pupils. Parents and teachers discuss the child's progress. Less frequently is it true that the pupil is involved in this discussion. The report may convey expressions of dissatisfaction but the pupil can be unaware of the ways in which he can modify his behaviour to achieve more effective learning. 'He could do better'. 'Haphazardly urging higher achievement'.[23] The inarticulated question of the pupil is often 'Yes, but how can I do this?' A related issue is: how does the pupil perceive himself in each of the learning situations? The teacher may feel he is doing well, but the pupil does not see it that way. Often he has no chance to express his viewpoint. Similarly, he may wonder why a particular teacher is complaining; as he sees it himself, all is going well. The tutor is able to help pupils to focus on the assessment of their performance in two ways. A questionnaire exploring progress to date and helping the pupils to identify areas in which they have advanced as well as setting goals for the immediate future is an activity for the group.[24] Talking through each pupil's progress with him, seeking to identify areas where the adult's picture of the pupil is at variance with his own so that these areas can be more fully explored, brings the tutor into a one-to-one relationship with members of his group.

Each school distributes information to pupils and parents through the year. However well written and presented notices and letters may be, pupils need to be helped to understand what is being asked of them. Information is disseminated at assemblies and in other ways and needs to be reinforced if pupils are to be able to respond. There is a programme of extra-curricular activities for which pupils volunteer and some need to be helped to participate in. Perhaps they have not grasped the facts and need information. Perhaps the pupil cannot cope with the social relationships implied in turning up and needs help. Perhaps he cannot see how to tackle the problem of how to get home if he stays after school. It is easy to dismiss a non-response as a lack of interest; this it may be. But for some pupils there is a need for them to be helped into such situations. Add to this school policies about punctuality, dress, the use of facilities and expected standards of behaviour and the tutor has the task of interpreting the school and its policies to the pupils.

Each of these issues can be raised in the group in a variety of ways which enable pupils to learn from each other. For example, it may be more effective to get pupils to work out in small buzz groups the reasons for uniform and to draw from their responses a list that each pupil makes up for himself, than to give each pupil the teacher's list. A noticeboard, built up by the pupils, of extra-curricular activities, with pupils asked to tell the group about their experiences of these, may be more effective in encouraging participation than the adult encouragement to take part. This may do little more than increase the stress which is preventing participation.

These classroom strategies provide no more than a sketch of a possible approach to tutorial work with the group and have to be set in the context of the changes that take place as pupils pass from childhood through adolescence to adulthood. Erik Erikson's description of the 'Crisis of Identity' in which the growing child asks the question 'Who am I?' both in the sense of 'what am I like now?' and 'what do I want to become?' provides a useful working model for the tutor.[25] The pupil is continuously gathering information about himself from home, from school and from his friends. The tutor, by his observations and by his silences, contributes to the pupil's forming self-image. Pupils are quick to sense the way they are valued by adults and take odd remarks as well as more intentionally directed remarks into their thinking about themselves. There is a tendency for teachers to draw more attention to failure than to success. Alerted to the possibility of commenting on successes and expressing positive valuation of the individual pupil and of the group can help towards the creation of a more positive self-concept.

The pupil's attempt to discover who he is in the sense of what he wants to become brings the tutor into discussion of the pupil's own choices.[25] The school will demand that a pupil needs to formulate his ideas in order that he can make choices of subjects for study and to decide whether he will continue in education or seek employment. This involves the tutor in a programme of work with the group exploring the possible course of action that can be taken. The tutor also becomes involved with each pupil, helping him to come to his own decision about his future. It is convenient for the school if the pupil is able to announce his career goal so that an appropriate programme can be devised to make this possible; assuming the goal is realistic. In reality many pupils do not find such a formulation easy, and in a context of unemployment many pupils have to be helped to make immediate choices without knowing the goal.

The institutional demands of the school, the learning experiences of the pupils, their personal growth needs and their discoveries about relationships provide an agenda for the tutor's work both with the group and with the individual. He can use the techniques of presenting stimulus material, buzz-group discussion, role-play and action research as well as one-to-one counselling in order to turn issues that he thinks need to be raised into practical learning experiences for the members of his group. His task is essentially an aspect of the school's programme of learning. He will continue to undertake the traditional form master's role in relating to parents and to fulfil the problem-solving role of identifying problem pupils and bringing appropriate sources of help to the situation; these roles are more readily understood.

Future Developments

The possibilities for tutorial work have grown apace since the 1950s. In this development there has been a tendency for the *demanding* role of the teacher to be opposed to the *caring* role of the tutor. I have argued that this division is unrealistic in the way that teachers work with pupils and have pressed for a change towards the view of the role of a member of staff, which incorporates the various sub-roles. Curriculum developments are also bringing changes in the style of relationships between teachers and pupils in the direction of co-operative participation in learning experiences. Relationships are changing in all aspects of the school.

The academic–pastoral division is also being crossed by the concept of the pastoral curriculum. I have argued that there is a tutorial contribution to the learning programme of the school, which is as important to pupils as the subjects that are studied. Michael Marland has suggested that a school has to decide to whom it will allocate aspects of the pastoral curriculum.[26] If all tutors are to take a full part in this developed programme, training is essential. Teachers are trained to define goals and to work with pupils in achieving these goals. The pupil in answering a question usually has a sense that the teacher knows the answer and is leading him to discover the answer for himself. Teachers also need to develop skills in working with groups and individuals in which questions are posed as a way of enabling pupils to come to their own answers. In these situations the teacher facilitates an exploration and discovery, believing that it is important that pupils participate in the process and leaving open the insights and conclusions that each may draw from the experience.

Perhaps the developed picture of the tutorial role will be seen to place too great a demand on all teachers, and some aspects of the work will have to be dealt with by specialists. Perhaps the 'pastoral head' will be the person who will 'teach' the pastoral curriculum within the time-table and will have to work out the interrelationship of this with the work of the other members of the pastoral team. Implicit in this is that the qualifications for pastoral leadership will include training in group work and in counselling skills and an ability to design the learning experiences of the pastoral curriculum, providing also resources for it.

As the possibilities for tutorial work have developed, so has the spectrum of teachers' ideas of what it means to be a good tutor. Teachers with whom I have worked in schools and on courses emphasize different aspects of the role that I have sketched and express different opinions about the importance of the work within the school. It is common to hear teachers say that they do not have enough time to do the work properly. Some schools have made no provision of time, and there is a need to review the place of tutorial work within the whole curriculum. Sometimes the question of time reflects the deeper issue of teachers who do not feel that they have the skills required to work effectively — there is a need for training. The question may also reflect the view of teachers who feel that they have been asked to cope with too many changes in recent years or who feel that they are employed to teach their subject and that too much attention has been paid to tutorial work.

A 'no change' stance could be upheld if it were not for the social changes going on outside school which press for changes within the school. I have described the way that teachers in some schools are seeking to respond to change so that pupils are able to gain fully from their years in school.

References

1   Crown Woods School, published by the School in 1963.
2   op. cit.
3   Robin Pedley, *The Comprehensive School* (Penguin, Harmondsworth, 1963).
4   op. cit.
5   Crown Woods School, op. cit. (note 1).
6   *The Times Review of Industry*, 10 November 1964.

7   Peter Daws, *A Good Start in Life* (Careers Research Advisory Centre, Cambridge, 1971). Education Survey 18, *Careers Education in Secondary Schools* (DES, London, 1973). J. Hayes and B. Hopson, *Careers Guidance* (Heinemann, London, 1972).

8   R. Howden and H. Dawson, *Practical Guidance for Schools — Educational and Vocational Guidance as Part of the School Curriculum* (Careers Consultants, 1973).

9   Schools Council, *Cross'd with Adversity*, Working Paper 27 (Methuen, London, 1970); Sir A. Clegg and B. Megson, *Children in Distress* (Penguin, Harmondsworth, 1968).

10 Schools Council, *Counselling in Schools*, Working Paper 15 (HMSO, 1967).

11 Patrick M. Hughes, *Guidance and Counselling in Schools* (Pergamon Press, Oxford, 1971).

12 op. cit., p. 193.

13 Douglas Hamblin, *The Teacher and Counselling* (Blackwell, Oxford, 1974).

14 Michael Marland, 'The Pastoral Curriculum', Chapter 11 in this volume.

15 Douglas Hamblin, *The Teacher and Pastoral Care* (Blackwell, Oxford, 1978).

16 Leslie Button, *Developmental Group Work with Adolescents* (Hodder & Stoughton, London, 1974).

17 Jill Baldwin and Harry Wells, *Active Tutorial Work:* 1. The First Year, 2. The Second Year (Blackwell, Oxford, 1979).

18 R. S. Peters, *Ethics and Education* (George ·Allen and Unwin, London, 1966).

19 *Developmental Group Work in the Secondary School Pastoral Programme*, Occasional Paper, Action Research Project, Department of Education, University College of Swansea, 1976.

20 *The Tutor* (Heinemann, London, 1975, paper 1978).

21 Leslie Button, op. cit. (note 17).

22 op. cit. (note 13).

23 Hamblin, op. cit. (note 13).

24 Examples of questionnaires are given in *Active Tutorial Work*, op. cit. (note 15).

25 *Identity, Youth and Crisis* (Faber, London, 1968, paper 1971).

26 Michael Marland, 'The Pastoral Curriculum', see Chapter 11 of this volume.

6   The Skills of Group Tutoring

Leslie Button

Social Education?

There are some who question the need for any special arrangements for
pastoral care: this is the function of the school as a whole, they would
say. There is no doubt that some social and emotional experience is
produced by every moment of a school life, but I fear that, in many
cases, this may be very different from what is intended.

Normal classroom activity has its covert as well as its overt meaning,
and the covert level of experience is part of the hidden curriculum.
Teaching may be seen as a cognitive exercise, but it will also be carrying
messages about the identity of the actors, their relative statuses, about
appropriate behaviours for teachers and scholars, and about levels of
personal significance. Over a period of time, this can amount to a conditioning that enters the self-feelings and personal identity of all concerned. Some young people find their school experience enlivening and
extending, but others are confirmed as failures, or made to feel that
they are people of little worth. Even pastoral work may be about conditioning rather than social education, for many pastoral systems are
much more about control and conformity than they are about the
growth of social competence, personal responsibility and maturity.

It is quite inevitable that the pupil's daily experience in school will
lead to some kind of conditioning, and to a cumulative influence on the
pupil's self-feelings. Even a denial that this takes place, or an attempt to
abdicate, merely leads to a different kind of conditioning. It is true that
the school is only one of the forces that bear upon the socialization of
the child, and what can be attempted at school is interactive with a
number of other influences. In adolescence, the peer group may be as
powerful as the family or more so. All this subsists within an atmosphere created by the local and wider community, including the self-
interest of the commercial world. But the influence of the school can
be very formative, and should not be underestimated.

This paper is written from the viewpoint that the school will be
wishing to help young people in their personal growth, in their social
skills, and in their responsibility and maturity. It is informed by experience gained through an action research project that I have directed,
concerned with developmental group work, and the work of the form
teacher as a group tutor.

Most social-education programmes seem to be about offering young people information. In some schools considerable efforts are made to involve young people in discussion, but here again the programme may be topic-based rather than about developing skills in the young people involved. It is like a camera panning from topic to topic, but at much the same level all the time. The discussion may touch individual people, but is just as likely to remain at the level of exchanging opinions about the topics concerned. It is possible to carry through an excellent cognitive programme of this kind without having any real impact on young people at an affective level.[1]

A very different kind of programme is required in order to help young people in their social skills and self-feelings. The young person must himself be the focus of the exchange. And a step-by-step exploration will be needed, where each step enables the young person to cope with the next, deeper step. The programme would proceed from a study of the situation in which they find themselves, to an examination of their own attitudes and behaviour, to their manner and skills in coping with other people — friends, peers in general, the opposite sex, their parents and siblings, with strangers, adults, and people in authority — and from there to the deeper self-feelings that influence every department of life so strongly.

These issues are at the core of personal development. This is not to deny the importance of information about sex, drugs, smoking, alcohol, race and hygiene, which seem to figure so prominently in social-education programmes. But I am suggesting that even the most lively programme including these topics can ignore the mainsprings of personal behaviour.

In social education the approach is also a major part of the content. New skills and behaviours will need to be actually practised in the classroom. But if we are really concerned with life skills, the programme must be about behaviour in the world outside and not only in the special environment of the classroom. So what we do in the classroom must lead to new and creative action in the world outside, which implies deliberate practice and self-help on the part of the young people concerned.

These are not new ambitions in our educational system, but their urgency and difficulty has increased, especially as a result of the progressive depersonalization and mobility in our society, and by changing attitudes, including a marked lessening of deference to authority. So how best can the school make its contribution? Whenever there is competition between a task that can be clearly stated and pursued, and the exploration of personal issues and feelings, the task usually wins. It is largely for this reason that time needs to be committed, within the school timetable, to personal exploration, and to the practice of life skills, which would not occur in normal lesson times. But unless teachers are ready with the knowledge and skills required to lead into this area of work, then an allocation of time may result in poor rather than creative experience for the young people.

It is true that much can be achieved through the general ethos of the school in setting situations that are generous and creative. But something in addition is required if we are to enable young people to pursue their personal development. Some schools include specific lessons for courses in social education, although this may appear under a variety of titles such as health education, common core, or as part of a careers programme. But if social education is to have the personal development of young people at its centre, someone in the school must be in a position to know individual young people sufficiently well to be able to see that they receive the help that they require for each new step.

It is often suggested that there will always be someone in the school who will strike a relationship with a specific child. The claim may or may not be valid, but that kind of contact does not amount to the help that I am suggesting here. Heads of Years and Heads of Houses have been appointed with these kinds of ideas in mind, but their work is not really about programmes of personal development. It is quite impossible for a single person to keep a finger on the stage of development of a large number of young people whom they meet only occasionally, or whom they teach in moving from class to class. Potentially, the key person to foster the personal development of young people is the form teacher.

Herein lies great potential, but alas, in many schools, it is a great weakness. Many teachers are insecure in the role of form tutor and are embarrassed by it. We have tended to say to the form teacher, 'Here is your form. This is not about subjects but about the young people themselves.' And then we have left them without the help and support that this many-sided operation must receive. How were teachers trained for this function? It seems to me that we have been quite unfair to the form teacher in expecting him to face this task with insufficient preparation and support.

Limitations of the Casework Model

The approach to pastoral work in most schools seems to be based on a casework model, which assumes that the help required by each individual will be provided through a counselling or helping relationship between a specialist worker and a client, in this case the teacher and an individual young person. The function of the specialist staff in pastoral posts, such as Year Heads or Heads of Houses, has been seen as helping individual young people who present problems or need specific help or advice. Referral systems exist, which seem to be based on the assumption that those occupying these specialist posts are in the focal position in the caring for individual young people. Unfortunately, they are often so swamped by these referrals that they have difficulty in preventing their role becoming mainly a corrective one.

There is a great danger of this practice devaluing the role of the form tutor, and urgent steps should be taken to enable form tutors to deal with far more of the caring for members of their forms than at present seems to happen in many schools. The role of the Year or House Head needs to change from that of mainly referral, to leading his team of form tutors towards the expertise that will enable them to cope more adequately at the level of the tutorial group as a whole. But when I have put this proposition to pastoral heads, quite a number of them have said that they would have some difficulty in serving as team leaders, since they are not themselves articulate about the expertise involved. The pastoral heads, in turn, have been offered very little help in developing the expertise required to support their role.

One of the basic difficulties is that many schools are trying to use the one-to-one casework or counselling model in work for which it is quite inappropriate. The approach, in most cases, is problem- or crisis-centred as distinct from educative or developmental. The main efforts should be directed at the roots of the problem rather than at their manifestations, and to the development of the pupil's personal competence and sense of responsibility that would reduce the need for corrective action. When young people reach the pastoral head, the situation may have gone so far that he has little choice but to take corrective or punitive action.

There is little point in approaching young people as if they were islands. Each one is caught up in a mesh of group pressures, and the proper area for 'treatment' is the young person together with those who are most influencing him. In school, this so often means his peers. Besides, most personal difficulties run much deeper than the presenting problem, and may involve basic social skills, or relationships with parents, peers or those in authority. This can only be learnt in contact with other appropriate people, through supportive group situations.

Some young people find themselves in fixed roles, such as clown or scapegoat, and will need to be released from these roles by their peers if they are to develop new modes of behaviour. The clown is an interesting case in point, and all teachers will be acutely aware of the diversionary influence of some clowns, who can neutralize the serious efforts of their whole class. The clown may be able to respond quite sensibly to the adult counsellor, but will revert to role immediately on rejoining his peers. He has to conform to the expectations that have been built up of how he should behave in their company.

In the case of the scapegoat, teachers tend to concentrate on the bullying that takes place, to the neglect of the way in which the scapegoat offers himself for persecution. The scapegoat may already have established a life-style that invites persecution. The conscious help of his peers will be required in order to enable him to escape from his present role, and to practise new and more appropriate behaviours toward other people. Unfortunately, as our own studies have shown, teachers can easily be trapped into confirming these roles in the process of coping with the normal pressures of the classroom. Some of the saddest cases we meet are those who have difficulty in forming relaxed and warm relationships with peers, and these may range from the shy and lonely to the true delinquent.

To approach these quite fundamental issues — and the sources of so many of our 'problems' — we need to be working with and through groups. If young people are to be enabled to break out of the restrictions that surround them, for example, to learn new behaviours toward their peers, then they need to be freed by their peers from previous expectations, and to have the opportunity of practising new approaches. A supportive group is required as an arena in which to practise these new approaches.

The appointment of counsellors to a number of schools has made its own special contribution, but it has also had the severe disadvantage of increasing the expectation that pastoral care is about problem-centred, one-to-one counselling. Not only is this approach quite inappropriate for many of the situations being faced, but it is also impracticable in terms of the large numbers involved. It can also have the disadvantage that the existence of a 'specialist counsellor' can give rise to the acceptance that he has very special skills to which others will defer.

The casework approach rubs off also on the form tutor. I have met many teachers who have exerted themselves to serve their pastoral group, but have done it by trying to offer themselves in a one-to-one counselling relationship to each of their thirty charges. I have even been asked by form tutors whether I could suggest activities that will keep the other twenty-nine youngsters usefully and quietly employed while they cope with a single person. Quiet chatting among the young people, finishing bits of homework, and even card games during the pastoral period are sometimes justified by a teacher as a legitimate occupation for the many, while he helps the few.

The casework style in the classroom can lead to a teacher seeking individual relationships with the members of his tutorial group like the spokes round a wheel, with himself as the hub. He sees himself as the total resource for the group, and is neglecting the contribution that young people can make to one another. Unfortunately, as I have found personally, it is possible for the tutor to be working very hard in this way to establish individual relationships with each member of his tutorial group, and yet the young people may be divided among themselves, unsupportive, even destructive of one another. The tutor's efforts to maintain individual relationships may even exacerbate this situation by introducing some competition for his attention. There is much less thought given to how the pastoral group can be welded into a small caring community. The first steps towards this can be so simple, but the individual casework-counselling concept gets in the way.

Working through the Group

To create a caring community in the tutorial group should be the basic aim of the form tutor. By this I mean actively caring, with young people learning how to help one another in a whole range of personal ways. The teacher, in the relationships that he or she offers to individual young people, is still an important resource, but the function of the teacher is extended to becoming a third party, who will enable the young people to respond to one another. The necessary approaches by which this can be achieved have to be learnt. There must be school structures through which teachers can learn techniques and strategies, and be supported in developing new models of work.

A growing number of schools are applying models of work that I have called developmental group work.[2] The models have been evolved over a number of years in association with teachers, youth workers, social workers and others who work with young people. Much of the work arose from some fundamental research into small-group structures among adolescents, into the patterns of friendships maintained by individual young people, and into the kinds of controls that operate within those groups.[3] The study was conducted through action research in which teachers and youth workers participated by researching into their own work situations.[4] The approach in the present programme of work remains enquiry-based, and proceeds by helping young people to explore, step by step, their own life space and personal behaviours and feelings. And in order that they should be free to acquire new social skills and approaches to life, the programmes are essentially active and experiential. The group itself becomes a practice arena, leading to new experience deliberately and purposefully undertaken outside the group meetings.

The Young Person at the Centre of his Own Development

Young people are not going to dare to face their own position, and even less to share their exploration with other people, unless they judge the situation to be supportive. The tutor will need to create that support, both by the style of his own leadership and through a number of activities that can help to nurture support. The tutor can enable but not direct the development of the members of the group; this needs a commitment by the young people to extend their experience, or develop certain social skills. This means that the young person must be at the centre of his own exploration — it is his understanding of himself and his situation, not the adult's knowledge, that is important. And since group work is about young people helping one another, the individual will need to share with his colleagues the relevant parts of his own exploration, so that they will know how to respond to him. This would include releasing him from unhelpful expectations, as mentioned above in the case of the clown or scapegoat.

In practice this may mean that the shy person will learn how to meet other people without so much discomfort, and possibly to reach out to people whom he or she would like to know better; or the friendless youngster, who always manages to alienate his peers, will learn about his inappropriate behaviour and develop new approaches, or the relaxed and mature young person will experience and value the kind of contribution that he can make to other people. It is important also that we should help young people to develop their capacity for creative leadership. It is not enough that the members of the group learn to operate more effectively within the confines of a protective environment. The test of its contribution is whether it helps the individual to operate more effectively in the real world outside. So there will always be an element of outside experience − of homework or fieldwork, through which group members can continue to practise their new roles and behaviours in their normal life both inside and outside school. This often involves learning how to cope with strangers, with authority figures, even with unreasonable people, and sometimes with an uncomfortable home situation.

There needs to be a sequence in the exploration. Many situational factors can be analysed at a fairly simple descriptive level, but the perception of patterns of relationships needs growing sophistication, and to reach the underlying self-feelings needs real penetration. The models we are practising offer this kind of framework, with a programme for each year backed by a set of working papers.

The Teachers' Expertise

Although many teachers have a natural flair for bringing young people into a collaborative as distinct from a directive relationship, we find that most teachers need to learn some new skills and approaches, as well as to become familiar with the concepts involved in this work. It is not difficult, only unfamiliar. We have found that teachers need:

(a)   to have the experience themselves of being a member of a group of this kind;
(b)   to come to understand the basic concepts that underlie the work;
(c)   to work through an initial programme with young people with close guidance through a support group of teachers who are following a similar experience.

The techniques to be learnt include such things as methods of promoting support and communication skills, role play, Socratic group discussion, action research, socio-drama and sociometric techniques. But the techniques only serve to lead to an exploration guided by a clear conceptual framework. In the course of this work, we have collected a lot of evidence about the valuable ways in which the new expertise learnt as part of the group work programme has entered the teacher's normal teaching methods.

It must be clear from what I have written above that this kind of expertise implies a certain amount of specific preparation and training. The level of training and sophistication required depends to some extent upon the level of support that can be offered to the teacher within the school. The teacher adopting this kind of approach as something new in his school will normally require significant and extended training and support through some kind of district training scheme. But once established in the school, there are a number of ways in which support can be offered, and the same level of pre-training may not be required.

In working with local education authorities, and through them with some of the secondary schools in their areas, I have found that a number of long-term strategies are required. The first priority is for the local education authority to produce an indigenous training team within the local authority area, who can take on one generation of teachers after another. Secondly, each of the participant schools will send a number of teachers as their representatives to be trained to a fairly sophisticated level of competence and security. A small nucleus of skilled teachers may then be built up in each school, possibly over more than one year, and this nucleus will be seen as a school-based training group, who will lead teams of form tutors into more effective tutorial work. But we have found that there is a big step between the skilled nucleus feeling competent and secure in facing groups of young people, and their taking on the role of school-based trainers and team leaders. They need to be trained and supported as trainers.

Training Methods

The training methods that have been evolved to support this programme are based on the premise that the only way to ensure that the trainees learn new approaches in their work with young people is to engage them, step by step, in actual work with young people. The training is, therefore, based on a structured programme of work with young people, accomplished week by week in their own schools. This is the core of the training. The meetings of the training group serve to initiate each step in the fieldwork, to help the trainees to examine their experience after the event, and to establish the conceptual framework on which the approaches are based. The material thrown up by the enquiry-based approach is used as the raw material for much of the theoretical discussion.[5]

The techniques and strategies that the trainees will attempt in their work with young people are first tried out by using the training group as a workshop. The trainee explores his own situation, his own pattern of relationships, his friendships and self-feelings, and his attitudes towards authority — as later he will encourage his young people to do. The prevailing feedback we receive from the teachers involved may be summarized by the teacher who said, 'Well, I hope this has been of some help to the young people -- it has certainly been of great value to me.'

It will be apparent from the training methods outlined above that there must be an extended programme moving backwards and forwards from fieldwork to the meetings of the training group. Several training guides have been produced to meet differing circumstances. The teacher in training is offered an outline programme suggesting the kind and sequence of activities that can inspire a regular programme with a group of young people. This runs to eighteen stages, each of which could occupy an hour or more.

It is recommended, for the initial programme of work with young people, that the teacher should seek a group of, say, ten to twelve young people, who are aware that they are assisting him in his own training. This sense of collaboration in the venture usually seems to add an extra dimension to the experience of the young people concerned, and is in accord with the general ethos of the work. As a next step in the training, the teacher is invited to undertake an adapted programme with a full tutorial group of twenty-five to thirty young people.

The teachers in training are advised to choose their trial group with some care — as far as that is possible when faced by the pressures of the school time-table. For their first attempt they should not make things too difficult for themselves. Often the most available group would be those young people who are at odds with the school, and sometimes teachers accept this kind of challenge because it is politically advisable. But most would be better advised to work with a reasonably co-operative group for their training experience. They will be able to turn to difficult youngsters with more assurance when they have first seen a programme through.

It is also important that the work should not be seen within the school as appropriate only to those in need of remedial treatment. The approaches are being used with considerable effect with alienated young people, with truants and other children at risk, and with delinquents.[6] But the work has just as much to offer to able and well-adjusted young people. Many valuable programmes have been conducted with sixth-form groups.

Application to the Pastoral Programme

One can be quite confident about being able to train a willing teacher to work with young people effectively in this way. That is not the difficulty. It is a much more difficult task to engage the school in the kind of developmental programme and institutional change that is required before this kind of approach can become the normal style of the form tutors. Most in-service training for teachers is seen to be about the skills of the individual teacher, who will apply the new approaches in the way in which he teaches his subject. In approaching the role of the form tutor, the operation is much more fundamental. In a large school, a year or house team may number ten to fifteen teachers, and it is very difficult for a single teacher to swim against the general tide. In any case, there may not be enough time to set aside on the timetable for any serious work to take place. An allocation of time would almost certainly involve a minimum of a total year intake, and a form period could be an acute embarrassment to form tutors who are without the strategies and materials to fill it. I have advised management teams in a number of schools against allocating additional pastoral time until they have the necessary teams of teachers ready to use the time vigorously and effectively.[7]

Long-term strategies must be foreseen. At the initial stage — that of building up a nucleus of skilled teachers who will become a school-based in-service training team — a good deal of *ad hoc* action will need to take place. Corners will need to be found in the timetable that will enable them to practise the methods, and to demonstrate to their colleagues that something of value can grow out of their work. Many schools have made use, for this purpose, of existing slots such as social-education or health-education programmes to which the approaches can be applied.[8]

The prime movers within the school must demonstrate that the methods can be applied to the normal pastoral group of between twenty-five to thirty young people, and within the limited spans of time likely to be available. They must also satisfy themselves that they have extended programmes available for a year's work at whatever stage they decide to begin. Some outline programmes have been produced as part of our project, which can be adapted to suit the circumstances of individual schools.

It is only at this stage that the school-based training team can, with confidence, recruit a team of teachers who are prepared to carry through a coherent programme with, say, a single year. Many schools have begun with an induction programme for the first-year intake, but some see other points in the school programme as most urgent or appropriate. Some workshops will need to take place with the team before the programme begins, and regular meetings must follow to support the team of tutors as the programme proceeds. In a number of schools the preparation has included work with fifth- or sixth-form young people, who have helped form tutors lower down the school.

It is essential to see the whole operation, not so much as about the skills of individual teachers, but rather as a developmental programme for the school as a whole. This must figure prominently in the early discussions before anyone from the school is recruited to initial training. And as the work proceeds, considerable efforts will need to be put into keeping other people in the school informed about what is happening. So conscious have we become of the importance of this side of the work, that we have structured it into the programme of initial training. Efforts are made to see that the school staff are consulted, so that the work can be seen as an experiment that is being undertaken on behalf of the school as a whole. Objective members of staff are invited to help

monitor and evaluate the scheme. Other staff members serve as visitors
to the trainee's group as part of the essential experience of the young
people concerned. Colleagues are asked to report on any specific changes
in behaviour, and written reports are required of the trainees for circu-
lation to other members of staff.
The prizes are considerable. Developmental group work is not only
about the approaches of the form tutor – it is inevitably about the
total ethos of the school. It is about a network of relationships, about
people caring for one another, about social skills and responsible action.
The approaches learnt on the programmes have immediate relevance
to normal teaching. And the identification of young people, first with
one another, and second with the staff, increases the attractiveness of
the school and what takes place in it, both for the pupils and for the
staff.

References

1 J. Baldwin, L. Button and D. Settle, *Developmental Group Work in the
   Secondary School Pastoral Programme – Working from Inside the School*,
   Occasional Paper No. 8, Department of Education, University College of
   Swansea, 1978.
2 For a description of the methods see Leslie Button, *Developmental Group
   Work with Adolescents*, (University of London Press, Unibook Series, 1974).
3 Leslie Button, *Small Group Structures Amongst Older Adolescents*, Department of Education, University College of Swansea, 1971.
4 Leslie Button, *Action Research as a Partnership with the Practitioner*, Department of Education, University College of Swansea, 1976.
5 For an account of the training methods, see Leslie Button, *Discovery and
   Experience* (Oxford University Press, 1971).
6 J. Jordan, *Developmental Group Work – An Experimental Programme with
   Pupils at Risk*, Occasional Paper No. 6, Department of Education, University
   College of Swansea, 1977.
7 Leslie Button, *Developmental Group Work in the Secondary School Pastoral
   Programme – Some Experiments at Ewell County Secondary School*, Occasional Paper No. 3, Department of Education, University College of Swansea,
   1976.
8 op. cit. (note 1).

7 Strategies for the Modification of Behaviour of Difficult and Disruptive Classes

Douglas Hamblin

Introduction: Basic Issues

Principles and constraints

This chapter represents a synthesis of a number of ventures undertaken by the writer in advising and helping teachers working with difficult and unruly classes. Incorporated into it is the writer's direct experience as a teacher of disturbed and delinquent pupils. The adolescents with whom this chapter will be concerned are not necessarily actively aggressive or grossly out of hand — often they will manifest apathy and inertia — resorting to passive and indirect forms of resistance to the educational process. This is more difficult to modify than active hostility. The approach to be discussed is a limited one, using only those *principles of behaviour modification* that are effective in the context of the comprehensive school where a fairly large number of teachers may be involved with a class. More important is its reliance on the principles and findings of social psychology related to group dynamics and perceptual processes, e.g. the concept of de-individuation (Zimbardo, 1969). This firm grounding in sound theory is stressed, for inadequate theory inevitably leads to inadequate practice.

The argument is simple and logical. It is that:

(i) Some classes develop negative characteristics as they progress through the comprehensive school. The associated behaviours become a salient part of the school identity of pupils in such forms, leading to habitual patterns of transactions of a very negative type between teachers and pupils. Once this has occurred, the problem can only be resolved by carefully planned *collective* action.

(ii) The problems posed by such a class will have complex causes and consequences, therefore simple recipes for action will be abortive, and, possibly, counter-productive. Each class will present a relatively unique combination of latent as well as manifest factors which has to be understood.

(iii) Hence preliminary exploration and diagnosis is crucial.

(iv) On the basis of this diagnostic assessment, those teachers who are responsible for the class can develop a set of procedures which should be implemented in a carefully phased sequence. The corrective measures will include skills drawn from counselling, behaviour modification, group interaction, also involving the use of games, role play and simulations.

(v) The remedies fall into two groups. First, there is the consistent application of the generally agreed strategy of coping with and modifying interaction between teachers and taught. This emerges from the diagnostic sessions, and is the responsibility of everyone who teaches the class. Second, there are the special measures taken by the head of house or year and the form tutor. As part of their specific pastoral role they should be responsible for inducing perceptual and attitudinal change, not only developing more positive views of school and academic work, but also providing any skills needed for success. Form-tutor periods will be used for this, although it is likely that additional periods will have to be allocated for these guidance sessions in the early stages of the project.

(vi) Periodic evaluation of the programme should be an integral part of the plan. Continuous monitoring of the objectives, especially of the intermediate ones, and the means of reaching them, means that arrangements have to be made for regular meetings during the diagnostic stage and during implementation of the proposals.

Certain standpoints held by the writer must be stated explicitly. First, any unnecessary separation of the pastoral and curricular is seen as unproductive. Indeed, I see discussion of the pastoral versus the curricular as a pseudo-question, diverting attention away from the fact that attention to emotions, perceptions and motivation is part of the professional task of the teacher. Next, teachers as professionals are seen as capable of modifying behaviour constructively, helping pupils to use the resources of the school. Finally, although the analytic framework which is presented may appear to be complex, its application is held to be within the competence of the teacher. This approach could be seen as unduly time-consuming, but it is designed to be economical by the insistence that action must always be preceded by careful diagnosis.

The method

The method is a problem-solving one which involves a team effort. The strategy outlined above allows all those who teach the class to work together, without losing their professional autonomy or resorting to ineffective actions based on frustration and partial understanding of the situation. The emphasis is on detecting underlying processes, and developing techniques which take account of the latent and less obvious. As teachers we must never forget that it is not merely the effectiveness of certain means in attaining immediate ends -- in this case, the modification of pupils' behaviour -- but their long-term consequences and their relationship to educational values. We need to keep in mind Daunt's (1975) principle of the equal value of every child, the desirability of building up a responsible form of independence and the need to adapt to the intellectual stage and preferred style of learning of the individual.

Doubts about the compatibility between behavioural modification and the educational process have caused many teachers to reject behaviourally based techniques as mechanistic. If we look at the work of

Krumboltz and Thoresen (1969) we see that behavioural counselling tailors the situation to fit the needs of the pupil. It requires the helper to conceptualize the problem in a way that allows him to detect the steps he needs to take to solve it. Those using behaviourally based approaches take a concrete approach rather than relying on vague abstractions such as 'inadequate' or 'aggressive'. Instead of labelling, the ways and *situations* in which the pupil is aggressive or inadequate are specified, and this is followed by examination of the steps which could be taken to remedy the situation.

The key concept in behavioural modification is that of reinforcement. It is very salutary to ask, 'What have I strengthened in this person?' at the end of a disciplinary interview. We may find we have paid more attention to the negative than to the positive: making gloomy predictions about his future behaviour, and attributing adverse personality qualities to him. We then wonder why no change occurs! The attempt at discipline is therefore self-defeating unless we consider what is being reinforced. A reinforcement is a reward, and when given as a response to behaviour, strengthens the tendency for that behaviour to recur. This sounds delightfully straightforward — perhaps banal — but complications will reveal themselves even in the diagnostic phase of the exercise.

One very frequent explanation of the reason for a pupil's behaviour given by teachers is that he is attention-seeking. Yet observation suggests that in the classroom we spend more time paying attention to the behaviours of which we disapprove than those which we hope to induce. What, then, is being reinforced? If we then see that in recent years a number of systems of behaviour modification have been developed which emphasize self-control, for example Goldfried and Merbaum (1973) and Thoresen and Mahoney (1974), it is possible to discard the notion that behaviourism is necessarily manipulative. It is concerned with anticipating consequences, identifying the triggers or cues which initiate automatic sequences of behaviour, and graduating demands to ensure the individual experiences success.

Yet difficulties do exist. Some forms of behaviour modification relying on the use of praise and other rewards as a means of shaping behaviour are difficult to apply in the comprehensive school. First, a number of teachers take each class — the more difficult the class, the more likely it is that the burden is shared as widely as possible — therefore it is hard to achieve the consistency of approach that exists in the primary school. Limits to the reduction of the number of those taking the class are imposed by the need for specialization. No easy solution is therefore possible. More crucial may be the fact that, in the situation where intervention is desirable, reinforcement based on reward is likely to be ineffective, perhaps counter-productive: Hargreaves (1967; 1972) has shown that teacher rewards can be noxious to the pupil. Punishment by the teacher becomes a reward because it brings increased admiration from the offender's friends, consolidating his reputation as tough and adult.

In classes where apathy and minimal performance are the norm, pupils often believe that success is dependent upon luck, and that the source of control lies outside themselves. They do not accept that they are responsible for their successes and failures. Phares (1976) states that when people see control as lying outside themselves, they do not apprehend the link between their actions and what happens to them. He suggests that behavioural modification is ineffective until this belief is changed. Low expectations of success and the tendency to blame others for what befalls the pupil often underlie passive forms of resistance to learning. It has been shown by de Charms (1968) that some adolescents see themselves as pawns, inertly acted upon by environmental forces, rather than being capable of determining their own fate. When such attitudes are well established, then reinforcements and rewards do little to change behaviour.

The situation becomes more complex when the dynamics of perception are taken into account. Heider (1958), Jones et al. (1971) and Weiner (1972) argue that behaviour is largely determined by the attribution of intent and purpose to others. Kelly (1955) shows that man's greatest ability is his capacity to represent his environment rather than merely respond to it. Yet this power to construct one's own social reality can be negative as well as positive, leading to a passive conception of life. If we are to be successful, those of us who have to lead the attempt to change the behaviour of pupils will have to contend with the partial and distorted sets of meaning held by many adolescents. These will be dealt with in the guidance sessions given by the form tutor and head of year or house, with other teachers intervening in appropriate ways during their lessons. Recognition that each classroom is a social system with a unique pattern of interaction shows the need for a team approach to be essential rather than desirable. Attempts at change must take into account the social-psychological concepts of a value climate, opinion leaders, bargaining and negotiation, which result in a definition of the learning situation which shapes the behaviour of teachers and taught, together with the mechanisms through which overt conflict is controlled and tensions reduced. These factors will be given fuller attention later — they are merely introduced here to show why we need a planned, team-based problem-solving exercise.

Wider issues

Insufficient attention is often paid to the indirect and less obvious passive forms of unco-operative behaviour compared with direct aggression. Superficial conformity and the 'tongue-in-cheek' mechanism may have more deleterious long-term effects on pupils and the school than straightforward hostility, although they may seem to be less inconvenient in the short run.

Part of the analysis which precedes action will be concerned with the unwitting contribution that staff are making towards the maintenance of the negative and unproductive behaviour of the class. Those engaged in the modification process must recognize that a well established and rigid set of negative transactions has emerged between pupils and teachers. Both sides maintain them, but we as mature adults must take the necessary steps to change them. The perceptual framework which maintains these transactions is not confined to the classroom setting. Staffroom comments and interaction actually strengthen our negative views of the group. Social-learning theory (Rotter, Chance and Phares, 1972) stresses the potency of expectations in shaping behaviour. Expectations can be defined as subjective impressions of the probability that certain behaviours and attitudes will occur. Negative expectations develop very quickly within a staff once the behaviour of the class becomes a source of discussion. These then govern our behaviours, making us act in ways which strengthen that of which we complain. These predictions can increase the anxiety of teachers who are uncertain of their capacity to cope, causing undue rigidity of perceptions and behaviour, which then prevent them from making realistic adjustments to the needs of pupils.

Let me be clear. None of the above denies the existence of manipulative and malicious pupils who can, with varying degrees of subtlety, indulge in 'teacher baiting' and who use the weaknesses and vulnerability of other pupils for their own ends. It merely stresses the pragmatic point that explanations of pupil behaviour couched solely in terms of the characteristics of pupils are incomplete. Failing to reflect reality, they are therefore unlikely to contribute to lasting change of the situation. The viewpoint set out above, which incorporates the idea of mutual contributions to the situation by both teachers and pupils, is not concerned with allocating blame. It is a hopeful and professional standpoint: for it restores the power to us by reminding us that we are not the hapless victims of a frozen social matrix in which change is impossible. However, rather than encouraging a search for some elusive 'cure-all', it requires us to adapt realistically to the full complexity of the situation.

In turn, this creates awareness of the need for evaluation of the strategies adopted. Failure to allow for the well-known 'Hawthorne Effect' — the positive response to novelty and attention — could mislead us. In planning this team effort — in which all who teach the class will be involved, although the head of year or house and the form tutor will have specialist tasks — decisions should be made about when and how evaluation will take place. The pressure of teaching is such that we have a tendency to demand quick — if not immediate — results, and if they do not occur we become disillusioned. Equally, it would be self-deluding to assume that an immediate positive response by the pupils meant that the problem no longer existed. The price of modification is prolonged effort and adaptation.

Evaluation implies statements of objectives that are clear enough for us to judge our success. We have long-term objectives which, when reached, indicate that the activity can be terminated, intermediate ones which mark progress towards the desired end-state, and — most crucially — immediate ones which are incorporated into the methods we use. All these gradually emerge from the analysis, but they are also given further definition during the exercise. It could be assumed without further questioning that a unilateral relationship exists between ends and means, i.e. that the goals are decided and we then choose the most appropriate means from the range of possibilities available. In practice, the ends rarely determine the means in this simple fashion. More probably, there is a continuous dialogue between ends and means as the exercise develops, and growing awareness of what is feasible and productive occurs. The early perceptions and definitions of the problem may be — almost certainly will be — modified as the team explores the problem, provided that they avoid early closure and maintain a basically scientific openness to evidence, even though it may be at variance with their earlier assumptions.

The Planning Stage

The early meetings of the team which precede action are part of an analytic and information-sharing exercise out of which should emerge the first steps in a policy designed to allow pupils the experience of consistency. There can be no constructive expression of concern without control, for consistent discipline provides the necessary framework for constructive expression of personal needs. Experience suggests that the kind of class under discussion is often the centre of widely varying and highly discrepant attempts at control by different teachers. Some teachers approach them in a structured and punitive way; some try to establish a regime based on a concept of equality which is unrealistic, and at variance with the beliefs and practices current in the school; others establish an implicit bargain or truce which incorporates unproductive mutual tolerance, psychological distance and minimal response. To establish and maintain constructive disciplinary demands may seem a lowly task, yet it is essential for creating an atmosphere of security, while simultaneously reducing the opportunities for exploiting the differences between teachers. Although 'Mr Brown always allows us . . .' or 'It's more interesting when Mrs Smith takes us . . .' and similar statements appear incredibly crude forms of manipulation when taken out of context, they still have an impact on the experienced teacher in the classroom as well as on the inept or the new entrant to the profession. These early meetings are likely to create a new awareness of the obvious — and yet unregistered — fact that the teacher is the subject of intense scrutiny by the class. Certain simple themes can be detected which act as triggers for misbehaviour or serve to justify it in the eyes of the pupils. Such justifications allow pupils to conduct themselves negatively with a good conscience! Hence it is vital that we understand them.

Tempting as it is for the group to ask immediately, 'How has the class become like this?', the temptation should be resisted, for it could be misuse of time at a vital point, and, almost certainly in the early stages of the planning, the answers would be misleading. The more productive immediate behavioural questions might be, 'What functions does the disruptive behaviour serve for them?' and 'What is the pay-off?'. We might then see that the pupils are maintaining an identity as a group within the school that gives them prestige with others in the playground; that they are avoiding challenges; that a picture of the classroom situation is being maintained in which the teacher is seen as an enemy whose defeat will enhance the prestige of certain pupils; that pupils have developed a pattern of interaction which insulates them from the demands of teachers without causing too many overt confrontations. The latter situation is one where we often remark, 'They're not bad kids, but somehow I can't get through to them.' The possibilities are manifold, and my experience suggests that one is often surprised at the answers that emerge to these simple questions.

Understanding the classroom environment
I have remarked elsewhere (Hamblin, 1978) that all too frequently in disciplinary discussions the plaint is heard that teachers have tried being hard, followed this by the reverse, and then are at a loss as to what to do next because the pupil has responded to neither approach. This seems to suggest a failure in clear analysis and assessment of the reasons for the state of affairs before taking action. This applies to the class as much as to the individual. Sound theory implies effective action, therefore a guide for the diagnostic phase is given below which encapsulates the implications of research cited in this chapter together with the experience and knowledge of the writer. The *content* is derived from what has been shown to be important in formulating teacher strategies for improving the social climate of the classroom and providing understanding of the reasons for pupils' behaviour. The *order* of presentation reflects the one that most teachers prefer, usually because it seems meaningful. It will also be obvious that there is a progression from the more obvious and concrete to the less tangible and abstract.

The assessment of classroom processes

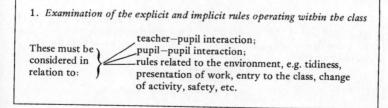

1. *Examination of the explicit and implicit rules operating within the class*

These must be considered in relation to:
- teacher—pupil interaction;
- pupil—pupil interaction;
- rules related to the environment, e.g. tidiness, presentation of work, entry to the class, change of activity, safety, etc.

2. Rewards and punishment

They are best treated as independent of one another, and it seems essential to consider the less obvious aspects. Therefore we explore them in terms of:

- the overt versus the implicit;
- the social and the material;
- their significance and meaning for pupils;
- the preferences of pupils;
- the relative emphasis given to positive (rewards) and negative (punishment) by teachers.

3. Recognition of the social structure of the class

This will involve understanding the functions of the:

- opinion-leaders who shape the viewpoints and reactions of others in the class;
- roles taken up by individuals which have an impact on their performance and that of others;
- ideal pupil and teacher roles inherent in the interaction between teachers and pupils.

4. Relevant perceptual processes

This is a key area, exploration of which leads to a deeper understanding of the latent processes. Questions have to be raised about the:

- attribution of intention, motive and purpose by the pupil to the teacher and vice versa;
- criteria for judgements of character used by teacher;
- expectations of the other operating in both teachers and pupils.

5. Key facets of the system of transactions

In this area, the group will pay attention to the significance and consequences of the:

- explicit and implicit bargaining processes operating between teachers and taught;
- leader–follower relationships within the peer group as well as between teachers and pupils;
- labelling and allocation of reputations both by teachers and pupils, including
  - teacher ⟶ pupil
  - pupil ⟶ teacher
  - pupil ⟶ pupil.

---

6. *The emergent definition of the learning situation*

This is the end-point in \
which one achieves   / nature of the teachers' definitions
understanding of why / of the classroom situations;
pupils behave in a   / pupils' perceptions of the classroom
certain way.   \ situation — there may be different ones for
It brings comprehension\ sub-groups;
of the: / awareness of areas of conflict and discrepancy
                        between them.

This diagram is more than a checklist, although it can be used as one. It structures discussion, while simultaneously creating awareness of the more subtle aspects of the diagnosis. Usually people constantly refer back to it, deepening their appreciation of the significance of the elements at each encounter. Each teacher will have his own perceptions and interpretation of the situation. Each one will contribute insights leading to fuller understanding, but undue sensitivity — perhaps idiosyncrasy — will be overcome by the opportunity to compare viewpoints systematically and examine contradictions and ambiguities.

It should now be clear that the writer is not stressing the pastoral—curricular dichotomy. The emphasis is on the fact that the teacher as a professional co-operates with colleagues to apply a key skill.

Diagnosis Preceded by Methodical Assessment

The diagram on pp. 87-9 draws our attention to the fact that:

(a) underlying classroom interaction is a continuous process of the development and consolidation of identities which shape the behaviour of both teachers and pupils;

(b) pupils actively contribute to the classroom climate in very subtle ways which are often not taken into account by over-general statements about 'poor backgrounds' and 'inadequate homes';

(c) as the last step in the diagram suggests, it is useful to consider the classroom as the setting in which pupils and teachers play out their roles, often with different and sometimes conflicting conceptions of those roles and the learning situation.

Such a general analysis brings the reward of deeper comprehension, but could lead to the point where the class is seen solely as an entity incorporating *mores* and holding norms which have a coercive effect upon its members. This is the case at one level of abstraction. We now begin to see the need for a thoughtful analysis, for apparent uniformity may conceal a rich diversity of response. A little thought suggests that, although a generally accepted climate and pattern of response to the classroom situation does exist, the basic forces outlined in the diagram impinge on individuals in different ways and to different degrees. Within the same classroom pupils will be experiencing different psychological climates: not only in terms of the learning situation, but also in the amount of time given to them by the teacher and the type of contact they have with him.

This point is worthy of further development. The issues of discipline and order dominate the teacher's perceptions and classroom interaction, in many cases from the first teaching practice until the day of retirement. Order is a necessary condition for constructive education, but sometimes this essential concern may restrict the way we function in the classroom and create a rigidity of approach that denies our own individuality and that of our pupils. It can lead us to create a system of transactions which stress teacher-dominance and unwittingly encourages pupils to develop strategies which insulate themselves against our influence and demands, resulting in the minimal performance necessary to avoid 'trouble'.

The fact that there are discrepancies between the teacher's attempt to secure uniformity of response from the class, and the fact that he simultaneously interacts in very different ways with individuals (as Brophy and Good (1974) demonstrate), illuminates the situation. What is not so obvious is that similar tendencies are at work among the pupils. Zimbardo (1969) takes up the theme of de-individuation in groups. Diener et al. (1973) shows that when experimental subjects were made anonymous, their aggression increased. Diffusion of responsibility has been associated with group processes, as Kogan and Wallach (1967) and Dion et al. (1970) have shown. Immersion in the group is a precursor to behaviours which are normally suppressed.

De-individuation is the state of affairs where, in Zimbardo's words, 'individuals are not seen or paid attention to as individuals'. They then believe that they are submerged in the group, and that evaluation of them is mainly on the basis of their membership of the group. Anonymity thus leads to the individual rejecting accountability for his behaviour. The pupil sees his behaviour as an inherent part of his membership of the class and therefore not his responsibility as a person. Unwitting collusion with this tendency occurs when we talk about 'that class' or over-emphasize in our actions and evaluations the idea of the class as a unit.

What is the impact of the tendency of the teacher to interact differently with individuals? At first sight it might seem that this cancels out the tendency to treat the class as a homogeneous and negative unit. Once a class acquires a reputation as difficult or deviant, the bias to respond to the negative rather than the constructive is strengthened. This orientation, in conjunction with our pre-categorizations and expectations, ensures that most of our interaction with a class which is out of hand reinforces their negative identities. While it is true that variations in the frequency of teacher responses to individuals do exist, it also seems likely that they are still largely phrased in negative terms, extending the pupil's sense of the primacy of being a member of a class with a bad reputation.

Important as these processes are, they do not constitute the whole story. Paradoxically, underneath this surface group-identity, pupils are building up situationally-based identities which have to be understood if effective change of the pattern of transactions between pupils and teachers is to occur. Before modification they operate to maintain disruptive behaviours, which take place within a context that stresses the diffusion of responsibility.

It is useful to pool experience and detect the unique set of roles and their significance in the class structure. One might find the 'resident cynic' who habitually devalues and antagonistically interprets the intentions and motives of the teacher. Another pupil might occupy the overt role of the 'trouble-maker' and yet be the agent of the 'delinquent leader', who, while maintaining apparent respectability, is actually guiding and using the trouble-maker. Like other machiavellian types, the 'delinquent leader' tries to keep his operations below the level of visibility, for his manipulation of others becomes ineffective once he is detected. The familiar classroom 'clown' and 'teacher's pet' will often be present, the latter serving the function of the deviant, who, by endorsing the values of teachers, coupled with his possession of unacceptable characteristics, therefore allows others to reject them with a good conscience. Sometimes a pupil occupies the role of defender of other pupils by interventions which attract the teacher's irritation, deflecting it away from his followers. Pupils might find it hard to verbalize their mechanisms in a precise way, yet my work in guidance often shows that they are aware of what is happening. The 'scapegoat' is the role of that member of the class who is manoeuvred into the position where he or she makes expiation for the offences of others. The person adopting this role commits his offences so clumsily and obviously that they incur the wrath of the teacher. Obviously the teacher is often aware of the scapegoat, but in a brief lesson period it may be more economical to respond automatically rather than spend time looking at the situation more closely. Equally, to ignore the behaviour may mean one runs the risk of being seen as endorsing it.

The above is suggestive rather than exhaustive, while the set of roles developed will differ from class to class. Identification of roles and their functions is merely the first step. Next follows consideration of the relationships between role-holders, bringing into focus the sequences of action which become habitual in a class. The clown may initiate the sequence by 'testing the climate' and, if certain reactions are present in the teacher, the 'trouble-maker' then begins to operate. Quite frequently, the first overt intervention of the 'resident cynic' comes at the point where — from the pupils' point of view — there is the danger that the teacher is going to interest and enthuse the class. He, in turn, often stimulates the 'time-waster', who diverts the teacher's attention away from the task by irrelevancies or by using the time-honoured tactic of asking questions, sometimes based on shrewd observation of the teacher's interests and willingness to be deflected in other directions.

I have pointed out elsewhere (Hamblin, 1974) that a sociometric survey will reveal those who are chosen by others, and the fact that they are so chosen gives them power over others. Therefore despite the de-individuation that exists at the general level of functioning, the class also contains opinion-leaders who have influence over the reactions and behaviour of sub-groups within the class. Studies of social influence show that a major factor is the perceived credibility of the source of the message. Katz and Lazarfeld (1965) showed the importance of two-step communication, in which the impact of the mass media was transmitted, not directly, but through individuals who acted as points of reference for others and as the source of validation for opinions and proposed actions. Hollander (1964; 1967) and Hollander and Julian (1969; 1970) argue from their studies that leadership can be seen as a reciprocal process of social influence in which leaders and followers are tied together in a bargaining relationship, yet it seems likely that the leader possesses greater influence over the followers. Indeed, Hollander's work on leadership focuses on the idea of 'idiosyncrasy credits', which allow the leader to innovate and deviate from the current state of affairs. People with the status of leader have conformed to group expectations at first as a necessary prerequisite for establishing their position, but can then initiate change and set new targets for the group.

Realization of the fact that the pervasive phenomenon of rejection of responsibility for behaviour is maintained by opinion-leaders allows us to see that economical strategies of attitudinal and behavioural change can be based — at least partially — on the identification and involvement of these opinion-leaders. Careful evaluation of the values they represent and of the rewards they offer to those whom they influence is essential if we are to code our messages to initiate positive communication with opinion-leaders. Consistent attempts to build on their strengths can overcome their initial suspicion. Too much warmth, crude or unrealistic praise, or abdication of our responsibilities would be self-defeating, yet we must change the sterile, if not hostile, relationships between them and us. Fortunately, it is only if we are insecure or hold rigid conceptions of having to exercise coercive controls that it becomes unduly difficult to build positive communication with these informal leaders.

Sherif, Sherif and Nebergall (1965) build on the image of latitudes of acceptance and rejection in discussing change of attitude. A message which is markedly discrepant from the recipient's own position not only produces resistance to the message, but can have a 'boomerang' effect which results in a hardening of the recipient's original position. This would then be reinforced by the responses of classmates. Hence the team should consider using what Freedman and Frazer (1966) and Baron (1973) have called the 'foot in the door' technique. This, in fact, represents the application of the principle of graduation of demands, which has been an important part of behaviour-modification theory. Initial small requests which gradually commit the individual rather than intimidating demands savouring of confrontation are more productive. Baron showed in his work that the small and initially probably non-threatening request led to later compliance more effectively than did moderate demands. This principle should be incorporated into our planning, together with the equally obvious, yet often forgotten one, that changes in behaviour should bring rewards for the opinion-leader. Graduation also applies to rewards, for initially these should be given in a casual way and not formalized.

Detection of points of breakdown

The preliminary diagnostic meetings are essential because each class is a social system with a relatively unique combination of factors. Social structure can be defined as consistencies in patterns of interaction, and one such consistency could be the point or points at which disruption tends to occur. Pooling of information often reveals regularities which have previously gone undetected.

Breakdown can occur at the point of entry to the classroom if the school is one where teachers remain in the classroom and pupils move. Equally, if teachers move, then a pattern may have developed in which teachers find themselves meeting disorder which then leads to a bad start in which hostility is generated. The teacher often tries to ensure that the 'pay attention' rule operates, but this can mean that energy is being deflected away from teaching into what is basically a custodial operation, which also reinforces the negative identity of the class. Perhaps this becomes clear if we realize that the situation overtly labelled as one of attentiveness actually may be one in which pupils are actively learning not to listen or attend. Habitual patterns of this type can act as instigators for the operation of the clowning role, or create the atmosphere in which the machiavellian techniques of the 'delin-quent leader' flourish. Walker and Adelman (1975), in a valuable book on classroom observation, include activities and materials which reveal the ambiguity and complexity of non-verbal communication in the classroom and provide some 'context awareness' games. The value of this is that in every class — disruptive or not — pupils learn to develop signals which are hard to detect. Although they are well-nigh invisible to the untrained observer or to teachers who are not well acquainted with the class, they initiate sequences of behaviour which, at best, impede learning. Recognition of such communication and its conse-quences leads to effective intervention.

In most lessons, particularly with younger or less able pupils, the teacher moves fairly quickly from the 'listen to me' rule to an activity which extends the experience of the pupils or applies the knowledge which has been given. Variation in the clarity of the instructions and the teacher's skill in classroom management is likely to be present at this transition. Yet it is only when teachers compare notes that they may find that certain pupils tend to focus on the change of activity as an opportunity to transfer the initiative from the teacher to themselves. Independently of the competence of the teacher at this point, one sometimes discovers that unnecessary delays or disruptive tactics appear, often not in an overtly aggressive way, but with politeness. Mechanisms of this type would be quickly detected in the primary school, but when a class is taught by a number of teachers who have relatively infrequent contact with the class, the more likely it is that they will become established.

The ending of the lesson provides further opportunity for breakdown. Difficulties often arise when the class has developed slow and slovenly ways of ending the lesson. If horseplay and chaos arise, the class finishes the lesson at a peak state of arousal. They then leave the classroom in a haphazard way and their progress to the next class is likely to be punctuated by incidents. Punishment of offenders alone is ineffective because it diverts attention from the cause of the offences.

Expectations, Evasions and Rewards

Rotter, Chance and Phares (1972), in their discussion of social learning theories, stress the importance of expectations in determining the positions people take up in the group. Kelly (1955) has similarly concentrated on predictions, and the way in which our predictions allow us to anticipate events, thereby gaining some measure of control over them. Through our predictions events assume meaning for us, while they cause us to act in a certain way. A pupil who predicts that his teachers will 'pick on him' may act on the basis of the prediction in a way which ensures they do just that. Storr (1970) from a different viewpoint stresses that we bring into unfamiliar situations in which we meet new people our 'prejudices of the past and our previous experience of people'. This is surprisingly true for both teacher and pupil.

Both pupils and teachers hold predictions which shape their interaction. Awareness of the simple fact that, if a pupil feels that when he does try to modify his behaviour his teachers will either not notice this or will misinterpret it, he is likely to decide 'not to bother', should help us to see that analysis of the predictions operating in the classroom is vital. Perhaps the notion that both pupils and teachers can anticipate the behaviour of each other accurately is not so disconcerting when we see that each group acts in ways which make their predictions come true. If this is so, then we can question in whose hands the power lies. Is it, for example, in the hands of those who maintain the most rigid set of expectations about their role partners? I have, for example, met on one occasion a group of teachers who held strong negative expectations about a class which, in turn, determined their actions in ways that maintained the behaviours of which they complained. Yet these experienced teachers seemed to be unaware of what they were doing.

Weight has already been given to the importance of pupils in producing the classroom climate. But can we assume that what is happening
is what they really want, despite their current attitudes and behaviour?
My experience suggests that the disruptive pupil or the unsuccessful one
does not want to be like this. Some years ago I found in an unpublished
investigation (Hamblin, 1968) that pupils in low streams who saw
themselves as failing in school and as nuisances wished to change the
situation, but did not know how to do it. This implies that at some
stage we will have to identify precisely the skills the pupils need if they
are to be successful.

This brings us to the question of conflict. The work of Miller (1951;
1964) provides a framework for the assessment of forces leading to conflict and evasion.

Types of Conflict

1. *Approach – approach*

   Two incompatible goals are desired.

   Example: A desire to learn and co-operate with the teacher and also
   to gain prestige with friends and acceptance by them,
   although they require the pupil to view teachers as enemies.

2. *Avoidance – avoidance*

   The pupil has to make a choice between two undesirable situations or
   lines of action.

   Example: Being blamed by the father (whom the pupil wishes to
   please) for failure to work, or being labelled by classmates
   as a 'creep'.

3. *Approach – avoidance*

   The situation contains elements which are both attractive and punishing.

   Example: The pupil wishes to progress and is likely to be promoted
   to a higher band, but he fears this will entail the loss of his
   friends.

Hargreaves (1967) points out that praise from the teacher can be
unwelcome because it reduces a pupil's standing with friends who have
rejected the values of school. This is undoubtedly often the case, although we have seen that pupils still desire success while predicting
failure. Therefore it is important for the pastoral workers who are involved to apply Miller's paradigm to the learning situation. Inevitably
this will lead to an examination of situations that create conflict and
trigger off avoidance strategies in the pupils. In an earlier discussion
(Hamblin, 1974) I underlined the importance of ego-defensive and
ego-expressive attitudes which, as Katz (1960) points out, serve important functions for the individual. The former serve to protect their

possessor from attacks on his self-respect and prevent valid, but distasteful, information from damaging the delusory picture of himself that he holds. We should note that ego-defensive attitudes are aroused by frustration and a sense of threat — indeed, change in such attitudes which protect us against threat is only likely to occur when the source of danger is reduced in intensity or removed. Certain frustrations are the product of poor educational organization and subsequent adaptations, for example an undue number of teachers teaching the class each week, a lack of co-ordination between the subjects taught, or inappropriate teaching methods. Removal of these sources of irritation and failure is crucial. Without this, the de-individuation inherent in the surface level of interaction between teachers and the difficult class, with its concomitant diffusion of responsibility, will maintain itself. This means that pinpointing the factors which consolidate or erode pupils' self-respect as learners is an integral part of the task.

Ego-expressive attitudes maintain a favourable picture of their holder, and function to indicate to others the kind of person one wishes to be. They are aroused and strengthened by comparison with other people, especially if those comparisons are negative. The opinion-leaders in the class function to exemplify the identities valued by the pupils; therefore we should eschew negative comparison of them with others. Instead we should build on their strengths, which can be developed in a way that brings them academic and school-related success.

This leads us into consideration of the punishment and reward systems operating in the particular situation. Rewards and punishments can be informal as well as formal, therefore general statements made about them in the policy documents of the school do not necessarily apply in a valid way. A class can attract, during the passage of time, a set of pre-categorizations which are weighted either negatively or positively, and which act as a framework within which the behaviours of members assume meaning. This then determines the bias towards either punishment or reward in teacher-interaction with that class. Also, we cannot, without careful thought, detect the meaning that punishments and rewards have for individuals within a class. If punishments confirm an identity as tough, while rewards diminish this valued perception of self, then the team has to think deeply of the self-defeating consequences of punishment. Although rewards and punishment seem to have independent effects, they both contribute to the adolescent's identity as a pupil and learner. To reduce the situations which lead to pupils meriting punishment is also to reduce the forces which encourage the pupil to reject the role of schoolboy or schoolgirl.

Evaluation of the occasions when to punish would be either unethical or counter-productive enters the diagnosis. For example, after certain points have been reached in campaigns against a pupil by others, normal disciplinary action directed at those who attack him can be counter-productive because they increase hostility against the pupil who is ostensibly being protected by the disciplinary measure. He may, in fact, become more vulnerable, feeling it is useless to complain because this increases the repercussions from others.

Punishments are mainly inhibitory and, as stated above, may have different outcomes from those anticipated. If the level of punishment exceeds a certain threshold (which seems to differ for each class), do we create hostility which leads to increased misbehaviour? In practice, over-reliance upon punishment seems to result in indifference rather than active hostility, which may be even more difficult to modify. Systematic analysis of who is punished, how frequently they are punished, for what offences, and with what results, is again a prerequisite for effective change.

Rewards are best based upon the setting of clear targets and goals which also provide the evidence of progress. Perceptions of success and the opportunity to use their preferred way of learning is essential. Rewards cannot be separated from methods of teaching, but this topic is beyond the scope of this chapter.

Varieties of Aggressive and Disruptive Behaviour

This section highlights some of the problems that the team will meet. The principle of selection has been that of calling attention to aspects that are sometimes neglected.

A pupil can occupy a scapegoat position which brings him chronic bullying. Help is obviously needed if his psychological development is not to be affected. But it may not be so obvious that he is actually maintaining the deviant behaviours and rejection of school values by those who scapegoat him. When he is seen as embodying the virtues appreciated by teachers, the class can reject them with a good conscience because they are associated with a despised person. Hence the frequency of the 'classroom creep' role — other pupils need him to maintain their own position.

Even if the victim is not a scapegoat we need to ask: from whom does he attract bullying? The status and position of both bully and victim within the class have to be borne in mind as we shape our strategies, for this will highlight the difficulties of intervention in each case. Next, we ask why is he the victim and not someone else? Does he provoke it by crudely assertive or infantile behaviour? Does he boast or carry tales? Does he provide entertainment by his tantrums? Therefore we look for signs of difference in the victim, bearing in mind that toleration of deviance is often very limited in adolescent less-able and disadvantaged pupils. Nothing is gained by denying this. Qualities which can be loosely labelled as 'effeminate', a different type of accent or speech, the possession of middle-class values and viewpoints, may be sufficient to unleash the bullying.

We have seen that a common explanation for the behaviour of pupils is that of 'attention-seeking'. This can be just as true of the victim. Does he get the reward of attention from the teacher, or is he trying to ensure that his parents will remain concerned about him? The victim may have a mother who foists harsh values and attitudes upon him. Sometimes such mothers teach the pupil to regard the less able and disadvantaged as inferior. Even when the majority of the pupils in the class fall into this category, the victim is unwise enough to display these perceptions. Like those who arouse jealousy by boasting about their possessions, they cannot understand why they are bullied. Insecure pupils often attempt to buy friendship, while those who are late entering puberty indulge in crudely assertive behaviour: both would deny their responsibility for what befalls them. Pupils like these are then allocated a negative role and wonder why! The form tutor and head of year will, of course, deal with some of these mechanisms through the programme of guidance activities.

The practical joker can be a skilled player of the game of indirect aggression. His jokes have negative and hostile components, for example making the recipient look foolish and feel inadequate, while keeping him in an impotent position — for heads or tails the joker wins. A complaint from the victim to the teacher brings a response of injured innocence, 'But it's only a joke, sir.' The victim is then made to feel he has failed to live up to the standards of his age-group, while the joker uses the incident to demonstrate to others that the victim deserves further rejection because he 'can't take a joke'.

The practical joker skilfully builds up the role of victim, proceeding, after some trial and error, to turn one pupil into the butt. Other members of the class will collude with him in this, thus the butt becomes the scapegoat who draws aggression away from other pupils, strengthening the bonds which hold them together. Practical joking also operates to direct attention away from the joker — a point which is made clear in the guidance sessions mentioned earlier.

Underlying difficult classroom behaviour may be psychological aggression, which is more important to those involved than the demands of learning. Destruction of reputations, the skilled use of innuendo, and the erosion of self-esteem have to be coped with. Gossip and rumour as a mode of indirect aggression is more common among girls, but it is not confined to them. Boys resort to it, usually restricting it to matters associated with traditional stereotypes of masculinity and to those who infringe the implicit rules about tale-bearing and who are over-eager to please the teacher. The object of psychological aggression is to make the victim feel isolated and increase his vulnerability, which again suggests the way to cope with it.

Passive aggression is the 'tongue-in-cheek' approach. Minimal responses and a superficial conformity, masking the lack of real response and active learning, create real difficulties. It is a hard fact that individual confrontations are unproductive, if not self-defeating, once this stage is reached. Homilies and exhortations often merely reinforce the *status quo*, while more active attempts by individual teachers only bring short-lived improvement. Such inertia is often linked with negative predictions about the likelihood of success, and a world-view in which pupils see luck and chance as playing a prime part. They see themselves as pawns and as oppressed by authority. The team must see that confrontations confirm this world-view if the pupils hold it, and strengthen their conviction that teachers are against them.

High degrees of indirect and passive aggression within the class indicate that the interactional system incorporates very negative perceptions on the part of both teachers and pupils. Wills (1971) in a different context pointed out that the mechanisms existing in the pupil group can reflect the punishments, rewards and controls operated by teachers. In the same way, the state of inertia which I have called passive and indirect aggression may reflect pupils' recognition of our low expectations of the class.

Strategies of Intervention

The analysis above, which shows what could be incorporated into the team's consideration, also indicates a number of measures that could be taken. In addition, the team will need to incorporate activities and approaches which emphasize the special contribution of the pastoral workers — the head of year or house and the form tutor. This means that planned guidance sessions which deal directly and indirectly with the problem are a central feature of the modificatory effort.

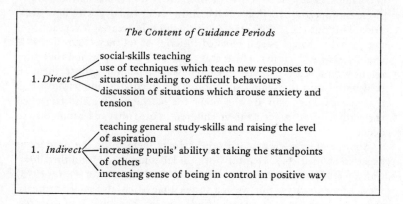

The Content of Guidance Periods

1. *Direct*
   - social-skills teaching
   - use of techniques which teach new responses to situations leading to difficult behaviours
   - discussion of situations which arouse anxiety and tension

1. *Indirect*
   - teaching general study-skills and raising the level of aspiration
   - increasing pupils' ability at taking the standpoints of others
   - increasing sense of being in control in positive way

Intervention may be necessary at different levels. In some cases, it has been useful for the head of year or house to offer individual counselling and help to one or two individuals suffering from some degree of maladjustment. This makes effective use of a key pastoral figure, allowing them to escape from the punitive role which is often allocated to them. Care is taken to inform those teaching the class of developments in the counselling, ensuring that the pupil is treated consistently. This is in line with the general aim of producing a safe and predictable environment in which ambiguity and opportunity for the exercise of machiavellian tendencies is reduced to a minimum.

The direct guidance programme

Attempts at modifying behaviour in the way outlined above often reveal that poor relationships, negative attitudes and unproductive behaviours are not so much the cause of the situation as the outcome of lack of basic skills leading to success in school. Hence, the main investment of energy by the form tutor and the head of year or house will be in the development and implementation of a structured programme of skills-based guidance. To utilize resources to the full, the drama and social education departments should be involved. The expertise within these departments is sometimes under-valued, and a potential source of ready collaboration is neglected. Incidentally, such co-operation alleviates some of the time-tabling difficulty, which appears to be a mundane consideration, but in practice is often an impediment.

In previous work (Hamblin, 1974; 1978) I presented an outline programme for the development of social skills. The themes of positive presentation of self, learning to co-operate and the management of tensions would provide unifying topics for the activities. Pupils could be aided to recognize their own contribution to the events they complain about, for example 'being picked on'. Understanding of the self-defeating — perhaps infantile — nature of their responses to frustration and failure can be productive, provided that pupils are simultaneously given appropriate new skills which allow them to cope with new situations. Without these skills, there is little point in creating awareness, for the path to change is still blocked. Studies of truancy (Carroll, 1977; Pugh, 1976; and Turner, 1974) leave one with the impression that poor relationships with parents, together with rebellion against them, is transferred into the school situation. This, in conjunction with the fact that the parents, who are the focus for rebellion, have also conveyed anti-authority attitudes to their children, means that re-learning has to occur.

Some aggressive or avoidance behaviours seem to be the product of negative comparisons. Helpful work on labelling theory and the allocation of reputations by Hargreaves (1972) and Hargreaves et al. (1975) should be consulted, but we can forget that labels also imply comparisons. A pupil who frequently finds himself the object of negative comparisons becomes resentful and develops a sense of grievance. Low self-respect also makes the individual vulnerable — a vulnerability which manifests itself as a readiness to feel attacked. The combination of low self-esteem and awareness of the existence of negative comparisons is one which is dangerous developmentally, and therefore has to be tackled resolutely. Comparisons deny individuality. To judge and react to someone through criteria based on some earlier experience with a brother or sister or some global notion about 'that family' also pushes the pupil towards the achievement of identity through opposition to those who compare and the institution they represent.

Behavioural modification techniques can be applied to help pupils learn new ways of handling problems and extend the range of possibilities open to them. Poteet (1974) gives a lucid account of the general principles. Tape recordings which present two ways of behaving, with different consequences attached to them, cartoons which show different responses to frustration, decision-making exercises, diagrams and variations of Kelly's (1955) fixed-role therapy and Bandura's (1969) social-modelling theory can be used. Role play and simple games can be developed to help the pupils take the standpoints of others. Activities which put pupils into a position where they have to make decisions, assessing the costs and consequences for others, are useful. The tutor must always use his skills as a teacher to help the pupils see the application of what they are doing. Transfer of training must be at the forefront of the tutor's mind and he must strive to stimulate it, otherwise the activities contribute much less to behavioural change than they could. The significance of standpoint-taking becomes clear when we see that it is a key element in moral behaviour — those who are unable to anticipate the reactions of others and see a situation from the other person's point of view are likely to be egocentric and impulsive. Standpoint-taking is the ability to construct, in imagination, the role of the other person, appreciating where necessary the pressures on the other, the expectations and obligations which impinge on him, and perhaps most crucially, the conflicts between various aspects of his role. Adolescence is a period when pupils try on a number of roles, and for sound development they need to appreciate the way those roles affect others, and why other people react favourably or otherwise to that role.

Examination of situations which produce insecurity and frustration can be introduced once the direct guidance programme is well launched. Too early an introduction could be counter-productive and reinforce long-standing attitudes. With this aspect of the direct guidance programme, care must be taken to guard against the danger of vagueness. Concrete situations with which pupils are familiar should be presented and the teacher should structure the discussion through presenting a list of two or three points to be explored.

A caution is necessary. Pupils will need time to adjust to the methods, and it is imperative that the head of year or house and the form tutor should constantly consult about the best way of using the methods suggested in this discussion. They are only as effective as the tutor makes them. Structure is crucial in guidance work with any class, but it is especially necessary when a class has presented difficulties. Without a firm structure and a clear statement of objectives pupils will misuse the guidance session.

The indirect elements

Pupils who experience prolonged failure, or who lack the skills necessary for academic achievement, still wish they could be successful despite their surface protestations of indifference. They put success out of court because they do not know how to achieve it. In a deeper exploration of study skills and achievement motivation (Hamblin, in preparation), I suggest that such pupils have not learned how to learn. A structured guideline programme which teaches the skills of listening, following instructions and competent presentation of work breaks into negative precategorizations of learning tasks in a meaningful way. When a class displays negative attitudes, undue passivity and a lack of investment of energy in academic work, then it seems sensible to boost their capacity through a vigorous crash programme of study skills which gives them a sense of potency and the ability to tackle difficulties. The aim is to develop their own style of study rather than impose recipes upon them. Exposure to a wide range of study techniques couched in suitable terms is therefore necessary. The programme would thus include instruction in the use of diagrams, active methods of reading and study, economical use of time, and competence in homework.

Exercises and activities aimed at increasing positive predictions of success and helping pupils to accept responsibility for their successes and failures without resorting to blame of others also play a part. The object is to change their beliefs about the nature of achievement and to build mature attitudes rather than to evade challenge defensively. The importance of supplementing the structural and direct measures by a programme of guidance for success lies in the need for change in attitudes and behaviours to be maintained. This will not occur when basic learning skills are absent. Without them, the results from the general attempt to modify transactions will be short-lived, yet the study-skills programme itself is unlikely to work without the preliminary interventions.

Other aspects

Both the direct and indirect elements of the special guidance programme allow pupils constructive expression of feelings, extend their repertoire of behaviours and — above all — develop the ability to see things from the standpoints of others, releasing them from the situation where they are prisoners of their own point of view. The growth of real autonomy depends on this.

The structure of the guidance sessions is simple: introduction of the activity with a clear statement of its objectives; the activity, which is conducted in small groups of three or four pupils giving maximum involvement; and the final section in which the tutor gathers ideas, structures them, and shows their applicability to life in the classroom. Two points must be stressed. The tutor has the task of ensuring that transfer of training occurs. Hence application of the ideas and activity must be given salience in the final section of the guidance period. Next, there is no necessary connection between activity-based methods of guidance and noise or disorder. If instructions are given clearly, the initial periods made rewarding and due thought given to the final section, few difficulties should be met.

This does not mean that the form tutor does not have to acquire skills. Many of us are unused to role play, games, simulations and exercises. Objectives must be clear in the mind of the tutor, and the theme of transfer of training be kept at the forefront if the sessions are not to degenerate into 'time-fillers'.

Imagination is essential — the re-orientating and skills-based guidance programme could involve several teachers in working with the small groups. In one school some years ago a programme of peer counselling existed, where sixth-form pupils devised activities aimed at attitude change and the development of learning skills with several different forms. The results were outstandingly successful. Perhaps we tend not to question our basic assumptions. Could change be better carried out by using other pupils as the agents of modification? In the situation mentioned, the writer, the school counsellor and the deputy headmaster acted as consultants to the pupils planning the peer-counselling programme.

There is no right way of tackling a problem, merely possibilities which are more or less effective in a given situation with the resources available. Evaluation is essential. Novelty alone is sufficient to produce short-term improvements in pupils, but after a short time it is likely they would resume their previous behaviours in a more entrenched way. Without the analysis and subsequent monitoring, the modification effort would fail and those responsible for it would almost certainly not see that they had foredoomed it to failure. Perhaps the greatest gain from evaluation is that it provides the team with insight into and classification of issues which can be used to prevent the development of such situations in the future. What is a remedial operation can become the inspiration for future preventative work.

Conclusion

In this chapter I have argued that the modification of the behaviour of difficult classes demands a searching diagnosis followed by carefully planned collective action. Both the initial assessment and the subsequent strategies rest on a wide range of theories and techniques, selected according to the needs of the situation and the resources available. Therefore no recipes can be offered for instant solutions for what often has deep roots. All who teach the class should be involved, although the form tutor and head of year or house will have special responsibilities.

References

Bandura, A., *Principles of Behaviour Modification* (Holt, Rinehart and Winston, New York, 1969).

Bandura, A., *Social Learning Theory* (Prentice-Hall, Englewood Cliffs, N.J., 1977).

Bandura, A. and Walters, R., *Social Learning and Personality Development* (Holt, Rinehart and Winston, New York, 1963).

Baron, R., 'The "Foot-in-the-Door" Phenomenon', *Bulletin of the Psychonomic Society*, 1973.

Brophy, J. and Good, T., *Teacher—Student Relationships* (Holt, Rinehart and Winston, New York, 1974).

Carroll, H. (ed.), *Absenteeism in South Wales* (University College of Swansea Faculty of Education, 1977).

Daunt, P. C., *Comprehensive Values* (Heinemann, London, 1975).

de Charms, R., *Personal Causation* (Academic Press, New York, 1968).

Diener, E., Westford, K., Dineen, J. and Frazer, S., 'The De-individuating Effects of Group Anonymity and Group Presence', *Proceedings of the 81st Annual Convention of the American Psychological Association, 8*, pp. 221-2, p. 1973.

Dion, K., Baron, R. and Miller, N., 'Why do Groups Make Riskier Decisions Than Individuals?' in Berkowitz, L. (ed.) *Advances in Experimental Social Psychology* (Academic Press, New York, 1970).

Freedman, J. and Frazer, S., 'Compliance Without Pressure: The Foot-in-the-Door Technique', *Journal of Personality and Social Psychology, 4*, pp. 195-202, 1966.

Goldfried, M. and Merbaum, M. (eds.), *Behaviour Change Through Self Control* (Holt, Rinehart and Winston, New York, 1973).

Hamblin, D., *An Investigation into the Ideal and Actual Selves of Boys in Secondary Modern, Grammar and Comprehensive Schools*, unpublished M.Sc. Research Report, Department of Social Psychology, LSE, University of London, 1968.

Hamblin, D., *The Teacher and Counsellor* (Blackwell, Oxford, 1974).

Hamblin, D., *The Teacher and Pastoral Care* (Blackwell, Oxford, 1978).

Hamblin, D., *The Teacher and Study Skills* (in preparation: provisional title, Blackwell, Oxford).

Hargreaves, D., *Social Relations in a Secondary School* (Routledge & Kegan Paul, London, 1967).

Hargreaves, D., *Interpersonal Relations and Education* (Routledge & Kegan Paul, London, 1972).

Hargreaves, D., Hestor, S. and Mellor, F., *Deviance in Classrooms* (Routledge & Kegan Paul, London, 1975).

Heider, F., *The Psychology of Interpersonal Relationships*, (Wiley, New York, 1958).

Hollander, E., *Leaders, Groups and Influence* (Oxford University Press, New York, 1964).

Hollander, E., *Principles and Methods of Social Psychology* (Oxford University Press, New York).

Hollander, E. and Julian, P., 'Contemporary Trends in the Analysis of Leadership Processes', *Psychological Bulletin, 71*, pp. 387-97, 1969.

Hollander, E. and Julian, P., 'Studies in Leader Legitimacy, Influence and Innovation', in Berkowitz, L. (ed.) *Advances in Experimental Social Psychology* (Academic Press, New York, 1970).

Jones, E., Kanouse, D., Kelley, H., Nisbet, R., Valins, S. and Weiner, B., *Attribu-*

tion: Perceiving the Causes of Behavior (General Learning Press, Morristown, N.J., 1971).

Katz, D., 'The Functional Approach to the Study of Attitudes', *Public Opinion Quarterly*, *24*, pp. 163-204, 1960.

Katz, E. and Lazarfeld, P., *Personal Influence* (Free Press, Glencoe, Illinois, 1965).

Kelly, G., *The Psychology of Personal Constructs* (Norton, New York, 1955).

Kogan, N. and Wallach, M., 'Risk Taking as a Function of the Situation', in *New Directions in Psychology*, Vol. 3. (Holt, Rinehart and Winston, New York, 1967).

Krumboltz, J. and Thoresen, C., *Behavioural Counseling* (Holt, Rinehart and Winston, New York, 1969).

Marland, M., *Pastoral Care* (Heinemann, London, 1974).

Miller, N., 'Comments on Theoretical Models: Illustrated by the Development of a Theory of Conflict Behaviour', *Jounral of Personality*, *20*, pp. 82-100, 1951.

Mlller, N., 'Some Implications of Modern Behaviour Theory for Personality Change and Development', in Worchel, P. and Byrene, D. (eds.) *Personality Change* (Wiley, New York, 1964).

Phares, E., *Locus of Control in Personality* (General Learning Press, Morristown, N.J.).

Poteet, J., *Behaviour and Modification* (University of London Press, 1974).

Pugh, G., 'Truancy — An Abstract of Research Findings', *Highlight*, No. 23 (National Children's Bureau, London, 1976).

Rotter, J., Chance, J. and Phares, E. (eds.), *Applications of a Social Learning Theory of Personality* (Holt, Rinehart and Winston, New York, 1972).

Sherif, C., Sherif, M. and Nebergall, R., *Attitude and Attitude Change: The Social Judgement—Involvement Approach* (Saunders, Philadelphia, 1965).

Storr, A., *The Observer*, 12th July, 1970.

Thoresen, G. and Mahoney, M., *Behavioural Self Control* (Holt, Rinehart and Winston, New York, 1974).

Turner, B. (ed.), *Truancy* (Ward Lock, London, 1974).

Walker, R. and Adelman, C., *A Guide to Classroom Observation* (Methuen, London, 1975).

Wills, D., *Spare the Child* (Penguin, Harmondsworth, 1971).

Weiner, B., *Theories of Motivation* (Markham, Chicago, 1972).

Zimbardo, P., 'The Human Choice: Individuation, Reason and Order Versus Deindividuation, Impulse and Chaos', in Arnold, W. and Levine, D. (eds.) *Nebraska Symposium on Motivation*, (University of Nebraska Press, Lincoln, 1969).

8   Pastoral Care and Careers Education

A. G. Watts and Beryl Fawcett

Pastoral Care and Guidance

Secondary schools tend to be self-validating institutions, insulated from society, and accountable in a pressing and immediate sense neither to their clients (the pupils) nor to their sponsors (the society of which they are part). So far as the clients are concerned, the fact that attendance is compulsory up to the age of sixteen produces an uneasy contract between the school and its pupils, teachers often feeling unsympathetic to unwilling pupils, and taking the compliant for granted. Schools frequently therefore lack a significant sense of accountability to their pupils.

Again, although schools are clearly accountable in an ultimate sense to society, this accountability tends to be mediated in ways which protect them from feeling its pressure. The main measure which tends to be used is performance in school-based tests or in public examinations. The examination system indeed provides the primary mechanism through which the school both justifies itself to the community and maintains control over its pupils. This system in turn is legitimated largely in terms of the career value of formal qualifications. But there is evidence that employers do not make such heavy use of qualifications as teachers often suggest (see Watts, 1978, pp. 44-5), and in so far as they do, this is frequently because qualifications are *convenient* rather than because they are *relevant* (see Berg, 1970). In short, examinations are validated not in terms of external criteria such as job performance, but in terms of intrinsic educational criteria related to the disciplines being studied within the school. Thus is the circle closed.

In this situation, 'pastoral care' tends to be viewed in an essentially supportive relationship to the school's teaching structure. It is often defined as a residual category: as Marland (1974, p. 8) points out, 'negatively one can say that the phrase covers all aspects of work with pupils in a school other than pure teaching'. In particular, it tends to refer to routine administration and to dealing with pupils' problems as they occur — often within a disciplinary (i.e. institution-centred) rather than a 'welfare' (i.e. student-centred) framework. Certainly some 'welfare' work is done, but simply in terms of the amount of time it consumes, it is clearly a marginal activity within schools. Hilsum and Strong (1978, table 4.3), in their study of the secondary teacher's day, found that on average 8.4 minutes a day were spent on 'pupil welfare' — i.e.

1.7 per cent of the working day. Moreover, such work is inclined to be concerned primarily with helping pupils to function effectively within the school's prescribed guidelines, and tends to be perceived as such by pupils (Best *et al.*, 1977; Lang, 1977; Murgatroyd, 1977).

Guidance, on the other hand, essentially addresses attention to the world outside school. As defined by the NFER (1953) – and subsequently elaborated by Morris (1955) – 'education, viewed as guidance, is the process of mediating between the growing child, his needs, powers, interests, and experience, on the one hand, and the needs, responsibilities, opportunities and values of adult life on the other'. In this view, the teacher's role can be compared with the guide on a long mountaineering expedition, in which 'the actual objectives, the routes, the stages, the pace and the equipment must all be chosen to suit the climber', and in which one of the aims is 'that the pupils should gradually become independent of the guide and able to climb unaided'.

Another analogy may help to distinguish guidance from other aims. If a young child is afraid of the dark and cries to have the light left on, alternative strategies are open to the parent. He may say, 'All right, dear, I know it is dark and frightening, so I will leave on the light, while you go to sleep'. The end of that scenario is a contented sleeping child, a contented parent who has soothed away the child's fears, and a problem which remains for the future. The child has been helped to cope within the existing frame-work, responsibility has been taken by the person 'in charge', but no real learning has taken place: indeed, to some extent the parent has colluded with fear of the dark, and, by implication, agreed that it is frightening.

Alternatively, the parent may say, 'All right, I know that it is dark, but there is nothing to be frightened of. Let's put the light out together, and I'll tell you a story'. This ploy may, in fact, take longer and it is still concerned with comforting the child – this time by remaining in close proximity with him – but ultimately, one would hope, it will invite the child to take a risk and discover that, when the parent leaves the darkened room, it is possible to survive. This is the guidance model, which does not advocate setting young people adrift, but by means of sensitive guidance aims to help them to cope with problems on their own.

Guidance is not the prerogative of the pastoral-care structure of the school. Indeed, if it is contained in this way, it is likely to be perceived as an essentially contingent and subsidiary goal, and thereby rendered ineffective. Some schools do establish a pastoral-care system which is quite separate from its academic system, thus separating 'caring' from 'teaching'. This is dangerous, not least because the appointment of teachers in specifically pastoral-care roles as heads of house or heads of year may lead to other teachers abdicating their traditional pastoral-care roles and referring all problems which are outside their specific subject domains. This tends to cast the pastoral-care head in a largely disciplinary role, thus creating a void so far as caring is concerned. Even if this does not happen, a pastoral-care system that is involved only in 'caring' and not in 'teaching' may well weaken rather than strengthen pupils, replacing coercion with an immature dependence as the controlling mechanism, instead of confronting the issues raised by the problems of learning and thereby creating a degree of independence for the pupil (Welz, 1978). Significantly, an HMI study of ten 'good' schools found that in all of them the pastoral and academic systems were closely integrated, usually by giving the form teacher a key role (DES, 1977, p. 21). It is also important that the concerns of guidance be given full attention in curriculum planning.

Guidance is conventionally broken down for purposes of convenience into three categories: educational, vocational, and personal. The implication that 'educational' and 'vocational' guidance are not 'personal' is patently absurd. Moreover, the further implication that young people can be considered from different viewpoints, and that each of these positions is somehow complete in itself, does violence to reality. If a pupil comes to a teacher and they start to talk about subject choices, this would seem to be concerned with educational guidance. If, however, the subsequent discussion moves into the realm of what the student wants to do on leaving school and the choice of subjects necessary for admission to an apprenticeship, it has strayed into the terrain of vocational guidance. And should the student also be suffering from constant rows at home about what he is or is not going to do on leaving, then − presumably − it becomes personal guidance. In the end, if guidance is to genuinely engage any of these three 'problems', it must be concerned with the whole person.

Nonetheless there is a case for some conceptual and even organizational distinction between the three areas. Careers guidance poses particular informational demands, and requires an orientation to the future and to life outside the school which are more imperative than in the other two guidance domains. American experience suggests that, if it is subsumed within a generic approach to guidance, these particular needs tend to be neglected (Ginzberg, 1972). It would seem therefore that there is some justification for giving careers guidance separate attention, while acknowledging that its particular concerns need to be met in a way which recognizes their ultimate interaction and interdependence with other guidance areas. It is with this essential caveat that we will now focus on the emergence of the concept of 'careers education' in schools.

Careers Education

Careers guidance in schools has undergone a major transformation over the past fifteen years or so. Traditionally, it tended to be an essentially peripheral activity. Indeed, responsibility for it was often almost entirely off-loaded on to an agency based outside the school − the

Youth Employment Service (as the Careers Service was then called). Even where the school appointed a careers teacher, his responsibilities were often confined to making arrangements for the careers officer's interviews, and distributing the pamphlets and leaflets sent to schools by organizations seeking recruits. In this model of guidance, not only was the main focus of responsibility outside the school, but guidance was confined to two central activities: *information*, typically in the form of a library of pamphlets and books containing occupational information; and *advice*, typically in the form of an interview in which the adviser diagnosed the pupil's attributes, related these attributes to the adviser's perceptions of the occupations which seemed most likely to match these attributes, and made appropriate recommendations.

These approaches to guidance have a number of critical limitations and assumptions built into them. Information is static and passive. A careers guidance service based simply on making information available makes four assumptions, all of which are of questionable validity:

(a) that the information is comprehensive, accurate and up-to-date;
(b) that pupils are motivated to use it;
(c) that they are capable of understanding it;
(d) that they are capable of relating it to their own needs.

As for advice, there must be important doubts:

(a) about whether an adviser, however skilled, can adequately diagnose an individual's attributes in, for example, the short interview which is still the main basis of operation in the Careers Service;
(b) about the objective accuracy of the adviser's perceptions of the occupational world.

Even if these doubts are discounted, it seems likely that a pupil who bases his decision on the advice of another will identify less with the decision, and that this may both reduce the effort he puts into the chosen occupation and the satisfaction he derives from it. Furthermore, he has learned little about the problems of decision-making, or about how these problems can be surmounted. The guidance process has not developed any skills or any conceptual framework which he can draw upon again in his career development. Indeed, the main learning likely to be derived from the advisory process is that the pupil has little control over his own destiny: the 'hidden curriculum' is that decisions have to be submitted to the agency of 'experts' who can mediate the social forces that ultimately determine the decisions.

Such concerns about the dangers of directive advice have led in recent years to increasing interest in a more client-centred approach to careers interviewing, focused not on advice but on *counselling*. In this approach, the object of the counsellor is not to diagnose the pupil's attributes and then recommend appropriate occupations, but rather to help him work through his problem, articulating his perceptions both of himself and of the options open to him, and subjecting them to scrutiny, until he is able to reach his own decision. The skills required of the counsellor, in short, are primarily not diagnostic but facilitative, and are concerned less with the outcomes of decision-making than with its process: as Katz (1969) has succinctly put it, they are focused not on helping pupils to *make wise decisions* (with the assumption that he knows what these should be), but on helping them to *make decisions wisely*.

It is not accidental that the concept of *careers education* has emerged more or less contemporaneously with that of counselling, for counselling is of limited value — or at least is likely to be a very lengthy and expensive process — if it takes place in a vacuum; whereas advice can be offered to pupils who know little about the options between which they are choosing, helping the individual to make his own decisions presupposes that he already knows a fair amount about the options open to him. Static, factual information is inadequate in this respect: the pupil also needs a conceptual vocabulary, a range of experiences, and a set of decision-making skills, to draw upon. Such concepts, experiences and skills may develop to some extent in the normal process of social maturation: indeed, the chief insight generated by the seminal research of Ginzberg *et al.* (1951), Super (1957), Super and Jordaan (1973) and Tiedeman and O'Hara (1963) is that this is the way they do develop, and that occupational choice can only be fully understood in terms of this developmental process. Careers education is based on the premise that such development can also be facilitated and, perhaps, accelerated by programmes of deliberate intervention, and that this is an important educational task, which merits a firm place within the school curriculum.

The emergence of careers education can thus be seen as part of a more general change in the way careers guidance is conceived, in which the limited notions of *information* and *advice* are being supplemented — and to some extent overtaken — by the more sophisticated and demanding notions of *careers education* and *counselling*. One of the implications of this educational conception of careers guidance is that it ceases to be seen as a peripheral activity within the school, and begins to be seen as one of its main educational functions.

Careers education has been defined by Law and Watts (1977) as comprising planned sequences of experiences designed to facilitate the development respectively of *(a)* opportunity-awareness, *(b)* self-awareness, *(c)* decision-learning, and *(d)* transition-learning. Each of these will now be examined in turn.

Opportunity-awareness means understanding on the part of pupils of the general structure of the working world they are going to enter, the range of opportunities that exist within it, the demands different parts of it may make, and the rewards and satisfactions that these different parts can offer. It also refers to awareness of the different paths and strategies — notably education and training — which are open (or closed) to particular individuals for gaining entry to those opportunities.

At the level of the individual it refers to awareness of the combination of demands, offers and strategies which match (or at least do not mismatch) a particular individual's characteristics.

Self-awareness means the sense of oneself as a unique individual, with personal characteristics which are like other people's in some respects but in other respects are not. It addresses the question 'what kinds of personal resources do I bring to the world of opportunities that exist for me?' In part it involves awareness of actual and potential personal strengths — qualifications, abilities, aptitudes, practical skills, personal qualities, and physical strengths. In part it involves awareness of limitations in these various respects. But it also includes awareness of personal needs, involving questions about what sort of satisfactions are sought, what kinds of interests are developing, what personal aspirations are being formulated, and what it is that is most valued in one's experience of the world. Some of the needs expressed by a young person will be deeply internalized and abiding, some will be situational and transitory. The converse of this exploration of needs is the exploration of frustrations — what is experienced as antipathetic, irritating, dissatisfying. To incorporate a self-awareness component into a careers-education programme in these ways is to pay attention to the importance of the self-concept in career development (Super *et al.*, 1963).

Decision-learning means understanding the variety of ways in which decisions can be made. It might mean, for example, understanding the various pressures, expectations and cues which are offered to someone in a decision-making situation. It might mean understanding the various styles in which decisions are made — intuitive, logical, etc. (Arroba, 1977) — recognizing that different people make different decisions in different ways, and that some decision-making skills are more appropriate for some situations than for others. There are also certain skills which pupils can acquire that will help them to make decisions in a manner more satisfactory to themselves — skills such as those of collating information and ordering priorities. At some point, too, individuals will need to take account of the risks involved in decision-making — balancing the desirability of different outcomes against the probability that they will occur. Again, it seems likely that pupils will need to learn to take responsibility for decision-making, accepting authority and accountability for the running of their own lives. What is being talked about here, then, are the skills and awareness that pupils need in order to integrate what they know of themselves with what they know of their opportunities, and in order to convert these two kinds of knowledge into an implementable decision. The skills involved are mainly generic ones for which career decisions are but one area of application (Watts, 1975).

Finally, *transition-learning* means the awareness and skills students need to cope with the transition consequent upon their leaving school. It could mean, for example, understanding how school life is different from work life — more attractive and manageable in some respects, less so in others (see for example Bazalgette, 1975). It could mean relating what they are learning on their courses to what will happen at later stages in their lives. It could also mean acquiring the skills and information they need to cope with the new situations they will meet — communication skills, interpersonal skills, budgetary skills, information about the roles of trade unions, information about hierarchical patterns of work, and so on. Transition-learning is, therefore, gaining a realistic appreciation of the environment into which pupils are moving — what sociologists term 'anticipatory socialization' (Merton and Rossi, 1957) — and becoming equipped with the skills needed to accomplish this transition appropriately and successfully. There will of course be considerable variations in the state of readiness of different pupils, and in the types of learning that they require: transition to work in a factory will present very different problems from transition to university. There is also a case for helping pupils to begin to anticipate the decisions which will need to be made after the initial transition — for instance, whether to stay in the job one has originally selected or to try something else. In general, transition-learning can help to anchor the tasks of opportunity-awareness, self-awareness and decision-learning to future realities, and to prepare students not only for *formulating* decisions but also for *implementing* them. A possible conceptualization of the relationship between the four aims is indicated in Figure 4.

Figure 4   *The aims of careers education*

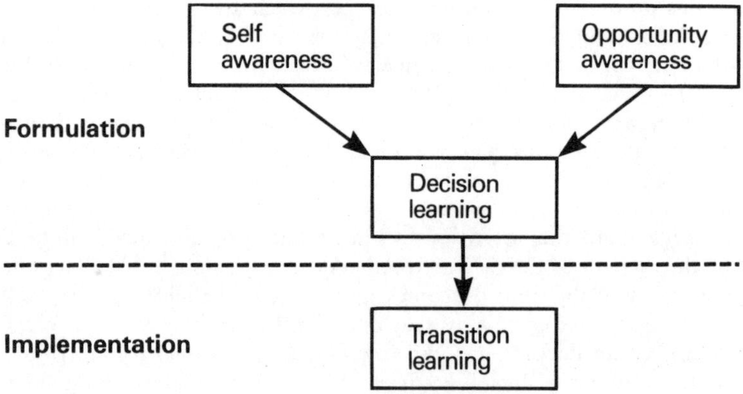

A survey conducted a few years ago by the DES (1977, p. 7) found that at that time about 70 per cent of secondary schools claimed to be giving careers education time on the time-table for at least some of their pupils. Most of this work is done in the fourth and fifth years, though some is done in the third and sixth years too. But the diversity of curricular practice between different schools makes it very difficult to be prescriptive about how programmes designed to achieve the aims outlined above should be structured into the curriculum. Five main approaches have emerged:

(a) Through traditional school subjects − e.g. studying local industry in geography and history, self-assessment in English, financial considerations in mathematics (see Avent, 1972).

(b) Through social studies − a number of CSE courses in social studies, for example, have included a strong 'world of work' component.

(c) Through courses in which personal values are considered − for example social education, moral education, humanities (see e.g. Elliott, 1975).

(d) Through a course in careers education as such.

(e) Through a course in personal, social and careers education (see Daws, 1971).

Each of these approaches has advantages and disadvantages (Watts, 1973, p. 8). It may be, however, that the approaches need not necessarily be regarded as mutually exclusive. In all schools the curriculum will already contain activities which are deliberately or incidentally concerned with meeting the aims of careers education. Arguably, a key role for the careers department should be not to ignore or undermine these activities, but to support and co-ordinate them.

Indeed, some would argue that there should not be a careers department at all. We do not accede to this view − at least not for the foreseeable future. The study of careers education in six schools by Law and Watts (1977) suggested strongly that a diffuse but co-ordinated approach to careers education tends to be the culmination of a process in which responsibility is first claimed and expertise developed by specialist careers teachers, and only subsequently related to the contributions of other teachers (see *ibid*, pp. 135-9). Moreover, co-ordination is a demanding and highly skilled task, and if it is to be effective, needs to be undertaken from a position of some strength in terms of both expertise and status.

It would seem therefore that, for the time being, a careers department is essential. Moreover, it is difficult to see how the head of such a department can hold his post as a sub-role dependent on a commitment to teach, for example, O- and A-level history. Sadly, it is still common to see advertisements for teachers to undertake just such a dichotomous position, which suggests that many schools do not yet fully acknowledge the importance of careers education. This will not have changed until schools recognize the need to appoint at least one member of staff with the time, space, commitment , status and financial encouragement to focus on their pupils' futures.

It may however be helpful if an important part of this role can be explicitly defined at the outset as being to co-ordinate and foster what the rest of the staff are doing in relation to careers education. One technique that may be helpful here is to log the existing activities in a grid, relating them to the four aims of careers education, and then to consider the best way of filling the gaps (see Law and Watts, 1977). Such a grid might include not only resources within the formal curriculum of the school, but also resources within its extra-curricular life, and indeed resources in the surrounding community — including the Careers Service, parents, former pupils, employers, trade unions, and colleges of further education. Young people do not only learn in classrooms, and they do not only learn from teachers. This is especially true in careers education. The professional role of the careers teacher is to harness the wide range of resources that may be helpful to pupils in preparing for the choices and transitions they have to make.

Careers Education and the Role of the Tutor

What then is the role of the pastoral-care tutor in relation to careers education? The relationship of the tutor to pupils is usually defined in an essentially 'individualized' way. Thus the HMI survey of ten 'good' schools, cited earlier, defined the test of a pastoral-care system as being 'the degree to which each pupil and his circumstances, aspirations and development are well known to at least one teacher and the extent to which such information is readily available and used' (DES, 1977, p. 21). But if the tutor and the pupil are to get to know each other, they clearly have to spend some time together. Many schools accordingly allot time on the timetable to 'tutor periods', during which the tutor can meet the pupils in his charge as a group. Such periods are often used essentially for administrative purposes — checking the attendance register, collecting dinner money, and the like. Sometimes, however, sufficient time is allotted to permit and encourage activities which have a learning function.

It is important to note that many schools which have attempted to do this have run into difficulties. As Button (1974, p. 170) points out, 'the structure of pastoral care has usually received more thought than the actual events that should make up a pastoral occasion'. As a result, tutor periods have often proved unpopular with staff. Lang (1977) reported that he had found 'many young teachers at a complete loss as to how to use the pastoral time that the timetable allocated them, and therefore dreading it, and seeking desperately for anything that will occupy the time'.

One possible solution to this problem is to integrate a curriculum in personal, social and careers education (approach *(e)* above) with the tutor period. Some schools have indeed done this (see e.g. Howden and Dowson, 1973). In principle it would seem to be mutually beneficial, providing a rationale for developmental group work (Button, 1974) which will simultaneously develop the tutor group into a living entity, and provide a supportive environment in which to engage in the often very personal exploration which these areas of the curriculum require. While not being impossible in groups of 25-30, which are the normal size for tutor groups in most secondary schools, such work would be likely to be much more effective if such groups were divided into subgroups of 12-15 (*ibid*, p. 167).

So far as careers education is concerned, some parts would seem to be particularly appropriate for the tutor period — particularly, perhaps, decision-learning (see Blackburn, 1975, pp. 104-105) and self-awareness. The tutor group may also be the appropriate place to examine the group attitudes and cultural forms which, as Willis (1977) has pointed out, are more important for many working-class pupils than the individualistic paradigm which characterizes middle-class people in their approach to working life.

There are, however, a number of difficulties in integrating careers education with tutor periods, and these need to be recognized and confronted. Some teachers may see it as an undue additional imposition, particularly when they are already under pressure to prepare and mark work for their main subjects. The resolution of the latter conflict will depend at least in part on the importance attached to the pastoral-care work within the school (see Marland, 1974, pp. 74-75): if it is clearly accorded little importance by the senior staff, and not rewarded in any way, it is more likely to be resented.

Furthermore, for some teachers careers education is likely to pose demands of a kind which they do not face in their own subject. Few teachers will have had experience of working in relatively unstructured groups within the classroom, and some will find this difficult and threatening. Moreover, some will find it easier than others to relate to their pupils in a way which will facilitate group work of this kind. On the other hand, the active tutor may see an imposed framework as yet another intrusion into his right to develop a relationship with his class. These factors all argue for flexibility in the implementation of such a scheme, allowing different tutors to adapt their approach to their own personalities and strengths, and providing a structure for those who want it rather than as an obligation for all. Materials may provide a useful support for some, and will be particularly useful if in themselves they facilitate the development of less formal personal relationships: many of the materials listed in the appendix are of this kind. Better still, a group of teachers within a school could work together to produce their own materials suitable for *their* particular pupils in *their* particular setting, thereby developing each other's confidence, and also fostering a powerful sense of ownership and commitment.

Finally, just as some tutors will feel uncomfortable with the *process* of careers education, so some will feel uncomfortable with its *content*. Certainly parts of opportunity awareness and transition learning, in particular, will require specialist information which they may simply lack. This is often *considered* to be less of a problem in the third year, when the main concern is with subject choices within the school: in many schools, indeed, the tutor is already more influential at this stage than the careers department (see for example Reid *et al.*, 1974, p. 221). Even here, however, some provision of resources from the careers department is essential to ensure that the pupils are fully aware of the vocational implications of their choice, and know something of the working world into which they are beginning to enter. And in the fourth and fifth years it may be best to leave parts of opportunity awareness and transition learning to be tackled elsewhere in the curriculum, with proper specialist support.

It would seem therefore that, while some schools may decide to make the tutor period the main base for careers education (and also for personal and social education), many will wish to regard it as one among a number of bases for such work. In this case, as we pointed out earlier, attention to co-ordination is important. Pastoral-care tutors need to know what is going on elsewhere, and to be able to draw upon it for their own work. Perhaps the most distinctive role which the tutor can perform in relation to careers education is indeed to pay attention to the ultimately *individual* nature of the areas with which it is concerned, and to ensure that opportunities are provided for pupils to *integrate* what they are learning. In other words, if the careers department has a responsibility for co-ordination of careers education at a curriculum planning level, the tutor has responsibility for integrating it at the level of the individual pupil.

This will need to be planned for, and explicitly stated. As Marland (1974, p. 86) points out, 'the very existence of a well-established careers teacher, with recognized status in the school, tends to draw a great deal of vocational work away from pastoral staff unless there is a definite policy to the contrary'. Yet in the end, the tutor is likely to have a much closer and more ongoing relationship with the pupil than the careers officer or careers teacher. If the careers officer has a primary concern with local job information and with individual careers guidance of a structured and informed kind, and the careers teacher a primary concern with the planning and co-ordination of careers education, then the tutor should have a primary concern for the career development of the individual — including supporting his enquiries as they progress, monitoring his applications once they start to be made, and involving parents where this is appropriate. Effectively harnessed, the resources of these three specialists can be far more effective than any one of them on his own.

As with any other professional role, however, the tutor requires training and support if he is to be expected to perform his role effectively. In the past this role has tended to be almost totally neglected in initial teacher-training: if — as we have suggested — it is to be regarded as an intrinsic part of education, rather than as an unwelcome addition, then this situation urgently needs to be rectified. Moreover, more in-service training in pastoral-care work is needed, both because of the past deficiencies in initial training, and because ongoing development of skills will always be important. Arguably, as Lang (1977) suggests, such training should include work with groups of young people in relatively informal settings, where the teachers' contribution will stem more from their sensitivity and character than from their skill as curriculum communicators. There also seems to be particular potential in in-service training conducted *within* individual schools (see e.g. Ellis, 1976), not least because it helps teachers to address attention to the particular characteristics of their own situation, and to develop the relationships which will facilitate co-ordination and mutual support in their work. In such training, the particular concerns of careers education merit due attention.

References

Arroba, T., 'Styles of Decision Making and their Use: an Empirical Study', *British Journal of Guidance and Counselling*, Volume 5 No. 2, July 1977.

Avent, C., 'The Integration of Careers Education with Other Subjects', *The Careers Teacher*, Spring 1972.

Bazalgette, J., 'The Transition from School to Work: an Organisational Approach', *British Journal of Guidance and Counselling*, Volume 3 No. 1, January 1975.

Berg, I., *Education and Jobs: the Great Training Robbery* (Penguin, Harmondsworth, 1970).

Best, R.E., Jarvis, C.B., and Ribbins, P.M., 'Pastoral Care: Concept and Process', *British Journal of Educational Studies*, Volume XXV No. 2, June 1977.

Blackburn, K., *The Tutor* (Heinemann, London, 1975).

Button, L., *Developmental Group Work with Adolescents* (University of London Press, 1974).

Daws, P.P., 'Careers Education in the Secondary School Curriculum', *Careers Quarterly*, Volume 23 No. 4, Autumn 1971.

Department of Education and Science: *Ten Good Schools: a Secondary School Enquiry* (HMSO, 1977).

Elliott, J., 'The Humanities Project on "People and Work" and the Concept of Vocational Guidance', in Elliott, J., and Pring, R. (eds.): *Social Education and Social Understanding* (University of London Press, 1975).

Ellis, A., 'In-School In-Service Training for Tutors', *British Journal of Guidance and Counselling*, Volume 4 No. 2, July 1976.

Ginzberg, E., *Career Guidance: Who Needs It, Who Provides It, Who Can Improve It* (McGraw-Hill, New York, 1972).

Ginzberg, E., Ginsburg, S. W., Axelrad, S., and Herma, J. L., *Occupational Choice: an Approach to a General Theory* (Columbia University Press, New York, 1951).

Hilsum, S., and Strong, C. R., *The Secondary Teacher's Day* (NFER, Slough, 1978).

Howden, R., and Dowson, H., *Practical Guidance in Schools* (Careers Consultants, London, 1973).

Katz, M., 'Can Computers Make Guidance Decisions for Students?' *College Board Review*, No. 72, Summer 1969.

Lang, Peter, 'It's Easier to Punish Us in Small Groups', *The Times Educational Supplement*, 6 May 1977.

Law, B., and Watts, A. G., *Schools, Careers and Community* (Church Information Office, London, 1977).

Marland, M., *Pastoral Care* (Heinemann, London, 1974).

Merton, R. K., and Rossi, A. S., 'Contributions to the Theory of Reference Group Behaviour', in Merton, R. K. (ed.): *Social Theory and Social Structure* (Free Press, New York, 1957).

Morris, B., 'Guidance as a Concept in Educational Philosophy', in *The Year Book of Education 1955* (Evans, London, 1955).

Murgatroyd, S.J., 'Pupil Perceptions of Counselling: a Case Study', *British Journal of Guidance and Counselling*, Volume 5 No. 1, January 1977.

National Foundation for Educational Research in England and Wales, *Statement of Policy* (NFER, London, 1953).

Reid, M., Barnett, B.R., and Rosenberg, H.A., *A Matter of Choice* (NFER, Slough, 1974).

Super, D.E., *The Psychology of Careers* (Harper & Row, New York, 1957).

Super, D. E., and Jordaan, J. P., 'Career Development Theory', *British Journal of Guidance and Counselling*, Volume 1 No. 1, January 1973.

Super, D.E., Starishevsky, R., Matlin, N., and Jordaan, J.P., *Career Development: Self Concept Theory* (College Entrance Examination Board, New York, 1963).

Tiedeman, D.V., and O'Hara, R.P., *Career Development: Choice and Adjustment* (College Entrance Examination Board, New York, 1963).

Watts, A.G., 'A Structure for Careers Education', in Jackson, R. (ed.), *Careers Guidance: Practice and Problems* (Arnold, London, 1973).

Watts, A.G., 'Teaching Decision-Making Skills', *General Education*, No. 25, Autumn 1975.

Watts, A.G., 'The Interaction between Careers Guidance and the School Curriculum in England and Wales', in Watts, A. G., and Ferreira Marques, J. H., *Guidance and the School Curriculum* (UNESCO, Paris, 1978, mimeo).

Welz, J., 'Caring for Learning', *The Times Educational Supplement*, 14 July 1978.

Willis, P., *Learning to Labour* (Saxon House, Farnborough, 1977).

Appendix

Some Careers Education Curriculum Materials

The Schools Council Careers Education and Guidance Project ended in 1977, and its materials are published by Longman. The third-year and fourth-year materials are entitled *Work* (Parts 1 and 2); its fifth-year materials are entitled *Work Out*.

In addition, a great many classbooks now exist for use in careers education. Many of them are CRAC publications, which are published by:

Hobsons Press, Bateman Street, Cambridge CB2 1LZ.

They range from general books like *Vocational Choice* and the Bull's Eye Series (*Choosing a Job*, etc.), to books dealing with more specific aspects of careers education like self-assessment (*Decide for Yourself*), decision-making (*Deciding*), and sex roles (*Male and Female*). CRAC also publishes some games and simulations, including *Speedcop*, the *Work Experience Projects*, and the *Esso Students' Business Game*.

Multi-media kits currently available include:

Schools Council Humanities Project, *People at Work* (Heinemann, London, 1971).

North-West Regional Curriculum Development Project, *Vocation* (Macmillan, London, 1972).

Childwall Design for Living Project, *The World of Work* (Arnold, London, 1973).

Source books for teachers include:

Hopson, Barrie, and Hough, Patricia, *Exercises in Personal and Career Devel-*

opment (Cambridge: CRAC/Hobsons, 1973).

Cleaton, David, *Exercises in Careers Education: Principles and Practice* (Careers Consultants, London, 1976).

Regular radio and television programmes on careers education are broadcast by BBC and ITV, and a list of these is available from:

Careers and Occupational Information Centre, The Pennine Centre, 20-22 Hawley Street, Sheffield S1 3GA

COIC also produce an annual *Catalogue of Careers Films and Other Audio-Visual Aids.*

All of these materials can be inspected at the Careers Education Resources Centre, NICEC, Bayfordbury House, Lower Hatfield Road, Hertford SG13 8LD (telephone Hertford 59001). NICEC is willing to run workshops for groups of teachers who wish to evaluate and select materials for use in schools.

9 Guidance and Counselling: changing patterns of care in schools

Patricia Milner

The term 'pastoral care' is redolent of parenthood in that it assumes that adults, and in particular teachers, are instinctively imbued with the skills needed to encourage young people in their life task of growing up. The reality is that the experiences of adults are becoming practically useless for their children, who have to live in a world which is fundamentally different, and teacher-training has long been conspicuous for its failure to clarify either the teacher's pastoral role or the contribution of pastoral care to the quality and equality of life in a school.

This reading argues for a development from the amateur status suggested by the traditional concept of pastoral care to the more informed and practised contribution of guidance and counselling in schools, an incorporation which signifies the arrival of a more professional orientation without reducing emphasis on the caring side.

Guidance in schools is usually thought of as a good thing, in much the same way, perhaps, that Christianity in the world is usually thought of as a good thing. A teacher or teacher-counsellor who plays the role of guide rather than instructor is often thought to be necessarily better, just as, for example, Christian marriage is often thought to be necessarily better than marriage based on secular or humanistic values. Perhaps the reality is that neither guidance nor Christianity are necessarily good things at all, that they may indeed be evil things under certain circumstances, and what kind of things they are depends upon the values implicit in their practice.

The intention behind this suggestion is not to belittle guidance or Christianity, for it is possible to have faith in both and few illusions about either; rather the intention is to challenge people to examine some of the implications of guidance practice, and in particular some of its pre-suppositions. This really means encouraging them to think about the theory of guidance, because the theory is concerned with trying to make explicit what is implicit in practice and thus to make what we do susceptible to constructive criticism. Practice without theory is blind; practice without theory can only achieve what we want it to achieve by intuition. To be right by intuition is a supreme gift, but, although it is important, it is insufficient as the sole basis of a practice which claims to be a reasoned one.

The view that guidance may be a bad thing is reminiscent of an ambiguous headline which appeared in an English newspaper during the last war. In large, bold letters it said: 'GENERAL FLIES BACK

TO FRONT'. The general was not really flying backwards, he was
flying back to the front line. Similarly, the suggestion that guidance
may be a bad thing means that it is necessary to fly back to our own
front line, where the action is, in order to think critically and constructively about what guidance in schools can and should be doing.
We sometimes assume that guidance is one of these new-fangled educational notions like the teaching of reading by the Initial Teaching
Alphabet, but in fact guidance is an ancient idea which has been used
by every culture in some way, perhaps to assist people in difficulty, or
to use and gather information, or to predict future behaviour and
success. Ever since people have lived together in groups there have
been choices and decisions to be made which caused conflicts of
interests and confusion of authorities. In the past the family, the
village, the guilds, religious societies, the professions — lawyers, doctors,
clergy or teachers — all contributed to guidance. They have all given
their time, their authority, their advice, their opinions and their help,
and this is a form of guidance which exists in every educational system
and in most human relationships.

At a national level the financial, medical, social and legal services of
the welfare state now provide a framework of guidance, in most cases
built upon many years of voluntary effort, for we have not always had
a national conscience for good works.

So guidance has been with us probably longer than the wheel, but
what is new is the way in which we organize it. In both England and
the USA the first organized form of guidance in education is usually
described as vocational guidance, and its origins placed in the early
twentieth century. However, in Europe, vocational guidance itself
and vocational guidance literature in particular can be traced back
almost as far as the first printed book in the fifteenth century. Slightly
over 500 years ago, an elderly Spanish bishop wrote a book called
The mirror of men's lives which was devoted entirely to the description
of different occupations. As a young university graduate, the bishop
had experienced some difficulty in deciding whether he should pursue
a sacred or a secular career. His book reflects his own decision-making
process by being divided into two parts, one describing all the positions
a person could occupy in a career in the church and the other part
describing crafts of various kinds, as well as the advantages and disadvantages of a number of secular careers from emperor to membership of
the learned professions. The book seems to have been a bestseller, for
in 1472 it was published in an illustrated edition and was later translated into Spanish, German and French. The learned people, often
priests, who used such a book to help young men to decide upon an
occupation must have been among the first vocational counsellors.

It was not until 1631 that the first book describing occupations
was published in England in English. Later, in 1747, R. Campbell
Esquire produced the *London Tradesman*: 'Being a compendious
view of all the trades, professions, arts, both liberal and mechanic,

now practised in the cities of London and Westminster, calculated for the information of parents and the instruction of youth in their choice of business.' Campbell notes that certain occupations require 'more strength than wit'; that a youth may become an apprentice 'without any particular education or genius' and that a lace-maker 'should be able to hand a lady to and from her coach without being seized with palpitations of the heart at the touch of a delicate hand'.[1] How times have changed.

This historical digression is a reminder that for five hundred years vocational guidance has been supported, indeed, sustained, by a small group of thoughtful people using a small, but comprehensive body of literature.

From the early days of universal education in England until well after the 1944 Education Act, the major responsibility for guidance in schools lay with the head-teacher. If a teacher had difficulty with a child the only person with any power to change the situation was the head. The head could largely decide what was taught and knew how, and when and possibly why. On the rare occasions when parents had to be consulted, it was usually done by the head. Vocational guidance, educational guidance, social and ethical guidance, on an individual and group basis, were mainly the prerogative of the head-teacher.

By introducing guidance and counselling programmes into schools we are seeking to bring rather more organized thinking and application to an area of education which has previously been carried out in an *ad hoc* way. We are seeking ways to do for the many what, in the past, we did only for the few. As a society we need to honour and to demand good work in every socially accepted human activity, however humble, and to scorn shoddiness, however exalted the activity. It has been pointed out that an excellent plumber is infinitely more admirable than an incompetent philosopher. The society which scorns excellence in plumbing because plumbing is a humble activity, and tolerates shoddiness in philosophy because it is an exalted activity, will have neither good plumbing nor good philosophy: neither its pipes nor its theories will hold water.

Now, in 1979, we are not really doing something new, we are trying to help more people and we are trying to do it better. In order to do it better we need to organize our thinking and our actions, our theory and our practice. The best theories are not something remote and academic: they offer a framework within which to think about what we do — they are working assumptions that we use until we find something more helpful.

One of the first tasks in organizing our thinking about guidance is to define what it means to us. In the early days of vocational guidance, one such definitiion was 'a process of assisting a person to choose, enter and progress in an occupation'. More recently, vocational choice has been seen by Donald Super as a matter of implementing a self-concept, and vocational guidance defined as a process of facilitating the clarification of a person's concepts about himself and of testing those self-concepts against the realities of the world.[2] When we have arrived at a definition, we need to think also about what we do, the functions we perform, or help others to perform. For example, the functions involved in assisting a person to choose, enter and progress in an occupation would probably include the provision of occupational information, making an occupational choice, placement in a specific job, and some kind of follow-up.

If we move from the vocational field to a wider appreciation of guidance in education we are likely to find that guidance is about helping young people to begin to find themselves, to develop their sense of identity, to begin to know who they really are, what they have and what they do not have; what they can do easily, what they can do with difficulty and what they probably cannot do at all, in terms of education, occupations, relationships, values and society. Despite the need to manufacture appropriate people-units for consumption in an industrial society, many schools have other concerns aiming to open choices and provide new experiences for their members, both of which are designed towards the serious purpose of helping people to be self-aware, confident and flexible, adequate enough to face their world with sanity and good humour, 'good enough' to encounter the hazard of being judged a success and remaining whole; stable enough to absorb failure with dignity, knowing their personal worth.

An organized programme of guidance and counselling in English education may be likened to a four-leaf clover and is probably as rare. The four-leaf clover of guidance consists of a philosophy leaf, a function leaf, a role leaf and an activity leaf. In one way or another it is already happening in schools.

(i)   As a philosophy, guidance is the conception that people have of the way in which the school should be related to the pupils.
(ii) As a function, guidance is a defined set of responsibilities which a school thinks that it can and should legitimately assume.
(iii) As a role, or set of roles, guidance can be seen to consist of designated positions that carry the obligation to dispense a school's responsibility in this area: for example head-teacher, careers teacher, school counsellor, house head.
(iv) As an activity, guidance may be said to describe the things that the occupants of these roles do to and for pupils that are consistent with the philosophy, the function and the role.[3]

What often happens in practice is that the aims of guidance are determined by a realistic, but rather negative assessment of a school's capacity to accomplish them. One aim may be 'to help new pupils to adjust to their school environment'; another may be 'to provide each pupil with occupational and educational information to help him to choose a job'. In England the equation for working out the aims of a guidance programme realistically often seems to be 'the aims of guidance equal what is desirable minus what is not possible'. When you visit some of our schools it appears that the answer to the equation is a very minus quantity indeed.

Under the general rubric of guidance in schools people do a variety of things: they administer intelligence, personality and achievement tests; they collect data on vocational interests and information about occupations and institutions of higher and further education; they group pupils according to various principles – house system, year system, curricular requirements; they interview pupils and their parents together or separately and provide both (and the school) with information; they advise pupils and teachers, make suggestions to heads of schools and engage in psychological counselling. They may also visit homes, contact social agencies, work co-operatively with child guidance clinics, arrange parents' meetings and attend national conferences to meet colleagues and to hear what is happening in other schools and in other countries.

Probably the most we can say about guidance in education at this stage is that it is a conglomeration of ideas and practices that different schools organize in different ways.

A fundamental question to ask in setting up guidance and counselling in schools should be 'What are schools for?'. It is important to raise this question because the purpose of education will determine the content of the curriculum, the teaching methods employed, the kind of schools we develop and the amount of education that we give to children and young people. This functional relationship is too often overlooked. We cannot discuss education without reference to the objectives and values of the community in which it is given – the purpose of society determines the content of education. Guidance is a part of the functional relationship between a society and its schools, and while not everyone likes this situation, that is the way things are.

A very simple definition of guidance describes it as a process of helping individuals, through their own efforts, to discover and develop their potentialities for personal happiness and social usefulness.[4] Guidance in schools could well pursue such aims in a society which severely restricts freedom of conscience and belief. Guidance is a technique, it is a means, and the ends it serves will be determined by the cultural tradition in which it operates and by the detailed way it interprets that tradition in its modes of operation. It is that interpretation which gives guidance the potentiality to be used for good or for evil.

Another definition of guidance describes it as a process of mediating between the growing child, his needs, powers, interests and experience on the one hand and the needs, responsibilities, opportunities and values of adult life on the other.[5]

The concept of mediation here suggests some kind of balance between the interests of society and the interests of an individual, and it calls for a thorough diagnosis and assessment of a situation before any action. It suggests the importance of helping a person to assess his own needs and powers and also the importance of analysing the situation with which he is faced, whether it is a question of conforming to school rules, overcoming anxiety in relationships, or choosing a career. The information which is gathered in the process of assessing a situation may then need to be evaluated and interpreted. To some people guidance is directive (it is often directive for teachers); to other people guidance is permissive (it is often permissive for school counsellors).

Those for whom guidance is directive might claim to see evidence of moral disintegration in the demands of some young people for independence, for the right to run their own lives and learning, for their refusal to be only what someone else wants them to be and their claim to self-determination in attitudes and values. Those for whom guidance is permissive might see these moves toward personal independence and autonomy as evidence of increasing maturity deserving consideration, respect and help, rather than condemnation and discipline. They believe that showing a respect for human differences among them may help adolescents to grow up tolerant of the differences they observe in others and concerned to understand rather than to condemn them. Those for whom guidance is directive are neither inferior nor superior to those for whom guidance is permissive, but their differences are significant. Young people need them both and both may be enabling.

Interpretation of this situation reveals that school society, like adult society, is *both* directive and permissive, and these are aspects of the same truth. This is an important discovery if a child is to try his powers, and test out the limits of sanctioned behaviour to discover his place in the world and reach an independent view of its meaning. Without freedom authority becomes tyranny; without authority freedom becomes anarchy.[6]

The introduction of an organized guidance programme makes provision for help in the form of guidance and counselling in a variety of areas and stages in school life, such as introduction to school, educational and vocational choice, preparation for work or further education concurrently with personal and group counselling, throughout the child's years at school. Guidance of this kind is given by means of guidance services provided in schools, which include:

(i) *An appraisal service* designed to collect, analyse and use a variety of objective and subjective data:
(ii) *An informative service* designed to provide pupils with a greater knowledge of educational, vocational, personal and social opportunities in order that the choices and decisions which they have to make may be better and more wisely made;
(iii) *A counselling service* designed to facilitate self-understanding and development by means of one-to-one or small-group relationships;
(iv) *A planning placement and follow-up service* designed to enhance

the vocational development of the pupil by helping him to select and utilize job opportunities within the school and in the outside labour market.

Although in each of these services there is something unique and different enough to set it apart from each of the others, each nevertheless functions in relation to the other and to one another. This outline is based on an American model, but guidance in English schools is not so clearly defined.

There seem to be a number of factors which are essential to the effective operation of guidance in all schools, but there are others which are peculiar to the circumstances in which each school finds itself. Not only are there variations between schools, as schools, but the organization of educational, vocational and personal guidance within them also varies according to the philosophies and strategies adopted by the schools, in pursuit of what they regard as their main educational objectives.

Certain broad factors stand out as being necessary for effective guidance in any situation.

Key Factors in Guidance

(i)   Knowledge and understanding of the pupil — his abilities, personal characteristics, aspirations, motivations, etc.;
(ii) Means whereby relevant information on education, vocational and personal matters is communicated efficiently and reliably to the pupil;
(iii) Time to pursue individualization in pupil guidance and to build up good tutor–pupil relationships as implied by (1), and as a corollary:
(iv) Adequate time, opportunity and context for sound decision-making at critical stages in the pupils' progress and development;
(v)   Co-operation and good liaison between school and parents, and with social agencies concerned with guidance;
(vi) Simple and effective procedures for communicating relevant information to others directly involved in the guidance process, including agencies outside the school.[7]

The majority of our secondary schools operate a variety of combined teaching and pastoral-care systems. These seem to be selected for administrative expediency or in an attempt to reduce the impersonality of a large school by breaking down the size of the group with which staff and children can identify. The alternatives vary from the more traditional horizontal year-grouping with form teachers or tutor groups to the vertical house system with tutor groups organized on a two to three-year basis, or possibly a more heterogeneous grouping of all ages. A developing feature of these systems is that for most practical purposes guidance is not only removed from the strictly academic setting, but is by design at the outset in the hands of someone who does not teach the pupil. Thus two changes are effected: educational guidance is put on a different basis and personal guidance is both unaided and unhampered by any specific teaching relationships.

There are two guidance functions which are not covered by the combined teaching and pastoral-care systems outlined. One is the careers guidance service and the other the counselling service of the school.

Tutors do not normally play a direct part in vocational guidance, and it is important to note that in a school where there is no counsellor or other specialized teacher, with a vocational guidance brief which allows a fair amount of time to be spent on the building up of relationships, pupils could be lacking in vocational guidance of any depth.

It is not many years since careers officers (formerly Youth Employment Officers) were attempting to carry almost the whole burden of the task of vocational guidance in secondary schools. In any reasonably self-respecting secondary school today, one can expect to find a wide range of careers literature (even a library section) indexed and regularly updated, frequent talks by careers officers and employers, films and television programmes on careers, with visits, involvement in work-experience schemes, careers conventions and separate pupil careers records.[8]

The attitude of some head-teachers that the limit of a school's function in vocational guidance is twofold, namely to provide a room in which the careers adviser can interview pupils, and to supply the information required on the Employment Service form, seems not only to misinterpret the scope of the work of the employment services, but also to miss completely the importance of an early approach to vocational guidance, which can only be met from within the school itself. The whole concept of vocational guidance in schools must alter radically in a situation in which the obligation of the school is to prepare young people for life, in a world where vocational pursuits are irrevocably linked with personal self-fulfilment.

Guidance is a term which encompasses much of our educational endeavour outside and sometimes within the area of subject teaching. Teachers, tutors, doctors, school secretaries, caretakers, dinner ladies, lollipop persons and friends may all at some time or another offer guidance help in the school setting, for interpersonal skills are present to some extent in all human relationships. The question is, how does the counsellor fit into such an organization?

The counsellor fits in as a specially skilled member of a guidance team, as a 'people person', for the house-head, tutor-group system is too often primarily an administrative expedient which makes the running of large schools easier. The administrative demands come first, because if they are not met it becomes difficult for the school to function. Children do not usually make a formal protest when they are neglected, but the tutor who neglects an administrative task is likely to be sharply reminded of where his responsibilities lie. Is it asking too much to make provision in education for a small group of people, namely counsellors, whose specific job it is to give priority to the needs of people in schools and to help others to do the same? Apparently it is, for on economic grounds, by default of educational administrators and lack of a clear lead, supported by financial backing from any government as well as some faint-heartedness from counsellors themselves, counselling is a non-starter certainly at primary-school level, and in much of secondary education also.

Perhaps counsellors are twentieth-century examples of the prophetic tradition; they certainly have some responsibility for acting as a thorn in the institution's side.

The appointment of a counsellor to the staff of a school can be likened to the estate of holy matrimony, in the sense that it is not to be undertaken lightly, wantonly or ill-advisedly, for despite the apparent similarity of objectives, a closer analysis of the organization of the school and the pressures to which it must both yield and respond indicates the conflicting criteria which inform the behaviour of the institution and that of the counsellor working in it.

The marriage between counselling and education may be an uneasy union, for the ambitions of each partner are sometimes contradictory — a not altogether unfamiliar state of affairs in matrimony. Counsellors are primarily concerned with individuals, sometimes with small groups such as the family or groups of children, and often with observing and interpreting to the school behaviour which results from individual pathology, family dynamics or institutional stress. Schools exist for the much wider purpose of preparing pupils to take their place in a particular culture and society, and although they may attempt to build a pastoral-care function into their structure, as we have seen, it is all too easy to take for granted that the personal problems which affect the educational progress of some pupils, and the numbers of those thus affected, will be adequately met by a de-centralized pastoral-care system, whose staff already have a great many other commitments to teaching, administration and school social organization.

In England, school counselling is one outcome of the intention to improve schools as caring institutions with a responsibility for maintaining, protecting and promoting the personal development and well-being of children. In theory, counselling in schools is basically a preventive mental health service.

There are certain aspects of a school guidance programme which may be particularly relevant to the work of the counsellor.

(i)   Individual counselling according to need on matters of personal, social, educational and vocational development.

(ii) Group counselling and group guidance.

(iii) Work with children who seem to have special needs.

(iv) Links with contributory primary schools and assisting with orientation of first-year pupils, together with orientation help at other points of change.

(v) Case conferences with tutors and teachers, to discuss certain children and their difficulties.

(vi) Liaison with parents and particularly with outside agencies.

(vii) Vocational guidance where there are no career teachers.

(viii) Assisting in the establishment of a cumulative educational records system.

(ix) Using standardized tests where this seems appropriate.

(x) Occasionally counsellors become involved in curriculum development and renewal.

There also seems to be a need for counsellors to be available during the process of subject choice-making to help tutors and pupils, with particular reference to both the personal and the possible future implications of the decisions.[9]

We have already noted that tutors and careers teachers are also concerned with these areas of development. What then can a school counsellor contribute? Basically counselling is an enabling process, designed to help a person to come to terms with his life as it is or to change it, and ultimately to grow towards greater maturity through learning to take responsibility and make decisions for himself. In its modern connotation, counselling is not meant to denote a process of advice-giving, of telling someone what to do, but rather of trying to provide the conditions under which an individual will be able to make up his mind, what, if anything, he should do. Sometimes a person needs help of a specific nature, for example, objective information about a job, or about his own limitations and capabilities, and information of this nature can be supplied by various people in the school, as we have already seen. Sometimes, however, what a person needs most is not information, but the opportunity to talk out in a calm, relaxed atmosphere, his innermost thoughts and feelings.

The essential contribution of the counsellor is to help people to see themselves in the light of the information they have, and to move towards answers to the question 'What sort of person am I?' and 'What do I want to make of myself and my life?' Counselling should not be just for people who are anxious, unhappy or unable to cope with the circumstances of their lives. In a complex and rapidly changing society, every individual must make choices fraught with important consequences for his future, and he should not have to take a psychological means test in order to qualify for a counsellor's help.

Children with special needs may involve the counsellor in working in a supportive role in conjunction with child guidance services, or with one or two cases of untreated mental breakdown, with a few children with some kind of emotional disorder such as anxiety, depression or hopelessness; perhaps with vulnerable children such as those from broken homes, others with physical handicaps, or those who have a low stress tolerance, and who are not able to cope with levels of stress that are well within the capacities of their fellows.

Counsellors may also be expected to work with children whose behaviour is difficult for the school to tolerate, such as delinquency or behaviour and disciplinary problems. Schools often regard these as a special kind of problem and often as the kind of children most in need of counselling. Difficult children are not necessarily children in difficulties, and behaviour which is unacceptable to the school may not be a problem for them.

All this seems very far removed from the situation in which for many years in English education the major responsibility for guidance in schools lay with the head-teacher. There is one very topical, often inconvenient and sometimes downright unpopular word to describe what has happened, and that word is 'change'. As our American colleagues repeatedly tell us, change — constant, accelerating, ubiquitous — is the most striking characteristic of the world we live in. But our educational system has not yet recognized this fact, that the abilities and attitudes required to deal adequately with change are those of the highest priority. It is not beyond our ingenuity to design school environments which can help young people to master concepts necessary to survival in a rapidly changing world, if we can recognize that these changes have advanced beyond the point where traditional pastoral-care provision is sufficient. There is no panacea even in a thoughtful guidance programme, but there is abundant evidence of growing areas of need in which trained counsellors could provide within the school a new dimension in the help available to young people and their parents.

References

1 D. G. Zytowski, 'Four hundred years before Parsons', *APGA Journal*, February 1972, Vol. 5, No. 6.
2 Donald E. Super, 'Vocational adjustment: implementing a self-concept', *Occupations 30*, 1951.
3 C. Weinberg, *Social foundations of educational guidance* (Free Press, New York, 1969).
4 Year Book of Education 1955 (Evans Bros, London).
5 NFER Statement of Policy 1953.
6 B. Morris, 'Guidance as a concept in educational theory' in *Objectives and Perspectives in Education* (Routledge & Kegan Paul, London, 1972).
7 B. M. Moore, *Guidance in Comprehensive Schools: A Survey* (NFER, Slough, 1971).
8 P. M. Hughes, *Guidance and Counselling in Schools: A response to change* Pergamon Press, London, 1971).
9 P. Mann, *Counselling in Education* (Dent, London, 1974; revised edition, 1979, Meridian House, 36 Park Vista, London SE10).

10 Psychological Theory and the Counsellor

H. J. F. Taylor

Introduction

Counselling is fashionable, and during the last twenty years has quickly established itself in many areas where professional relationships exist between people. The increasing number of counsellors, and of training courses for counsellors, has raised a number of problems for the psychologist. Among these problems is the continuing confusion over what is meant by counselling,[1] and a parallel confusion over the appropriateness for counsellors of much psychological theorizing.[2]

Within this context, the objective of this chapter is necessarily a limited one. No attempt will be made to argue the case for preferring one psychological theory to any other in terms of its utility for counselling. Nor will the different strategies and methods employed by counsellors be evaluated. Rather, I shall attempt merely to prepare the ground for a consideration of such issues by outlining the problem as I see it. To do this, I shall briefly discuss the nature of theory in general and of the relationship between psychological theory and counselling practice in particular, and then proceed to outline the main groups of theories which confront the counsellor and which might inform him in his practice.

The chapter is exploratory rather than definitive, but my hope is that it will at least indicate in which direction subsequent analysis ought to move.

Theory and Practice

After reviewing the evidence in several areas of research relating to counselling techniques, Shapiro was forced to conclude that it was 'not possible to make firm recommendations for the practice of counselling on the basis of present knowledge'.[3] Such a conclusion might seem rather severe, or disappointing, to the ever-increasing number of people who try to offer psychological or personal help to those with relationship or adjustment problems.[4] And yet it is not too surprising when one bears in mind the dissolving power of research and of a critical and scientific approach to knowledge and to a 'science of the mind'. It emphasizes that counselling is more of an art, perhaps, then a science, and that there can be little help from 'scientific' psychology for the moment.

Shapiro points out that counselling is

firmly rooted in a humanistic ethic, emphasising the inherent potential
for growth and self-actualisation . . . [which] leads to the assumption . . .
often uncritically accepted, that a certain type of counselling relationship
is good for any client. On this basis, a professional tradition of counselling
has evolved, in advance of any scientific validation.[5]

As counsellors well know, it could be argued that for certain kinds of
personality, counselling is inappropriate — those who, for example,
benefit most from a highly structured framework for learning — or who
are too inarticulate in a one-to-one encounter where the difference in
intellectual levels and in expectations between counsellor and client is
too wide. Again, in group counselling those who find it difficult to
relate to a group benefit little and seem to need a one-to-one relationship.[6]

The experimental psychologist makes a similar point when emphasizing that the amount that is not known with any certainty is always so
much greater than the amount of secure and well-founded knowledge
that merits confident application.[7] The present position is much the
same as when I wrote in 1971:

In his everyday work the counsellor is continually faced with people who
need psychological help with problems that need to be understood and
that demand containment or action. No general laws about human behaviour exist that have universal validity and current resources often break
down when confronted with complex human problems. The counsellor, in
order to make sense of this situation, must draw on different theoretical
approaches. In becoming aware of the difficulties in gaining precise knowledge and of the lack of scientific data to support his work he acquires a
humility of approach based on uncertainty rather than on certainty. The
limitations of theory force him to select ideas from many sources that
appear useful in understanding others as well as in studying himself. He
will then realise the broad truth that in so far as the counsellor 'knows'
himself, so he can begin to 'know' other people.[8]

The rapid development of counselling during the 'sixties and 'seventies was not the product of a single, well-established body of knowledge,
scientifically validated, waiting to be put into practice, but more the
product of a growing awareness of the *need* for the development of
counselling services — in medicine (for example genetic counselling),
in social work (family counselling[9]), in marriage guidance (marriage-
guidance counselling), and in education (the role of the school counsellor).

Counselling today, then, is characterized by a growing number of
psychological approaches and techniques. The number of descriptive
terms attached to 'counselling' in the literature gives some idea of the
bewildering array of perspectives which confront the practitioner:
Gestalt[10], 'non-directive'[11], 'client-centred', 'behavioural'[12], 'existentialist', 'rational-emotive', 'relationship', 'friendship' and 'psycho-
analytical' counselling all receive a mention, and even this list is not
exhaustive.

It could be argued that such a proliferation of 'new' approaches may well be hindering the development of effective counselling and the selection and training of counsellors, and that the benefits coming from such a wide range of theories to support these approaches is illusory. Patterson writes:

> But what is discouraging — and disturbing — is the lack of or the inadequacy of, theory and concepts supporting the new methods or techniques; the ignoring, or ignorance of, the research supporting what has come to be known as the 'core conditions'; the evangelistic fervour with which many of the approaches are advocated; the lack of concern for any evidence of their effectiveness except possibly testimonials; the failure to recognise that what is called counselling . . . can be for better or for worse — that people can be hurt as well as helped; and finally, the eagerness with which the approaches are commercialised.[13]

Patterson writes about the position in America and it is arguable that some of his statements do not have, as yet, too much relevance to what is happening in the UK, although there are indications of their potential applicability in the near future.

There is also considerable confusion over the definition of counselling as a professional activity. Venables attempts to clarify the position when she argues that counselling needs to be distinguished on the one hand from 'advising or informing, guiding or teaching, and on the other from psychotherapy and psychoanalysis'. Her definition of counselling would be acceptable, I think, to most field-workers when she writes: 'Counselling as distinct from other activities discussed is primarily concerned with feelings — with dilemmas springing from emotional difficulties connected with personal relationships and the self-image'.[14] It is clear that psychology should be one of the more appropriate disciplines to contribute a theoretical background to counselling conceived in this way, but there are doubts about the appropriateness of much psychological theorizing for the field-worker,[15] and some acute dilemmas are present for the practising psychologist as well as for his academic counterpart. Westland's analysis of nine 'crises' in psychology indicates clearly that by its very nature psychology is a discipline in which differences of opinion, conception, definition and approach are inevitable, and this is by no means necessarily an unhealthy state of affairs.[16] One has to accept that the strict behaviourist and the existentialist (or phenomenological, organismic or self-) psychologies will not be able to agree on fundamentals. One might hope, however, that the extremes might at least occasionally communicate with one another!

For the practitioner in counselling the message is plain: there are limitations in any one approach and few applied psychologists are committed to either behaviourism, psycho-analysis or 'third force' models. A judicious eclecticism may well be the wisest course, and Zangwill's point made some time ago is still, perhaps, true: that 'every psychologist has perforce to create his own psychology'.[17] Some, however, consider such eclecticism to be an obstacle to resolving the contradictions inherent in a theory—practice dichotomy for the field-worker. Sheldon outlines the disadvantages of an eclectic approach for the student when he is confronted by 'logically incompatible theories alongside each other . . . leaving the choice to the student.'[18] This, he says, is

> closer to academic licence than academic freedom. It perpetuates a situa-
> tion where knowledge is merely stored rather than sifted or refined. If we
> have no established criteria against which to judge the validity, reliability
> and practical utility of concepts, then it is difficult to know [when] it is
> safe to let go.

While Sheldon is writing of social work, the same arguments against eclecticism have been used by applied psychologists but with uncertain effect. Thus, Westland is forced to conclude that eclecticism seems the only way forward as 'the hope of a unified discipline of psychology is a chimera'.[19]

It seems to this writer that the very concept of 'theory' is one that needs clarification in the literature of counselling. Though much employed, it is plainly used to convey very different meanings by different writers and, one suspects, owes something of its popularity to the prestigious aura of 'science' which accompanies its application. It is perhaps helpful to distinguish two major usages of 'theory', both relevant to our enquiry, but representing different levels of abstraction and of complexity.

In the first sense, a theory is a system of ideas which seeks to incorporate a variety of 'facts', gained from observation and experiment, and which can be used to generate hypotheses to guide further experimental work. It entails an ordering of these 'facts' such that the theory in some sense *explains* how they are related to each other, and how the situation comes to be as it is and not otherwise. 'Facts' which are not consonant with the theory cannot be ignored, and it is part of the process of science that the theory is amended, in the light of experience, to accommodate such 'facts'. In short, the theory is refined in the face of new evidence.

H. J. Eysenck, in a chapter entitled 'The Role of Theory in Science',[20] elaborates the important part that theory has to play in the development of a science. He asks 'Why do we need a theory? The most obvious answer is that only the possession of a good theory will tell us where to look in our search for results.' In this sense, theory provides the framework of concepts and assumptions without which the prediction and testing of hypotheses would not be possible. That is to say, it is through theory that our expectations of the world are articulated and measured against reality. The spirit of science has always insisted on the primacy of good theories, though there are many who would doubt that 'good theories' are as easily identified as Eysenck seems to think.[21]

The second main use of the word 'theory' is in the sense of 'guidelines' for the counsellor when different theoretical approaches are combined, and drawn on, depending on the nature of the problem or problems confronting the counsellor. The level of reasoning and thinking is here less complex and difficult. The purpose here is to use these 'guidelines' to make sense of the material that is brought up in the counselling interview. Even though the counsellor wants, perhaps, to reject theories, denying their utility and even becoming anti-theoretical, he will inevitably be guided by some general theoretical notions, however simply expressed or unwittingly formulated. Rejecting theory (or guidelines) and relying on intuition, common sense, natural perceptiveness or what you will, is a very hazardous basis for approaching people with problems.[22]

A major danger for the counsellor has been highlighted by Hamblin,[23] and applies particularly to the counsellor working in isolation:

> The process of attributing motives to people and giving causal meaning to behaviour is very open to error . . . even more serious is the way in which the needs and implicit personality theory of the counsellor can distort the idea he has of a pupil. Some check on perception of behaviour and motives is nearly always needed.

In other words, in an important sense the counsellor *never* works without theory, for some sort of theory, however vague and unarticulated, is present in the way he perceives the counselling activity, and the assumptions he makes about himself and his client.

While it is clear from the foregoing discussion that some theoretical background is presupposed by the very existence and practices of a counsellor, there is as yet no evidence that the actual psychological or developmental theory favoured by the counsellor has much bearing on his effectiveness. This is not to minimize the importance of theory, but merely to direct attention towards another very important area to be considered: that of the qualities of personality which appear to be necessary if counselling is to be successful. It is widely accepted that the three 'necessary and sufficient conditions for constructive personality change' are empathy, non-possessive warmth or unconditional positive regard, and genuineness or self-congruence. These are felt to be crucial for effective counselling. Although strict experimental evidence for their effectiveness is, according to Shapiro, sparse, it is likely that they function by reinforcing self-exploration. The time may be fast approaching when 'hard data' on counselling effectiveness may be more important for the field-worker than the present elaboration of theories.

However, the theories that often seem to have the most relevance to counselling relate to general ideas on human development and to the nature of personality. They seem to fall into two very broad and very different (if complementary) approaches. On the one hand there is the work stemming from Ellis, Freud, Rogers and the psycho-analytic school where the stress is on the subjective, the introspective, and the self-report. (In the light of his especial influence on the development of counselling, Rogers' contribution can usefully be treated separately.) On the other hand there is the work stemming from behaviour modification and behaviour therapy relating to the work of Eysenck, Skinner, Rachman and Watson, where the stress is on the objective, the observable, the measurable, and the processes of learning and unlearning. It is to a consideration of these broad groups of theory that I now turn.

Counselling and Psychological Theories

The psycho-analytic approach to personality

From the work of psycho-analysts such as Freud, Bowlby, Klein and others, the importance of early experience in determining later personality characteristics has been established. According to these approaches, the main structure of adult character and personality are laid down in early childhood (below the age of five years). There may be, for example, critical periods during which a young child's separation from the mother between the ages of six months and three years can prove severely damaging. It is easy to exaggerate the importance of these early influences and to neglect the influence of social forces that mould the personality. Reinforcement of early learning in babyhood and early childhood, and that which occurs in later childhood and adolescence, may be just as influential, if not more so, in determining the lines along which the growing person will develop. There is some evidence that the lack of an easily available 'extended' family (aunts, uncles, grandparents) can create difficulties for some parents who are then relatively unsupported and are thrown back on their own resources, which may be quite meagre. As I wrote in 1977,[24] it is noticeable in young parents, especially those perhaps who have no easily available family models, that they need help in developing parent skills, and increasingly systematic and sophisticated attempts are being made to respond to these needs.

Obviously there are influences in personal and family history that can hinder or facilitate psychological growth. Various forms of breakdown between the parents and their offspring can occur at any age. At one extreme the parents can abandon the infant, and failure to provide consistent, reliable, and loving parent figures can prove damaging to the growing child. At the other extreme there may be no outward signs of breakdown, yet the parents may be crucial in inducing other effects on their children that are not necessarily damaging. The parents can determine not only interests and attitudes but the kind of career or job that may be taken up. For example, L. Hudson suggests that 'There is an excellent case for believing that the origin of the future scientist's bent for analysis lies within the family. Some features of his relations with his parents must discourage an interest in people, and encourage one in objects.'[25]

Psycho-analysis is at once a method of helping people who are in psychological distress and a method of investigation into human motivation. In the former case by means of a personal analysis (which is costly both in time and money) it is a form of individual treatment which aims to alleviate, change or 'cure' symptoms. The efficacy of such treatment is difficult to prove in a strictly scientific sense, and when specific hypotheses have been developed from the theory the evidence for effectiveness is considerably less satisfactory than that gained from the evaluation of behaviour-therapy treatments. Even so psycho-analysis appears as a body of doctrine or as an attempt to present a unified theory of personality development which many claim is useful in education and in social work. Such a viewpoint induces strong emotion at times in its adherents and in its opponents, although such extreme attitudes are inappropriate for the practitioner who wishes to cull from this approach all that is best and most useful for his work. The psycho-analytic study of children either through forms of child analysis or through other forms of psychotherapy has been fruitful in detailing what goes on in the mind of the 'disturbed' child, as well as throwing light on 'normal' child development and on the education of very young children.

The first few years of life, when the developing child is learning to relate effectively to the parents and to the family, are critical in determining the direction in which a person will develop. How the parents see the child, and how they deal with him, determines how he will regard other people when he becomes adult. How he sees people (either as threatening, hostile, indifferent or apathetic) depends on how his parents have treated him. Fairly characteristic attitudes of suspicion, aggression or submission will be induced. How the young child reacted to the family structure and system of relationships can often throw light on puzzling aspects of the grown person. It is claimed that the successive stages in infantile sexuality can have great importance in linking certain personality traits in adults with early childhood reaction — for example oral and anal impulses may persist into later life at an unconscious level. Such a view of the importance of the earliest social environment can, it is held, bring out significant relationships between parental upbringing, personality and cultural background. These ideas have been fruitful in influencing what goes on in 'children's centres' (set up by Social Services Departments) and in day nurseries attached to day schools (infant or first schools).

According to this view present behaviour is determined largely by the interplay between conscious and unconscious forces. Unconscious forces are present in everybody in the sense that people are not always able to give a full account of their actions and are often puzzled by them. Subsequent reflection can sometimes reveal the unconscious determinants in our behaviour, and the perceptive reader will be able to supply many examples from his own experience. A dislike, for example, of a person may be based on infantile feelings of hatred against an important childhood figure. These primitive feelings may be re-aroused much later in life by an adult who resembles this childhood figure either in physical appearance or in manner or attitude. The re-arousal of these primitive feelings may be unpleasant, and not acceptable to consciousness. They may be suppressed and hidden yet they may quite unwittingly still be a factor determining relationships with certain people. In this way too the destructive young person at school, or the management problem in the home, often has these unconscious forces unwittingly reinforced by 'authority' figures — teachers, parents and social workers — in such a way that special arrangements have to be made for their education in special units or schools, or in 'refuges', 'free schools' or in 'education guidance centres'.

If these unconscious forces in the personality exert such strong influences on behaviour that relationships with others are greatly affected, then it is claimed that behaviour change cannot occur without finding out the nature of these forces. Many psychological processes such as denial, resistance and rationalization, might have to be overcome before the unconscious conflicts can be understood.[26]

Some consider that psycho-analytic doctrine should be taught to all those who are going to work professionally with young children and young people. For example, Halmos says:

> It is my belief that at the present time a unified theory of personality development must be pivoted on the psycho-analytic theory for no other theory of human motivation available today can offer us explanatory hypotheses of equal scope, depth and predictive power. Nor is there any other theoretical system as helpful as it, both in the handling of human relations in general and in the techniques of professional work in particular.[27]

Halmos' views are related to a value or belief system which includes the following propositions:

(i) Man has found a way of relieving human unhappiness by a 'faith' in the success of counselling people. By helping others to achieve insight into themselves and to know how they developed as persons, so people will be enabled to make a better and more satisfying adjustment to living in a mass society. In such a society, and especially in education, it can happen that young people sometimes feel overwhelmed and degraded by mass impersonal teaching, where the techniques of instruction can become more important than the nature of the learner. The large size of groups alone can be felt as overpowering; especially if little or no attempt is made to compensate for size and impersonality by contriving an environment where the individual can feel wanted, secure, important and of significance to others.

(ii) One of the primary tasks of all those professionals engaged in counselling and psychotherapy is to find ways and means of helping others develop insight into themselves. This task is very much part of the belief system of Western philosophic and religious (Christian) tradition, and links with Eastern forms of thought can also be detected. Insight is defined by Halmos as 'the individual's ability to relate the effect of a present experience to that of a past one provided the latter determines the basic quality of the former.'[28]

(iii) Each person is of value in and for themselves and 'love for the other' is the basis on which counsellors approach their clients. Help is offered not on the basis of advice-giving or prescription, nor in outlining the causes or reasons for maladjustment, but those counselled are invited to discover the truth about themselves in a non-directive way. This does not mean that the 'fiction of non-directiveness' can be permanently maintained, as some direction based on moral commitment must inevitably take place, however unwittingly. The 'faith of the counsellors' has 'implicitly retained the notion of an unanalysable proclivity and need to love and to be loved'. The re-emergence of behaviouristic and 'mechanical' ideas based on Pavlovian methods has made 'a mutual accommodation with tradition moral images of love impossible' while 'the vitalistic psychological training of psycho-analytically oreintated counsellors has . . . underpinned and perpetuated traditional moral confidence in a humanistic and noble conception of human love.'[29]

The Rogerian approach

An approach to personality in some ways related to the speculative psycho-analytic viewpoint has been developed by the American C. R. Rogers.[30] It has been given different descriptive labels such as 'non-directive', 'self theory', and 'client-centred'. The essence of his system is a belief in the person as someone who is able to determine what problems should be discussed and who is able to seek his own solutions for them. The person is capable of self-direction; the counsellor's main role is to avoid direct intervention, or to keep such intervention to a minimum.

The most helpful attribute of the counselling interview is seen to be a warm, positive, permissive, accepting attitude on the part of the counsellor, which creates the easy environment necessary for change in attitude towards the self to occur. In such a climate, relatively free from threat and anxiety, a move can be made towards accepting those parts of the self which are distasteful or unpleasant. Rogers observes: 'When a person's view of himself changes, his behaviour changes accordingly and to puzzle over this is the beginning of both theory and science.'[31] He analyses the processes making for understanding, such as a feeling for (or empathy with) the other person in a one-to-one situation and a recognition of the reciprocal relationship achieved as one 'imperfect human being' is brought face to face with another 'imperfect human being'. Effective communication in the counsellor–client relationship appears to depend partly on the belief that the individual is capable of self-direction and able to take his own decisions. The

person is looked upon as someone who is ready to respond to any or
every stimulus outside the self, which performs a control function
by searching, sifting and selecting such stimuli on the basis of past
experience, of his sense of values, and of social norms.
Rogers defines the self as the 'I' or 'me' part of the mind.

> The self-concept, or self-structure, may be thought of as an organised
> configuration of perceptions of the self which are admissible to awareness.
> It is composed of such elements as the perception of one's characteristics
> and abilities; the percepts and concepts of the self in relation to others
> and to the environment; the value qualities which are perceived as associa-
> ted with experiences and objects; and goals and ideals which are perceived
> as having positive or negative valence.[32]

Such a self is subject to the same laws as any other aspect of nature
and offers research hypotheses which can be experimentally tested.
(Rogers' ideas have proved fruitful in producing such experimental
work.) When the individual's image of himself agrees fairly closely with
the image others have of him then a degree of stability in adjustment
is arrived at. When, however, there are wide differences between such
images then instability is a likely result. A self-image is gradually built
up partly on the introjection of admired individuals, both inside and
outside the family. This self-image can so distort his views of himself
and the outside world that he defends himself by psychological processes of denial, projection and rationalization. Rogers considers
that progress in personal adjustment is likely to come about when
the historical and emotional basis for such distortions is brought to
awareness. In this way a more flexible response to experience without
such disabling and distorting personal factors is achieved. The counsellor or therapist is seen as a catalyst who helps forward these processes
in a relatively unhurried way. The self-image changes through a process
of self-acceptance although no definition is offered of the end product
or finished state. The individual is always in the process of 'becoming'.

The behaviourist approach
Behaviourism claims to be objective and scientific and its foundations
are laid in learning theories or in conditioning theories. It rejects the
approaches to counselling so far considered — namely by concentrating
on what people can tell you about their own state of mind (self-report),
on the subjective and introspective, on feelings and emotions, and by
paying attention to inner experience. The behaviour–therapy approach
appears to exclude at first sight nearly all the hypothetical ideas put
forward by the psycho-analysts. Since most human behaviour is acquired
by learning then it ought to be possible to contrive conditions in which
undesirable behaviour can be 'unlearned' and desirable behaviour either
learned or re-learned. To modify behaviour, a degree of 'manipulation'
is inevitable, and new learning conditions are consciously planned
based on learning theory and the results of experimental work. From
a behaviouristic viewpoint the counselling can be seen as a means of

re-arranging environmental conditions based on conditioning techniques. These techniques, rigorously planned in an objective way, deal directly with individual problems and symptoms. Any attempt at understanding, at gaining insight, or at empathy is consciously avoided. The approach to the person is made by isolating the problem (and this can be anything from a reading disability to compulsive masturbation) and by designing an experiment that may modify or eliminate such a problem. Attention is concentrated on separate elements of behaviour, and some success has been reported. One variant of these techniques is known as behaviour-therapy or behavioural counselling, and the utility of this approach is described at length in the works of Eysenck, Woody and Rachman.

The Skinnerian model is often taken as an example of applied science where an attempt is made to shape behaviour using procedures derived from widely accepted theories and experimental practices rather than from those which appear to be unduly speculative. Skinner's ideas seem to be characterized by a tremendous optimism about their beneficial outcome or end-result and by a strong faith in the value of his reinforcement techniques.

Skinner maintains that the learning of any task must be split up into many small successive steps and that as each step is carried out it must be reinforced. He defines reinforcement objectively as anything which increases the probability of an action being repeated. Reinforcement can take many different forms such as material rewards (for example a sweet) or a reward such as praise by a teacher, or even the awareness that the action carried out is the correct one. Each step must be mastered properly and correctly, and be reinforced appropriately before the learner goes on to the next step. Each step is worked out in such a way as to appear to follow on naturally from the preceding one and becomes in its turn a preparation for the next. The overall aim is to ensure a rapid and immediate success in mastering each step. It is more effective to reinforce correct learning than to criticize the incorrect adversely.

The model offered by Skinner has been used as a basis for educational programming (for example in teaching machines) as well as for providing a theoretical background for dealing with severe behaviour problems in schools. The utility value of Skinner's approach is seen in a study by Wagner,[33] where he shows how it is possible to apply Skinnerian ideas in order to eliminate a severe behaviour problem, the compulsive public masturbation of an eleven-year-old girl.

Wagner assumed that certain desirable behaviour changes were necessary — the girl had to stop compulsive masturbation in front of the class. To stop this behaviour he selected certain reinforcing agents as a form of reward. These proved momentarily inhibiting to the child when introduced. These reinforcing agents were activities she particularly enjoyed, such as painting, handing out and collecting papers, helping the teacher, and so on. Whenever masturbation stopped a reward was offered immediately, thus ensuring that the desired response pattern was repeated. Unwanted responses went unrewarded and soon vanished because of non-reinforcement. The number of rewards increased as the desired behaviour gradually became more frequent. For example, when one full day had been completed without masturbation a special note was sent to the parents to say how well she had behaved that day. By arrangement with the parents it was agreed that they would reward her successes suitably on receiving these notes from the teacher. The position was eventually reached when the desired response pattern was regularly being shown. The experimenter also manipulated other variables such as the spacing of rewards, thus ensuring experimental control of the desired behaviour.

Behaviourist ideas based on learning theory have also been fruitful when used in a more general way as guidelines, for example, in dealing with an emotional problem,[34] or in relieving phobias in children by a few sessions of a systematic desensitization procedure.[35] Both these approaches can be incorporated in the techniques which the counsellor can use.

The principles behind Skinner's approach are perhaps fairly easy to grasp, although any serious attempt at experimenting with behaviour-therapy methods needs to be carried out by someone specially trained in their use. As Broadbent observes, 'the whole virtue of Skinner's attitude is that it draws attention to the concrete realities of behaviour',[36] although obviously one of the dangers can be that alternative explanations and theories may be ignored or neglected. In the example given above, for instance, the same result might well have been achieved by a different method of approach, or the result achieved may have been due to the skilful, co-operative and understanding teacher who regularly received support from someone outside the school, thus reducing any anxiety which may have been present.

In any counselling situation, there may be many factors leading to successful results. The faith and confidence in a particular outcome can induce greater efforts among participants. The desired behaviour may be produced by cues, hints and suggestions given unwittingly or subconsciously. Again, observations may be biased by rigidly pre-conceived ideas — expectations and prophecies become self-fulfilling and you find what you expect to find. Factors other than the ones put forward as influencing results are mentioned in discussions on the introduction of a new alphabet (ITA) for the teaching of reading in schools. The success claimed for the experimental classes could be accounted for by factors other than the introduction of such an alphabet (for example the teacher's faith in the new method, an inability to control all the variables satisfactorily, the change of attitude when a reading drive is started in a school, increased enthusiasm for a new method, and so on). This, the well-known 'Hawthorne Effect', could well account for the results achieved by behaviourism, or for that matter any other theory, when applied in a counselling situation.

Conclusion

This, then, is the situation which confronts the counsellor. On the one hand he perceives an array of psychological theories which we have grouped and briefly outlined under the headings psycho-analytic, Rogerian, and behaviourist. Each group has its advocates both on the theoretical level and across the broad spectrum of counselling situations in which these theories are applied. That each has an internal logic and has some appeal to common-sense experience would seem to be evidenced in their continued co-existence.

On the other hand, the counsellor's success seems as much to be due to a host of intangibles that characterize his own personality, intangibles that do not seem to rely on one or other of these theories for their effectiveness. The main dimensions here seem to be intelligence, sensitivity to others, capacity for caring for people, genuineness (honesty, integrity), and a capacity for relating to others with warmth and understanding. It seems at times that the least important attribute is the level of sophistication of one's theoretical background.

So how is the counsellor to proceed? Should he go it alone and pin his faith on those intangibles which, he hopes, characterize his own personality? Should he rely on those methods which, in his own experience and that of others, have been found to be effective? If so, what part is theory to play in the training, preparation and practices of counselling? Or should he strive to master the competing theoretical positions that psychology offers him so that he can, at best, make an informed decision to become a Freudian, Rogerian, Skinnerian or whatever, or at least opt for an eclecticism which utilizes that which is of value in them all? The absence of 'scientific' validation for either the psychological theories which underpin counselling or the practices of counsellors hardly constitutes grounds for abandoning them. For the growth of counselling is not a product of science but a response to the need in people to attach themselves to another for help in meeting, understanding and attempting to resolve the contradictory feelings, personal dilemmas, puzzlements and anxieties involved in social life.

Attractive as it would be to have a single, coherent psychological theory supporting a tried and trusted set of counselling techniques, this is surely impossible at the moment. This does *not* mean, however, that theory is to be ignored or neglected. It seems to me that the best in counselling will be achieved by those who are both endowed with those qualities of warmth, empathy and genuine caring for others *and* who have at least been made aware of the complexity and inconclusiveness of the psychological theories they confront. An awareness of the problematic nature of those very theories would appear to be essential if they are not to be naively embraced and employed by the counsellor as he seeks some theoretical justification for his daily practices.

It has been the object of this paper to highlight just how problematic this relationship between psychological theory and counselling practices really is.

References

1   A. E. Venables, 'Theories about Counselling', *British Journal of Guidance and Counselling*, Vol. 2 No. 1, 1974.
2   D. A. Pond, 'What shall we do with applied psychology?', *Bulletin of the British Psychological Society*, Vol. 30, Jan. 1977.
3   D. A. Shapiro, 'Counselling', in H. J. Eysenck and G. D. Wilson (eds.), *A Textbook of Human Psychology* (M.T.P. Press, London, 1976).
4   D. McConochie and A. Petrie, *Child Guidance* (Macmillan, London, 1974).
5   op. cit.
6   H. J. F. Taylor, 'Some Problems in Group Counselling of Adolescents', in *Occasional Publications of the British Psychological Society*, 1979.
7   O. Zangwill, *Introduction to Modern Psychology* (Methuen, London, 2nd Edn., 1962).
8   H. J. F. Taylor, *School Counselling* (Macmillan, London, 1971).
9   H. J. F. Taylor, 'The Development of Family Counselling in Schools', *A.E.P. Journal*, Vol. 4 No. 4, Spring 1977.

    Winston, New York, 1975).
11 C. R. Rogers, 'A Theory of Therapy in Personality and Personal Relationships', in Koch, S. (ed.), *Psychology: A Study of a Science*, Vol. III (McGraw Hill, 1959).
12 H. J. F. Taylor, 'The Behaviour Modification Approach to Childhood Problems', *A.E.P. Journal*, 1974.
13 C. H. Patterson, 'New Approaches in Counselling', *British Journal of Guidance and Counselling*, Vol. 5 No. 1, Jan. 1977.
14 op. cit.
15 D. A. Pond, op. cit. (note 2).
16 G. Westland, *Current Crises in Psychology* (Heinemann, London, 1978).
17 op. cit.
18 B. Sheldon, 'Theory and Practice in Social Work', *British Journal of Social Work*, Vol. 8 No. 1, 1977.
19 op. cit.
20 H. J. Eysenck, *Sex, Violence and the Media* (Temple Smith, London, 1978).
21 For a discussion of the criteria of a 'good' theory, see Sheldon, op. cit. (note 18).
22 B. Sheldon, op. cit.
23 D.Hamblin, *The Teacher and Counselling* (Blackwell, Oxford, 1974).
24 H. J. F. Taylor, 1977, op. cit (note 9).
25 L. Hudson, *Contrary Imaginations* (Methuen, London, 1966).
26 For a discussion of some of these 'ego defence mechanisms' see C. Rycroft, *A Critical Dictionary of Psycho-analysis* (Nelson, Sunbury, 1968).
27 P. Halmos (ed.), *Papers on the Teaching of Personality Development*, Sociological Review Monograph No. 2, University College of N. Staffs.
28 P. Halmos, 'The Personal Service Society', Inaugural address at University College, Cardiff (University of Wales Press, 1966).

29   P. Halmos (ed.), op. cit. (note 27).
30   C. R. Rogers, op. cit.
31   op. cit.
32   op. cit.
33   M. K. Wagner, 'A case of public masturbation treated by operant condition-
     ing', *Journal of Child Psychology and Psychiatry, 9*, pp. 61-65.
34   H. J. F. Taylor, 1974, op. cit. (note 12).
35   A. W. Bolgar, 'Systematic Desensitization as a Counselling Procedure',
     British Journal of Guidance and Counselling, Vol. 6 No. 1, Jan. 1978.
36   D. E. Broadbent, *Behaviour* (Eyre and Spottiswoode, London, 1961).

SECTION C

Bringing Learning Back In: the fundamental issue?

Introduction

In the previous section we saw how in discussing the role of various specialists (form tutor, counsellor, careers teacher and so on) the boundaries between the academic teaching of knowledge and the pastoral care of children have to be blurred if those roles are to be developed in a meaningful way. Whereas contributors to that section saw this as implied by a consideration of specific strategies for guidance and counselling at all levels, the three chapters in this section argue in various ways that the breaking down of this distinction is fundamental to a clear understanding of how pastoral care is related to education. Moreover, such a fundamental re-definition of pastoral care has far-reaching implications for curriculum design and implementation, and for the organization of school structures within which the curriculum is to be taught.

Michael Marland outlines such a pastoral curriculum, and discusses how it might be divided up and allocated to various teams within the school. Derek Williamson points to the way in which existing pastoral-care structures may actually mask serious inadequacies in the academic provision of the school, and in the process absorb valuable resources that might be more fruitfully employed in other ways. John Buckley criticizes the academic–pastoral distinction on the grounds that it entails a fundamental misunderstanding of the concepts of education and learning, and goes on to propose a particular set of structural arrangements whereby teams of teachers would be responsible for *all* aspects of the education of a group of children throughout their school career.

The concept of the team is applied quite explicitly in the programmes outlined by both Marland and Buckley, and is one which we saw also in a number of contributions in the previous section. It is, by implication at least, also part of Williamson's case for a more reasoned and carefully designed academic curriculum, which would significantly reduce the 'need' for pastoral care. Many teachers will perhaps be surprised that 'teams' should be offered as some sort of solution to the problem of care. After all, they may say, don't pastoral-care teams already exist in most schools? What else is the House Master (or Year Tutor) and the group of form tutors for which he is responsible?

Perhaps it is not insignificant that so little is said about such 'teams' by any of the contributors to this volume. Where teams are advocated they are always conceived of as fairly new alliances, or as different combinations forged from existing roles, and not merely as the elaboration of existing structures. Is this not a tacit admission that existing so-called 'pastoral teams' are not, as a matter of fact, *teams* at all; that they are simply ineffective groupings which are perhaps purely nominal and make little corporate contribution to the pastoral endeavour? Perhaps the identification of a group of teachers as responsible for specific aspects of the pastoral curriculum (Marland) and for a specific group of children (Buckley) is one way of creating teams which are teams in *fact* as well as in name.

It may also be a necessary prerequisite for a new 'contract' between teacher and pupil, which transcends the sterile and demoralizing relationship that too often exists. As both Buckley and Williamson argue, the inadequacy of learning situations that are characterized by apathy and antagonism is something that no pastoral structure separately conceived is likely to make good.

The argument in this section is that global problems must be tackled on a global scale. Piecemeal tinkering with existing structures or the refinement of specialist roles will be of strictly limited consequence. What is required is an altogether more basic reassessment of the organization of schooling which includes both curricular design and role-definition.

11 The Pastoral Curriculum

Michael Marland

The word 'curriculum' simply means a list of those activities which a school is trying to provide fairly deliberately for its pupils as some kind of learning experience. There is thus nothing very difficult or impressive about the word. From that point of view, even an informal school journey or parents' outing for their children have a kind of curriculum; a school camp has a curriculum; the school assemblies have a curriculum . . . and so on. Incidentally, whether you write it down or not, you still have a curriculum. A school, or a section of it, must have a curriculum, even if it requires a team of researchers to come and observe what you are doing and write it down and say, 'That is your curriculum'. I shall speak of this listing of a deliberate provision of activities from the pastoral point of view, in seven sections.

1 Curriculum Content and Pastoral Needs

Obviously a total pastoral-care system has many complementary elements, from a clear responsibility structure for individual casework to good relationships with parents. However, if the academic curriculum is not included any list of elements is incomplete. This is because all kinds of pastoral care in school work with, and depend on, the pupils' ideas, attitudes, skills, knowledge of facts, and knowledge of concepts. What the pupil actually knows, is capable of, and brings to a particular pastoral encounter are among the key factors which vary the effectiveness of the pastoral care that is offered.

Consider some examples:

(a) Supposing one of us has decided to spend forty minutes after school with a fifth-year pupil to counsel him privately and personally about post-fifth possibilities. We have learnt about Rogerian counselling, and we know that counselling should be non-directive, and that our task is to act as a neutral sounding-board, to respond, and to clarify. But, after about five minutes, it becomes very clear to us that this boy of sixteen actually doesn't know the difference between FE and HE; he doesn't know the different ways in which you can get into an occupation — by proceeding with general education and moving across later, or by going into a specific kind of vocational education earlier, and so forth. What then happens to that precious forty minutes?

Instead of being a non-directive counselling session, it becomes a *lesson* in the structure of education, because we find we can't move into counselling without giving the necessary information. Therefore we are forced back to putting over content even though we didn't mean to. Only in the last three minutes do we actually get round to helping the boy clarify his own wishes; we haven't been able to reach counselling because we had to fill a knowledge vacuum.

(b) Take a fourth-year boy having problems with his work-load: he has recently moved from the Lower School where, as in the first three years of a typical comprehensive school, the pupil hasn't been obliged to read very much. Now, suddenly, he has hit this Middle School reading load in his new range of option subjects, with new homework demands, and a new burden of problems. His tutor decides that he will spend fifteen or twenty minutes on a purely individual basis trying to help this boy sort things out. What does the tutor find himself doing? He is actually giving a lesson on organizing time, a lesson on note-taking, a lesson even on reading to learn. In other words, what looked like a purely pastoral session, has willy-nilly been converted into a content session. The tutor can't get to the counselling because of the information vacuum: advice has become instruction.

(c) Moving gradually to the more intangible, take a third-year girl, having rows about being late home at night, who has turned to her Head of Year for advice. Even here the Head of Year finds that before he can give advice, he has a good deal of information to give. He actually has to remind her of what it is like to be a parent; he probably even has to remind her about parents' legal responsibilities, that parents themselves aren't allowed to go out and abandon children under a certain age at home, and so on. Once again, an advice session has become an instruction session.

(d) Even if we move to the most intangible, the situation is the same. A tutor takes a second-year girl to one side because she is being picked on: she's unpopular. This is perhaps the most intangible, the most personal piece of counselling you're likely to give. Helping a pupil cope socially requires more than 'counselling'; it requires 'information' and 'tuition'. The comparison with adult situations is interesting. In a report of an apparently successful prison after-care experiment, the key point was that prisoners were given certain social *skills*; various of these ex-prisoners maintained that it was this tuition which helped them not go back to prison. We talk as adults of how you have to 'work at' friendship. It's quite a common adult phrase, yet we don't give this sort of advice to pupils. I had a relevant experience when I went along to the English-Speaking Union to be briefed about an eight-week scholarship to go to America as a guest of the English-Speaking Union. I looked around, and there we were, middle-aged men and women, writing notes on the social skills expected of visiting English people by American hosts. I found myself going home with notes saying: 'Don't forget to write thank-you letters', and 'Don't forget to take a little pile of nice presents, which have to be British'. None of us objected to being given that advice — it was a *content* session.

These are all examples of the impossibility of focusing on individual help and guidance without considering the curriculum content that lies behind it. My first and most idealistic reason, then, why every school should create a pastoral curriculum is to establish the concepts, attitudes, facts, and skills which are necessary to the individual.

There's another reason, apparently a more mundane one: there would never be sufficient time for all the pupils in a school to have all the necessary guidance given individually; it's just not possible. Anybody who researches into the pastoral system of a school finds this lack of guidance. Here, for instance, is part of a research report on the transition to work in a number of comprehensive schools:

> For the normal, untroublesome child tutorial care and counselling still went on mainly in crises. This seemed equally true for the personal guidance areas of careers and vocational development, for attention to interpersonal development, and for keeping an eye on the development of an imaginative approach to life and job.[1]

And also, in that research report, a comment about one pupil' 'Lake School's inability to provide an effective, available tutor for Susan and her peers occurred despite having launched a programme to do just that.'[2] It is physically impossible to give every student totally adequate care individually. Of course, at the lowest level, there is also the need to occupy the time if yours is a school where you are not rushed down to assembly five minutes after getting into the tutorial room. It has been interesting to see the first wave of comprehensive schools pulling back from assemblies and giving more and more time to tutor periods, and then many of them pulling back from that, and people saying, 'There's too much time around and teachers don't know how to deal with it'.

Unless we have an agreed background curriculum, we are depending on children having crises before we can offer them any help; that way we don't know their problem until they know their problem — and often they don't know their problem until it's too late to help them with their problem. Thus, to rely too heavily on pastoral help given individually is actually a let-down for the majority of children. Of course, I am not in any way denigrating individual help, but it must depend on a curriculum background — and if you rely on working entirely with individuals, some pupils are going to miss out.

Thus I would say that *the art of the pastoral system is to help all the individuals without always giving individual help*. Therefore, a school must find ways of preparing for the expected needs, following up the discovered needs, and giving the necessary basis for a personal seeking of advice. This preparation and follow-up is largely going to be in the group situation: that must mean that we should have a curriculum behind it. What I want to argue, then, is that *the most effective individual guidance and counselling depends on the background of concepts, facts, and skills which the individual client brings to the counselling session.* I would therefore suggest that individual counselling has to depend on whole-group exploration of this necessary background. Drawing up the list of what should go into that background is essentially a curriculum matter. The curriculum components which relate especially to individual and personal growth I would call the 'pastoral curriculum'.

2 Curriculum Planning

It can, sadly, be shown that there is little curriculum planning in our schools. Most of us get the cart before the horse: we have a department called History, and we discuss what it ought to do. Or, occasionally if we are modern, we say you put together history, religious studies, and geography, and sometimes English. There are a number of good motives for such a move, such as reducing the number of teachers a pupil meets, showing a 'seamless web of knowledge', and so forth. However, another reason is the sharp awareness of a lack of curriculum planning in the school, and an intention of healing the cracks or fissures between the departments. I am not arguing against such 'integration' — but I should like to point out that it does not solve the problems of curriculum planning. At its best it produces only planning in one particular area, and it can produce an even deeper chasm between the new faculties than the original fissures between the smaller departments. Certainly, it doesn't make the problem of across-the-board curriculum planning one jot easier. Indeed, with the new, larger, more powerful barons, holding sway over their Faculties of Creative Arts, for instance, it can be even harder to get proper curriculum planning across the board.

What, then, is a curriculum, and how should curriculum planning be carrried out? The starting point must surely be the putting of the fundamental question: 'What should the pupils' for whom we are responsible gain from our school?' Thus the beginning of a curriculum (or the beginning of a revision of the existing collection of school syllabuses) is rather like drawing up a shopping list. We should gather a list of the 'learning' or the 'growth' that we hope will embody these. This 'shopping list', in fact, will be based on our understanding of what a pupil is likely to need. It will not be merely a list of facts, nor will it be merely cognitive, but is likely to include concepts, facts, attitudes, and skills — which can be seen as the four main components of a curriculum list. (There will be other starting points for parts of the list, such as the need for the foundations of certain disciplines.) I strongly recommend that everyone in the school concerned with the planning of the curriculum should have no preconception about who should be responsible for any part of the list. It is dangerously limiting to think in terms of which department, which subject, or which teacher-team should undertake any part of the list. It is even inhibiting to proper development of the list if you think too early in terms of which age of pupil suits any particular item. Such pre-conception starts to affect the contents, which are then shaped to suit the school's teaching and organizational pattern rather than our perception of the pupil's needs. If we take the shopping-list metaphor further, you could say that you draw up the initial list according to the need not according to who will make the purchases. Once the list is drawn up, parts of it can be given to various members of the family.

Let us consider one aspect — library-user education and study skills. If you start by presuming these aspects are to be taught by, say, the English teacher, or by the librarian, you are probably defining, inadvertently, what will be taught and how it will be taught. You are, for instance, de-contextualizing the majority of the skills (as neither of those people are themselves responsible for factual research activities with pupils). Similarly, a decision that the ability to 'read' technical drawing is to be taught by 'craft' teachers, by removing it from town planning, mapping, and architecture, changes its nature.

Similarly, at this stage a curriculum list does *not* fix learning or teaching methods — that comes later. If you take the change from a traditional mathematics syllabus to an SMP or modern maths syllabus, there is a considerable change of content, but not necessarily a change of teaching method. *Curriculum planning in its early stages does not control classroom method*, and I stress that in the pastoral context because people seem to begin to get worried at this point that 'curriculum' means didactic lectures. Also curriculum does not imply the mode of relating to the pupils. The formality of listing what you propose to do does not imply a formality of relationship when you do it. The list of things you propose to do on holiday might be put on paper — one, two, three, four, five. It does not mean that the formality of that list has to be replicated in the formality of your relationships, or even in that order. Indeed, the same curriculum aim can be met in a didactic way or a discovery-orientated way, in an authoritarian way or in an intimate way.

Nor should it be considered that the curriculum is mainly to do with the cognitive. For instance, I have included 'attitudes' as one part of any curriculum. This is entirely legitimate. Aims concerned with attitudes or emotions have always been part of the curriculum. A music curriculum is bound to include the aim of increasing 'enjoyment' or 'appreciation'. A religious studies curriculum would probably include the aim of improving 'understanding' and 'sympathy'. A biology curriculum that didn't include some notion that you were helping to improve pupils' respect for living matter would be a poor kind of curriculum. Indeed, many parts of the so-called 'academic' curriculum, the readily accepted curriculum, have aims as subtle and as intangible as parts of what I am calling the 'pastoral curriculum'. Science, biology, history, music all have the development of attitudes in their curriculum, and this should be stated and the desired attitudes made explicit in the curriculum description.

The pastoral curriculum, as I see it, would be those items on the shopping list which are essential for the personal growth of individuals, for their learning growth, and are not there mainly because it is part of the logic of a subject. It is quite right, for instance, that at a certain point in mathematics, negative numbers must be tackled. Negative numbers are tackled because they are part of the logic of the mathematical structure. That is proper. But I am suggesting that we have to have a check-list also for that which should be there because it is necessary for the growth of the individual.

3   Curriculum Division

The 'shopping list', then, makes up the curriculum as a whole. To make the list comprehensible and to start seeking ways in which responsibility can be given to teams of teachers, the items on the list have to be grouped. This grouping creates divisions, and the divisions can be seen as aspects of a school's work. It is important to stress that nothing in my argument is either for or against what is normally called 'integration' in curriculum-planning (or, more accurately, time-table-planning). The integrator brings together previously separate but already defined subjects. The process I am describing starts before those subjects have been defined.

The question of how to divide up the huge list of items is confused by our metaphorical problems. What shall we call the 'gatherings' of items that we wish to see related? The HMIs in the DES curriculum 'red paper' *Curriculum 11-16* (December 1977) choose the apparently quite reasonable word 'areas', and they 'identify 8 broad areas of experience': aesthetic/creative, ethical, linguistic, mathematical, physical, scientific, social/political, and spiritual. Although the anonymous authors are at pains to stress that 'there is no wish to divide experience into mutually exclusive categories', most of the rest of the booklet is a series of statements by 'subject committees' of the Inspectorate, who were invited to consider the contributions of 'their' subject, and the 'core' or 'common' curriculum is soon argued in subject terms.

I deeply dislike the metaphor of 'area', and it is especially unhelpful for the planning of the pastoral curriculum. 'Areas' have what the dictionaries call 'more or less definitely marked boundaries'. However much people wish to talk about 'blurring' the boundaries, and however much it may be true that one area 'shades off' into another, the basic concept embodied in the metaphor is of physically adjacent places. Even if you're not always sure if you are in one or the other, you can be in only one at a time. There is no way in which one 'area' can be said to permeate all the others, for that is a contradiction in terms.

I prefer to think of the curriculum as a multi-faceted object, like a gem-stone (see Figure 5). In the initial division of the curriculum list, each facet can have central characteristics which link them. For analysis and discussion, we can consider primarily one facet, but all the other facets are still there, and are always part of what is being looked at. Indeed, looked at from the apex, all can be seen simultaneously, and all meet.

Figure 5 *The relationship of curriculum facets*

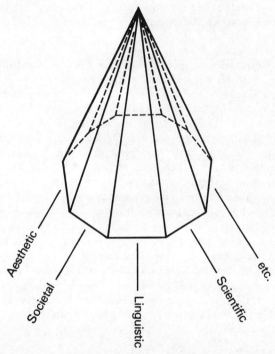

These facets can be defined in different ways, but I should not wish them to be given subject labels. I prefer to give them broad labels such as 'societal', a facet covering everything that needs to be known about society; another covering the understanding of everything scientific from the growth of the world, through living things, to technology; another concerned with communications; another with the visual arts. I suggest that one of these facets should be labelled 'pastoral' — that is, the school curriculum looked at for the moment solely from the point of view of the personal needs of the pupil resolving his individual problems, making informed decisions, and taking his place in his personal and social world.

4. *Curriculum Distribution*

So far we have gathered a list of the pupils' needs, and grouped many of them as 'personal', that is, those which underpin pastoral care. The curriculum has been divided only for grouping of items and for analysis. However, even though I have recommended postponing the distribution into teacher teams until as late as possible, it is obviously necessary at some point to distribute the curriculum among the teachers so that syllabus-planning can follow.

In the primary school the distribution is simple: the class teacher in the 'self-contained' class (to use the American term) takes the whole curriculum, except for a few fragments of facets such as music or physical education. In the secondary school there seems to me to be three main methods of curriculum distribution:

(a) The specialized

This, the most common, gives a particular group of curriculum facets to one team of teachers. Usually the curriculum facet or facets) is then called a subject and the team of teachers a department. It is probably the method that heads like best because it is obviously practical and has the advantage that you can appoint somebody on Scale 4 and simply tell them to get on with the job. Some facets lend themselves fairly readily to that. Modern languages is probably one. It's noticeable that that has been the way most schools have planned their curriculum hitherto. Thus, everything 'scientific' goes in the Science Department. When you get something like Health Education, you're in trouble: you either look to one of your old departments, wait until your Head of Home Economics retires, and ask the next one to take that on; or you introduce a new subject, as some schools in the UK have done, creating departments of 'Personal Relations', with a 'Head of Personal Relations'. This team is treated like a subject team and the subject is seen as discrete. 'Careers' is another facet you can give to a 'Careers Department'. That is the first method: call your facet a subject, give it a teaching team, and give it a team leader, called a Head of Department.

(b) Multi-team

Some facets are distributed between a specified and limited number of teams. I mentioned earlier the facet of library-user education and study skills. This could be given to one team, but at Woodberry Down School, for instance, we have distributed it between five teams: the tutors (library induction, general study-skills), the English Department (fiction and dictionaries), the Humanities (parts of books, especially index, classification, search strategies), and the Science Department (with similar tasks), with each option in one pool providing fourth-year revision. Notice that there is still one overall syllabus, but it has been divided up and handed out. We do something similar with Health Education, which is divided between Science, Home Studies, Tutors, and Social Studies (called 'Common Core Course'). A third example is the Drama programme for the first three years at Broughton High School, Lancashire, which is largely based on the school's pastoral curriculum. (This differs markedly from so-called 'integration', as the multi-team approach has one unifying syllabus cut up, with sections inserted into other syllabus sequences.)

(c) Whole-school policies

The whole-school approach is the third method. In this a facet is given to all the teams, and is expected to feature in every part of the school's activities. Thus the facet of 'preparation for work' can be seen not as a separate subject, but as a way of focusing all subjects; reading can be seen not as a separately taught skill, but a skill taught in each subject and through the material of that learning activity. I should myself argue that there are a number of facets that should be whole-school policies: visual literacy, moral education, health education, careers, and certainly language. As attempts to develop policies for 'language across the curriculum' have shown, whole-school policies are difficult to start, to implement, and to monitor. When everybody is in theory doing something, in fact nobody might be properly involved. They do, however, relate especially to the pastoral curriculum.

Those are the three methods of distribution. I have stressed that one should not make the decision until the shopping list has been drawn up and the facets grouped. The choice of methods will vary from school to school, and various combinations are possible. You can obviously combine (a) and (c), i.e., the 'specific' with the 'whole-school', the 'specialized' with the 'disseminated'. Thus, you could have both specific careers teaching in one subject and disseminated careers teaching throughout the whole school. However, the more complicated you get, the more difficult it is to make sure the work is actually being done.

Let us take a facet which is undeniably related to a school's pastoral concerns: preparation for work. A humanities team might have the topic of 'jobs' in a first-year integrated humanities syllabus. This would be part of the humanities team's covering of its own syllabus aims — to show how human beings relate their human needs to the environment. Thus a first-year class might study the Common Ground film-strips called 'Life-styles'. One, for instance, shows the work and life of a university professor in a university in Ghana. At that moment the pupils are not 'doing careers', but meeting one part of the Humanities objectives through careers-related material. Similarly in English in the older years it is possible to do a unit on 'Work'. Most English departments have much literature focusing on the family, growing-up, and relationships in the family environment. All of these may be excellent books, but if the overall balance of reading is considered, why not include some of the also very good literature on what it is like to be at work? This then also becomes a contribution to the whole-school careers policy, and it meets the point that you can't think about work unless you know what various situations *feel* like.

These are two examples of subject teams contributing to whole-school policies from the pastoral facet. Again, this is not the same as integration. *It is that some aims of those subject teams have been made synchronous with the main aims of the careers policy.*

We then have to ask ourselves which part of our pastoral facet should be covered by whom; this is a two-way process, because it means the pastoral team must speak to the curriculum planners in the school, and must indeed be part of the curriculum planning to ensure that the pupils' pastoral needs are covered somewhere on the curriculum. We must then decide what parts of those needs will be covered by the pastoral team. *I am not saying that everything on the pastoral curriculum should be taught by the tutor. Some of the content should be distributed to others.*

Some parts of the pastoral curriculum are likely to be well covered by the team called 'English'. It would be very rare that there would be a school in which the English Department didn't cover some parts of it, because the medium of literature makes objective discussion of a large number of pastoral problems easier. It is easier to talk about family problems in the situation of a fictitious story than with the individual pupil. I think both should be done. Other parts could be distributed to those responsible for Health Education (which will of course be different subject teams in different schools). No doubt the 'Humanities', whatever subject headings are used in a school, would satisfactorily take on key parts of the pastoral curriculum.

Certain schools may wish to distribute other parts of the pastoral curriculum to still other teams, but finally there will surely always be some parts of it which must properly be the responsibility of the pastoral team, the tutors. A substantial part of their work will be concerned with practical help to individuals and their families, but some of it will be 'covering' parts of the pastoral curriculum.

Figure 6 shows the kind of relationship that there can be of teacher teams to the pastoral curriculum. The centre circle represents the pastoral curriculum, and part of this is covered by three of the subject teams: English, Health Education, and Humanities. The tutorial team similarly take part. The area outside the inner circle is the remainder of that team's work, which in the case of the tutor team is the individual counselling and practical help. The tutorial team's part of the inner circle can usefully be called 'the tutorial programme' (see Figure 7), and this is described further in Section 6.

Figure 6   *The pastoral curriculum and teacher teams*

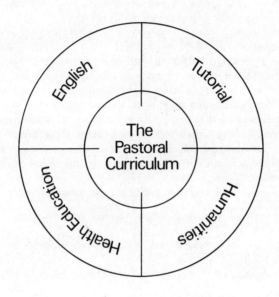

Figure 7   *Pastoral duties of the tutorial team*

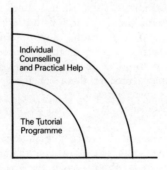

The Pastoral Content

A curriculum is not a teaching scheme; it is arranged in a logical order, not necessarily in the order we should teach it. The first thing on the curriculum is not necessarily the first thing we teach, or the first thing we offer as a learning experience. There are commonly thought of as three aspects which make up pastoral guidance: *(a)* personal, *(b)* educational; *(c)* vocational. The content can be usefully gathered under those three headings. Each school should draw up its own list, but here are some of the points which might go in:

(a) Personal
There is a common fallacy that all personal guidance must be given in person. This is not so. Everybody has had a great deal of personal help, in the sense that it affected them more than or differently from the way it affected their neighbour, by communal, public activities. It is often presumed that if a thing is personal, it is too personal for a curriculum. I think that is so for some things; some things are far too personal for most schools. However, that does not mean that everything that is personal is too personal for the privileged position of the classroom.

The points which might go in this section would include:

(i)   the self: what makes up a person's temperament, personality, and needs;
(ii)   how to assess, understand and cope with physical and emotional well-being;
(iii)   the individual in relation to family, neighbours, friends, growing up;
(iv)   getting on with people, skills and attitudes (when I look at the trouble that our pupils get into with various members of the public, Underground ticket collectors, bus conductors, old ladies, and the rows they get into, I think it is partly due to a lack in our pastoral programme);
(v)   rights and obligations as an adolescent, as a young adult; the legal framework (it's a pity to wait until a seventeen-year-old has a brush with the Law, has a row with a policeman, gets into trouble, and then try to mop up the pieces, when you could have actually explained, for example, that a policeman has the right to stop and question you in certain circumstances: better to actually prepare them for these situations than just mop up the trouble afterwards);
(vi)   choice and choosing; how to prepare for choice and how to evaluate;
(vii)   using the services and facilities that society offers (it's not enough to just say: 'There's a counselling service down the road', or 'There's a library down the road', or 'There's a GP down the road': *how do you make use of these services?*);
(viii) the personal conventions of society; meeting, introduction, letters, telephone conversations;
(ix)   other people's difficulties: charity; understanding;
(x)   recreation: hobbies; using time; opportunities.

(b) Educational

This, I believe, should be the predominant part of the pastoral curriculum for the following reason: the activities of education are all around the pupil, and it's therefore the easiest of the three to cover. After all, we believe in field trips, we believe in taking pupils to see things *in action*. The great advantage of teaching the educational part of the pastoral curriculum is it is in action all round you, and you are only too obviously part of the action. It's worth stressing that the many aspects of educational guidance within the pastoral curriculum should be done thoroughly – not only for their own sake, for instance not only to make sure that the pupil makes the wisest choice, but also because it is the only choice that will be made within the influence and help of the school: *the educational part of the pastoral curriculum is a preparation for analagous activities after school.* Thus, for instance, how to cope with different teachers is not only valuable because it helps the pupil cope with those teachers and make best use of them, but also because it is an analagous preparation for coping with different people in work, society, and so forth. I am stressing that the educational list contains matters done for their own sake, but also for the sake of the fact that education is at hand and, therefore, very good learning material.

What do we include?

(i)   The school itself: its people; its hierarchy, building, and facilities – for two reasons – both because they need to know these in order to be able to use the school, but also because we have to teach pupils about organizations since much of what they need for the rest of life is encountered in organizations. If we teach them how to use the school organization, we will better teach them how to use a hospital organization. John Bazalgette has declared, after his research into the transition from school to work, that many have difficulty in the transition because they can't understand their work organization. He said that he discovered that this was because they didn't understand their *school* organization. (He went on to make a rather nasty dig that that was because the teachers who taught them didn't understand their own school organization!) If we don't teach the pupils how to use the school organization then we aren't teaching them how to use another organization.

(ii) Study strategies, library skills,[3] and revision approaches.

(iii) How to *use* classes, small groups and teachers.

(iv) Subject choice: for its own sake and as a paradigm of choosing wisely. Somebody said that it doesn't matter if you make a wise choice; it does matter that you choose wisely. I think that is why the subject-choice part of the school programme is desperately important, not only so that the pupils make the wisest possible choice, but even more so that they have the experience of choosing wisely on an important matter.

(v)   The examination system in the UK: this is not understood by
       many pupils, and yet part of the pastoral system is going to be
       to help them use the data they get from the examination. Fre-
       quently they haven't been taught. The relationship between
       CEE, O-level, and CSE is difficult, but it's a bit mad that we
       put people in for these examinations and we tell them to use
       that data to decide what careers to go into if we don't help
       them to interpret that data.
(vi)   Examination entry: administrative arrangements.
(vii) Other educational agencies outside school.
(viii) Informal education: newspapers, broadcasting, museums, maga-
       zines.
(ix)   The sharing of the educational and teaching experience of mem-
       bers of the group with those who do not study that subject.
       When I go into some tutor groups and see the desultory chat,
       the building-up of peer group 'prisons'[4], I realize that we're
       almost denying the purpose of comprehensive education: we have
       given them a wide range of activities and options, but we have
       found no way of feeding some inkling of some of those options
       into the group as a whole. What is the point of being in a school
       where a few pupils learn Classics, if the rest of us don't actually
       get a little inkling of why they should be doing it, and isn't the
       pastoral programme one place in which you do it?
(x)   One very important part of the educational element of the
       pastoral curriculum is to help pupils make use of the feedback
       on their learning performance that the school gives them. It has
       been conclusively shown that 'deterioration in quality of intellec-
       tual problem-solving performance is generally independent of
       proficiency at the task'.[5] That is, in the face of partial or complete
       failure what characterizes those who go on to achieve better
       results is not those individuals' ability. Carol Dweck and her
       research associates at the University of Illinois have shown that
       'persistent, mastery-oriented children view failure as carrying
       information about specific aspects of the performance that are
       modifiable'. What she calls 'attribution retraining', that is, specific
       steps to help children analyse their difficulties and utilize criticism,
       has a greater effect on a young person's response to failure than
       a long history of previous success. This view, which is contrary
       to much of teachers' assumed folklore, implies a definite pastoral
       task.

(c) Vocational

The paradox for our pupils is the great diversity but the reduced
knowledge. In the Lancashire mill town in the 'twenties where my
father grew up, there was only the choice of the foundry or the mill –
unless you ran away as he did when he was seventeen! In the Suffolk
village where I live now, you can see and even join in the main work

occupations, and by the age of six you know what each is like. However, in all our cities, there is instead the paradox of the widest opportunity range of types of job that the world has ever offered people, but very little sight of what they do. I remember one girl going home in tears following a careers talk at school, saying, in effect, 'They tell me there are so many thousand jobs I can do, but I don't know which one.' This was because she could not comprehend what was involved in them. Where can you learn about what it is like to do jobs? The portrayal of the world of work in the media is often inadequate.

Most of what is necessary by way of help is open to all teachers: characteristics of different walks of life, different ways of earning a living, team work in different jobs, and so on. I wish here not to specify the content, but to stress that it is not the more obscure details of specific professional careers advice I am referring to, but those more general points that can be handled by all teachers, given the appropriate help and materials.

The Tutorial Programme

Supposing you have worked from the shopping list of the overall school curriculum, then divided out the pastoral curriculum, and then distributed that pastoral curriculum. There is still the need to draw up an actual tutorial programme. You have decided what should be covered elsewhere, you have decided what will be taught specifically and what in a disseminated way, and what will be taught by whom. If there is a tutorial team, I suggest that it is the responsibility of their team leader to make sure in collaboration with them that there is a tutorial programme. *It will not look at all like the list I gave in 5*, because that is in a logical order, and you don't necessarily teach things in a logical order. The tutorial programme, then, takes those points from the pastoral curriculum which have been agreed in this school to go to the tutors. This will vary from school to school. Some of them − like induction into the school − are likely to apply in every school, but not inevitably.

The programme then finds pupil activities to embody those curriculum aims, because all learning in a school has to be translated from an *aim* into a learning *activity*. The science teacher, for instance, has the pupil observe a particular chemical reaction that carries a particular learning charge. We, similarly, have to find things for the pupils to *do* that will carry the tutorial charge of the tutorial programme. The activity should have a sensible correspondence to the aim. Individual work will be part of it, but only some of it. The misunderstanding that pastoral care is by definition for individuals alone has caused gross difficulties. As Dr Leslie Button has put the problem:

> The predominance of the case-work model, through which the teacher seeks to deal with one person at a time, seems to be one of the major difficulties. The teacher tends to see his value to the young person in

terms of his relationship with each one, rather like the spokes around
the hub of a wheel. The relationship between the teacher and the young
person is, of course, important, but we have tended to neglect the relationship between the members of the pastoral group, and the urgency of
creating a caring community within a class. The purpose of group work is
to facilitate the reciprocal help and support between the members of the
group.[6]

Those processes have to be tackled in a programme devised for the
groups, but leaving teachers considerable freedom. The organizing
principle can be that of the sequence of the school years provided care
is taken. Douglas Hamblin has argued that what he helpfully calls
'critical incidents' can be 'used as a framework for pastoral care'.[7]
'A critical incident', he explains, 'is a major task which emanates
firstly from the organization of the secondary school and secondly
from the adjustments that society demands of adolescents, and each
one can be broken down into a number of smaller tasks that demand
certain skills.' I should argue that these critical incidents can be one
of the main organizing methods for the pastoral programme.

This programme would have to divide that curriculum into aspects,
then into years, and then into activities. By 'into years' I certainly do
not mean that one whole topic would be left to one particular year. It
is particularly a problem in year-based schools, because there a year
topic can very easily be seen as the only topic for the year, and be kept
out of the other years. Thus the over-rigid pattern becomes:

Year One: Induction
Year Two: Family
Year Three: Subject Choice
Year Four: Study Skills
Year Five: Examination Preparation, Careers, and 'Life'.

It may appear logical, but I don't think the programme should be like
that. Instead I think the programme should be seen as having a number
of main themes which are kept in sight in all years in varying degrees.
Such a pattern could be shown as a grid, with across the top axis the
different aspects: knowledge of the school, choosing subjects, self,
careers, family; down the side of the grid should be the years of the
school. In any one year, one of those different aspects will swell out,
like an hourglass, and then slim down again, *but none of them would
disappear from any year*. Thus, the careers part, the work part, of the
tutorial programme would be there in every year. Certainly, it would
expand in Year Four, perhaps narrow in Year Two. Similarly, induction
into the school is not a Year One activity alone; pupils don't need to
know everything about the school in Year One. So that would be quite
big in Year One, would narrow in Year Two, and would then expand
again in Year Three, when you have to take a fresh look at some parts
of the school. The same is true of 'the family' as a theme. In a way it
should never leave the programme, even though in some years it will
be more important than in others.

When you come to think about it, there aren't many activities pupils can do in rooms in schools. If we put aside the ones we don't want them to do, we've only got a handful: listening, discussing, talking, investigating and project work, drawing, reading, question-naires, and writing. We might add various kinds of practical work, but they are a bit difficult to handle in tutor rooms. I would suggest that we have to list the kinds of activities that we think pupils can carry out. Then we can list 'the curriculum content'. If, again, this is done in the form of a chart with one list across the top and the other down the side, there is a series of boxes. Then, in each box we can put down suggestions for activities. This, therefore, is the penultimate stage in the working out of a tutorial programme.

There are fallacies in some schools that these activities are to do with time-filling; there's that awful fallacy of the phrase 'Tutorial business', and tutors sometimes say: 'Of course there sometimes isn't much time left after the tutorial administration.' *I suggest that most of the tutorial administration should be a vehicle for the curriculum aims.* Take an example from examination entries. How is that adminis-tration problem handled in most schools? In many schools, a day after the deadline when examination entries have to be in to the Board, the Head of Year rushes around to the tutors and says: 'Get these checked and give them back to me by lunchtime.' The tutor rushes around his tutor group and tries to get the entries checked. When you come to think about it, that bit of 'admin' or 'business' could be a most impor-tant element in the most central, educational part of the tutorial pro-gramme, embodying the pastoral curriculum. What does it contain? It contains not so much decision-*making* as decision-*checking*, which is almost as important as decision-making.

How might you set about it? A tutor might have, a long time in advance, a *pro forma* for the pupils to fill in, in which he puts down what he *thinks* they've entered for. Then, when they get what they *have* been entered for, they have a cross-check opportunity, and they have to query any discrepancy. It involves explaining to them about different syllabuses, and different Boards, and different modes. It involves getting them to sign, so that they have the emotional weighting invested, having corrected it themselves. That is a sketch of something like a three-session programme that embodies a part of the pastoral programme in the form of what some people make just an 'awful bit of business'.

In American high schools the 'home-base teacher' is regarded simply as a filing clerk by many principals. We shouldn't let it be like that. We must find ways of seeing that there is no mere 'business', and even such things as checking the addresses on the school records can be made a teaching activity. It is baffling to see in some schools teachers who in a music lesson or a science lesson would make everything into a learning activity, even putting away the magnets, restricting certain activities in the tutor room as being merely business.

It is interesting to see that although in most American high schools the allocation of 'discipline' to the Vice-Principal as a specialist; of 'counselling' to the Guidance Department, with its training specialists; and even in some schools of attendance to a special Attendance Department, has left the 'Home-Base Teacher' as an un-led, programmeless, minor functionary, some schools are making determined moves towards a more unified approach very reminiscent of our integrated 'pastoral care'. Thus in 1978-79 Evanston Township High School started a 'Home-Base Program', the ten purposes of which cover very similar ground to a tutorial programme in this country, including such purposes as:

5   to help freshmen better understand the curriculum, co-curricular, career, college, and social opportunities at ETHS.
6   to promote and develop positive study skills and habits.

Each teacher has a massive loose-leaf document drawn up by a 'Task Force' of parents, teachers, students, and counsellors, and including specific activities and worksheets. This is precisely a tutorial programme.

Materials

Very few schools even have a budget for their tutorial programme — a sure indication of the real lack of seriousness; very few have any learning materials for the tutor to use. I suggest that the final stage in planning the pastoral curriculum is to translate it into support materials. Material should not dominate the programme, for certainly every session should not start with a worksheet! Indeed, semi-structured discussion is likely to be a major mode of working. Nevertheless, one of the most effective ways of helping tutors without dominating them is the provision of material.

Material is likely to be very simple, and to include such things as lists, pro formas, questionnaires — each of which can be a way to help a young person to explore thoughts. More elaborately, there might be drawings, photographs, tapes, slides, perhaps to help evoke matters for discussion. Some of this may be drawn from existing published schemes in such fields as Moral Education, Health Education, Citizenship. Others might be filched from other schools and teachers' centres.

Working with groups is likely to require 'materials' if it is not to be all teacher talk or to dissolve into desultory pupil chatter. However, often the material should be minimal, and the temptation to over-supply should be avoided, both because of the shortness of the time for group work, and because of the need to leave elbow-room for personal variety.

The Schools Council's Moral Education 8-13 Project is an example of translating aims into learning materials.[8] For instance, there are 'Photoplay' kits, which are designed 'to increase children's awareness of the verbal and non-verbal aspects of behaviour', including to 'heighten perception and sensitivity to other people's needs, attitudes and feelings'.

The material developed by teachers working at the Blackburn Curriculum Development Centre, Lancashire,[9] also shows how some of the seemingly intangible aims can be given a concrete practicality in possible classroom tasks. Thus self-assessment is given a *pro forma*; the objective 'for the pupil to show respect for other people's property by returning borrowed articles promptly, handing in lost property through proper channels, etc.' is translated into an activity: 'Pupils are asked to describe (written or oral) their most precious possession and imagine how they would feel if they lost it or it was stolen.'

As another example, the objective: 'for the pupil to demonstrate an understanding of the difference between constructive and destructive criticism, or negative and positive comments' is translated into a game, involving cards pinned on each pupil's back, on which other pupils write positive comments on each other's cards. These and other published schemes can be of considerable help, though it is still likely that schools will have to produce much of their own material. Therefore the kind of consortium pooling carried out through the Area Teachers' Centre clearly has a great deal to recommend it.

Conclusion

Schools up and down the country are at the moment searching for a way of backing up their one-to-one pastoral care with a structured group approach. In Avon there are groups working at the Avon Teachers' Centre. In Bexley the 'Pastoral Care Committee of Secondary Teachers' have had a series of meetings, including such specific topics as study skills. Their secretary writes: '. . . they have found that the very keen but inexperienced subject-specialist often has considerable difficulty in devising suitable activities for his or her pupils during tutor periods from a pastoral view-point.'

Dr Leslie Button of Swansea declares:

> We do seem to be really helping schools with developing tutoring skills to enable teachers to make something creative of their pastoral occasions. Wherever I go this seems to be a yawning gap in the schools' approaches to young people. And although it is a very small part of the total time-table, it seems to pervade the whole spirit of the school, the general attitudes of the pupils, and their relationships with those who teach them.[10]

The problems are explained by the historical growth of pastoral care as a concept, and the promotion methods accepted so far, together with virtually complete lack of help in initial and in-service training.

Paradoxically, schools with powerful traditions of individual pastoral care often have great difficulty in planning tutorial programmes precisely because of their strength: the group approach seems to threaten the tutor's rightly cherished work with individuals. Their greatest difficulty is often their very strength: tutors feel that any 'curriculum' will come between them and their charges. They often elevate 'getting to know the pupil' (which is, of course, useless unless the knowledge is made useful to the pupil) above supporting the pupil except retrospectively after crises. *The real barrier between tutor and tutee is the insulating vacuum of having no purpose other than helping when difficulties arise.*

The paradox is that a proper programme of support for the tutor, which involves drawing up likely learning experiences within a pastoral 'curriculum', makes the tutor more useful to the majority of tutees, and thus enables her or him to be *closer*. The curriculum is only a part of pastoral care, but it is a most important one. It cannot involve all the most personal facets of personal relationships, but in covering the more general public ones it can give real personal help. A school which places emphasis on caring for its pupils and offering them access to all forms of educational development cannot leave personal, educational, and vocational guidance to each of the tutors individually, however keen they are. A pastoral curriculum is necessary to help the tutors help their pupils.

References

1   J. M. M. Hill and D. E. Scharff, *Between Two Worlds*, (Careers Consultants Limited, 1976), p. 147.
2   op. cit., p. 171.
3   The 'Need to Know' project, funded by the British Library, is an interesting attempt to fill part of this curriculum need. It attempts to define what information the individual requires for his or her personal life and how that information can be found. It then devises teaching strategies. Further information may be obtained from the British Library.
4   This is the term John Bazalgette uses for the self-defensive friendship groups which pupils build up and then can't free themselves from (see 'The Pupil, The Tutor, and the School', paper presented to the Organization in Schools Course on Pastoral Care, Churchill College, Cambridge, July 1978).
5   Carol S. Dweck, 'Learned Helplessness and Negative Evaluation', in *UCLA Education*, Vol. 19 No. 2, Winter 1977, University of California.
6   Leslie Button, *Developmental Group Work in the Secondary School*, Occasional Paper No. 1 of the Action Research Project, Department of Education, University College of Swansea, n.d.
7   Douglas Hamblin, *The Teacher and Pastoral Care*, (Basil Blackwell, Oxford, 1978).
8   Longman, 1978.
9   Years 1 and 2, by Jill Baldwin and Harry Wells, have been published by Basil Blackwell under the title *Active Tutorial Work*, 1979.
10 Personal communication.

12 'Pastoral Care' or 'Pastoralization'?

Derek Williamson

Introduction

Most teachers in comprehensive schools are, I believe, fairly happy about their situations as *teachers*. They feel they have a definite function to perform, one which the pupils expect and one which, given a little experience, they can perform reasonably well through tried and trusted methods. However, their role as *tutors* within the school is something they are less happy about. Perhaps this is because the recent concentration of attention on curriculum matters has been accompanied by a failure to consider the overall pattern of life within the school. Or it may be that 'pastoral matters' are less easily defined, observed and measured than the traditional academic or instructional activities of the school. Whatever the reason, many teachers feel themselves to be working in an area which is vague and uncertain, and in which the roles they are expected to perform are often ill-defined and confusing.

The aim of this paper is to begin an analysis of the pastoral-care aspect of the teacher's role, by considering it in the context of *(a)* the instructional function of the academic side of schooling, and *(b)* the changing nature of schools as formal organizations. In attempting this task I shall be exploring some concepts and theoretical approaches which may cast light on our topic: in particular I shall be outlining some of the theory of organizations deriving from Weber's model of bureaucracy, and suggesting how it, together with more recent approaches to the curriculum and pedagogy, may ground our understanding of pastoral care in a wider understanding of educational structures and processes.

I shall also be advancing the thesis that pastoral care in the large comprehensive school, though lacking a unified philosophy and in need of a more stable framework of agreed practice, is essentially a means of *support* for the school as it performs those tasks expected of it in terms of our present conception of education. This support can be seen in the thousand and one odd jobs which are performed daily by Form Tutors, Housemasters and Heads of Year, jobs which are conceived of under the umbrella of 'pastoral care', and which can be seen to be part of 'making the school work'. But it would be false to think that these tasks constitute a single, undifferentiated activity. On the contrary, I hope to show that support is given to our present form of 'product' teaching in two quite different ways: on the one

hand are the more recognized methods of supporting the able child
through a system to which he quickly adjusts, and on the other, those
activities which are aimed at resolving the problems posed to the
system by the not inconsiderable numbers of children who are unable
to benefit from 'product' teaching, and who may rebel against its
constraints. This distinction cannot be too strongly stated, for it calls
into question some widely held notions about the functions of pastoral-
care systems and those who operate them. In short, while some children
are 'guided', 'counselled' and 'supported' through a successful school
career, others (the 'less able', the 'disadvantaged' etc.), are 'processed'
to accept a system in which they are destined to be failures. For want
of a better word, I shall call this processing *pastoralization*.

Finally, I shall argue that 'problems' which pastoral-care systems
supposedly exist to solve, may perhaps be solved only by a much wider
consideration of the nature and processes of teaching and learning.

Pastoral Care and 'Pastoralization'

The pastoral system is usually thought of as bearing responsibility for
the non-instructional aspect of the child's school experience; i.e. for
the educational and social *welfare* of the individual pupil. In dis-
charging this duty, the pastoral system works in conjunction with the
academic system (Heads of Department and subject teachers), the
executive (Headmaster and deputies), and out-of-school services where
necessary. A key person in the pastoral system is the Housemaster or
Head of Year, who might be thought of as integrating these various
aspects of the school experience around and through the pupil. It is
he or she to whom each child should be able to turn for guidance
within the school and who should be the person to form the essential
links between the school and the child's parents.

To ensure that each pupil within the comprehensive school has
immediate access to at least one particular member of staff, the pastoral
system is broken down into units known as tutorial or form groups,
under the care of the form tutor. Each group, consisting usually of
about thirty pupils, meet their tutors for two daily registration periods,
at specified periods during the week designated tutorial periods, and
for formal assemblies. In this way pupils and tutor get to know each
other, in both a formal and informal way. The pupils come to know
what is expected of them in the routine procedures of school, standards of dress, punctuality, behaviour towards others, behaviour within
the school in general, attitude towards work, and so on. Seeing the
pupils twice daily places the tutor in an ideal position of responsibility for the pupils within his group. It is also from the tutor, through
this daily contact, that the child gains the necessary confidence to
seek personal advice. This advice may concern emotional difficulty,
academic failure or aspiration, choice of career, or type of further

education, the broad intention throughout being to support the child within the general framework of the school. It is the responsibility of the form tutor to develop a relationship of mutual trust between himself and the pupil. It is because of this position of mutual trust that the tutor is able to make sense of the many varied and complex learning experiences the school has to offer. Pupils normally recognized within the school as the 'more able' accept readily the types of teaching situation prevailing, experience little difficulty in learning through traditional methods, and generally can be seen to be making progress. The type of help these pupils require is normally limited to answering a few general enquiries about timetable difficulties, subject-option choices and so on, and perhaps providing a sounding-board for the occasional 'beef' about having to wear school uniform and attend 'boring' formal assemblies.

It is through a similar position of mutual trust that other pupils, particularly those who experience difficulties in learning through the traditional methods of teaching, and who find it hard to make sense of the varied and complex learning situations they encounter, are led to accept the hours of boredom which the current practices of education entail for them. With these pupils, normally identified as the 'less able', the tutor frequently uses the relationship of mutual trust, knowingly or otherwise, to deflect legitimate grievance away from the inadequate types of learning experience offered within the school. It is this 'pastoralization' which makes possible, or is even a precondition of, the continued existence of what might be called 'product teaching'; i.e. if education is approached as the production of a standardized commodity, the raw materials (children) have somehow to be induced to stay on the conveyor belt and accept the practices of the assembly-men (teachers) as legitimate. When children question the adequacy of the learning situations provided, the tutor is faced with the difficult task of finding answers which will, at least, avert an open rejection of the school and its practices. The type of explanation he gives for these inadequacies leads, initially, to a spirit of glum tolerance among the pupils. Of serious concern for the secondary school is the way in which, as the pupils progress through the school, this glum tolerance gives way to a variety of attitudes of resentment towards the school in particular and society in general.

Thus the role of the tutor is to give support to the academic–instructional aspect of the school's work by (a) helping children to make sense of the variety of learning situations the school offers, and (b) pastoralizing those children who do not appear to benefit from the current form of product teaching.

The positive aspects of the pastoral responsibility are essentially concerned with helping the individual to get the maximum benefit from the experiences the school offers. This can take the form of advice to the individual in preparation for various educational choices, helping the individual in his day-to-day relationship with others, both pupils and staff, and where personal advice cannot be offered, ensuring that the pupil knows where to get the advice through the various services that exist both inside and outside the school. These positive functions of pastoral care are concerned first and foremost with helping the individual to develop his or her life-style within the framework of the school. The wider the variety of activity within the school, the greater the flexibility of the learning situation, the greater the number of career lines (in the Chicago school sense[1]) available to the pupils, the more successful the school will be in offering all its pupils the possibility of enjoying their time at school in a positive way.

Where this variety and flexibility are absent, where because of lack of basic skills, know-how, knowledge, intelligence, experience, call it what you will, only a limited percentage of pupils can really take advantage of the types of situation the school offers, special structural devices and practices are essential. Within the school these devices and practices perform the negative function of pastoral care. The reduction of resentment felt at the lack of opportunity offered and at the limited learning experiences provided is achieved at the personal level, between tutor and pupil. It is this negative function which I have called 'pastoralization'.

We can begin to see how the process works through a consideration of the school as an organization, and in particular, by looking closely at the type of bureaucracy that has developed in the comprehensive school. In this way it can be shown that, while the comprehensive school attempted to cater for children of all abilities, this was not accompanied by any radical change in the types of learning experience provided for the pupils. Thus, although there are organizational differences between the comprehensive and the traditional grammar school, these differences are not marked in the area of central concern: that of providing learning experiences for the pupil. Here, there has been little change.

Schools and Bureaucracy

The nineteenth century produced a number of brilliant descriptions of bureaucracy; it was, however, Max Weber who began the systematic study of this phenomenon. Weber attempted to define a 'pure type' of bureaucratic organization by what he considered its most characteristic features. He hoped in this way to provide some type of 'measuring rod' against which specific bureaucratic structures could be compared in future investigations.

Fundamentally, for Weber a bureaucracy is a rational arrangement of offices designed to achieve a specified goal, and providing certain means for administration and control of the office-holders' actions. Officials entering the bureaucracy expect security, specialization of function, and seniority and salary based upon achievement and examination. Offices are hierarchically arranged so as to facilitate demarcation of responsibility and accountability. Weber's concept of bureaucracy included the following criteria:[2]

(i) There is a clear division of labour, and regular activities are distributed in a fixed way as official duties.
(ii) The organization is hierarchical: each lower office is under the control and supervision of a higher one.
(iii) There is a system of rules, and operations are governed by the application of these rules to particular cases.
(iv) The conduct of officials is impersonal, and duties are performed without hatred or passion and hence without affection or enthusiasm.
(v) Employment is based on technical qualifications, it is protected against arbitrary dismissal and it constitutes a career. There is a system of promotion according to seniority, or to achievement, or to both.

Weber's account of bureaucratic organization has received close scrutiny and has been put to some empirical testing. The original dimensions of bureaucracy have been refined and elaborated, and in the process a number of problems have emerged. In a chapter entitled 'The Advantages of Bureaucracy' Frank Musgrove[3] makes the important point that all aspects of bureaucracy as developed by Weber have not developed in unison over a period of time. Using ideas from Hall[4] and Pugh, Hickson, Hinings and Turner,[5] Musgrove indicates the independent features of bureaucracy by showing that an organization may have a well-defined system of rules without being particularly hierarchical, or may emphasize technical competence without placing stress on either specialization or impersonality of official conduct.

Classifying organizations in terms of crucial patterns of interaction led Blau and Scott[6] to regard schools as service organizations. They saw the main problem as one of establishing a balance between the professional expertise of the staff and the wishes of the pupils. In considering the schools historically it can be seen that attending to the wishes of pupils is a comparatively recent innovation: so much so that one could generalize to show that the more formal types of school resemble the Weberian model of bureaucracy, while the recent informal types resemble a model which, though derived from Weber's bureaucracy, differs markedly from it. While neither type of school will constitute a 'pure type', different types of school organization clearly have bureaucratic elements which are becoming more significant as they develop.

In his 'Models of Bureaucracy that permit Conflict' Eugene Litwak[7] synthesizes from the study of complex organizations what he calls the 'Professional Model'. Using Litwak's approach it is possible to show how the more traditional schools, particularly the public and grammar schools, correspond fairly closely to Weber's model of bureaucracy with their stress on *secondary* relations and organizational *rules*. The more recent comprehensive schools, by stressing *primary* relations and organizational *goals* conform more closely to the later model. Moreover, it is a feature of Weber's theory that the pure bureaucratic structure is the most efficient form of organization for large institutes dealing with uniform situations. Problems confronting its officers are relatively constant and predictable, so a high level of specialization is appropriate. The traditional grammar school fits well into this model, for the task to be dealt with is recurrent in time and concerns subjects which are, for all practical purposes, 'identical' (i.e. students of equal ability). Specialization in the grammar school has been seen as essential, and to a great extent it held the key to that efficiency for which such schools won repute. However, in terms of the argument here being presented such experts in their specialist fields must be regarded as somewhat similar to supervisors on an assembly-line, churning out the same type of product year in and year out. The demand for impersonality within grammar schools also assumes uniform events. Members of staff faced with a non-uniform problem, which cannot be covered by school rules and routine procedures, lack independent action and tend to resort to a higher authority.

Reference has been made to specialization within the grammar school, and this involves stressing the traditional areas of knowledge as opposed to social skills. By 'social skills' or abilities is meant the actual capacity to communicate with others, to motivate them to work, to co-operate with others, and to internalize the values of the organization. Granted Weber's assumption about traditional areas of knowledge, his model does not necessarily lead to efficiency when part of the job requirement stresses social skills. It is within this area that the new conceptions of the recent comprehensive schools differ from the grammar schools. The features of bureaucracy outlined by Weber are related to and upheld mainly by the subject departments of the school, the area of the school responsible for the teaching. Here the actual organization of teaching has changed little. In some cases new labels have been attached to old systems, but generally neither material provision nor educational thinking and practice has been applied to providing the resources and techniques needed to meet the very wide range of individual needs within the comprehensive school.

What happens within the comprehensive school is that the problems of the individual child become apparent through the pastoral system. The relationships developed with the child and possibly the child's parents, reveal to the tutor the demands which the individual child places on the school. But, in most cases and in most schools, these demands are not met. The pastoral system, with its intimate knowledge of the child, uses this knowledge to a large extent to socialize the child into a teaching system which is based primarily on a search for talent. This procedure of searching for talent utilizes a syllabus based on subject specialization, as developed within the grammar school. This means that comprehensive schools on the whole do not dispense with specialization, although in some schools integrated subjects do affect subject-area boundaries. In a theoretical paper Bernstein (1971)[8] shows concern for the social organization and transmission of educational knowledge, and particularly with discerning the difference between what he describes as 'educational knowledge codes' of the 'collection' and 'integrated' type.

Collection curricula are characterized by 'closed' compartmentalized relationships between the subjects, integrated by an open relationship. Further to this Bernstein maintains that such curriculum types have other distinct features, that collection types involve subject loyalty on the part of the teacher, a range of different subject ideologies, strong boundaries between subjects, didactic instruction, and a hierarchical concept of valid knowledge and oligarchic control (vertical hierarchy of staff) within subjects. By contrast he maintains that integrated types involve weak subjects, a common pedagogy, mixing of the categories of knowledge, early initiation into basic principles and strong horizontal relationships among staff.

Bernstein's analysis presents a theoretical basis for understanding the social-organizational, as well as the intellectual, differences between subject-specific and integrated studies. In an attempt to meet the wide range of individual academic needs the comprehensive school has by and large offered a broad array of subjects with an attendant increase in specialization. Together with this increased specialization, however, goes a definite emphasis on social skills. Thus, while the organization of teaching subjects becomes more specialized, the pastoral system is increasingly involved with generalized social skills, skills which the tutor is involved in developing as he deals with those tutorial responsibilities which arise from day to day. Moreover, the all-ability school involves no standardization of raw material, and this is reflected in ideas about the finished product. Such a range of ability puts a premium on knowledge and understanding of the *individual child*, as opposed to knowing what is suitable material for a class of thirty or so 'standardized' children. Where social skills are concerned the impersonal social relations of Weber's model are hardly appropriate. If the transmission of traditional knowledge areas is the task of the subject teacher, the development of social skills is more the task of the pastoral tutor. Together, the system represented by the pastoral tutor and the class teacher combine in an attempt to produce efficiency within a non-uniform organization. This is most vividly revealed in the hierarchical and horizontal relationships that exist within these schools. Within the departmental areas of the school, hierarchical relationships which lead to efficiency have been established; within the House system, however, or that part of the school responsible for pastoral care of the children, participation in decision-making across the hierarchy is essential. Put differently, decisions involving social skills, rather than specialist skills, might be carried out more efficiently under a horizontal structure of authority, which permits all individuals to participate equally in decision-making.

The Limits of Change

It is now pertinent to consider how far the emergent structures of comprehensive reorganization we are witnessing are an administrative exercise rather than an educational reform. It is an achievement to have arranged for an increased number of pupils to pass through one school door rather than three; it would be a hollow one however if all that happened through the one door was simply a re-hash of the traditional teaching methods as developed in the grammar, technical and secondary modern schools. In many schools the most serious of these difficulties is related to the methods of teaching used.[9] For although comprehensive reorganization entails structural changes, these are superficial: the traditional pattern of academic organization persists, and continues to be unduly influential. Given this, it is hardly surprising that methods of teaching have changed so little. The type of teaching that has dominated educational practice in the past is still the dominant form within the comprehensive school. Methods designed for uniform situations are imposed on to non-uniform groups. The pre-occupation is still with the child's capacity for learning, that is, the antecedent qualities which he brings into the school, his intelligence, his motivation and various aspects thought to be the product of home background. The child is thought to come into the school with a notional potential, or from a more pessimistic point of view, a 'deficiency rating' which has important bearing on his ability to reach a particular level of achievement in the school. Schools vary in the degree to which they are prepared to wait before deciding that potential has become more or less clearly established, and that the child can be placed in a teaching group appropriate to his ability. Of course this is not an entirely passive experience. The pupil is able to exercise some degree of control over his achievement level through the amount of effort he or she is prepared to put into the work.

Achievement is still recognized in terms of mastery of specific bodies of knowledge, mapped out into areas which coincide with particular stages in the pupil's career. It is still the task of the teacher to arrange and present these bodies of knowledge to his pupils. The focus of interest of the teaching still tends to be on the products of learning, not on the process, which is assumed to be the same for all pupils. And learning is still thought to be most effective when a teacher expert who knows the subject-matter structures it and imparts it to those who do not. Within this system of teaching the teacher imparts knowledge to recipient pupils. Those who fail to respond or to accommodate the knowledge are called 'less able' children. Learning within the school is still required to be collective in the sense that a nominal pace, sequence and structure for the subject content of the lessons are imposed on all pupils in the class together. In this light the problems for the teacher tend to be those of order and discipline and are seen in terms of getting children to sit in orderly ways so that they can be taught. This recognized form of teaching is the norm, whether applied to the streamed or mixed-ability type of class organization. This remains the problem of the comprehensive school: how does one involve children of all abilities in learning situations? That the present system is inadequate is apparent to the informed observer. That the inadequacies of the teaching system are supported by the pastoral system is something less apparent. Support of learning situations is a positive function of pastoral care; its support for inadequate teaching methods is an immediate cause for concern.

Pastoral Care or Organizational Prop?

As I have argued, pupils who cannot adapt to methods of 'product' teaching are 'pastoralized', and this process can be effected in a variety of ways. The pupil may be referred to the Head of Department, the subject specialist with expertise in his subject but little or no knowledge of the individual child. Or he may be referred to a member of the pastoral staff, his Form Tutor, Year Head or Housemaster. Rarely in these meetings, however, is the teaching organization brought into question. What is clearly a *learning* problem is perceived in terms of the ability (or rather, the *in*ability) of the pupil to adapt. The pastoral staff may be sympathetic to the needs of the pupil, but they have a difficult task in trying to reconcile the inadequate teaching to the unresponsive student. Seldom does the tutor tackle the problem by criticizing the teaching techniques of the staff involved; more readily will he exploit the relationship he has developed with the pupil to divert attention from such a sensitive area. Through the position of mutual trust built up over many hours of personal contact, out-of-school activities, school visits, weekend holidays, sports teams, and meetings with the pupils' parents, the tutor becomes instrumental in getting the pupil to accept resignedly that the failure is his, that there must be something lacking in his understanding, that he must be at fault since others seem to be coping reasonably well. Those who do seem to be coping must be allowed to do so, the system cannot be disrupted, the Pastoral Tutor cannot allow that. All children in the school have an equal opportunity to do well, and if the child cannot use the opportunities provided, then the failure is his. In this way the comprehensive school becomes for many a legitimation of failure, while at the same time insulating and supporting the inadequate teaching system.

That 'pastoralization' is a special structural device essential to reduce resentment is a necessary condition of our present system of education. Where the young are encouraged to high motivation but limited by structural opportunities, where many aspire to high status but few can achieve, where education leads to classification and classification to division, such a system is essential. That our schools provide increasingly for this division can be seen in the increasing attention given to younger children by the Careers Research and Advisory Centre.[10] Having worked in the past to abandon selection at eleven plus, teachers within the comprehensive system are now faced with 'Your choice at thirteen plus', an essential guide for choosing O-levels and CSEs. Choice at thirteen plus leads to choice at fourteen plus, then at sixteen plus and on to eighteen plus. Surely it is time to ask, choice for whom? For under our present system of education we certainly seem to be determining and reinforcing a system of out-of-school opportunities. In *Classrooms Observed*[11] Roy Nash has demonstrated that children's attitudes to learning are formed to a large degree in the primary school. Perhaps more significant than this, for the present argument, is the fact that Nash sees the primary school as teaching hierarchical levels of personal worth more successfully than anything else. A process starting in the primary school is consolidated within the comprehensive school and gains realization with employment.

When considering the dual role of pastoral care, on the one hand as a support system, on the other as a 'pastoralizing agent' for those unable to benefit from what the school offers, it seems likely that the pastoral structures actually prop up and conceal the ailing academic work of the teacher and the school. While it is widely recognized that low achievement and poor motivation in academic terms may originate in personal background problems needing pastoral care, it is less frequently realized that a good curriculum, well taught, may be an essential agent of personal development, and if it is not provided the pastoral organization may be overloaded with what are mainly self-imposed problems.

If the school is to provide learning experiences for its pupils, within a non-uniform system, then it must develop more flexible teaching strategies. 'Growth' learning, with its emphasis on an active rather than a static notion of the mind, appears to offer the most rewarding avenue for future development. Within this proposed approach the pupil's processes of thought are not simply reducible to the possession of intelligence. They do instead seem to be part of a highly complex personal system of interpretations, intentions and recollections. While accepting some genetic limitations on the structure of human thinking, it is held that cognition is a 'growth process' and that the mind is capable of unlimited development.

The main focus of 'growth learning' is on the process of knowing, and the child's organization of meaning into large schemes of knowledge. It explores the ways in which the child categorizes and perceives logical connections between data, and how his patterns of inference lead to increasingly complex chains of meaning. This kind of enquiry has led to the view of learning in which the structuring of knowledge is seen to be fundamental to the development of understanding. For the teacher the essential problem is to understand the logic of the child's process of knowing, to understand how he interprets and accommodates new knowledge. The relationship between the structure of meaning which the child habitually uses and the structures which are presented to him by the teacher is a critical one. The classroom interaction which follows from an acceptance of this paradigm is likely to allow the pupil more control over the structuring of his curriculum knowledge. The teacher becomes more a guide than an instructor: thus the pupil is given increased responsibility for his own learning. The essential element in the pursuit of more active learning experiences must be the feeling of common interest. It must involve pupils and staff alike, and should arise from the involvement of all in a programme of education which forms the main justification of the school. Such a programme would reduce the need for 'pastoralization'. For where time is spent on planning and co-operating in the creation of meaningful learning situations, where considerably more satisfaction than frustration is provided, pupils will experience personal growth, and personal growth they will find rewarding enough in itself.

References

1 E. C. Hughes, 'Institutional Office and the Person', *American Journal of Sociology*, Vol. 43, November 1937, pp. 409-10.

2 M. Weber, *The Theory of Social and Economic Organizations* (Oxford University Press, New York, 1947; Collier-Macmillan, London, 1964).

3 F. Musgrove, *Patterns of Power and Authority in English Education* (Methuen, 1971).

4 'The Concept of Bureaucracy', *American Journal of Sociology*, 1963, Vol. 69, 1963.

5 'Dimensions of Organization Structure', *Administrative Science Quarterly*, Vol. 13, 1968.

6 Peter M. Blau and William Richard Scott, *Formal Organizations: A Comprehensive Approach* (Routledge & Kegan Paul, London, 1963).

7 *American Journal of Sociology*, Vol. 5, 1966.

8 'Classification and Framing' in M. F. D. Young (ed.), *Knowledge and Control* (Collier-Macmillan, London, 1971).

9 See G. Esland, 'Pedagogy and the Teacher's Presentation of Self', Open University Course E282, Unit 5 (Open University Press, Milton Keynes, 1972).

10 *Beginnings: Choosing the right 'O' level and C.S.E.s.*

11 Roy Nash, *Classrooms Observed* (Routledge & Kegan Paul, London, 1973).

13   The Care of Learning: some implications for school organization

John Buckley

The school is a caring community. Such a statement may be found at the beginning of many a handbook issued by schools to intending pupils and their parents. Heads and deputy heads who are attending courses in management at the Centre where this writer works often make the same statement when asked to express succinctly the aims of their schools. The significance lies in the priority which is now given to this aim. It frequently appears as the first of a series of aims, as if to summarize the ethos of a school. The assertion represents a genuine concern of teachers for their pupils which has long been present, but the priority it is now given represents a shift of emphasis in the role which schools see themselves playing in contemporary society. Increasingly schools fulfil a role as agencies of general social welfare. '

A head of a primary school or of a comprehensive school on a large urban housing estate is aware that social problems 'home-in' on the local school. The class teacher daily meets pupils who need time and energy devoted to their behaviour, their attitudes and their values. One response of secondary schools to these pressures has been the development of pastoral-care systems. The problems could no longer be dealt with satisfactorily within the framework of normal lessons but were to be dealt with by special teachers, at special times, in special rooms, and those handling such problems were given telephones, secretarial help, special payments and the status which these facilities confer. To a head who was developing such a system this was how it felt. It seemed to work and many of the teachers who took on these tasks performed them with dedication and distinction. However, there is now a growing dissatisfaction with this form of organization. The pastoral and academic structure seems to have divided pupils into two halves: creatures to be 'taught' and creatures to be 'cared for', to have divided teachers into two groups: 'teaching teachers' and 'caring teachers', and to have divided an individual teacher into two halves, sometimes 'teaching' and sometimes 'caring'. This chapter seeks to explore some ways in which these two roles might be brought closer together in school organization.

Some Features of Teaching and Learning

The purpose of any organization is to fulfill certain aims. In the case of a factory producing motor cars or plastic cups this may be expressed in terms of maximum production. A school has no such inert product and consequently there is far less unanimity about its aims. In fact there is considerable confusion in our society as to what the aims of schools are. Some see them as places for socialization, others as places for individual development. Faced with this dilemma one seeks to identify those activities which characterize a school and distinguish it from other caring institutions. The organization may then be designed to enable these activities to take place more effect- ively. The activities which characterize a school are teaching and learning. The main participants in a school are teachers and learners. The problem of organization lies in the fact that the two sets of participants may conceive these activities differently. Their attitudes to and expectations of teaching and learning may vary. It may be helpful in approaching the organization of teaching and learning to examine some of the features of these activities and some attitudes towards them.

The first point to note is that teaching and learning represent a form of relationship between teacher and learner. If it is effective there is some change in the learner. The relationship and the change are essential features of teaching and learning. They may be considered as a sequence. There must be an effective relationship if there is to be effective learning. The relationship must be right if learning is to happen. There is a social task before there is any change in development. The notion of 'care' for a teacher is the creation of that relationship from which learning may follow. The teacher who 'cares' is the one who teaches effectively. This is the essential 'hidden' curriculum of values and attitudes which must animate any other curriculum if there is to be effective teaching and learning. Much therefore depends on the way people in a school treat each other, talk to each other, consider each other, develop mutual respect for each other, reject each other, love or hate each other. Collectively this is the ethos of the school. The purpose of developing such an ethos in a school is in order that teaching and learning may take place and not in order that the institution may feel cosy and comfortable.

The next feature of teaching and learning is far more complex. It is the skill, some would say the art, of communication. Communication is essential if teaching and learning are to take place. This skill recognizes the essentially complementary roles played by teacher and learner. Particularly important is that role played by the learner because it is with him or her that communication begins.

The person who initiates or teaches requires skills of presentation but is utterly dependent upon the learner, who must pass through various stages, each with its own sophistication, before learning can be said to have happened. There must be awareness and attention on the part of the learner before perception can happen. Much depends upon the acceptability and credibility of the teacher before the next stage of reception can take place. With a message comes a person, who must be acceptable, before understanding can begin to happen. At this stage the significance of meaning is crucial. We strive in teaching and learning for a mutuality of meaning, a common understanding of words used. Each word or other symbol misunderstood or misinterpreted may cause a relationship to falter. Eventually may come acceptance and involvement by the learner in what the teacher has sought to teach. A learner may then come to 'possess' what is taught. The image is not of the oracle but of communion. Herein lies the quality of 'care'. The theologian Martin Buber describes this form of relation as 'inclusive':

> Its elements are, first, a relation, of no matter what kind between two persons, second an event experienced by them in common in which at least one of them actively participates. A relation between persons that is characterised, in more or less degree, by the element of inclusion may be termed a dialogical relation.

And again: 'The relation in education is one of pure dialogue.'[1] The teacher to be effective must not only know where the learner is but know 'what it feels like to be there'. It is rather more than empathy — simply transposing oneself into the place of another and feeling as they feel. The 'dialogue' described by Buber has the characteristic of a genuine conversation which 'derives its genuineness from the consciousness of an element of inclusion'. It is a 'making room' for another person in one's reality. The reality exists 'between' the teacher and the learner. There is mutuality. The inclusion is not mutual, however, because the learner cannot experience 'being taught'. The teacher stands at both ends of the common situation, the learner only at one end. If teacher or learner were to jump the 'spark' gap the learning relation would change and become one of a different type such as friendship. Both teacher and learner must retain their roles but communication and dialogue must continue.

Buber's definition of the teaching and learning experience refers also to 'an event experienced by them in common'. The task commonly experienced would seem to be a third significant feature of the teaching and learning relationship. Learning seems to happen more readily when the relationship is formed and focused round a task. This is the long-known lore of the apprentice and his master and it is as true in the inner-city school metalwork shop as it was in Renaissance Italy. Teachers of crafts in workshops, teachers of PE on playing fields, on mountainsides and in boats have often found discipline a little easier than those requiring pupils to be in desks, in straight lines, facing the front.

One further factor seems necessary for a teaching–learning relationship to form and this is 'time'. Teacher and learner need to spend an adequate amount of time together. Long stretches of consecutive time may not be necessary, although to complete a creative entity such as a pot, a painting or a pie long periods may help. A modern language may require a period of daily prattle, typing a daily tap. The periods of time may vary but all teaching–learning relationships seem to need time to develop and mature.

Three conditions seem to be necessary for the formation of the teaching–learning relation. These may be summarized as: two people, a task and time. Communication and dialogue imply a person-to-person involvement. Although much teaching and learning must perforce take place in groups, in clusters, or even in crowds, at times, if only momentarily, it must be one-to-one. The task provides the neutral ground on which teacher and learner meet. Time allows the growth of mutual confidence. It is this style of relationships which embodies the 'pedagogic care', the care of learning which is the proper prerogative of the teacher. It is the rigorous concern of the good teacher as to whether a learner learns or does not learn. When a teacher cares he or she makes demands on a learner. When a teacher makes demands on a learner he or she is caring. This style of pedagogic care may be distinguished from the concern for the general welfare of a learner which seems to characterize some pastoral systems. The 'spray gun' approach of generalized care for all is a diminution of a teacher's proper function. For a teacher to 'care' is not enough if it means a soft-centred concern for general welfare.

This is not to say that in the present state of our society there are not youngsters who are in urgent need of the care and attention of a parent-substitute because their family situation has not provided the security, support and love which a family should provide. The existence of many such problems is the justification for the appointment of trained social workers and psychologists to the staffs of schools, so that these youngsters are treated like others with physical and mental handicaps. Many teachers have taken on the role of social workers and psychologists because they have become disenchanted with the delays and frustrations of dealing with outside agencies. What is more, some teachers are very good at playing these roles, which may beguile and seduce them away from their proper role as teachers.

The Teaching–Learning Contract

The relationship which is described above may be looked upon as a form of 'contract' between teacher and learner. As with all contracts it needs to be renegotiated from time to time in the light of prevailing conditions. These conditions are the realities of both teachers and learners.

Radical changes have taken place in society and particularly in the world of the young adolescent. The impact of a media-charged reality is transforming learning patterns. Schools no longer have a monopoly of the teaching business. Media-packaged information is available in more attractive forms than many a 'boring old school lesson'; tabloid newspapers and magazines are produced more attractively than most work-sheets. The fantasy world of the disco assails the eye with a kaleidoscope of colour and the ear with a cacophony of sound. The young arrive at school familiar with a battery of teaching devices such as television, transistor radios, cassette players, music centres and pocket calculators, each of which may at times make a drab, dreary or boring teacher seem redundant. The micro-processed society is but a further short step away, and while it may not deschool society, at least it may reduce school to but one element among the learning experiences of young people. It is not surprising that some youngsters have already become disenchanted with the menu offered by some schools, which seems dull and sometimes irrelevant to their experience outside school. These changes and others are reasons for the decline in the authority of the teacher. Such authority is no longer legitimized by his or her office but needs to be earned by a demonstrable evidence of skill as a teacher. The young are questioning those traditional aspects of a teacher's role which involve the omniscient stance, and may also question the more recently adopted role of woolly and luke-warm caring, which many can well do without. Some youngsters go further and actively reject such teachers. When hectored or harassed by teachers expecting automatic acquiescence to the old-style authority the result may be open confrontation.

The conditions in which learners now find themselves seem to reinforce their requirement that their teachers should above all be able to teach effectively. Do not most learners in schools readily rate their teachers in order of their teaching skill? The kindliness or severity of a teacher may have little influence over his or her reputation as an effective teacher. The conditions of teachers have changed too. Their job has become much more stressful and nervously exhausting, particularly in inner-urban areas. Teachers are assaulted verbally and occasionally physically. As a result they have become insecure and less sure of themselves. There has been criticism of teachers from outside schools, arising from a vague sense that 'things are not what they were in our day', rather than from really hard evidence that teaching and learning are less effective. The crisis of confidence has led to reactions, some of which concern the organization of schools. On the one hand there has been a retreat to hard-line doctrines such as more discipline and more corporal punishment, or on the other hand to soft-line doctrines of 'sanctuaries' or 'sin-bins'. These are understandable reactions to the problems of disruptive pupils, but perhaps can only be temporary expedients which evade the fundamental issue that it is a school's job to teach people, not merely to custodially contain them. The explanation of much disruptive behaviour may lie in the failure of teachers and learners to comprehend each others' reality. The onus for renegotiating the contract must lie with the teachers and clearly makes great demands upon their imagination, sensitivity and understanding. It also requires nerve and a readiness to listen and be communicated with. In short it needs dialogue. Perhaps the greatest adjustment which contemporary teachers need to make is the abandonment of the omniscient stance of 'teacher knows best', in favour of the equally important and more realistic role of consultant, entrepreneur or orchestrator.

Other adjustments that teachers may have to make in any negotiated contract are a readiness to allow a greater degree of participation and 'doing', as opposed to sitting and listening. There will also be a need for negotiation over what is to be learned and how it is to be learned. However, while becoming perhaps more opportunist in meeting short-term needs, teachers may have to bear the responsibility for maintaining stability of values amid the wilder fluctuations in the demand for knowledge and skills. Indeed the demonstration of values in their teaching styles may be the most significant function of future teachers. Values do not readily emanate from computers, nor is morality easily miniaturized or micro-processed. Such changes in role do not diminish the role of the teacher; they enhance it. The voice may no longer boom from the oracle but a still, small voice may be equally effective if it is in communion with the pupil.

Learning Units and Teaching Teams

If 'pedagogic care' means the formation of teaching–learning relationships, and if these relationships are to involve communication, dialogue and the provision of adequate time, then the school organization will need to be designed to enable these things to happen. The structure of relationships will need to provide for the following:

(i)   A group of teachers to be responsible for the 'whole' development of a group of learners.
(ii)   Dialogue between those teachers who teach the same learners.
(iii) Decision-making about those learners and their learning to take place as close as possible to those learners in the total school structure.
(iv)   Dialogue between teachers and learners about the effectiveness of the teaching and learning.

If the organization is to provide these conditions it would seem logical to concentrate the 'care' for individual development of a learner in the hands of those who teach that learner for a substantial part of his or her learning programme. In a primary school this is achieved by a class teacher who teaches the class for a substantial part of their time in school. In a secondary school there are bound to be a number of specialists who will share the teaching of a particular group of learners. The ratios of teachers to learners being what they are, a solution would seem to be the creation of a unit of organization which is large enough to accommodate a number of teachers.

This 'learning unit', as it might be described, would be composed of, for example, some 90 learners and 4 teachers, or alternatively of, say, 110 learners and 5 teachers. In a particular year of a secondary school this 'unit' might represent the complete intake or it might represent half the intake. In the latter case the year would contain two 'learning units' and each unit would be the responsibility of a 'team' of four or five teachers. The 'team' of teachers is already familiar in an academic department or in a group of year tutors or house tutors. The 'teaching team' proposed is a group of teachers who are brought together by the fact that they teach the same group of learners. They share together their essential professionalism.

The 'teaching team' would be the basic unit of school organization and other departments, such as subject departments, a remedial department, careers departments, together with resources centres, or libraries, psychologists or social workers, would provide a servicing function. To certain meetings of the 'teaching team' would come representatives of the learners. Consultation between teachers and learners would not be either necessary or desirable in every area of the teaching—learning activity. The planning of a syllabus or the design of a work-sheet would remain the prerogative of teachers, but the pace of a learning programme or the difficulties experienced by certain learners may well involve consultation between teachers and learners.

The setting up of such consultations between teachers and learners will inevitably create some problems for some teachers. Attitudes change very slowly, and only gradually would the areas of competence be hammered out and delineated. This is the way in which the 'contract' between teachers and learners may be continually renegotiated as the world of teaching and learning changes.

Much of what is being suggested was achieved by the 'old-style' form teacher, particularly if he or she taught the form, say, English or Mathematics for five or six periods a week, but a cross-disciplinary team may give a further dimension to knowing where learners 'are'. For example, the English teacher in the team would shed a continuing light on the slow development of reading skills which may be inhibiting the progress of some learners.

The form teachers' role became more difficult as forms became more mobile, visited a variety of departments, and became more fragmented into sets or into option groups. Also no one teacher had the monopoly of knowledge, wisdom or patience needed to relate to thirty or so learners. Some became too possessive, others retired, some resigned or were promoted. What seems essential is a continuity of good relationships for as many learners as possible, and in a 'team' there is more likelihood of at least one teacher making a good relationship with each learner. Furthermore, while a team may, in a year, lose one member it is less likely that the whole team will be dispersed. Other advantages of the 'teaching team' might be as follows. The team may provide a powerful source of support for teachers beset with an increased number of behaviour problems. Teachers may confer more readily with colleagues over learners causing mutual concern and deal more quickly with those who pose problems. Such a 'team' may also absorb new and inexperienced teachers and provide more immediate support for such teachers than a professional tutor or a deputy, neither of whom share the mutual experience of teaching the same learners.

The 'learning unit' and its associated 'teaching team' may be thought of as 'a school within a school' in that it is a relatively autonomous unit. It is larger than a form or tutor group and smaller than many year groups or house groups. Instead of one teacher being associated with it, as in the case of the form, a group of teachers is associated with it and this team is responsible for the 'care' or development of the 'whole' child. Each teacher teaches all the learners at some time in their learning programmes and may therefore be in a position to comment on the intellectual and social development of individual learners.

For discussions between members of the team to be effective there is clearly an optimum size for such a group. Perhaps the combination of four teachers and three learners, making a total of seven (at times when learners are involved) will be most effective in terms of successful group dynamics. The question will be asked as to which teachers should participate in 'teams', and this is not easy to answer. The composition of teams will clearly be a question that would preoccupy the management team of the school. Two factors will need to be borne in mind, namely the personalities of the individual teachers and the subjects they teach. The likelihood is that most teachers would perform two roles. They will be a member of a 'team' and they will also teach in some other part of the school. While the secondary-school curriculum is not the concern of this chapter, the way that curriculum is organized cannot be ignored when discussing which of the teachers who teach a 'learning unit' should make up interest here, as there have been a number of attempts to implement the system of 'a school within a school' in the USA. Such a school is Evanston Township High School, Chicago, which was visited by the writer and where the experience is usefully described by Halstall,[2] drawing on the work of Plath particularly:

'Ideally to gain the greatest advantages of personal relationships, a pupil's classes in "a school within a school" should all be scheduled with students and teachers in his unit. Two factors may prevent this: highly refined ability grouping, an elaborate setting system and a large number of optional subjects.' Halsall concludes: 'If a large school wishes to work "a school within a school" organization in any real sense very fine ability grouping has to be discarded.' Thus the type of organization being advocated is more easily adopted where there is a high degree of mixed-ability grouping and where there is either a common curriculum or at least a large common-core curriculum and limited options. Consequently, at the present time, it would be easier to adopt in years 1 to 3 of the secondary school than in years 4 and 5, where there is still a large number of option choices in the curriculum.

However, if there is a concerted move towards mixed-ability grouping, individualized learning or a common curriculum from 11 to 16, the suggested style of organization may be implemented more easily. In fact this writer would say that the desirability of this style of organization may be one reason for moving towards a more common curriculum. Another factor which would render the adoption of such a system easier is the reduction of teacher specialism in secondary schools. If teachers were less specialized and were able to teach more than one subject to their 'unit', this would reduce the number of learners taught by one teacher and might improve the quality of teacher—learner relations by increasing contact time.

'Team' Organization in Relation to the Present Organization of Schools

There are clearly difficulties in implementing the above style of organization within the structures of schools as existing at present. In order to examine some of these difficulties it is necessary to consider some of the broader issues of school organization. Most schools are organized on a hierarchical principle, and the appointments within the hierarchy are related to the salary structure. This hierarchy commonly features a top management team, composed of a head and up to three deputy heads, now frequently enlarged to include up to three senior teachers. On paper, their titles may differentiate their responsibilities, very simply, as for example head of curriculum studies, head of pastoral care, head of resources, head of lower school, and so on, or they may have quite elaborate and detailed role definitions which set out their responsibilities in, say, a staff handbook. The second level of the hierarchy, or middle-management structure, commonly features the heads of academic departments, and the heads of pastoral divisions such as years or houses. A third level of teachers of subjects and form teachers or group tutors completes the structure. These hierarchical structures may exemplify the pastoral—academic divide, and various attempts have been made to solve this dilemma by redefining the roles of year heads or house heads, in order to make them responsible for both the academic and social development of their charges. Thinking at the North West Educational Management Centre has been concerned for some time to solve this problem by a complete and radical restructuring. Fred Tye, writing in 1974, asked:

> Why not, when planning a school organization, abandon the first step, the
> creation of titles and definition of roles at the top, and start instead at
> the bottom? It ought to be possible to write down all the tasks which will
> have to be carried out by a school for and on behalf of pupils. These tasks

can then be sorted into piles of jobs, which in some sense go together, making a self-consistent package and a satisfying total commitment.[3]

This task has proved to be a very difficult one, and existing hierarchies have obstinately resisted any attempt at radical restructuring. It is in the nature of hierarchies to resist change and to seek to maintain the *status quo*. More recent thinking at this Centre recognizes that the existing hierarchies and salary structures will not be charmed away but that two distinct 'modes' must be recognized in the management of large schools. One mode is 'management for stability' and the other mode is 'management for development'. The first mode is concerned with such matters as security, safety, rules, routines, maintenance and discipline, all of which are necessary for the stability of any social institution, as a supportive framework for both teachers and learners. The second mode of management for development is concerned with innovation and change, which is equally necessary in schools where change is going to be a constant fact of life, where curriculum will need to be subjected to continuous review, and where teaching methodology will need to be frequently scrutinized and updated. How are these two modes of management to be expressed in organizational terms? It seems that those management functions concerned with stability might be performed by members of the hierarchy grouped in such arrangements as standing committees. However, a conscious effort will be needed to form alternative groupings which cut across the hierarchy and seek to arrange for all members of the professional body to participate, if they wish, in the decision-making which is concerned with development. Such a grouping may be a working party responsible for undertaking a developmental task, such as curriculum review, improving liaison with primary schools, or seeking greater involvement with the local community. Such groupings of teachers may often include teachers from all levels of the hierarchy and may benefit from the contribution of young teachers, who would thus feel that they have some share in determining future developments.

The 'teaching team' advocated in this paper may be seen as one such grouping, including as it would both experienced and inexperienced teachers, and it would certainly be concerned with some developmental tasks. However, in the long term much would depend on how teams evolved, and this leads to consideration of the crucial issue of leadership. There are two possibilities. Members of a 'team' might take turns in being chairman, thus deliberately dissociating the 'team' from the hierarchy, and emphasizing the participation of all members in the decision-making. Alternatively, a team-leader might be appointed and then inevitably this appointment would eventualy fit into the existing hierarchy. The most likely inheritors of such posts would be the present year heads and house heads and their assistants. The status of such team leaders would gradually evolve and they would be likely to rank with the heads of subject departments. The more 'open' style of team would have the advantage of building into every teacher's role, not only performance as a teacher but some obligatory participation in decision-making and some obligatory sharing of chairmanship. The two latter activities would be a valuable form of staff development. The disadvantage of the 'open' system is that the team might lack status when dealing with the 'barons' who head faculties or departments and who might not take kindly to the servitude of providing a service. Some conflict there may always be between those individuals and those committees concerned to maintain stability and the *status quo* on the one hand and those individuals and groupings concerned to pursue development on the other. This may be no bad thing but will certainly place demands on the top management in keeping a balance between stagnation and headlong haste.

In the early days of its existence the teaching team would be in the developmental mode. How it would evolve is difficult to foresee, but its future would depend very much on the style of leadership exercised within it. The evolution of such teams would not be without tensions and conflict, just as the growth of pastoral systems produced jealousies and dissension. Today's stability is yesterday's development.

Examples of Teaching Teams

Three examples are offered of how the team approach may be applied to managing teaching and learning. The first two are drawn from contemporary experience in English comprehensive schools. The third is a suggested pattern advocated by the most recent reforms in the Swedish comprehensive system.

(i)   The first example illustrates a move towards a team approach which was developed because of dissatisfaction with the pastoral–academic divide and wish to involve those with pastoral responsibilities in teaching those for whom they are responsible.

The team is composed of the head of year and two other teachers (the heads of other years). Together they teach an interdisciplinary course to their year group of 270 learners in groups of 90. The course in this instance is one in Personal and Social Education. It is a highly structured course, is taught by team-teaching methods, and includes elements of careers education, health and sex education, community responsibility, group dynamics, religious education, and so on. The course is taught in years 1 to 5 as part of a common curriculum. The team prepare the course together with the help and advice of the Head of the Faculty of Personal and Social Education. The course is itself unexceptional, and team teaching of such a course is common. What is of interest is the value reported by the teachers of having their common experience of teaching the group as a reference, when discussing other aspects of the development of individuals. However, the time devoted to the course is only 2 hours 20 minutes per week, and the course has had to struggle to gain status in the curriculum because it is not examinable. A significant and unusual feature of the course is the fact that each year all pupils are required to answer a written questionnaire which evaluates the past course and invites suggestions which may be incorporated in future courses. Although this team does not perform all the roles associated with pastoral care, it is a deliberate attempt to show that certain pastoral activities properly belong within the classroom.

(ii) The second example is also taken from a large comprehensive school where a purpose-built and very well equipped humanities block has become 'a school within a school'. Here a team of teachers of English, history, geography and religious education teach an integrated humanities course to all forms from years 1 to 5.

In years 1 to 3 a team of seven teachers and a remedial teacher teach a highly structured course by individualized learning methods to the whole year-group, which is blocked on the time-table for ten periods per week. In the first year particularly, the number of teachers by whom pupils are taught is kept to a minimum. In years 4 and 5 the year is divided up into two half-year groups, each of which is taught by a team of four teachers. The teams of teachers have spent much time and energy in the production of their own teaching material, which has a very professional look about it. The faculty common-room has a healthy but not over-hectic feel of bustle and activity. Teachers again report the advantages of this team approach as being very supportive, particularly to new arrivals to the staff. They also report being able to handle most of their behaviour problems within the faculty area. The disadvantages have been the number of meetings and the difficulties of keeping a hard-working staff motivated to prepare new material. The fact that the faculty is favoured by facilities and very ably led has meant that deliberate attempts have to be made to avoid becoming isolated from other faculties in the school.

(iii) The third example is drawn from a Swedish comprehensive school catering for young people from 9 to 16 years of age. When visited by the writer, this school was taking part in the trials of the most recent reforms to affect Swedish schools. These reforms were concerned with the 'inner working', or what was going on in the Swedish comprehensive schools, which have been in existence since 1962. In 1970 a Royal Commission was set up to look at various unsatisfactory features of comprehensive schools.

Among the causes for concern were lack of motivation or 'school fatigue' on the part of the pupils and a curriculum which was not sufficiently in touch with contemporary society. Among the proposals which were being tried out in the school visited were those of the 'learning unit' and the 'teaching team'. The intake to the school was about 180 pupils and they were divided into two mixed-ability 'units' of 90 pupils. Each 'unit' was looked after by a team of four teachers.

There was a team-leader, two specialist teachers and a remedial specialist. Together this 'team' taught the 'unit' for a large proportion of their learning programme. Most teachers taught more than one subject, not without complaint in some cases. The whole 'unit' enjoyed the services of the remedial specialist. At some time during the week each teacher taught all the learners, except in the case of the remedial specialist, who dealt only with those needing special help. The team leader was directly responsible to the principal or his deputy and there was no intervening year head or house head. Team meetings were held weekly and in addition to team members, a psychologist or social worker might attend if requested. The 'team' was thus the focal point for case conferences over young people with problems. The team meetings were also attended by three representatives of the learners. At the time of the writer's visit the role of the team leader and his or her remuneration was exciting much interest and controversy among the members of teacher associations. The original proposals were to transfer a proportion of the budget previously allocated to heads of departments to the holders of the new posts. The associations have opposed this move and have also sought additional payments for the extra meetings necessitated by the new proposals. The decisions about these financial issues have now been delegated by the government to local authorities.

In the pilot area visited by the writer there was a cautious but fairly general welcome for the 'teaching team' idea among the teachers questioned. Some of their reasons for favouring the scheme were as follows:

(i) Planning is made easier and courses are more coherent.
(ii) Most teachers find the team supportive. Weak and inexperienced teachers are particularly helped.
(iii) Team teaching takes place more often.
(iv) Learners are known better and discussed more knowledgeably at meetings.
(v) More concerted action is taken to deal with difficult pupils more speedily.
(vi) Remedial teaching is more readily available and is more often provided in the ordinary class situation.

(i) There seem to be more meetings than before.
(ii) Teachers have to spend longer hours in school.
(iii) Many teachers found the presence of learners at meetings very threatening and were not reconciled to this idea.

The point must also be made that most teaching is in mixed-ability groups in Swedish schools. There is limited setting in mathematics and in modern languages at ages 14 to 16. Also, there is a limited option scheme at ages 14 to 16. Only five out of thirty-five hours of schooling are allocated to optional subjects. Teams have been more difficult to operate in these years. Teachers of older pupils have a long tradition of specialization. This tradition is less strong among teachers of ages 9 to 14. Nevertheless, the mood of many teachers was cautious optimism. The head of the school visited was very deeply concerned to establish a dialogue between teachers and pupils, rather than adopt the traditional autocratic, paternalistic or didactic stance of 'teacher knows best'. He expressed his concern thus: 'We must now be more open to the thoughts and feelings of our pupils and of their parents. As a head I must spend longer looking at and listening to people. I must see my school with clearer eyes.'

Conclusion

The suggestions in this paper for the organization and management of learning are attempts to focus the schools' care and concern for the individual within the teaching–learning situations in the belief that for a teacher that is what 'care' means. The teacher who 'cares' is the teacher who teaches effectively, in the same way that the doctor who 'cares' is the one who treats his patient effectively. Similarly nurses and social workers have their professional concepts of 'care'.

An attempt is also being made to recognize the need for the learner to be involved in his or her own learning, not simply as a recipient of what is deemed appropriate, but by participating in a dialogue which may reveal what is appropriate to both teacher and learner. From such dialogues, gradually and continually, the contract between teachers and learners may be renegotiated. The readjustment of the traditional relationship between teacher and learner will be accompanied by discomfort, unease and insecurity on the part of both teachers and learners. The duty of care will remain, but the notions of 'pastoral care' and of *in loco parentis* at the secondary level of education may become less appropriate. Both have connotations of authority and paternalism which may be increasingly called into question by future learners, who may enjoy a variety of learning experiences in and out of learning institutions but may yet seek the services of the teacher as soothsayer, priest, magician, confidant or confessor, who cannot be replaced by machines, robots, computers or microprocessors.

References

1 Martin Buber, *Between Man and Man* (Fontana, London, 1971), Chapter 3, 'Education'.
2 Elizabeth Halsall, *The Comprehensive School* (Pergamon, Oxford, 1973).
3 Fred Tye, *Educational Administration Bulletin* (BEAS) Vol. 3 No. 1, Autumn 1974.

The schools referred to in the examples given of teaching teams on pages 192 to 195 are:

1 Marple Ridge High Street, Stockport (Headmaster, David Styan, B.Sc (Econ.).).
2 Tarporley Country High School, Cheshire (Headmaster, R. N. Wrigley, B.A.).
3 Madesjöskolan, Nybro, Sweden (Headmaster, Gerhard Gustafsson).

SECTION D

Structure and Process: three case studies

Introduction

In Section A of this book, the failure of educational researchers to analyse rigorously and systematically the realities of pastoral care in schools was forcefully expressed. The 'conventional wisdom' was criticized on several grounds and the inadequacies of the concept of pastoral care itself were considered. In particular it was suggested that there may be a serious discrepancy between what is written about pastoral care and what it actually means for practising teachers in actual schools.

The following chapters represent three attempts to give empirical referents to the theoretical conjectures of that section. All are sociological in orientation and focus upon the context of pastoral-care activities.

Peter Corbishley and John Evans provide some valuable insights into what pastoral care might mean in their comparative study of two very different comprehensive schools. They bring out the importance of the historical and environmental factors which pose organizational problems unique to each school, and demonstrate the significance of the resultant administrative structure for the way pastoral care is conceived of by the teachers. The importance of the head-teacher's philosophy and its translation into a structure in which responsibility is delegated within the role-structure is well established, but the comments of many teachers show how such features may be interpreted and evaluated in very different ways. A pastoral-care system may justify a school's claim to care, but teachers' accounts show how great the gap may be between stated aims and their attainment. Problems of role definition, inadequate time and resources, the demands of policing a large and rapidly expanding institution in a difficult area, and the internal tensions of a medium-sized bureaucracy are all important factors in determining the success of a school in all aspects of its work. In so far as conventional prescriptions for pastoral-care provision fail to take account of the social, historical and organizational complexities involved, Corbishley and Evans' paper amply demonstrates their inadequacy. In drawing on teachers' verbal accounts to document their case, Corbishley and Evans direct attention to the fundamental importance of how teachers construe their actions and the context in which they are effected. This is a common theme through all the chapters in this section.

Mike Taylor adopts a socio-linguistic perspective to analyse what actually goes on in a counselling session between a tutor and a fourth-year pupil. He demonstrates the complexity of pastoral encounters, drawing attention to the variety of contextual features of the situation in which they are enacted. The constraints of teacher–pupil role expectations, available time, physical location and so on are shown to be potentially as significant to the outcome as the stated aims and objectives of the tutor. In the process Taylor develops a model which teachers might use in analysing their own pastoral-care activities and contributing to the in-service training of themselves and their colleagues.

The final chapter is a report of a piece of on-going research in one particular school. It, too, emphasizes the importance of actors' constructions of the realities they face in their daily routines. Drawing on interview transcripts and observations, the authors identify a number of distinct perspectives which teachers adopt towards their roles and the context in which they are played out, and argue that an understanding of such perspectives is essential to the planning of institutionalized pastoral care.

Taken together these chapters offer substantial evidence for the need to consider pastoral care as a product of a very complicated set of developing social relationships. They provide useful insights into the realities of pastoral care in a number of schools, some of which may be bitter pills to swallow for those who have written optimistically about the subject in the past. But there can be no point in ignoring harsh realities because they are unpalatable. There can be no short cuts to the effective organization and provision of something as fundamental and worthwhile as the care of our children. A grasp of the tensions between educational ideals and the historical, organizational and material constraints which obtain in particular schools seems an essential prerequisite for success in this endeavour.

14   Teachers and Pastoral Care: an empirical comment*

Peter Corbishley and John Evans

Introduction

Empirically-based literature on pastoral care is rare. Gleanings are available from the NFER studies of comprehensive schools on the national pattern of pastoral organization.[1] But books or articles tend to be about prescription and counter-prescription as to 'how to do it'. Their central basis tends to be personal experience (albeit sometimes lived and working) rather than research. In a large number of them, issues seem to divide neatly on a political left—right spectrum. Rhodes Boyson, it is sensed, is against a pastoral emphasis and in favour of a return to 'teaching'.[2] The Teachers Action Collective argues that pastoral care is not really 'pastoral' but another means of preparing pupils for the discipline of the work-place.[3] The Right to Learn Group, politically on the left, argue for a need to re-emphasize classroom teaching, the position of the form tutor and the associated dismantling of pastoral-care systems.[4]

The bulk of the comment is directed however at several previous contributors to this series, centring on Michael Marland.[5] The views of Douglas Hamblin[6] have also provided another major horizon to which we felt it necessary to refer ourselves. It is our view, based on the two case-studies to be presented, that both authors underestimate the organizational ramifications and socio-historical contexts within which pastoral care is effected. To this extent their comments are unhelpful to teachers who wish to assess the possibilities for modifying their practices in the light of, among other things, the Great Debate, a multi-cultural society, and falling rolls. Marland does this by tending to substitute the promotion of the personal growth of the adolescent for an emphasis on the curriculum. Hamblin achieves it by arguing that the pastoral staff are there to teach the study skills which are necessary for a pupil to learn the curriculum proper. It must be hoped that our

*This article arises out of the SSRC-financed project 'Pupil Identities and Teacher Strategies in Mixed-Ability Curricula'. We would like to thank Brian Davies and Catherine Kenrick for their comments and support in producing this report. The research is based on a case-study of two schools which were 'lived in' for the academic year 1977—78. We were not specifically interested in studying pastoral care. Our conceptual approach assumed that events in classrooms are not separable from overall school organization. We produce this article therefore as a 'spin-off' whose possibility rested on our concern to consider all aspects of school life in their bearing on work in classrooms.

article does not lead readers to ignore other valuable comments both
authors have to make, as our focus is specifically on pastoral care
within school organization.

Hamblin is somewhat easier to comment on than Marland. The
crucial aspect of pastoral care for him is its integration with the curriculum. In this, Hamblin sees himself as going one step further down the
lane pointed out by Marland. He realizes too, if not in so many words,
that the Great Debate is only an early stage in the critical scrutiny of
the comprehensive school.[7] The pattern he suggests is a straightforward
one and involves identifying critical stages in a stylized pupil's career.
Induction, option choices, work for exams, career choices, and entry
to sixth form are for him typical occasions requiring positive intervention by pastoral staff. It is the responsibility of pastoral staff to
teach study skills at all stages of a pupil's career. This is not the sole
emphasis, but it is at the core of his position. 'Once this is accepted,
we see the sense of making the pastoral task the production of open
minds . . .'[8] 'Study skills' is, of course, too narrow a phrase. Hamblin
elsewhere argues: 'we have already seen that the pastoral team will
be giving deep thought to the processes through which pupils learn
in the sometimes troubled period of development we call adolescence'.[9] Hamblin's problem pupil, the one to be identified by pastoral
staff, submits to authority, uses a context-bound language and has
little capacity for independent learning. Particularly indicted, therefore,
in Hamblin's critical perspective on existing pastoral organization, is
the school which reinforces a pupil's reliance on external authority and
devises a pastoral system with the primary function of punishment.
The pastoral system, for Hamblin, has a role *vis-à-vis* staff, too. 'Coali-
tions, factions and near feuds will mar staffroom relationships, and it
may need a well integrated pastoral team to bring such conflicts out
in the open and increase commitment to the task'.[10] Hamblin, therefore, like so many others, is working on a dimension of schools as
'closed' and 'open', which, however fashionable, is often too pro-
grammatic to be helpful.[11] Hamblin, likewise, stresses the school as
a caring community. But his particular orientation to the curriculum
— which retains separate professional expertise for curricular and
pastoral staff — is potentially more fruitful than Marland's.

Marland is not, as he is at great pains to point out in his conclusion, advocating educational softness: 'Even love must have method'.[12]
He continually points to the practical consequences of particular
organizational patterns. One of the aims of pastoral care is 'discipline',
or in his own words, the maintenance of 'an orderly atmosphere'.[13]
Like Hamblin he has much to say of practical usefulness. In a subtle
shift, however, he repeats the unstructured progressivists' emphasis
on the whole child.[14] He centres the link between pastoral and curricular in the adolescent status of the pupil who has 'to find himself and
find meaning for his studies and his life'.[15] In this emphasis the whole
atmosphere of the school is pastoral and teaching—learning takes

place within 'that elusive quality of care'.[16] Educational knowledge
is 'only part of the greater need'. The curriculum itself is to be 'pastoralized' and unlikely to become 'almost independent' except in the
'development of physical skills'.[17] Education in the narrow sense exists
within the other forms of guidance: disciplinary, vocational and personal.[18]

Marland's view represents a shift which has been found to have its
dangers for the status of learning in American schools.[19] The secondary
school as the school of adolescence, of 'the crisis of identity'[20] may
belie the perspectives of adolescents themselves. Although no further
mention will be made of it here, it is clear from our own work that
few pupils consider themselves to be individuals in isolation from
their friends.[21] By the third year self-chosen peer groups are fully
established and it is within these, in and out of school, that pupils
live out their differing adolescent statuses. Ethnicity of any kind
tends to reinforce these divisions. Teachers in turn have access to
these groupings only on the pupils' terms. Teachers can listen to conversations but the truth revealed is only partial. The rationalization
of the concerns of adolescent sub-groups through education will meet
with resistance, then, if only because teachers are adults.

Pastoral organization for Marland is not principally a backup to the
academic. It exists to create a certain ethos or spirit. It may well be,
therefore, residual in its calls on staffing. Pastoral heads will work
directly with teams of form teachers who in turn will be allowed
autonomy, for instance, direct representation in meetings with parents.
Marland characterizes his preferred tutor role as ascendant (rather
than neutral or subordinate). Like Hamblin he underemphasizes the
likelihood of internal staff dissension and the effects of variations in
career motivation and aspiration. It seems particularly important to
emphasize that, given the plethora of talk about pupils, pastoral systems also entail the organization and thereby the control of teachers.
It is accepted that schools label pupils. It needs to be said, too, that
schools can help to create both 'good' and 'bad' teachers and that the
pastoral system plays its part here, however caring the school community.

History

It is not perhaps accepted as axiomatic that all empirical studies should
have an historical element. But present practices do grow out of past
ones. Writers like Marland and Hamblin are themselves conscious that
the meaning of the term 'pastoral care' has changed even within the
last ten years.

A historical approach is not necessarily developmental, though,
and even a brief consideration shows up one paradox. In 1800 the Head
of a public school introduced a pupil to his school by roundly telling

him that 'the school is your father. Boy, the school is your mother . . . and all other relations, too'.[22] Boarding schools are directly *in loco parentis* for all of a pupil's curricular and extra-curricular daily existence. In State schools till recently, the organizational import of the 'house' has been restricted to games and non-academic activities.[23] Yet in more recent times, as the willingness to attribute parental authority to teachers has become more conditional *and* more attenuated, pastoral systems with complex effects on schools have become more general.

It may be ambivalence over the precise degree to which a school takes over from where the home has left off, if it should at all, that has led to the variation in the scope and experience with which schools attempt pastoral care. This article will highlight some of these difficulties while arguing that influences broader than confusion over the articulation of home and school are at work. We will not try to argue the relative merits of vertically or horizontally-grouped pastoral regimes, although the article rests on a comparison of two schools with such different organizations. School V has a vertical house system and School H a horizontal or year system. They are different too, in a variety of other respects. Like all schools, both operate under constraints which although different, may be thought to lie somewhat easier on School V. As will be seen below, H is a more than typical inner-city 'comprehensive'. Its hesitations over the pattern of pastoral care to adopt or the rigour with which its present form must be implemented are endemic to low-status schools in British education. If School H 'improved', another with similar problems would take its place, as some administrators but not many politicians seem to realize. The well-developed pastoral organization at V brings a success which hides omnipresent strains. Both schools face the curricular and other pressures of the Great Debate. As will become clear, it is not a paradox that an emphasis on curriculum will create problems for pastoral care in V, while in School H it might help to solve them.

On reorganization, School H was tripled in size overnight in the amalgamation of three schools. Conflict between staff and pupils from the different schools ensued.[24] Ideal did not meet practice. The tragedy of insufficiently planned-for reorganization enacted itself. The buildings were unfinished. Problems over the three-day week and pre-Houghton teacher anxieties exacerbated this historical legacy. Teacher turnover in the next few years was huge. The pupils increasingly began to come from a variety of multi-ethnic backgrounds, predominantly West Indian from the British Colonies, for whom little preparation was made. Pastorally, as with many schools in the early stages of becoming comprehensive, the issue was that of size. The Head organized a series of mini-schools for the lower, middle and upper ages. The model of pastoral care remained that of the smallish secondary modern or grammar school, which had been the province of the Head and Deputy. The new Heads of School simply took on the traditional powers, which included those over curriculum. They dealt with admissions, reports, and liaison with parents, and they administered corporal punishment. In the words of one School Head, we were allowed 'to be headmasters, he used to come into our offices and thank us, saying what a wonderful job we were doing'. A School Counsellor was appointed to supplement these heads. In the staff guide form tutors were asked to 'regard themselves as having a special concern for both the pastoral care and learning . . . of members of their form.' A tutor was clear about the responsibilities of the job, and in the words of one 'knew exactly where his leader was'. A fully formed pastoral system, retaining a balance with the academic, had apparently been formed.

It was another three years, upon the arrival of a new head, before a year system was also adopted. The horizontal system, according to Monks, is characteristic of schools which reorganize late. School H fits this pattern, undergoing as it were a second reorganization. The tone with which pastoral care was now approached became more liberal. The traditional system, even with the addition of a school counsellor, had of itself proved incapable of establishing disciplinary control. Fears both as to the size and social composition of the school roll were an ongoing worry. The school counsellor now began to be phased out. Pastoral care was to be organized in a more complex way and became less dependent on semi-autonomous professionals such as the counsellor. The status of the school heads became particularly ambiguous. The measured ability of the school's supposedly comprehensive intake, though now improving, is still worse than when the school opened as a secondary modern.[25]

School V had a different historical legacy, reorganizing two years earlier than School H. It had consistently worked to realize certain forms that closely identified with the development of comprehensives. It adopted mixed-ability groupings, an open sixth, a personal guidance programme integrated with critical moments in a pupil's career, as advocated by Hamblin. It built up strong links with parents, and a strong Parents' Association. It was oversubscribed. The Head is now attempting to move towards a community-school role, with premises used after school as a social centre. The Head summed up the underlying motivation as 'our philosophy is that none of us is entitled to put a frontier of limitation — either actually or psychologically — to the march of any pupil'. Originally School V appointed six heads of house, each with a small office. The Monks survey suggested that schools of V's size had particular difficulty in staffing a pastoral system while balancing academic requirements. Three years after reorganization, problems over allowances (but as importantly over the number of staff required) led to a contraction in house staff. Six houses remained for pupils, but were now staffed by three teams, each servicing two house groups. For parents strong links with houses remain as their children follow each other into the same house. Unlike School H, this reorganization caused no problems for the staff concerned, perhaps because it involved a contraction on the pastoral side. Unease continues, however, about the effect of innovations which are defined as pastoral. Unlike School H, for instance, parental and staff pressure for examination results calls into question such key features of the school as the open sixth, which the Director of the Sixth Form saw as pastoral — 'if we felt the child could benefit in any sphere, they should be taken back'. As the other schools in the area have reorganized the intake has 'improved', with now some 20 to 25 per cent who could have entered grammar school, and a small tail of 10 to 15 pupils with a reading age below 9. There is a feeling among the staff that parents of the more able children are demanding better results. Some staff now want the kind of academic emphasis in allowances characteristic of schools organized from a grammar-school base.

Organization 1977–78

The two schools have the following organizational pattern. School H is eight-form entry, with a ratio of one member of staff to fifteen pupils. Excluding form tutors, 17 per cent of the staff are involved in pastoral care. School V is six-form entry, with a ratio of around one to seventeen: 21 per cent of teachers are involved to some extent in pastoral work, defined as either the disciplining or counselling of pupils, or both these roles. Both schools work to a weekly timetable of 23 hours 20 minutes, as do the bulk of schools.[26] School H divides its week into twenty periods in order to reduce movement rather than to facilitate curriculum innovation. Movement is a problem in V too, which works on a time-table base of forty periods but teaches mostly in doubles, while gaining flexibility for single and triple periods in some subject areas. The normal teaching load in H is 19.40 hours. In V it is 18.40 hours. It is these figures which are taken to represent 100 per cent in either case. Individual teachers may have slightly bulkier time-tables but not typically. The percentage figures in brackets in Figures 8 and 9, therefore, do not have the same meanings in each of the tables in terms of teaching hours. These are always higher for School H. But the figures enable a comparison of teaching loads *within* a school. It is this which is uppermost in teachers' minds.

The allocation of scale points to individual teachers is not published in School V. A note in the teachers' bulletin which itself indicates some anxiety about the overall pattern reads as follows: '. . . allocation of points to staff with pastoral responsibilities equals twenty-four. Allocation of points to staff with departmental/faculty responsibilities equals forty-six. (This number also includes senior staff with overall responsibility for discipline and general school administration).' Roughly a third of allowances (34 per cent) therefore went for pastoral purposes, which is somewhat greater than the 24 per cent expected according to Monks.[27] In School H the allowance points were published. About

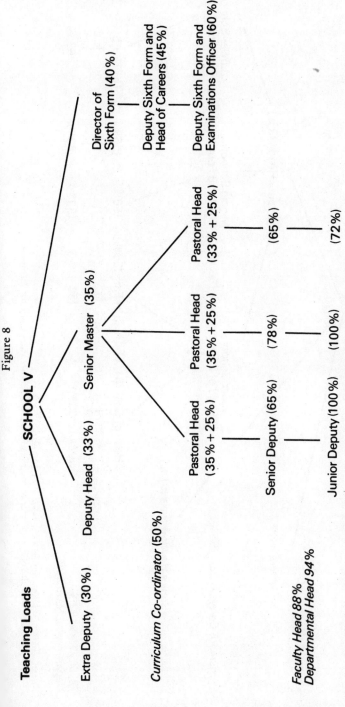

Figure 8

Teaching Loads

SCHOOL V

Extra Deputy (30%)

Deputy Head (33%)

Senior Master (35%)

Curriculum Co-ordinator (50%)

Director of Sixth Form (40%)

Deputy Sixth Form and Head of Careers (45%)

Deputy Sixth Form and Examinations Officer (60%)

Pastoral Head (35% + 25%)

Pastoral Head (35% + 25%)

Pastoral Head (33% + 25%)

Senior Deputy (65%)

Junior Deputy (100%)

(78%)

(100%)

(65%)

(72%)

Faculty Head 88%
Departmental Head 94%

Notes: [1] 25% of a pastoral head's teaching time is spent on a personal guidance programme.
[2] 100% = 18.40 hours taught. Time-table was 23.20.
[3] Figures after the plus sign refer to teaching for pastoral rather than academic purposes.

Figure 9

SCHOOL H

Teaching Loads

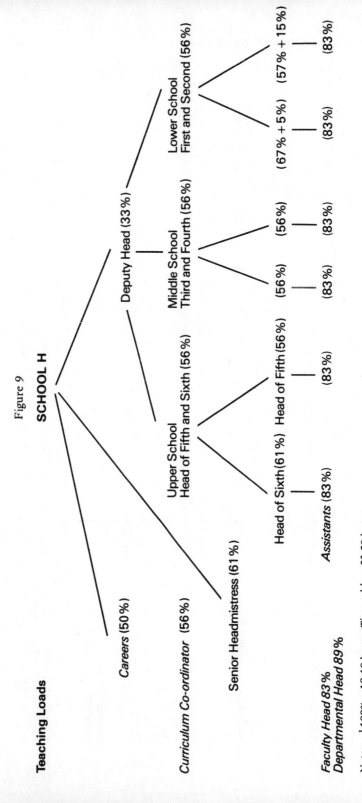

Careers (50%)

Curriculum Co-ordinator (56%)

Deputy Head (33%)

Senior Headmistress (61%)

Upper School
Head of Fifth and Sixth (56%)

Middle School
Third and Fourth (56%)

Lower School
First and Second (56%)

Head of Sixth (61%)   Head of Fifth (56%)

(56%)   (56%)

(67% + 5%)   (57% + 15%)

Assistants (83%)

(83%)   (83%)

(83%)   (83%)

(83%)   (83%)

Faculty Head 83%
Departmental Head 89%

Notes: [1] 100% = 19.40 hours. Time-table = 23.20 hours.
[2] Figures after the plus sign refer to teaching for pastoral rather than academic purposes.

28 per cent of the points went to the pastoral side, as would be expected
by Monks. It may be useful for readers to bear both these sets of information in mind while reading teachers' comments, especially on the
balance or split between pastoral and academic. In School V it is clear
that in terms of subject-teaching time the pastoral heads are part of
the senior management, while their deputies are more favourably
placed in respect of teaching loads than faculty or departmental heads,
including the one pastoral teacher who is a craft teacher for 78 per cent
of the time.[28] In School H the pattern of resource allocation is somewhat more ambiguous, but one interpretation would suggest that in
terms of teaching loads the Heads of School, together with the Heads
of Third, Fourth, Fifth and Sixth year, form a second-tier group along
with the three curriculum co-ordinators, whereas Faculty Heads and
Deputies form a third tier. The Heads of year one and two between
them teach a further four periods in the lower-school sanctuary. In
fact these periods were not evenly divided, as one year Head was a
modern-language specialist in a department with staffing shortage
problems. The overall impression, then, in terms of staff involved,
teaching loads, and points allocation is that the pastoral organization
is more pervasive and central in School V. In H it remains more separate,
self-contained and perhaps more distant from the Head.

These comments should not be taken to mean that the pastoral
system in School H is less central to the day-to-day running of the
school than that at School V. In V the pastoral heads met with the
main management committee once every four weeks, but met with
their form tutors one week in three. In H the pastoral heads were part
of the management group which met every week, and met fortnightly
with the deputy and head specifically to discuss pastoral matters.
Senior pastoral staff rarely met with their form tutors as a group.

School H – The Contemporary Perspectives

The teachers regard their work in the school as difficult and challenging.
Classroom teaching, in terms of material and resource preparation
required, together with the amount of attention demanded by pupils,
is seen as extremely demanding of time and energy. It is difficult,
additionally, because a disproportionate amount of time which could
be directed to learning, teaching and caring, has to be spent in the
seemingly endless and exhausting pursuit of pupil discipline and control. Organizationally, as has been seen, the school has a well defined
if rather separate and specialized pastoral structure. In the staff guide
these arrangements are made to look after 'the academic and personal
welfare of each and every pupil'. For the form tutor this involves
talking to pupils about their work; checking on homework books;
and contacting subject staff about their pupils' work and behaviour.
Pastoral heads are *ex officio* members of the Board of Studies, which

as its name indicates is responsible for curriculum appraisal. But as one head of school, agreeing with a colleague that they are faced with the 'pastoral need' of pupils from an area of 'economic and social disadvantage' argues,

> although I'm officially responsible for pastoral and academic progress of the children, really and truly, I feel the pastoral side is the one I should look after. We've got a very strong faculty system — many people who are paid high salaries to look after that side. And I feel I don't want to interfere too much. All I ever do is at management, I can make the odd comment . . . but I don't lay down the law.

The role of the school head is no longer perceived as equivalent to that of a headmaster, but only as the head of a specialized sub-division within the school.

The pastoral structure provides the evident justification of the Head's message to parents that the school is one 'which cares for its pupils'. In the school prospectus parental concern is held to focus on size, 'the size of the school, that so many parents distrust is in fact the major asset because of the extra services it can offer in terms of care . . .' While this is the present rationale, it does not reflect the school's history. The pastoral system in its current form was not a response to size alone. The thrust of the Head's emphasis is seen further by noting his comment to parents on the 'key figure' of the form tutor and on the role of the form period in which 'there is every opportunity to achieve a thorough understanding of every pupil'. Year heads in turn (to whom, alongside subject teachers, form tutors are to relate) are 'expected to develop a meaningful relationship' with pupils. In short it is 'a structure [which] thus ensures that every pupil is well known to every senior member of staff. There are also points of contact for parents who wish to get in touch with us.'

The official image as presented to both staff and parents is of a responsive and caring structure which goes beyond being a device to obviate the anonymity of a large school. The honesty and genuineness of the intentions behind this presentation are not at issue. As one head of school put it:

> I want every child to fulfil his or her potential. I want every pupil to feel that he or she can go to the form tutor with any problem and that any problem will be referred to the year head or to me . . . I want teachers to get to know as much about pupils and their backgrounds as possible . . . I want every child to fulfil his or her full potential.

All these comments, in common with the manifestos issued by heads in other schools or by writers on pastoral organization, have the emphasis on care and knowledge of the individual. One nevertheless senses a failure to grasp history accurately, or a wishfulness in the present, that belies the reality of School H. The comments are prescriptive rather than descriptive.

If we turn to how heads of school and year interpret and appraise their intentions as they are translated into practice, a grimmer picture emerges. 'I would love to do more pastoral work, but I can't. The Headmaster would love to see me standing in the corridor every minute of the day . . . I'm a policeman, that's all I am.' This comment from a head of school is echoed in that of a head of year: 'Not enough of my time is taken up with pastoral work. I hope to spend more of my time seeing how tutors are working . . . usually my time is taken up seeing about five prize-nutters and about a quarter of my time is taken up with secretarial stuff.'

In part, some of these comments reflect the change in system: 'In Mr X's time I did pastoral work. I had an excellent administrator Mr J. and this released me to do pastoral work. Now, if the Head saw me with a pupil, he'd be annoyed . . .' Another head of year remarks 'there was more emphasis on pastoral care in Mr X's time . . . then, I was responsible for social and academic responsibilities.

It might be thought that the creation of further layers of responsibility in pastoral care would free the school heads for even more pastoral work. Cearly this has not happened and the reasons are somewhat up in the need to implement certain policies in the non-academic sphere.

On arrival at the school. the Head had defined his problem as attracting a 'better clientele', 'to ease the burden placed upon teachers who are confronted with a preponderance of low-ability children.' In his view, given parental choice and falling rolls, schools are now firmly entrenched in a 'market economy situation'. He recognized that both parents and primary-feeder school heads judged the school less on the merits of thorough curricula than the public symbols of educational excellence: order, the wearing of uniforms and respectful children. Many teachers readily and sometimes critically perceived the amount of time and effort the Head devoted to changing the public image of the school. He chose the route not of curriculum change but of establishing control. He chose the route not of curriculum change but of establishing control. The pastoral structure therefore has a dual aspect. It is an advertisement for the school — real evidence of its care. It is also the means for creating the internal order and coherence which is commonly supposed to lie behind a good public image. It must be realized therefore that the position of a head is extremely unenviable. The expectations of parents, LEA personnel, and teachers create constraints which inevitably distort any straightforwardly held pastoral ideals.

The extention of the pastoral system under these conditions bore most heavily on school heads. But a cycle of personal recrimination was also set up which moves from the year heads to form tutors, back to senior staff and so on, in turn, to the pastoral staff or form tutors. One year head argues for instance that 'teachers want to have a very friendly relationship with their pupils, they don't organize their classes so that *they* [her emphasis] are in control.' Another year head criticized his tutors, who 'are not in the classroom on time and have poor discipline, time after time, pupils swear at them and nothing is done to them . . .' Members of senior management regard the discipline as 'only barely adequate' or 'very poor'. For them 'the structure is right'. It simply 'needs pruning' of its 'inadequate staff' followed by 'their replacement with teachers with a much higher level of expertise.' Allowances are given to those identified (rightly and wrongly) as professionally able teachers to encourage them to stay.[29] Those who remain unrewarded in turn can have their criticisms: 'A good pastoral system affects discipline generally. If the pastoral system worked better then one's classroom teaching would be less interrupted by discipline problems. But pastoral heads are bogged down in paper work.'

Less generously, others argue that 'there is no systematic approach to detentions needed as a deterrent'. Or there are 'no effective sanctions for persistent offenders'. One teacher goes further and relates the problem back to the lack of a traditional system to back up pastoral staff: 'There is insufficient support from deputy heads and headmaster; there is an unwillingness to accept, to do anything which may affect the façade that the school attempts to present to the external world. Suspensions and expulsions make for a bad press.' Those who do not regard the system so critically, who perceive it as 'quite good' or working 'fairly efficiently' are form tutors who ask for more to be 'loaded into the form teachers' hands, i.e. checking out absences and more contact with parents of children in the form.' (Ironically, the staff guide outlines considerable responsibilities to the form tutor.) This is a call for greater tutor autonomy. In contrast, it is those who accept the outlines of the system who most criticize its failure to work. One dominant response then to the more complex division of labour has been that of buck-passing in the area of greatest failure.

It would be wrong, however, to simply characterize this as a 'distorted' system in which pastoral care 'is conceived largely in terms of complaints, investigations of these complaints, and finally of punishments'.[30] This was not the official intention and generally perceived purpose of the system. And it does not reflect the reality of those form tutors and pastoral staff who clearly define their practices more 'pastorally'. But an organizational innovation is not adequately characterized by the intentions of its authors. It may be that the division of labour as introduced is a more serious source of disorder than intentions which are hardly likely of realization given the conditions outlined above.

It should not be thought, either, that the system does not work. It does offer constructive and positive assistance. One form tutor notes that it functions 'generally quite well. And there is usually someone a pupil can be referred to . . . ' But once again the efficiency is seen as dependent on personal abilities. 'Some are not as good as others: some are excellent, they follow up everything and care for kids . . . others are useless.' Labelling has been strongly emphasized in analyses of the way teachers relate to children. It is important to note the same process at work in staffrooms, in this case via a junior member of staff. But at all levels, as has been seen, there is clearly a search for culprits rather than causes, with a serious effect on staff morale.[31] An institutional irrationality is developed in which demands for greater and tighter control are made upon a system which is currently unable to deliver this systematically. Tutors emphasize the 'lack of good pastoral control', demand 'improved chasing after children'. It all seems a matter of 'not letting things slide'. Other comments from form tutors reveal a professional resistance to the organizational structure itself, in the catch-phrase 'there are too many chiefs and not enough indians'. There is the feeling that people could be involved less in 'administration and more in teaching'. If there were less need to attend meetings there would be 'more involvement by pastoral staff in the classroom situation, [they would] see exactly what is going on. Students would be kept on their toes if they knew that they could be visited unexpectedly by senior staff.' The prevalent anxiety about control is present in these comments, but the central problem created by the extension of pastoral care is also present. There exists 'too much bureaucracy, not enough communication'. There is, and this is a point taken up by some staff in School V, a 'lack of communication between pastoral staff who have access to important information'. In fact, as one form tutor emphasized, even decisions 'just float down to people in a garbled form'. The teachers' response is to ask for more open meetings; 'many meetings are not open to general members of staff'. The open meetings are not in themselves an adequate response because the lack of communication that such meetings are designed to solve is intimately related to the weight of administration and bureaucracy entailed in the new system.

There are those too, it should be noted, who argue that problems originate outside the school in 'lack of parental control' or in 'strong cultural differences breeding mistrust and suspicion based on ignorance'. This contrasts with School H. But even in these cases it is ultimately placed back to a pastoral system which is 'still not fully efficient'.

There are points of contact between the prescriptive typologies of Hamblin on the distorted pastoral system and Marland on the subordinate tutor, with the evidence presented here. It might be thought, then, that School H is a representative case of what Hamblin and Marland criticize. Enough has been said, however, to indicate that we do not think this is so. Pastoral heads do want autonomy, do want to care, and form tutors want more responsibility. They criticize the paper work, call for better upward communication, and all in all want to assert, even if they do not put it into so many words, the values of professional autonomy against those of centralized direction and control.

There is a perennial struggle being enacted here. It may be helpful to note its emergency, particularly in the area of pastoral care, and to go some way towards explaining its occurrence before going on to examine the other implications of the evidence from School V. Imagine for the moment that we can regard pastoral-care systems as small sub-system bureaucracies employing less than twenty professionals. An American study of such organizations suggested that the employment of professionals rather than clerks led to greater demands for upward communication, required a more dispersed management, and led to a greater interest in and a desire to contribute to all aspects of the organization.[32] The characteristic structure of subject departments in a school meets these criteria. Heads of department are numerous and in the main relate to small groups who are regarded as colleagues. A definite autonomy is granted to subject departments by senior management in schools. This is extended to individual teachers and is symbolized in the tentativeness with which senior management enters through the classroom door. However, pastoral care, as traditionally defined in the tripartite system, was basically an administrative task. It covered dealings with parents, feeder primaries, and other outside agencies. Discipline, too, whatever its psychological significance for the individual, is a question of maintaining that order within which the main purpose of the school can be carried on. Attempts to define the pastoral aspect of the teacher's responsibility in professional terms have historically come later than the systems designed to meet the new administrative requirements caused by increase in size and reorganization. The traditional relations to parents and others have also become more complex, with changed attitudes on both sides. Pastoral care is therefore marked additionally by a management need for downward communication geared to maintaining the school's good standing. Centralization of certain functions follows particularly in relation to discipline to implement appropriate policies. In the extension of traditional duties downwards, there is an increase in administration and a formalization of certain duties, particularly for the form tutor. The overall effect is to treat professionals as clerks. The ambiguities and irrationalities within School H relate, apart from local contingencies, to this tension between a demand to implement centrally-directed policies and a professional's own sense of the autonomy due in most aspects of school life. It is also the point, which the evidence from School V illustrates more fully, at which the professional feels the split between the pastoral and the academic. In pastoral-care systems of the type outlined, teachers are treated less autonomously than in their capacity as subject teachers. They attempt to overcome this difference by calling for a reduction in the scope of pastoral organization through limiting the allowances it takes up and by calling for greater autonomy for the form tutor. These are demands, however, which senior management, given pressures from the press, parents and local politicians, may feel unable to comply with. Pastoral care may be ideally about community. It may become, under certain conditions, in its organizational aspect, a prime focus for dissatisfaction, and possibly one source for turnover among staff.[33]

School V — Contemporary Perspectives

Staff in School V are, in contrast to those in H, satisfied with the pastoral system. Most regard it as the most successful feature of the school. Their comments, even when critical of the weight of the pastoral system within the school, are positive about the members of pastoral teams. As one head of department noted, 'If ancillary staff took over the mundane jobs landed onto the house staff (e.g. filing) this would ease the teaching load. If more weight were given to subject teachers' ideas on framing pupils' course choices we would all be grateful. On the whole the house staff are committed, hard working and overstretched.' This is a complex comment. It indicates the administrative nature of much of the work of house staff and points to a solution which would certainly be welcomed by the Head if the local authority would provide the staff. But it is also critical of the influence pastoral staff have on the balance of subject options in third and sixth years. This is an intrusion into the autonomy of heads of department.

The mention of pupil files indicates further one aspect of the nitty gritty of pastoral work. These files contained examination results and other academic reports. They also included all information on a pupil's conduct in school, positive and negative, as made known to teachers. They aim thus to provide a running record of pupils' involvement in school, but would also contain summaries of staff interviews and meetings with parents. Staff contact with outside agencies such as the police or psychological services was also recorded. These records were the source of references to employers and others and pupils were told of this. Care is (perhaps inevitably) being mixed with control. They were also the basis for a leaver certificate designed for the early leaver and for the pupil with a poor rate of success in public examinations. In this full form such records constitute a centralization of information which formerly could have lain with many departments or have remained privy to the Head or Deputy. In the grammar or secondary-modern school some of this information would perhaps never have been written down.

As one teacher noted, none of the pastoral staff had any professional expertise in 'personal guidance'. The capacity of the social and educational welfare agencies, too, was limited by the policies of the local authority. Referral was not a realistic option in the case of more than a tiny handful of pupils *within* the authority. The information pastoral staff had to rely on, then, was their own common sense. Often their guidance would take the form of a re-explanation of the school's purposes and of the benefits of conformity. The rationale for a pupil's difficulties could go beyond the normal teacher attribution of laziness. It was often based on family breakdown: death, single parenthood, impending or recent divorce, difficulties with parents. Possible problems form tutors were asked to look for were identified as 'a sick parent/anxiety, extra responsibility, etc.; impoverished family/uniform difficulties, over-strict parent, etc. etc.'

The category of 'over-strict parent' in this, the 1978 list of form-tutor responsibilities, had in fact replaced that of 'very large family' in an earlier one, a recognition perhaps of changed attitudes to authority in the wider society which shall be mentioned later. Explanations in terms of family pathology are the counterpart of a real knowledge and firm liaison with most families.³⁴ Inevitably this knowledge appears private and personal as it involves the intimate lives of others. To be effective, some version needs to be given to the staff at large if wayward behaviour is not to be unfairly punished. But there is a requirement for it not to become gossip. As the pastoral roles become specialized in a formal delegation of what was previously the Head's concern, there is also a tendency to deny a pastoral role to subject teachers. The young teacher who wished 'that the pastoral system wasn't seen as the disciplinary force in the school' could therefore comment that 'communi- ׀ cation between pastoral and teaching-only staff is a bit lacking as I found when I started here'. Another commented similarly that 'the ֊ pastoral system too frequently gets associated with the disciplinary system' and that 'more information should be passed on'. The words of another reveal the mechanism of vagueness which safeguards the specialized knowledge: 'I would like pastoral heads to pass on information about a child if I ask rather than replying "he/she has lots of problems" and then refusing to explain what they are.' The same teacher then commented how this affects relations to parents in that 'rather a barrier is formed between parents and other teachers as all contact is by pastoral teachers'. It is of course not only one's standing as a professional subject teacher that is at stake. Broader understandings of the psychological and social conditions for learning have become part of professional training in recent years. The refusal to disclose information runs counter to this emphasis.

The hidden link between care and control has been indicated, but the explicit association between discipline and the pastoral system is as obvious to teachers as to most pupils. Teachers are the ones, after all, who have to decide to use it. So other teachers welcome its disciplinary function. The pastoral system is 'just a discipline chain but is really only pastoral for a few, difficult cases. It could be a little tougher in its approach.' Another added that the 'pastoral system doesn't let pupils get away with much' and that 'perhaps the cane could be used a little more on certain children who are bumptious to every teacher they come across'.

The continuity between the new pastoral-care system and the traditional is highlighted in another quotation. The contrast with School H is straightforward in this respect. But, as the quote indicates, School V, with this continuity, has defined its problems, although it has few of them. 'In some cases, the more serious, I believe it is, the senior members of staff and senior house staff have a good grip of the problems.' One consequence is that it is thought to compensate for staff weakness. The pastoral system is involved in 'too much doing discipline for weak teachers who can't be bothered to instil their own'. More neutrally, another comments 'it works as a sort of telling-off system for teachers who don't do it themselves'. It is of course those teachers who have recourse to the system, as they are encouraged to do, who are defined as weak. One quote brings out this point again, indicates the relation to children already discussed, and points to the mechanism. The pastoral system 'is seen as both a pick-up mechanism for others' weakness, and a means for counselling children and a major bureaucratic tool'.

The standardization and formalization that the pastoral system entails requires further comment.[35] The abrogation of discipline by the pastoral system in respect of certain 'weak' teachers has further unintended organizational consequences for departments. One subject teacher stressed 'I believe that departments must be strong enough to do some of the disciplinary work themselves and the pastoral system is not the first line of defence. Strong departments are essential and this must not be allowed to fall down because of a too strong pastoral system.' In this teacher's view, one aspect of a strong department is 'more teachers with responsibilities within departments'. Issues of emphasis and ethos within the school are encapsulated in the old issue of allowances, 'a proper structure in all departments' as this teacher again put it 'to somehow reduce the continual pressure on teachers'. In this matter, teachers in School V face the same difficulties of care and control as in School H. The job is not any the less challenging for being in an 'easier' school. Perhaps in this last quotation there is another reference to the issue of teaching loads (which are anyhow lighter by an hour on average for School V). As one teacher comments,[36] in a direct echo of School H, 'perhaps if the experienced staff in it were out in the classroom more, there might be less need for them in the pastoral system'. One senses again the pursuit of an ideal state which cannot be achieved given the compulsory nature of schooling and the problems of control that then ensue even among generally well-motivated pupils.

A strongly established pastoral system has in fact then become the spinal cord of the school. Messages about school routines and duties are elaborated downwards. Messages about difficult pupils and difficult teachers are passed upwards. Pastoral systems play their part in school politics whether the 'P' of pastoral stands for principles (educational), parties (political) or simply personalities.

They cannot be simply dichotomized into contrasting types straightforwardly or even very usefully. Teachers do have different values, too, outside their position within the school. For some, the personal guidance programme was 'indoctrination' or 'a very dubious term'.

The question of teacher weaknesses, which in School H was assumed rather than anticipated as in V, has its broader facets too. Jean Floud commented in the early 'sixties that as the teachers' 'moral authority dwindles, so that of the peer group waxes and the pedagogical devices to establish his *personal* authority over his pupils are rendered both more necessary and more difficult to carry into effect as his institutional position weakens'.[37] Parents too, in matters varying from punishment, attendance at school events and even the curriculum, no longer give teachers uncircumscribed control. Teachers in V felt the parents were behind them, in part owing to the pastoral system, 'but the underlying atmosphere is because the kids are brought up to be polite'. Even given this support there was an undertow of comments indicating that the state of discipline was progressively if slowly worsening. The following quotation indicates something of a teacher's own ambiguity over discipline at a time when attitudes to authority have been changing. Discipline was 'better than most schools. Probably not as good as it was, but deteriorating more slowly than most'. And then in the next sentence this teacher goes on to comment that discipline is 'imposed and our children have no more and possibly less self-discipline than the other schools, for instance see their behaviour at bus stops'. The phrase 'bus stop' can strike an immediate sense of anxiety into any Head's heart, particularly in a more suburban area. Similar issues are a commonplace in the newspapers. But such anxiety does not only or even chiefly centre on pupils. It is perhaps the relatively recent pre-Houghton staffing crisis which, especially in London, focused anxiety on the quality of the teachers accepted by Heads.[38] The growth of in-service education, and within schools positions such as that of teacher-tutor may be seen as attempts to fine-tune teacher-quality controls. But pre-eminently, real and imaginary pressures on Heads have led them to the realization of the possibilities that pastoral-care structures afford for centralizing discipline away from certain teachers, so directly strengthening their own control.

Time has been spent in delineating some of the pressures that teachers can feel when designing the pastoral system. The effect can be to treat professional teachers more bureaucratically, and perhaps even without intending to, split the pastoral from the academic. On the one hand the pastoral tends to become equivalent to organization. There is, one teacher suggested, an 'inability to make changes in a petrified pastoral/organizational system'. This system seems to mean 'committees and hierarchies which lead to the feeling of powerlessness for those not in the know', and 'an administrative burden placed on ordinary teachers and form teachers'. The effect can carry over to pupils: 'Although providing a good education for a pupil, I do sometimes feel that in organizational matters and dealings with pupils, we can be too rigid.' There is 'a failure to present knowledge as worth while for its own sake. Learning was continuously bolstered with bribes of house points.'

The traditional reluctance of any Head to intervene within a subject department in part derives from the ignorance any teacher feels about another's specialism. The institutional space for extending organization lay in the field of pupil guidance, especially of the less able. One focus for conflict between the pastoral and the academic can be the matter of option choices. The pastoral staff, with their reserved contact with parents, are best placed to consult them and their children about these. To do so, however, removes the centrally valued function from departments. Numbers in options also crucially affect future staffing requirements. 'Many kids take advice from pastoral staff that is not necessarily what departments would agree with.' So 'there must be close contact between departments and pastoral work'. In fact the time-tabling arrangements that would allow this are fraught with difficulties bordering on the impossible.

Departmentally, the issue that has been indicated is one of 'not purloining departmental staff for pastoral roles, which effectively diminishes the impact of the classroom programme'. The proposed resolution is 'an improvement in the balance' between 'academic and pastoral areas'. Enough has been said to indicate that this is only an area of marginal change. Pastoral staff are now seen as essential to the running of the school.

In the classroom the split becomes more apparent. 'Teachers are particularly deflected from the intense effort needed for *real* class-room teaching by too much superficial "office work".' Or again, 'we are expected to behave both as system-supportive civil servants *and* creative innovative teachers'. Others see it less as a question of creativity than as one of poor examination performance, the 'result of undervaluing the work of *teaching* and the needs of academic attainment'. The school may be well organized pastorally but the school is less successful, 'generally speaking, in academic arrangements and the curriculum'. This judgement, of course, may or may not be correct.

A similar contrast appears at the level of the form-tutor role. There is little real information on how form tutors actually functioned in unreorganized schools.[39] No doubt there is a tendency for retrospection to make individual memories more rosy. In some grammar schools the form tutor taught across a range of subjects in the first year so as to ease new pupils into secondary school.[40] In a secondary modern this pattern could continue into the second and third year as more generalist teachers were employed. Interestingly Dale points to the academic duties of a form tutor in teaching non-subject-specific general learning skills of reading and memorizing.[41] In an appeal for greater autonomy, one teacher echoed this, calling for 'a greater concentration of form teachers on the academic problems faced by pupils'.[42] This teacher goes on to refer to 'indoctrination'. In his turn, the Head put the emphasis on personal guidance:

> Some teachers do not fully appreciate the vital importance of the role. They see it as a daily chore of routines to be got through – registers, returns, passing on information, etc. To these, personal guidance is no more than another such chore; it all adds up to a 'dilution' of the purity of their 'real' purpose as subject teachers.

It may have been that the less routine form periods allowed for the kind of contact with teachers that several of them recall as one of the most important features of their own school life: in several cases to be in contact with subject staff in the area teachers now taught.

One quoted 'the presence of some caring science teachers'. Others talked more generally of 'help and guidance by certain teachers', or again 'certain teachers with whom I had very good relationships and who always encouraged me to try harder'. These kinds of pupil relations with staff do still exist, but the specification of form-tutor duties removes one occasion for their occurrence. The call for a re-emphasis on the academic may in part be due to a feeling that this is so.

A Final Comment

It would be invidious to finish without some tentative resolution of the problem of professionals within small bureaucracies. Given all that has been said about the way in which local pressures and complexities limit practice, it can only be done with a due sense of caution and hesitation. The temptation to prescription remains strong. But pessimism too needs to be avoided. In fact both schools in their own ways are already moving in the potentially less self-defeating but even more complex direction of curriculum change. Pastoral care which aims solely for control will be self-perpetuating in an unfortunate fashion. But pastoral care in the less extensive form of a team of senior pastoral staff is here to stay, for the reasons outlined. It might perhaps be better however if pastoral heads related and worked along with selected teams of tutors, say, in the first, third, and fifth years: in the first to help pupils' transition into secondary school, in the third to advise on option choices, and in the fifth to ease transition into work or on into the sixth form. They might still be the prime foci for parents, though perhaps joined more regularly by form tutors. They could usefully, as in School V, handle a personal guidance programme for all years, in order to get to know all pupils better. They would retain strong liaison with career staff, and so on. But if their deputies were removed they would be less easily available for dealing with routine discipline matters. The onus might well return more to departments. The administrative burden of pupil files in some form is also likely to remain. But it might prove a useful part of a probationary teacher's induction to be engaged on such a task, perhaps with a lessened teaching load. However, a clear need would emerge, we suggest, for appointments within curriculum areas, for staff with pastoral as well as academic responsibility. The precise duties of such, the dangers of overlap if the curriculum areas are departments or faculties, are obvious. But such an arrangement would keep staff identified primarily on the curricular side. Such appointments might create a sense of pastoral responsibilities within, say, a Department, many teachers of which will also be form tutors. Perhaps most importantly it would not, from a Head's point of view, dangerously decentralize pastoral care, but in turn might allow for a greater collegiality among those who have specific pastoral responsibilities. Like all such proposals this is only 'a thought'. Perhaps enough has been said to elucidate some of the underlying organizational factors that point in this direction. In any context, the design of a superb formal structure is only the first step along the path to adequate organizational practice.

References

1 The NFER studies (otherwise referred to in the text as the Monks studies) are (1) *Comprehensive Education in England and Wales*, ed. T. G. Monks (1968) (2) *Comprehensive Education in Action*, ed. T. G. Monks (1970) (3) *A Critical Appraisal of Comprehensive Education*, ed. J. M. Ross *et al* (1972).
These books form a general background to the chapter, but specific references will be found as follows:
   (a) Time-tabled periods and teaching load (1) p. 70, (2) p. 53
   (b) Ability intake into comprehensives (1) p. 26, (2) p. 63, (3) p. 32
   (c) Distribution of allowances by history and type of school (2) pp. 31-4
   (d) Duties of senior staff (2) pp. 40-1
   (e) Late tendency to horizontal systems (2) p. 40
There are of course more extensive references to a wide range of items including form tutors. These references here are simply signposts.

2 Mr Boyson's position seems to change, but M. Marland's insistence that pastoral care is not 'soft' is an argument made with the 'Black Paper' people in mind; see R. Boyson *The Crisis in Education* (Woburn Press, London, 1975) about the loss of the central function of good teaching.

3 'Stripped of all the romantic connotations, the pastoral staff in reality fulfils one of the basic functions of schooling: the disciplinary function necessary to the economy has become a separate category, divided from the academic, i.e. the skill and grading function.' Teachers Action No. 5, 1976; cf. also No. 3 for another article on Pastoral Care.

4 'School *does* Matter', *Right to Learn*, 1974.
This perspective is apparently similar to Rhodes Boyson's. But while both left and right advocate relatively minimal structures of pastoral care, they see this as having different educational and social outcomes. On the one hand there is the belief that pupils and teachers should achieve success without the *expectation* of large-scale pastoral support. While for the Right to Learn group it is the increased hierarchy associated with pastoral provision that reduces personal autonomy for both teacher and pupil, both no doubt would regard a lessened emphasis on learning as a luxury of those who have never had to make it or are a dominant group in society.

5 Principally, therefore, M. Marland, *Pastoral Care* (1974). But the article was also written after reading P. E. Daunt, *Comprehensive Values* (1975), and K. Blackburn, *The Tutor* (1975).

6 D. Hamblin, *The Teacher and Pastoral Care* (Blackwell, Oxford, 1978). It is important to note the dates of publication of books on pastoral care as later publications inevitably rely on earlier ones. In 1971 A. Rowe wrote on *The School as a Guidance Community* (Pearson Press, Hull, 1971). Hamblin, in a different tradition, also has a more developed position than that of the schools reported in Monks as to what pastoral care entails.

7 Hamblin, p. 140.

8 Hamblin, p. 19.
9 Hamblin, p. 17.
10 Hamblin, p. 16.
11 M. Holt refers to the educational debate conducted 'all too often' in terms of fashionable dichotomies: classical versus romantic; or subject-versus child-centred; or open versus closed; or the product versus the process. Much of this has been tiresome and unhelpful.' *The Common Curriculum* (Routledge & Kegan Paul, London, 1978), p. 27. A more analytic approach is available in 'Consultation and Educational Ideologies: some issues raised by research into children's judgements of teaching performance' by R. Meighan in L. Barton and R. Meighan, *Classrooms and Schooling: a critical reappraisal* (Nafferton, Driffield, 1978). It too questions the usefulness of such dichotomies, particularly in relation to the role of the teacher.
12 Marland, p. 205.
13 Marland, p. 10.
14 One reading of N. Bennett, *Teaching Styles and Pupil Progress* (Open Books, London, 1976) would suggest that structured progressivism is the most efficient form of teaching. What seems to be required is to have a well-grounded and differentiated view of the child as opposed to a vague and woolly one.
15 Marland, p. 12.
16 Marland, p. 204.
17 Marland, p. 10.
18 Marland, p. 12.
19 Cf. J. S. Coleman *The Adolescent Society* (Free Press, New York, 1961) and B. Davies, *Social Control and Education* (Methuen, London, 1976), pp. 148-50.
20 Marland, p. 2.
21 We hope to comment on pupils' perspectives more fully at a later date.
22 Marland, p. 5. It is a statement by the Reverend Boyer, Headmaster of Christ's Hospital, quoted in J. Morpurgo, *The Christ's Hospital Book* (Hamish Hamilton, London, 1953), p. xi. This is not perhaps the only influence from public schools on pastoral care. Harold Silver has noted the absence of corporal punishment in early monitorial schools: 'Aspects of Neglect: the Strange Case of Victorian Popular Education', *Oxford Education Review*, Vol. 3, No. 1, 1977. After noting the accounts in *The English Vice: beating, sex and shame in Victorian England and after* (Duckworth, London, 1978) one wonders whether the institutionalization of caning in state schools was an inheritance from the public schools via the school inspectorate, most of whom in the late nineteenth century came from public schools.
23 R. Gross, *British Secondary Schools* (Open University Press, Milton Keynes, 1965). Perhaps the most comprehensive collection of self-reports on different pastoral-care systems in public, grammar, secondary modern and comprehensive schools.
24 As the headmaster put it at the time, 'four different groups of people each with different histories, traditions, attitudes and age ranges were thrown together'. The fourth group were the newcomers who had been at none of the pre-existing schools.
25 A straight comparison on the same tests is not possible. IQ scores for the first year of entry as a secondary modern cateogirzed on a 10-20-40-20-10 percentage distribution (from low scores to high, left to right) were 2-23-71-3-0. In 1977-78 the first year intake on the NFER AH2/3 (general reasoning) scored 30-32-28-7-2. These differences cannot simply be the product of test differences. The number of pupils with a reading age of 9 or below on entry was about 26 per cent in 1977-78. The figures for School V were 3-10-43-

30-13 and 6 per cent for reading ages of 9 or below, though here on a different test than in School H.

26 Cf. Note 1, or more fully, DES *Statistics of Education Special Series Survey of the Curriculum and Deployment of Teachers: Secondary Schools (1965-6 part I)* (HMSO, 1968).

27 Cf. Note 1.

28 It has been suggested that teachers of non-academic subjects saw avenues of promotion in pastoral care. There was certainly evidence of this in School V.

29 Gerald Grace in *Teachers, Ideology and Control* (Routledge & Kegan Paul, London, 1978), p. 130, notes that a preponderance of those designated as 'outstandingly good teachers' by Heads of inner-city schools worked in the pastoral system. Good teachers were not characterized in terms of their professional pedagogic skills.

30 Hamblin (note 6), p. 6.

31 Heads frequently gather a disproportionate amount of the available opprobrium. Given their enormous formal powers in the British system they can be judged to be both cause and culprit in a way which overlooks the real constraints upon their possible actions. Similarly subject teachers can overlook the organizational pressures requiring some form of pastoral care.

32 P. M. Blau, W. V. Heydebrand, R. E. Stauffer, 'The Structure of Small Bureaucracies', *American Sociological Review* No. 31, 1966, p. 179. This article defines professionals as those having a degree. In sociological literature teachers are often considered to be semi-professionals, referring to a certain lack of autonomy. Certainly their autonomy in schools is generally limited to subject teaching as such. Issues such as school groupings policies, the overall curriculum, and as outlined here, school discipline, are reserved to senior management.

33 Cf. Blau *et al.* (1966) 'Yet if management seriously frustrates professionals in the exercise of their responsibilities, it not only courts the danger of dissatisfactions and defections from the organization but also fails to take advantage of an important resource at its disposal, which includes professionals' interest in perfecting operations as well as expert knowledge.' (p. 184).

34 A discussion document on *disruptive pupils* produced by a pastoral head began 'It is generally agreed that a favourable family background (particularly in pre-school years) has an important influence on satisfactory emotional development as well as on the development of specific intellectual skills. Aspirations of children can be closely linked with that of parents. If parents have low aspirations for their intelligent child, this can affect performance in school as well as behaviour.

Whilst it is dangerous to label and categorize humans, for the purpose of this discussion it may be helpful.' The last comment indicates that the teacher is not just generally naive.

35 R. King, in *School Organization and Pupil Involvement: a Study of Secondary Schools* (Routledge & Kegan Paul, London, 1973) comments directly on this, arguing that comprehensives were more ritualized than either the grammar schools or secondary moderns he surveyed. He also commented: 'similarly the formalization of pupils' activities also controls the teachers' (p. 138).

36 Quotations when unassigned are from subject teachers, including heads of department.

37 'Teaching in the Affluent Society', *British Journal of Sociology*, Vol. 13, 1962. Note also the comment from parents in Kirby, Liverpool. 'One of the criticisms that is made by many parents was that teachers were too friendly

with their children and that discipline (as judged by memories of their own school days) is slack': J. Mays *et al.*, *School of Tomorrow* (Longman, Harlow, 1968), p. 109.

38 Cf. the comment by Sir William Alexander, Secretary of the Association of Education Committees, quoted in *Teachers in Turmoil* by V. Burke (Penguin, Harmondsworth, 1971): 'In the last ten years very large numbers of young people have been poured into the profession so there is now a high proportion of teachers in the first five to ten years of teaching. Many have come through the universities at a very militant time in student politics. As a result, these new young entrants have been much more militant than their predecessors. Also, one gets the feeling that they were not quite so committed to teaching.' More recently there has been militancy in teacher training over closures. These anxieties can also extend to whether all teachers are capable or willing to teach the less able in comprehensive schools. Monk has found teachers themselves expressed most anxieties about their preparedness for teaching these groups. Cf. Note 1.

39 But in addition to R. Gross, see J. Walton (ed.) *The Secondary School Timetable* (Ward Lock, London, 1972), pp. 10-11, 45-46, for some of the time-table /curriculum reasons for the pastoral/academic divide.This is not perhaps receiving wider recognition over a range of issues. In another discussion of Ruffwood (Mays *et al.*, *The School of Tomorrow*, op. cit.) in E. Halsall, *On Becoming Comprehensive* (Pergamon, Oxford, 1970) it was stated that 'the fact that Ruffwood was purpose built for a house system was a condition in fact that appears to have led to a modified form of non-streaming so as to integrate both the social and academic aspects of the school life' (p. 267). In 1978 Maurice Holt however was arguing strongly that mixed-ability teaching was to be justified only on academic and not on pastoral grounds.

40 R. Dale, *Downstream* (Routledge & Kegan Paul, London, 1965), p. 62. Dale specifically mentions the form tutors need for a 'briefing from the Head' about any 'special cases', emphasizing the existence of what has here been called the traditional pattern of pastoral care.

41 R. Dale, p. 62.

42 R. Dale, p. 64.

15   The Language of Pastoral Care

Mike Taylor

Why Look at Language?

During recent years, the relationship between language and learning
in secondary schools has been explored and documented in some depth.
As a result of this there is now some general recognition in schools
that the kinds and quality of learning that pupils engage in across the
curriculum are closely related to the language opportunities they are
provided with, both as producers and receivers, in the classroom.
Moreover, since the publication of the Bullock Report, many secondary
teachers have been encouraged both to survey the language demands of
their discrete subject areas, and to reflect upon the uses made by
teachers and pupils of language-for-learning opportunities. Such activity
has often been enhanced by scrutiny of classroom data. Tape recordings,
pupils' writing and participant-observation of learning-in-action have all
been beneficial in focusing attention on the textures of teacher—learner
discourse and refining teachers' awareness of potentially problematic
aspects of language in use. Guidelines for this kind of classroom eth-
nography (see for instance Marland 1977 and Torbe 1976) are now
widely available, and continue to provide the basis for fertile curriculum-
policy discussion and documentation within schools

The purpose of this chapter is to provide a simple model for the
extension of such language-policy discussion into the area of pastoral
care. Although much of the work of pastoral-care tutors inevitably
involves the written word, the following analysis will be restricted
to face-to-face contact between tutors and pupils. I hope it will provide
a tentative but coherent framework within which tutors can monitor
and critically reflect upon those aspects of speech behaviour through
which many of the processes and functions of pastoral care are most
characteristically mediated. With the help of such a framework and the
support of tape-recorded examples, it is hoped that groups of tutors
may be encouraged to enrich their own informal in-service activity by

(i)   talking their way towards more perceptive and comprehensive
      insights concerning 'what goes on' during pastoral-care encounters
      and the types of talk they value in particular pastoral contexts;
(ii) refining their own listening by gaining a heightened awareness
      of those aspects of the communicative context that may influence
      and determine the kinds and quality of meaning transacted
      between pupils and tutors;

(iii)   feeding this awareness back into their individual pastoral activity
        and exercising a refined listener-reflexivity during the course
        of their everyday encounters with pupils.

As an illustration of the kinds of insight afforded by an investigation
of the language of pastoral care, the chapter includes a specific example
of pastoral-care in action, which is analysed in depth. Before proceeding
further, however, it might be beneficial to place this analysis in a
broader context by offering some general remarks about conversation,
learning and the school.

Making Sense of the World through Conversation

In everyday life, conversation serves a range of functions, but a particularly significant one is the role it plays in negotiating and validating
that sense of shared reality which forms the necessary social backcloth
to the acting out of our individual identities and endeavours. Chatting
and gossiping with friends and acquaintances we create and exchange
verbal representations and interpretations of aspects of experience
(both trivial and significant) — the performance of the local football
team; the cost of living; the current scandal. Often the people we
choose to chat with at any length are those whose systems of belief
and sentiment accord most closely with our own, and this mirroring of
viewpoints therefore offers us the close reassurance of confirming our
personal identity within a wider framework of social solidarity and
communality of feeling.

However, it is unusual for there not to be some divergence of opinion
in even the most socially supportive of friendly conversations, and once
alternative frames of reference are brought to bear upon our individual
interpretations of experience, the function of conversation, while
remaining socially cohesive, extends to the elaboration and improvisa-
tion of inter-subjective viewpoints. For instance, two friends talking
about the vagaries of a mutual acquaintance may differ somewhat
in the kinds of human sympathy, moral standpoints, or range of evidence they bring to bear upon their discussion of the matter. In this
circumstance they can either tacitly 'agree to differ' or, by suspending
their own viewpoint and 'taking the role of the other', place themselves in what is potentially a learning situation, enlarging their own
understanding and reconstruing their interpretation of events through
the alternative frames of reference offered by their partner in dialogue.
This aspect of everyday talk which allows the participants to mutually
reflect upon and assimilate experience has been termed by James
Britton 'spectator-role' talk. He argues that rather than being disparaging
about gossip and casual conversation we should reocgnize them as
fundamental psychological necessities (Britton 1972). Through daily
conversation we assume a mutual spectatorship upon aspects of our
own and each others' lives, thereby not only enlarging our repertoire

of potential experiences, but by 'revisiting' our own experiences from a wider range of reference points than are accessible to us in the 'here and now' of our everyday transactions, we can imbue them with richer significance and interpret them more comprehensively.

More simply, in our conversations with others we are repeatedly sharing the stories of our lives, fictionalizing our felt and lived-through experiences in an attempt to pin them down and validate their 'reality'. Sometimes while the narrative is familiar enough the meaning remains illusory. Conversation provides the necessary context for inviting collaborators to help us in the telling.

Conversation as Communicative Context

However much the enlargement of personal meanings assumes a major focus within any conversation, the communicative process demands that we also attend to the social dimensions of the task. In these terms, conversation involves the representation and communication of at least two different kinds of meaning. One kind of meaning is focused upon those ideas, observations, feelings or intentions we are giving utterance to; the second is focused upon the kind of emergent or ongoing relationship we perceive between ourselves and our participants in dialogue. The linguist Michael Halliday has termed such meanings 'ideational' and 'interpersonal', and the essentially polyphonic nature of language allows both of these themes to be stated and developed simultaneously in those more or less improvisatory exchanges we call 'talk' (Halliday 1973).

In any speech situation, therefore, the words we choose, the particular grammatical patterns we select to structure them, and the intonation, stress and paralinguistic patterns which reinforce or enrich meaning, are all orchestrated (Halliday's 'textual function') in response to our perception of the total context of communication in which we find ourselves. Moreover, as well as 'what we are talking about' and 'to whom', this total context also includes such inter-related features as 'why', 'when', and 'where'. Indeed, in extreme cases the 'why', 'when', or 'where' of a potential speech context may have such an overriding influence that the act of talking, however desirable, is precluded altogether (as in betraying compatriots under torture, during a two-minutes' silence, or standing outside the door of a recording studio).

Each speech situation, therefore, generates a certain range of expectations among its participants; expectations or hypotheses about the kind of language encounter in which they are engaged. Often these expectations are derived from previous experiences of similar encounters, and it is likely that the wider our social experience the wider will be the range of language resources we can draw upon to match the implicit demands of the different communicative contexts in which we find ourselves. In linguistic terms such a repertoire would be a reflection of our 'communicative competence' as individual speakers.

Thus, when people talk together, part of the process of constructing meaning is focused upon negotiating a reciprocal understanding of the social context in which the talk is operating. This involves its shifting functions, the relative status of the participants, their feeling responses to each other, and the relation of their speech acts to the wider context of linguistic and behavioural expectations operating in the surrounding physical and cultural environment.

Often, of course, during everyday conversation such reciprocity of perspective is not achieved. As speakers we sense that 'we didn't get ourselves across', that our 'intentions were misunderstood' or that we 'may have caused offence', though, more often, we are inclined through self-protection to blame our audience — 'he was totally unreasonable', 'they just couldn't understand'. Such breakdowns in communication can sometimes be explained by the fact that our linguistic responses to what we perceived to be a shared situational context did not completely match our audience's expectations. In other words, for each of us the situation 'triggered-off' different 'rules' of discourse. An equally valid explanation might also lie in the wilful undermining by one of the parties of such 'norms' of discourse as a signal of personal hostility or as an act of individual self-assertion. Such 'norms' are, of course, in no sense deterministic. Nevertheless, if the linguistic improvisations which we each play upon the theme of our individual authenticity extend too far beyond the harmonic frameworks of social expectation, mutual meaning-making inevitably flounders into the obscure or explodes into the discordant.

Learning, Conversation and the School

There are a number of reasons why this brief exploration of the themes of conversation, learning and communicative context provides a relevant backcloth to the investigation of pastoral care. For instance, if everyday conversation provides a means of organizing and making sense of experience, how can we, as pastoral-care tutors capitalize upon this potential on behalf of our pupils so that they are encouraged to talk their way towards a richer understanding of themselves and their school-related 'realities'? In theory it is a generally accepted prerequisite that, to be effective, pastoral care should take place in a relatively relaxed and conversational climate where pupils can make themselves known to a particular staff member as rounded individuals with individual gifts, hopes, aspirations and troubles. Again, in theory, this 'learning conversation' serves the dual function of affording the school richer insights into and necessary background information about pupils; while pupils through access to a sympathetic adult interlocutor are drawn into the verbal elaboration of those aspects of subjective meaning which focus on school-related matters, thus clarifying and illuminating their paths through the complexities of secondary schooling in particular and adolescent experience in general.

But how often does this happen? Conversations in school are often very different in kind and function from everyday conversations. For instance, conversations outside school are usually freely entered into by parties who accept or negotiate *en route* equality of status. So long as certain minimal proprieties are observed (they will of course be different proprieties depending upon the context of talk and the culturally derived expectations of the participants) conversation can peter out, be unilaterally broken off, or submit itself to the ebb and flow of rapidly changing purposes, perspectives and subject-matter. By contrast, school conversations are often teacher-instigated and the topics teacher-initiated. Moreover, the situation is also asymmetrical in terms of status, the tutor's residual authority as 'teacher' creating further imbalances. These and related aspects represent important features of the kinds of communicative context through which the purposes and meanings of teachers and pupils are necessarily filtered during the process of talking in school, a communicative context often quite different, in terms of the expectations it generates, from conversational contexts in the world at large.

Similarly, in the classroom learning situation, the dominant role of the subject teacher often so influences the communicative context that powerful constraints operate upon the kinds of language pupils can use and the kinds of meanings they can make and exchange with others. Of course, in cases of legitimate social control, this might be beneficial; nevertheless, the rules of normal classroom discourse as revealed by many studies (Flanders 1970, Bellack 1966, Barnes 1969, Sinclair and Coulthard 1975) reflect an endless litany of narrow intellectual and social orthodoxy rather than that individual elaboration and exchange of meaning through the 'transforming power of the word', which renders learning self-justifying and makes it one's own. Pupils in these contexts learn 'what it means to learn' in the largely non-negotiable terms the teacher offers them. 'Good' pupils fulfil the teacher's expectations − expectations implicit in his language, tone of voice, gestures, stance, and the way he receives pupils' replies. They take on wholesale the teacher's frames of reference and construction of the communicative context. 'Bad' pupils, on the other hand, reject the teacher's interpretation and play the language game deliberately against the rules. (Many other pupils probably spend several years puzzling over the nature and function of the rules themselves.)

In short, all our transactions with pupils are interwoven within a verbally mediated backcloth of social relations and institutional expectations. The very 'taken-for-grantedness' of these contexts, particularly by teachers themselves, often obscures their crucial importance in fostering or frustrating a communicative climate in which both they and their pupils can exchange those mutually significant meanings necessary to true learning. The competent but disillusioned teacher is, therefore, defeated not by his choice of what to teach, or by his ability to teach it, but by his unawareness. He has not seen that there are features of the school community in which he works, the boundaries it sets up, or its 'message systems' or its attitudes to learning or to language for learning which have come between him and his pupils. (Thornton 1974)

Mapping the Communicative Context of Pastoral Care

To what extent are the characteristics of classroom discourse equally attributable to pastoral care? How important is the total communicative context to the success of pastoral care? To what extent do our expectations and strategies as teachers foster or frustrate the exchange through such encounters of significant meanings? The remainder of this paper will focus upon such questions by identifying some of the essential features of those communicative contexts through which pastoral care characteristically operates. Figure 10 provides a simple framework for such a map, and as an illustration of its usefulness as a tool for reflection and discussion a particular example of pastoral care-in-action will now be analysed in some depth.

This example, which is transcribed in full at the end of the chapter, took place recently in an urban comprehensive school and involved the fourth-year tutor and Lorraine, a fourth-year pupil. With Lorraine's permission the tutor tape-recorded their conversation, having explained that it was for a friend 'interested in language in school'. The tutor also provided the following brief description of the encounter in the form of a spoken postscript to the tape.

> This recording is an interview with a fifteen-year-old girl whose mother had enquired about her at the end of last term, who was not known to me so I looked at her continuous assessment (C.A.) which we have once every half term and wrote a letter to her parent based on that continuous assessment. The interview was to follow up on the letter which established that she really wasn't getting along very well with her homework and there were one or two areas which she was having difficulty with. So it wasn't a heavy interview. It was in the nature of an enquiry; I was trying to find out what her difficulties were. Also to establish whether she was likely to stay on at school or when she would be leaving so that I could reply to the enquiry from the County about her train pass. The interview was fairly friendly. She was rather nervous at first about the tape and also rather aggressive about the fact that I had written to her mother I think. I got the impression that she started off rather aggressively but calmed down a little bit afterwards.

(Before proceeding further, readers are advised to turn to p. 244 where they can read the transcript in full.)

How?

The kinds of meanings transacted during the course of this conversation and the linguistic choices through which those meanings are encoded are represented by the 'HOW' of the model (Fig. 10) — that is, the message forms (both verbal and non-verbal) being exchanged by the participants. A great deal of this is represented in the transcript itself, though we must remember that without the key information provided by accent, intonation, stress, speed, voice quality and pause lengths the transcript is only a crude representation of the source material. Similarly, we are totally denied access to those vital non-linguistic features of communication such as gesture, posture, eye-contact and facial movement which interact so closely with linguistic meanings by reinforcing, contradicting or commenting upon them. The linguistic textures reflected in HOW are, therefore, a partial representation of the fluctuating efforts of two people to negotiate a degree of communality of perspective on their shared (and to some extent institutionally defined) situation while retaining their authenticity as individuals. This situation is defined for each speaker by the way they perceive, and the kinds of significance they ascribe to, those specific variables listed within each of the other boxes: About what? Why? Where? When? and to whom? and each of these will now be considered in turn.

About what?
The shifting spiral of themes within the conversation seems to cover the following topics:

(i)   Lorraine's mother (domestic/academic)
(ii) Problems with homework revealed by the continuous assessment report (academic/behavioural deviance)
(iii) Attitudes to class work (academic)
(iv) Irrelevance of 'school' knowledge/importance of passing exams (academic)
(v)   Necessary qualifications for nursing (career)
(vi) Problems with learning chemistry (academic/behavioural deviance)
(vii) Problems over homework. Lorraine's mother (academic/domestic) (interruption)
(viii)Information about bus pass (administrative/academic/career) (interruption)
(ix) Teacher's suggestions as to how to better the academic situation (academic/domestic/career)

Why?
The tutor described the encounter as 'in the nature of an enquiry' and this is borne out by the fact that she asks almost fifty questions (Lorraine asks four). A simple classification of the question is set out below (after Barnes 1969).

(i)   Eighteen questions asking for factual information

  e.g. 'Who do you have for chemistry?'
       'Have you got somewhere where you can sit and write OK . . .?'

In a pastoral-care context factual questions are likely to vary in

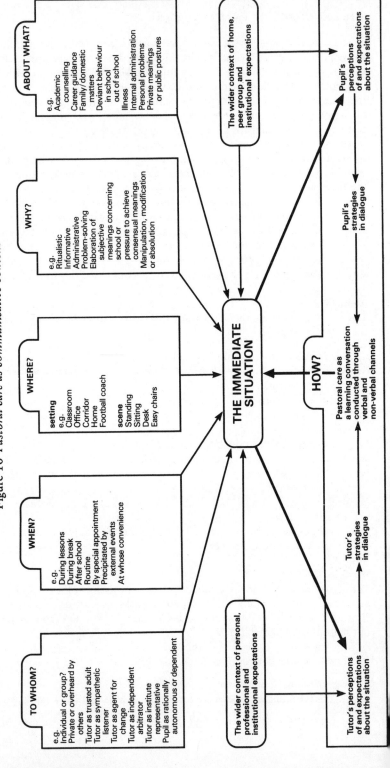

Figure 10 *Pastoral care as communicative context*

'key' from 'questioning' to 'probing'. This is a significant factor since some questions will clearly infringe upon a pupil's personal space more than others. If the tutor hasn't legitimized the right to ask questions directed at more personal areas of experience (home, family life, affective state) then answers are unlikely to be forthcoming. Similarly, where answers to such questions are likely to prove incriminating in any case, direct answers will be avoided. Questions may then be repeated or reframed in a manner which is interrogational rather than conversational.

(ii) Twelve apparently 'open' questions inviting elaboration of the pupil's subjective viewpoint

> e.g. 'Well what do you mean she's getting worse?'
> 'Do you think that is a fair assessment of you?'

Questions in this category appear to offer genuine opportunities for students to elaborate upon their subjective interpretations of school events in the role of spectator, thereby enhancing the potential of the context as a 'learning conversation'. Nevertheless they are often defensively interpreted in context as invitations to justify deviant attitudes or behaviour, as in

> T 'So . . . what happens in class work . . .'
> L 'Yeah but that Maths teacher you can't do nothing.'

Thus, however friendly a tutor may appear, his residual role as teacher and representative of school values may initially create an asymmetrical situation which provokes defensive postures. The extent to which this asymmetry is rectified will depend upon the kind of audience the tutor is offering (see 'To whom', p. 237).

(iii) Thirteen semi-'closed' questions, often tag questions, inviting shared agreement with the tutor's frames of reference and interpretations

> e.g. 'Then it just . . . gets into the mess it's in *now* doesn't it?'
> 'Well that doesn't get you very far young lady does it?'

(iv) Three semi-'closed' questions inviting the pupil to make a contractual-like statement about future action

> e.g. 'Have you talked to Mr Y at all about it?'
> 'No, I haven't.'
> 'Well, don't you think you might?'
> 'Um, so what can you do about that?'

Both of these question-types seem directed towards the shaping of behaviour. The extent to which they are 'invitations' or 'demands' and the degree to which they are open to challenge by the pupil will, again, depend upon the kind of person the tutor is projecting herself as. Often pupils' answers to such questions signal grudging acquiesence to the language-rules of a game which is heavily weighted in the tutor's favour (the 'hidden curriculum' of pastoral care). They give the 'right' answer (as we might suspect, Lorraine repeatedly does towards the end of the encounter), the behaviour modification thus indicated seldom going any deeper than the shaping of surface verbal behaviour.

(v) Two 'soft' directives — standard polite ways of directing behaviour —

e.g. 'Can you sit yourself down?'

This brief analysis of the tutor's questions demonstrates that although the primary purpose of the encounter was conceived of as 'enquiry', its function extends well beyond the finding out of information or the exploration of the pupil's perception of affairs. This is also endorsed by the tutor's non-question contributions, the functions of which can be crudely categorized as follows (after Mitchell and Cangemi, 1977):

(i) *Understanding and accepting* This includes any utterance in which the tutor signals sympathy, understanding of the pupil's situation, or acknowledges the validity of a viewpoint.

e.g. L The exam paper's a waste of time . . .
     T Might well be . . . I mean there's a lot of people would agree with you.

(ii) *Explaining and informing* Here the tutor provides background information to clarify the context of the talk or other specific information relevant to the pupil's needs.

e.g. T Well, what happened, see, was that when I got the enquiry I looked at the last continuous assessment . . .

(iii) *Restating, clarifying and interpreting* If we subscribe to the view that one of the principle purposes of pastoral care is to structure opportunities for pupils to make better sense of themselves and their school and school-related activities through 'learning conversations' with empathetic adults, then this category of tutor talk is crucial. Here the tutor mediates between the pupil's perceptions of himself, the home—school 'realities' in which he operates and possible alternative constructions and interpretations of these realities. This process of mutual 'reconstruing' comes close to Kelly's model of the psychotherapeutic interview (Kelly 1955) from which Britton gained illumination in his exploration of specta-tor-role talk (Britton 1972). In this encounter the tutor some-times mediates between alternative interpretations of a shared reality:

> T   See I mean after all if you think about it Lorraine . . .
> um you know its *your* maths lessons. They're not for
> the teacher, not for your Mum —

She sometimes points to inconsistencies in Lorraine's reasoning:

> T   No, you're more or less saying to yourself well I can't
> be bothered with them, therefore I can't be bothered
> to . . . er take the exams, therefore, erm, erm I am
> saying I can't be bothered to enter nursing.

On other occasions she engages in a kind of 'Rogerian' debate, trying on what she perceives to be Lorraine's viewpoint and limit-testing it by deliberate overstatement.

> T   You know in a sense Lorraine what you are saying is
> you're sitting back in the chair and you're saying
> 'OK teacher, . . . interest me.' Aren't you really?

(iv)   *Directing, advising and moralizing*   As well as those questions which serve as semi-directives, other contributions endorse the feeling that as this encounter progresses its emphasis upon direct influence becomes increasingly marked. The tutor repeatedly impresses upon Lorraine the need to make the most of classwork and 'sort out the homework situation' and suggests some specific strategies for doing this.

'Just tell him why you haven't been doing your homework.'
'You've got to say "All right, so my mum's nagging me but it doesn't really matter" . . . '

In summary, the 'why' of this communicative situation as enacted by the participants points towards a complex multi-functionality in which a combination of sympathetic enquiry and direct influence on the part of the tutor is a high priority. From Lorraine's perspective the functions of the encounter are more difficult to postulate since, unlike real conversation, she was neither a co-initiator of it, nor of equal status within it. Nevertheless she seems to perceive it as

(i)   an opportunity to express her true feelings about her mum,
   particular teachers and the curriculum in general with an
   impunity which would doubtless have been denied her within
   those contexts.

(ii)   a confrontation of viewpoints in which she tenaciously resists
   any suggestion that she herself is responsible for what the
   teacher defines as 'the situation'.

Thus, although she exercises within the supportive framework of the discussion a range of linguistic freedoms possibly denied her elsewhere (a therapeutic function maybe), she does not accept the situation as one in which to seriously reconstrue her position through a 'learning conversation'. We might ask ourselves whether this is

(i)   a product of the situation itself
(ii)   a product of experience of teacher—pupil talk in school at large
(iii) a product of wider linguistic allegiances.

In fact although we don't *know*, it is possible that in contrast to the tutor's account of the talk as 'enquiry' Lorraine may well have legitimately regarded it as a 'telling off' or 'warning about homework'.

Where?

The physical setting is often a significant factor in constraining or facilitating different kinds of talk. Not all of us respond to such potential constraints in the same manner. Nevertheless, few of us would shout across the interior of a church unless dire necessity demanded it. The geography of furniture often works in concert with the formality of a particular speech situation and provides additional signals as to the status of the participants. Desks, the distribution of chairs, enforced standing and sitting postures and the surrounding decor can signify ease, confidentiality, formality or dominance, and such signals inevitably influence the kind and quality of the ensuing talk. In school terms we recognize that disciplinary matters are often signalled by markers of different status (pupil standing in prepared spot—teacher sitting) and by a symbolic décor reflective of institutional authority and stability (study, desk, photographs, sports cups). On the other hand, more personal meetings are often transacted more readily in a climate of physical relaxation where reciprocity of status among the participants can be negotiated (football coach, coffee bar, workshop).

Lorraine's interview took place in the fourth-year office. The tutor sat at her desk and Lorraine sat beside her next to the electric fire. It was very cold. No one else was present in the office but the accessibility of the tutor meant that the conversation was punctuated by two interruptions. The second of these was possibly crucial, since Lorraine seems to be approaching a revelatory outburst just as Sandra comes in

'I'm getting so fed up with all of it. I'm fed up with everything at the moment. Everything's boring that I do.'

The interruption aborts the development of this theme and allows the tutor to shift the topic at the point of resumption to a purely administrative one.

When?

The conversation took place in school time and had been previously arranged by appointment. It was tutor-initiated and was a direct product of an enquiry made by Lorraine's mother about her half-term continuous assessment report. The 'when' dimension could be an important contributory factor in the dialogue for a number of reasons. The timing may affect the duration of the talk. The elaboration of inter-subjective intent and a rich exchange of personal meaning is only likely to occur in circumstances unthreatened by the conversation's sudden curtailment. If one of the participants feels threatened or inconvenienced by the timing, discussion will not be entered into or sustained so freely. Conversely, in some circumstances, pressures of time may precipitate the 'head-on' confrontation of issues which in more leisurely circumstances could be more adequately prepared for. Also if such meetings take place outside school time this could in some circumstances carry connotations of being kept behind as a punishment.

To whom

(i) The tutor as audience

We have noticed that the functions of this pastoral-care conversation extend well beyond the bounds of 'enquiry'. The tutor spends a lot of the time informing, explaining, contradicting, advising and directing. Also some of the questions she frames and her evaluative responses to Lorraine's answers interact with her residual status as teacher and representative of institutional norms to shape the nature of Lorraine's responses towards desired goals. To this extent her behaviour mirrors that often observed of teachers during 'normal' classroom discourse.

However, there are also significant ways in which she diverges from the norms of teacher–learner discourse. For instance, she tolerates and even tacitly endorses criticism of certain colleagues. In offering advice she focuses her appeal on practical strategies and the learner's personal interests rather than on conformity, social obligation or institutional loyalty: for example, 'you've got to be more *selfish* about it'. In these and other ways she is presenting herself to Lorraine as a particular kind of audience; taking the role of 'trusted adult' (Britton 1975) rather than institutional representative or judge. How else does she try to negotiate the kind of informal social relationship which will encourage a rich exchange of meanings between tutor and learner? Is she successful? What kinds of affective information does the language carry about the kind of social encounter this is?

One immediate and striking feature to those who listen to the recording of the conversation is the incidence of 'downward convergence' in accent on the part of the tutor. As linguists have demonstrated (Labov 1966) it is characteristic of speakers to signal informality of social context and warm affectivity both by a perceptible 'broadening' of accent/dialect features and by a degree of 'matching' in accent pitch, voice quality and speech style. (Apart from the ubiquitous 'yeah' this is impossible to represent in the transcript.) The tutor's accent and voice quality are closely matched to Lorraine's during much of this discussion (they both originate from the same area of

London) although interestingly, again, in confirmation of empirical findings, the tutor's more formal summary recorded for me at the end of the tape conforms much more closely to received pronunciation.

Similarly, but from a grammatical point of view, the tutor's speech includes instances of mazes, false starts, fillers, hesitations and convoluted syntax in proportions which may well test the credibility of readers unfamiliar with transcriptions of everyday speech.

> 'So really in a way there's a certain . . . how can I say . . . re . . . not so much a responsibility, perhaps that, but if you like I mean I would like to be able to say to you and to some of the others, well . . .'

Such features are characteristic of what has been termed the 'consultative' style of speech (Joos 1961). This lies in the middle of a spectrum of styles or 'keys' of discourse each of which reflects the degree of formality of context or social distance perceived by the participants. The predominance of the consultative style here is a reflection on the tutor's part of the collaborative nature of the enterprise as she sees it. The false starts and 'loose' syntactical structure share two functions. Firstly, they suggest that some of the tutor's contributions are being thought through at the point of utterance and that she is not merely rehearsing a set of ritual platitudes. An example of this is in her reply to Lorraine's rather aggressive assertion that the exams are a waste of time. The tutor seems anxious to formulate a response to this which acknowledges the partial validity of Lorraine's viewpoint, while pointing to the practical advantages of mathematics in real life. Her language reflects this process of 'thinking on her feet'.

> 'Might . . . might well be . . . I mean there's a lot of people would agree with you on that er you know there's a lot of people say what . . . at least Maths to some extent is er of some practical use . . .'

A second function served by many of these features is that of stylistically reinforcing a sense of tentativeness which will invite some degree of qualification from the partner in dialogue. The 'trusted adult's' viewpoint, unlike teacher assertion, is relative and thereby open to a degree of challenge. Perhaps this is why Lorraine feels it legitimate, in terms of signalled status, to interrupt the tutor several times with her own alternative constructions of her 'school reality'.

Yet another interesting feature of the tutor's speech is the repetitive use of phrases indicating 'sympathetic circularity' ('see'; 'you know') a feature first associated by Bernstein with the use of the restricted code (Bernstein 1971). They may of course be little more than fillers, but cumulatively they seem to act as repeated appeals to Lorraine for confirmation of a shared sense of context and communality of purpose.

Finally the episode is introduced and completed by references to the cold weather which seem to acknowledge the essential equality of the two participants in the wider context of humanity. The teacher's initial 'ugh', presumably accompanied by appropriate grimaces and gesticulations, is referred back to in the final signing off. These simple friendly utterances at the casual/intimate end of Joos' spectrum underline the institutional role-play of the encounter itself and place it in its proper context.

> T You got cold hands?
> L Yeah.
> T Mm I got cold toes . . .
> L Yeah.
> T See you.

(ii) The tutor as listener

Over and above the perceived necessity to present oneself in such audience roles as non-assertive, trusting or authoritative, a pastoral-care tutor must also be a 'good listener'. Close listening ensures that maximum meaning and significance are being derived from what is being said, and, equally important, that those aspects of subjective meaning, the articulation of which might prove particularly beneficial in helping the pupil to make sense of his experience, are focused and sustained through the tutor's questioning strategies (Tough 1979).

Such listening with understanding is a highly active process. Rather than passively 'reading off' the semantic content of messages as they are sequentially delivered through syntax and speech sounds to the ear, the listener actively projects into the emergent meanings of the speaker as they are articulated at the point of utterance. He samples and scans the spoken output, testing it against his own predictions about what is going to be said; predictions which are confirmed or modified in the light of the unfolding information. Where prediction is confounded he is then most likely to interrupt the flow, and by taking over the role of speaker, seek clarification.

In a pastoral-care context we might, therefore, assume that a 'good' listener is someone with sufficiently wide frames of reference and empathetic insights to assume, however temporarily, the interpretative frameworks, value-systems and modes of construing of a partner in dialogue. This capacity for empathetic projection enhances the opportunity for correct prediction and rich comprehension and maximizes feedback to the speaker in the form of those relevant comments and questions which assure him that he is being understood.

Part of the art of listening also lies in reading those complex meanings which often lie behind superficially simple utterances.

Behind every thought there is an affective-volitional tendency which holds the answer to the last 'Why' in the analysis of thinking. A true and full understanding of another's thought is possibly only when we understand its affective-volitional basis . . . to understand another's speech it is not suffic'ent to understand his words — we must understand his thought. But even that is not enough — we must also know its motivation. (Vygotsky 1962)

From this perspective the act of comprehension involves the penetration of a veil of words to seek the subtext of thought which lies behind them. As we listen we are not only projecting into linguistic meaning but posing the question 'what does the speaker *really* mean?' Each utterance has to be cumulatively glossed or translated and the clues which provide the keys to meaning are often to be found in those paralinguistic and non-verbal signals which operate alongside, instead of, or in counterpoint with language itself. Voice quality, eye contact, facial and bodily gesture, posture and proxemic behaviour, all provide a range of cues to which we respond as listeners in our efforts to comprehend the 'affective-volitional' basis of other people's speech.

At the beginning of Lorraine's interview we can, perhaps, glimpse some of these complex processes at work. How are we, as listeners, to interpret Lorraine's comments about her mother? Clearly, their subtext is far richer in significance than the words themselves. It seems as if Lorraine is seizing the initiative by testing the tutor's trust and negotiating an understanding of the kind of encounter she is engaged in (the presence of the tape-recorder may also have exacerbated this challenge). In these terms a part of the meaning of 'she's nosey, she always wants to know what's going on' might be glossed as follows:

'Where do we stand? Whose side are you on? Are you likely to be sympathetic to my side of the situation? How much unbridled personal opinion will you tolerate? Will you feel obliged to side with my mother (or authority in general) against me?'

It is arguable that the tutor herself seizes something of this complex of meanings. Her comment that she thought Lorraine 'was rather aggressive about the fact that I had written to her mother' is significant in this respect, and also in her hesitant response 'well that may well be . . . so . . .' she is anxious to avoid passing judgement, defusing the situation with genuine, though somewhat nervous, laughter.

Whether or not this suggested 'reading' is true is beside the point. The only valid meanings of the encounter are those which the participants themselves are negotiating as the conversation proceeds. Nevertheless this brief example serves to indicate the enormous complexity involved even in 'conversational' listening and helps to explain why pastoral care and counselling activities are often far more tiring than teaching, where (lamentably perhaps in most cases) listening on the part of the teacher is a relatively under-used skill.

The wider contexts of language in use
The preceding pages have summarized some of the essential landmarks which between them stake out the linguistic territory of pastoral care. However, the picture is incomplete without brief reference to the

wider linguistic allegiances that participants might bring to any situation, allegiances that add yet another dimension to the relative ease with which they can share significant meanings. For example, for many adolescent pupils, that verbal elaboration of subjective intention and personal meaning which has been suggested as one of the implicit demands of pastoral care may elsewhere be a low-priority function of language and one for which they feel particularly ill-prepared. There may be a number of reasons for such potential inadequacy outside those generated within the immediate context itself. One may be that the characteristic patterns of language which the child has experienced at home may have precluded from an early age opportunities for the verbal elaboration of intersubjective meanings (Bernstein 1971, Tough 1974). Such pupils may, therefore, have little experience of 'learning conversations' in a domestic context on which to base their expectations about the nature and function of this kind of discourse. Similarly, the school subject curriculum as enacted at secondary level often does little before sixth-form level to encourage the verbal formulation and elaboration of individual learning or the testing out of higher-order thinking strategies through 'expressive' talk (Rosen 1972); and those 'learning conversations' examined by Barnes in his analysis of collaborative learning activities are sadly still a rare phenomenon indeed (Barnes 1976). Thus, irrespective of the more favourable situaton in terms of teacher—pupil ratio and any shift in functions of the talk, both pupils and tutors engaged in pastoral care may well cling onto those verbal strategies more widely reinforced through their roles in the curriculum at large (e.g. teacher as interrogator; pupil as agenda-guesser).

Another interesting linguistic allegiance has been highlighted by Rutherford, who shows that irrespective of their normal fluency and penetration as individual speakers many adolescents may not choose to talk analytically about certain key aspects of experience. He suggests that any topics which lie close to adolescent preoccupation, particularly those susceptible to fantasy, will become temporarily 'unanalysable'. That is, their only linguistic representation will be through a covert and semi-secretive argot characterized by non-logical, imprecise language. There is a difference between this and adult expectation.

> . . . not because the basic 'rules' are different, but because the language refers to unanalysed concepts in an alien but related sub-culture which has its own set of totems. An adolescent going through a sullen silent stage may be suffering a particularly painful form of the bi-culturalism which afflicts exiles. How can one talk about totems in a way that will appeal to adult logic? (Rogers 1976)

It may well be the case that Lorraine's repeated and typically adolescent use of the words 'boring' and 'stupid' fall into this category, concealing, but hinting at, a far more complex sense of *anomie*.

Finally, the tutor, too, may have wider linguistic allegiances which preclude him from taking up all of the options in discourse hitherto suggested. For instance, if the linguistic climate of the school is one in which friendliness towards pupils, humour and casual conversation are construed as threatening the foundation of 'good' discipline, then tutors are more likely to operate pastoral care from a standpoint of greater linguistic formality and wider social distance. Similarly, in such circumstances, the highly articulate pupil whose language reflects a refined sense of individuality of viewpoint may be seen as institutionally threatening or getting dangerously 'above himself'. Clearly, neither of these is the case in the present example, where the tutor's questions and advice, however insistent, are offered within a skilfully contrived climate of warmth and friendly informality.

Summary

By providing this linguistic commentary upon a particular example of pastoral care it has been my intention not so much to produce case-study 'research' insights, but rather to offer tutors a detailed agenda for their own in-service activity and reflection. A further list of questions for consideration is now appended to provide a clearer focus for the discussion of teachers' own tape-recorded examples.

About what?
Which topics lie within or outside the legitimate concerns of pastoral care?

Which particular topics might be construed as legitimate by a tutor but not so by the pupil? Would this be true for all tutors or pupils? What about topics initiated by the pupil?

Why?
What do tutors' questions reveal about their own purposes in pastoral-care situations?

What do pupils' answers reveal about theirs?

Do pupils ever interpret pastoral encounters as opportunities to elaborate their own subjective viewpoints about themselves and 'school' realities? What evidence is there of spectator-role talk or the thinking through of insights?

Is there a 'hidden curriculum' within pastoral care?

How does the language the participants use reveal it?

Where?
How often do pastoral-care encounters whose function includes the elaboration of personal meanings in a climate of confidentiality and trust take place in counterproductive physical environments? Where accommodation is limited, how do we make the best of a bad job?

When?
How often are pastoral-care conversations

    (i)   routine or time-tabled events?
   (ii)   precipitated by external factors?

    (iii) tutor-initiated?
    (iv) pupil-initiated?

To whom?
In what ways do the parties concerned signal their relative status during pastoral care? How appropriate are these messages to the functions of the encounter?
What kind of audience is the tutor presenting himself as?
What affective links underpin the relationship, and how are these negotiated?
To what extent may false expectations have distorted our listening?
What aspects of meaning become accessible at a second hearing which were not 'heard' during the conversation itself? Why might this be?
Which particular pupil utterances seemed to have the most powerful sub-textual meanings?

The wider context
In what ways does the language climate of the school at large support or subvert our attempts to create appropriate communicative contexts for pastoral care?
What other aspects of 'linguistic allegiance' may be operative factors?

By analysing their own pastoral-care encounters in terms of these various dimensions of the context, tutors can adopt a critical yet positive perspective on their performance of this important aspect of their roles.

References

Barnes, D., *From Communication to Curriculum* (Penguin, Harmondsworth, 1976).
Barnes, D., *et. al. Language, the Learner and the School* (Penguin, Harmondsworth, 1969).
Bellack, A., *et. al. The Language of the Classroom* (Teachers College Press, New York, 1966).
Bernstein, B., *Class, Codes and Control*, Vol. 1 (Routledge and Kegan Paul, London, 1971).
Britton, J., *Language and Learning* (Penguin, Harmondsworth, 1972).
Britton, J., *et. al. The Development of Writing Abilities (11-18)* (Macmillan, London, 1975).
Flanders, N., *Analysing Teacher Behaviour* (Addison-Wesley, London, 1970).
Halliday, M. A. K., *Explorations in the Functions of Language* (Edward Arnold, London, 1973).
Joos, M., *The Five Clocks* (Harcourt Brace, New York, 1961).
Kelly, G. A., *The Psychology of Personal Constructs* (Norton, New York, 1955).
Labov, W., *The Social Stratification of English in New York City* (Centre for Applied Linguistics, Washington, 1966).
Marland, M. (ed.), *Language Across the Curriculum* (Heinemann, London, 1977).
Mitchell, D. W., and Cangemi, J. P., 'Interactional Analysis and the Counselling Interview' in *College Student Journal Vol II*, August 1977.
Rosen, H., *Language and Class* (Falling Wall Press, Bristol, 1972).
Rogers, S., *They Don't Speak our Language* (Edward Arnold, London, 1976).
Sinclair, J. M., and Coulthard, R. M., *Towards an Analysis of Discourse* (Oxford University Press, 1975).

Thornton, G., *Language, Experience and the School* (Edward Arnold, London, 1974).

Torbe, M., *Language Across the Curriculum: Guidelines for Schools* (Ward lock, London, 1976).

Tough, J., *Focus on Meaning* (Allen and Unwin, London, 1974).

Tough, J., *Report of 7-11 Schools Council Project* (in preparation) 1979.

Vygotsky, L. S., *Thought and Language* (Wiley, New York, 1962).

Lorraine's Interview with the Fourth-Year Tutor

T   Lorraine?
    Ugh (indicating the coldness of the room) Can you shut the door?
    (indistinct) Can you sit yourself down?
    Couple of things. First of all . . . um . . . I can't remember what prompted your mother to phone up.
L   She's nosey, she always wants to know what's going on —
T   (Interrupts) No (laughs) (pause) well that may well be . . . so . . . but . . . um . . . she phoned up about something quite . . . incidental . . . er . . . er . . . I think it was . . . maybe it was to give her . . . her business work number.
L   No she had to come and get me didn't she because I wasn't well —
T   Oh that's right.
L   and she saw you in the hall so she asked you if she could have a report on me.
T   No, she phoned me up. I spoke to her on the phone.
L   Did she?
T   Yeah. Well I didn't speak to her, she spoke to one of the secretaries.
L   Oh she's getting worse.
T   Well what do you mean she's getting worse?
L   She's always nosey, she's always trying to find out what I'm doing.
T   Well don't you think it concerns her what you're doing?
L   Not really.
T   No? Why not?
L   Well it's up to me isn't it.
    (Short pause)
T   Do you think she's interested in what you're doing?
    (Short pause)
L   Not really.
T   Well, she, she enquiries about you so that shows some interest doesn't it?
L   She usually does that so that she can get annoyed with me when she finds out there's something wrong.
T   Well did you see the letter?
L   Yeah.
T   So you know what was said.
    Well what happened, see, was that when I got the enquiry I looked at the last continuous assessment and as far as I was concerned um . . . there was nothing else that I could go on because I've not had . . . er . . . you know any kind of conversation with any members of staff about you, you know you just seemed to be getting along OK. And then when we looked at it, when I looked at it . . . um I don't know if Mrs X had spoken to you about your C.A. — had she?
L   Yeah.
T   Yeah well now there seems to be a couple of . . . problems with it. The one area that seemed to show up on quite a lot of them was the fact that you're

not really doing your homework.

(Slight pause)

L It's too boring.

T What, the homework's boring?

L Yeah, all of it's boring.

T The lessons are boring.

L Yeah.

T You're fed up with it generally.

L Yeah.

T So . . . what happens in class work, see, I mean look, er, it says like for Maths 'poor work and behaviour and homework'.

L Yeah but that Maths teacher you can't do nothing. All the others are all mucking about you can't hear what she's saying, and she always picks on us anyway we're sat up the back all the girls you know all my mates we're all sat up the back so whenever something goes wrong she always shouts and points at us (Teacher laughs) and everyone else is doing the things and so we can't hear what she's saying so we don't know we're supposed to be doing.

T Well why do you all go and sit up the back? Why don't you sit at the front where you *can* hear?

L Cause that's where the people are all mucking about.

T But you're *not* mucking about.

L We sit and talk cause we can't hear what she's saying anyway.

T So you sort of abandon it.

L Yeah . . . that's be the word for it.

T Well that doesn't really help does it?

L (Quietly) No.

T It's . . . it's very difficult . . . I know those kind of situations . . . but if you're in a class you know where people are mucking about if you must sit and natter as well it makes it really impossible for anything to happen doesn't it. I mean I *know* that that difficulty exists. You haven't told me who that teacher is but I known from your description who it is because I know, I've had the same conversation with several other people who say that they can't get on in the lessons either. So really in a way there's a certain . . . how can I say . . . re . . . not so much a responsibility, perhaps that, but if you like I mean I would like to be able to say to you and to some of the others, well, you know if you could do your bit to see that you're not mucking about and not talking, you know, when you shouldn't be then at least the people who are moderately well behaved like you, you know, can be getting on with something and then it only leaves the teacher to worry about, you know, the real people who mess about a lot but if *you* just abandon it and all the other kind of people who get on with you, you know, *sort* of get on don't make any attempt even then it just kind of gets in the mess it's in *now* doesn't it?

L Um, yeah.

T See I mean after all if you think about it Lorraine . . . um you know it's *your* maths lessons. They're not for the teacher, not for your Mum —

L (interrupts) Yeah but the stuff we're doing is so stupid. You don't need it. I mean when am I going to know want to know how to make the . . . what is it . . . percentages into decimals. I'm never going to use that. I don't see the point in doing half the stuff we do. There's no use to it and drawing pretty pictures and putting in nodes and three joins. Ugh! Phugh! That's more like an art lesson than a maths lesson. It's stupid. It's a waste of time.

T   Well . . . it has one distinct application which is not at all that much of a waste of time and that is . . . that it serves so that you can answer the questions that are on the exam paper.

L   The exam paper's a waste of time an' all then if that sort of thing's on it.

T   Might . . . might well be . . . I mean there's a lot of people would agree with you on that er you know there's a lot of people say what . . . at least Maths to some extent is er of some practical use to you you know, I mean when you're at work or perhaps you know when you've —

L   (interrupts) I could understand with normal maths you know the multiplying and taking away and all that sort of thing. You use that. But all this square roots and everything. Unless you're gonna go into a specialized subject which you take a course in it anyway to do that specialized subject you don't need it. I don't see the point in doing it.

T   Well as I say you know all right if if you accept that then the point that you must accept that there is in doing it for *you personally* because you're not going to go into it as a specialized subject is so's you can pass the exam, and that's just the same as the reasons for doing all the other subjects that you do.

L   (Pause) Yeah.

T   Because you know we live in a world where people say you know you have to have a piece of paper proving how good you are . . . to get a job . . . or . . . you know to get an opportunity of a job. You know the old thing. If there's five people up for an interview say for a secretarial job or something and one person has got a you know a whole range of examination subjects they automatically stand a better chance even if the five people might all be of the same ability.

L   (Pause) Yeah.

T   Have you thought about what you're going to do when you leave school?

L   Going to do nursing.

T   Well you see I mean nursing is . . . is a classic example you can't get anywhere in nursing without passing your exams.

L   (Pause) Umm.

T   I mean you have to have passes you know er CSEs and 'O' levels to get *in* and then when you're in you have to go through exams all the way through don't you. So you *know* that however stupid it might seem that the exams —

L   (Interrupts) Yeah but when it comes to that . . . I don't mind working for something that I'm going to use I'm going to need but when it comes to subjects I don't think I'm going to use or nothing then I can't be bothered with them.

T   No, you're more or less saying to yourself well I can't be bothered with them, therefore I can't be bothered to . . . er take the exams, therefore erm erm I am saying I can't be bothered to enter nursing.
(Pause)

L   No not really. All I'm saying is I'll I'll work for the things that I know I'll need . . . but anything that I think is unnecessary for me I won't bother with.

T   Well you're going to need . . . five . . . good passes to get into nursing aren't you . . . I think . . . I'm not sure.

L   Don't know.

T   What are you going to do between the time you leave school er well you know I mean like the end of the fifth year and . . .

L   Don't know I don't want to get a job though. I don't think it's worth getting a job for two years.

T Would you want to go to college and do a pre-nursing course?

L Yes something like that.

T Well you could do that either at school in the sixth form or you could go to college.

L I want to get a very good biology them sort of things you know and chemistry if I can and I want I wanted to take an 'A' level in them if ever I got good enough you know get an 'A' level in them two so I want to stay on and go to a college or something like that.

T Aha . . . well you'll need also English and Maths.

L Um.

T And you'll probably need a couple of other things as well at least one other if you've got biology chemistry English and Maths I think you'll find you need five —

L (Long pause) Um.

T — really. So I mean you know . . . but look you see it says 'Chemistry'. Ah, 'Improved classwork, poor homework'.

L Yeah but I don't understand a lot of things they're going on about I get sort of left behind you know. In chemistry they give you an experiment to do. They give you a worksheet and you have to write down off the worksheet, do the experiment and write up on the experiment. I don't get enough time to get it all finished . . . 'cause it takes me half an hour. I read all the worksheet copy out a lot of the stuff off the worksheet and I got to do the experiment, takes you something like a half-hour to do that. Then you've got to write down all the results from the experiment and I don't get the time to finish it and then (laughing) I get into trouble for not doing the experiments.

T Yeah, who do you have for chemistry?

L Um . . . Mr Y I think.

T Um is . . . I mean are your friends in the same position are other people in the class in the same position?

L Yeah.

T Or is it —

L You know some people manage to get it done you know people who work really fast or something like that but the people I sit with and myself I don't get it done and they don't get it done either I mean without having to copy it off someone else you know.

T Well — ask yourself really. I mean are you not getting it done because you're spending quite a bit of time nattering . . . that there's a group of you you know not *really* working as hard as you could if . . . you say that the group you sit with don't sort of get the work finished. Do you think you'd get more work done if you were on your own?

L No I probably wouldn't get any work done if I was on my own.

T Because there'd be nobody to ask and nobody to copy from.

L Yeah.

T Um . . . well that's not I mean allowing for the fact that that's one of your most important subjects that's really . . .

L Um.

T Not very good is it? You'll have to sort something out about that. Have you talked to Mr Y at all about it?

L No, I haven't.

T Well, don't you think you might?

L I don't really know what to say to him though.

T Well just say to him what you've just said to me you know you find it hard to get the work done during the lesson so you're not quite sure what it's about and so you're not able to do your homework.

L   Um.

T   And he'll give you some help won't he? Are you going to be able to do that ... do you think?

L   Yeah talk to him about it.

T   Well . . . quite a good idea you know if you don't want to tell him in front of other people in the class about it, I mean it's say a bit difficult at the end of a lesson unless your lesson is like onto breaktime or lunchtime, is to go and see you know to go over the science office at lunch time, 'cause they're usually around there aren't they in the science office and just have a word with him. Just tell him why you haven't been doing your homework. Because he probably thinks that you haven't been doing your homework because you're just you know a bit lazy over it.

L   Yeah.

T   But generally what about the homework anyway?

L   I don't know I find it all boring to sit down and do work.

T   Have you got somewhere at home to do it?

L   Yeah I can go and sit up in my bedroom.

T   Is that sort of satisfactory, I mean have you got somewhere where you can sit and write OK or do you sit and listen to records or something instead?

L   I sit on my bed and do it.

T   Does your Mum nag you about it?

L   Yeah . . . non stop 'Have you got no homework, got homework, done your homework, done your homework, where's your homework'. It never stops.

T   But you're not doing it anyway are you whether she nags you or not.

L   No . . . well . . . it gets my back up once she keeps going on about it so I just tell her I haven't got any. Stick it in the drawer.

T   Well that doesn't get you very far young lady does it?

L   No . . . just fed up with her nagging me. I just try and get out of it all the time. Go out and stay away from her.

T   And I dare say that makes her nag you more does it?

L   I'm never there so she don't get the chance to 'cause whenever I can I'm out.

T   Well . . . the result of that is that if you're not doing your homework because you're trying to keep out of your Mum's way, you're getting yourself into difficulties, getting behind in work and getting poor grades when you could get good ones.

L   Mm.

T   There's erm — a report coming up in you know in about March. What's going to happen then?

L   It'll be another bad one probably.

T   You're accustomed to having bad ones are you? I don't know what your reports have been like up to now.

L   Well they always say that . . . usually they say that I'm a nice character very friendly . . . er distractive — things like that . . . you know distract other people. Keep talking.

T   And is . . . do you accept that? Do you think that is a fair assessment of you?

L   Yeah. That's what I do because I get bored.

T   Um, so what can you do about that?

L   Dunno . . . I can't really make the lessons more interesting can I?

T   (Pause) You can't make the lessons more interesting by doing what you have being doing because you're still finding it boring but maybe you could make

it in some way more interesting by being involved in it. You know in a sense
Lorraine what you are saying is you're sitting back in the chair and you're
saying, 'OK teacher (you know whatever subject it is) interest me.' Aren't
you really? You're asking the teacher to say, 'Ah this is going to be really
wonderful Lorraine and you won't be able to er you know think about anything else for the next fortnight.' Well I mean it doesn't really sort of work
like that does it? The way it works is you saying —

L   But I start off trying.

T   to yourself well here's the lesson what can *I* get from the lesson?

L   Yeah but I start off trying sort of thing you know you get a page a couple
    of pages of good work and then after a couple of pages it gets boring 'cause
    you go on with it for so long. You get one chapter and you get all these
    questions in it so you start off and do the first two pages and then you get
    the same things on them. And it's boring. Same sort of thing that *you'd*
    get if you kept just reading the same book doing the same things with that
    book that you just did with the book before.

T   Um.

L   You just seem to be repeating over and over again you know — just a bit
    fed up with it.

T   Well listen I mean we've only had one term of it so far Lorraine: we've got
    another two terms of this year and about two-and-a-half terms next year.
    (Pause) Well what can you do about it?

L   Dunno. Not much I can do really. Grin and bear it.   .

T   Well I think in some ways you've got to do more than just grin and bear
    it. You've got to make it . . . um so's that you can make it actually work
    because at the moment it's not, not really is it? I mean it *is* in some subjects
    but if you're getting comments like this then it's not really working.

L   I'm getting so fed up with all of it. I'm fed up with everything at the moment.
    Everything's boring that I do.
    (Knock at the door)

T   Come in Sandra.
    (Sandra comes in)
    It's break time do you want to . . . what have you got after break?

S   I've got Biology, I can go to that.

T   OK. Um what about this afternoon?

S   I've got to go all the way up to the top floor. I'd come back in swimming
    time.

T   What have you got, what subjects?

S   Spanish and English.

T   I'll try and get you some work over lunch time, OK?

S   OK.
    (She goes out)

T   Well look there was one other thing . . . um . . . which I think . . . you know
    . . . regarding your nursing is probably self-explicit. You get a bus pass. Erm.

L   A train pass.

T   Um a train pass. OK well now . . . (reading from a letter) 'regarding season
    ticket for above information required by the County Council' . . . whereabouts
    do you live?

L   Er Sanwell near the station.

T   So the County pay for your train pass.
    They want to know when you will be leaving. (Pause) Now I looked up in the
    register and your birthday's in September.

L Yeah.

T So you *could* leave —

L Next September.

T No not next September. Next Christmas.

L Is it Christmas?

T Yes . . . oh no I tell a lie, it's not Christmas.

L Easter.

T It's Easter.

L Easter.

T You could leave next Easter but obviously if you if you still want at that stage to do your nursing things you won't want to leave because you'll be staying on to do your exams. If you leave at Easter you see you won't be able to do any of your exams. To do your exams you'll have to stay on until . . . erm you know after the . . . into the summer. So . . . what do I write and tell them? Do I write and tell them that you will be staying on for the next two . . . you know until the summer?

L Yeah . . .

T Because otherwise if I write and say that you I mean that's why they're asking because you are old enough to leave at Easter you see.

T So you want me to say that you'll be staying on. But in any case there's not going to be a lot of point in staying on unless we can be a bit more successful about it than this is there?

L No.

(Buzzer goes)

T Hallo, come in.

P Can you give me a lock for my locker, someone put this (indistinct) down and it's taken off the lock.

T I haven't got any locks, um Mr Z is the man to see. Can I suggest you come back before afternoon registration about quarter to two. OK?

(Pupil goes)

Um . . . I've been talking to Mr X about the Maths kind of thing so I'm not trying to blame all the Maths kind of stuff on you Lorraine you know because I know that this is a situation in the class. But certainly you can do something about the Chemistry if you talk to Mr Y and the English you see I mean the comment for English there was that your work was inconsistent. Like you said you do *some* good work but you get fed up with it and you know you go off again.

L Yeah.

T You you you know you've got to think about what you're doing here. You've got to think about as I say it you've got to be more *selfish* about it. You've got to say 'All right so my Mum's nagging me but it doesn't really matter er you know yes I would prefer to sit and talk to my friends but . . .' You know you've got to think about yourself a bit more. Think about what it means to you.

L Um.

T I tell you honestly I've seen . . . you know . . . you get so sorry when it comes round to about this time or maybe sort of Easter with people in the fifth year and they think 'Oh gosh I'm never going to make any of those exams I wish I'd worked' . . . it's too late then . . . So it's up to you. I think you know we'll have to talk about it another time really because you know it's into break time now and we haven't really had much time . . . Now you see I . . . I don't want to get you into trouble with your Mum but obviously since I've written her this letter as I say until I looked at the C.A. I wasn't aware of what the situation was with the homework. Um I think that you know what you need to do Lorraine is to try and sort out the homework situation and not let you know your rows with your Mum or your kind of er disagreements with your Mum get in the way of that, I mean, you know do that homework get that homework sorted out you know then by all means keep out of your Mum's way. Have a think about it. Did she have a go at you when she got the letter?

L   Yeah.

T   When's the next C.A? I don't know it'll be, erm, about three weeks' time. Let's . . . you have a think about it and let's you and I have a look and have another chat about this next C.A. and see what it says and you in the meantime you have a try and see if you can get down to things yourself. All right? You got cold hands?

L   Yeah.

T   Mm I got cold toes . . .

L   Yeah.

T   See you.

16 Interpretations: teachers' views of 'pastoral care'

Ron Best, Peter Ribbins, Colin Jarvis and Diane Oddy

Introduction

In Chapter 1 of this volume we expressed concern at the failure of educationalists generally, and of educational researchers in particular, to give careful consideration to the design and implementation of pastoral-care provision in schools. Relatively little has been written for publication in this field, and to date there have been few attempts to investigate the growth of pastoral-care systems as we know them.

In the absence of a comprehensive investigation of this phenomenon, a 'conventional wisdom' has emerged which lacks any sound theoretical basis and is characterized by unsophisticated analysis. Thus statements about pastoral care are inclined to be woolly prescriptions for what it *ought* to be rather than realistic assessments of what actually goes on in schools. The picture which has emerged is one of pastoral care as intrinsically a 'good thing', providing 'care' and 'concern' for the social and emotional well-being of children, 'guiding' and 'counselling' children in the resolution of problems of educational, personal and vocational choices, and generally creating a warm, convivial and re-assuring climate in which they might develop their potential to the fullest. In bringing about this highly desirable state of affairs, the design of pastoral-care systems (Houses, Years and so on) with their attendant role structures (Heads of Year, Heads of House, etc.) is seen as an essential prerequisite.

This rosy picture is not one we could accept without qualification. Our own experience as teachers and lecturers with pastoral responsibilities to discharge led us to conjecture that there is some disjunction between the 'conventional wisdom' about pastoral care and what it actually means for 'chalk-face' practitioners. We also advanced an alternative explanation for the growth of pastoral structures, arguing that perhaps they have more to do with resolving the problems of teachers and administrators than those of the children for whom they supposedly cater.

This chapter describes some of the findings of an on-going piece of research[1] that is designed to check the validity of our conjectures. Drawing on field notes and interview transcripts compiled in a concentrated study of an 11–18 comprehensive school, we posit a number of distinct teacher-perspectives expressed in identifiable languages, in which a concern for the pastoral needs of children is not foremost in teachers' minds. The picture that emerges has rather little in common with that of the 'conventional wisdom', and this has some far-reaching implications for those whose task it is to institutionalize pastoral care.

However, an understanding of the reality of pastoral care can be achieved only in terms of an appreciation of the nature of social interaction itself, and it is to this we now turn.

The Context of Social Interaction

It is necessary to begin with some assertions about social action and the context within which social action is effected.

The theoretical tradition which informs our position is that of *Verstehen* sociology, a tradition stretching at least from Weber, and articulated by the symbolic interactionists and social phenomenologists, notably Mead, Schutz and Goffman. For Weber, important distinctions were to be made between 'action', 'social action', and 'behaviour'.[2] 'Action' was distinguished from mere behaviour by the fact that the actor attributes a subjective meaning to his actions. Any explanation of social phenomena therefore has to take account of how the actors involved construe their actions and the context in which these actions are effected. Action becomes *social* action the moment the actor takes account of the actions of others in formulating his own. Social action is most fully exemplified in inter-personal relations where a number of actors negotiate reality in the light of the perceived meanings which 'significant others'[3] attach to the situation.

For the actor, there are three dimensions of any social situation in which he is involved:

(i) There is the actor himself, who exists as a subjective consciousness, making sense of the situation, and seeking to make the situation manageable as he goes about the rational accomplishment of certain actions and the pursuit of certain goals.

(ii) There are other actors, who, although 'other' for the actor and therefore part of the objective reality which confronts him, are apprehended as other subjective consciousnesses like himself.

(iii) There is the objective reality which all actors agree to exist as external to themselves, and whose objectivity resides in their nature as the objectification of inter-personal constructs.

Therefore, for any actor, his actions take place and must be formulated in the context of a socially constructed objective reality within which other actors are pursuing their own planned actions and in doing so expect certain sorts of action from him. Thus, the social situation confronts the actor as a set of objective circumstances within which he effects his actions and pursues the realization of his plans. At the same time it constitutes a dynamic context which includes significant others and which imposes important constraints upon the possible courses of action open to him.

In the process of making reality manageable, actors identify characteristics of situations as coming under certain generalized categories. Each new situation is interpreted, at least partly, in terms of generalizations made in previous encounters. Moreover, social interaction would not be possible unless the actors concerned shared the categories in terms of which interaction is effected. Put another way, social life is lived through sets of *typifications* which make reality meaningful and shareable by the members involved.[4] Actors make their actions-in-context rationally accountable, not only to themselves but also to others, in terms of such typifications. The identification of key categories in actors' accounts is therefore important for an understanding of distinctive attitudes which actors adopt for particular aspects of their lives. When applied to the study of pastoral care, we shall see how such typifications can be grouped to identify distinctive teacher perspectives and associated languages.

An important feature of the shared reality of social actors in an institutional setting is the framework of expectations objectified as the roles and statuses of the institution. Successful accomplishment of one's action is in a real sense the successful performance of the duties attaching to a position in the role structure, which entails the satisfaction of the expectations of those playing other roles (complementary, reciprocal, etc.). Applied to the study of pastoral care in schools, that part of the objective reality which is embodied in the organizational arrangements of the school (divisions into subject departments, Houses, Years and so on) and their formal roles (counsellor, form tutor, Head of House, etc.) will obviously be of significance.

However, it must be remembered that such structures exist in a real sense only in so far as actors agree that they exist, and accept their prescriptive force for their own actions. Social structures like a house system are therefore constantly being produced and reproduced by the teachers and pupils who 'work' them and work *within* them. Other, less formal, structures may also exist in so far as actors bring them into existence, and although these are not institutionalized in the formal designation of roles and statuses, they are no less significant. In both cases, the actor's successful negotiation of his daily routine relies at least partly on his ability to understand the constraints such structures impose upon him and to exploit the opportunities for action that they provide.

It would also be wrong to reduce all social interaction to the level of meeting the expectations of others. As Goffman[5] and Fletcher[6] have argued, successful management of one's identity as a *self* or *person* is of crucial importance. It is not merely the approval of significant others which has to be achieved (i.e. a satisfactory public image), but also that self-approval which is part and parcel of one's *self*-image. Persons require a measure of dignity and self-respect for their own well-being as much as for the effective performance of the complex of roles which they have to play. To be satisfied with one's inter-personal *qua* inter-*personal* relations is a potent motive in guiding social action, and, as Goffman has pointed out, actors adopt all manner of strategies and ruses to protect and enhance their public- and self-images, often resorting to collusion to 'save face' for themselves and others in the tense encounters that characterize social life.[7]

The picture is thus infinitely more complex than that given by those who have written and spoken about pastoral care in the past. We shall argue that the realities of pastoral care cannot be grasped in the easy prescriptions of educationalists nor in the design and analysis of structural arrangements alone. Rather, such understanding will come by an exploration of the tense relationship between actor and context, as the teacher exploits such space as exists or can be made within the constraints he faces, in his ongoing pursuit of effective role-play and personal self-fulfilment.

Social Interaction and the Role of the Teacher

In our earlier chapter we suggested the existence of two versions of pastoral care: an 'official' version couched in terms of the conventional wisdom, and an 'unofficial' version held by many practising teachers. Whereas the former conceived of pastoral care as a rational and wholly desirable activity, the latter sees pastoral care as 'impractical, unnecessary and counter-productive; at best being an administrative device and at worst acting as a powerful force for emphasizing and reinforcing the labelling activities of the academic side of a school's work.' This model was to some extent patterned on Nell Keddie's analysis of 'Classroom Knowledge'.[8] She argued that the accounts teachers give of their actions depend upon the context in which the account is produced. Thus a particular philosophy or doctrine may be expounded in the *educationist* context (for example, explaining the school's policy to an outsider), but be contradicted by what is said in the *teacher* context (for example, staffroom gossip). She argues that a distinction must be made between words and deeds, between doctrine and commitment and between theory and practice in investigating the gap between what is said to happen in schools and what actually happens. While sharing these sentiments in regard to pastoral-care provision we would argue that the model of two versions or two contexts is an over-simplification.[9]

In the course of any day, a teacher has to manage a variety of types of situation, each of which entails particular expectations of him and more or less difficult problems to be resolved. No role is simple or unifaceted. Part of the variety of situations the teacher faces stems from the diffuse nature of the teacher's role, at once being an administrator, disciplinarian, welfare agent, instructor, and so on. Appropriate action for the teacher will partly depend on which of these aspects of his role he is being expected to perform at a particular time. Moreover, demands made upon him are to some extent a function of the status of those with whom he is interacting. Thus it is not merely that the teacher is acting as an administrator that is significant, but also whether the other with whom he interacts is acting as an administrator, instructor, disciplinarian or whatever. At the same time, each teacher is attempting to negotiate the situation in a way which is personally meaningful for him, and which protects or enhances his own self-image, which gives him some feeling of identity and self-respect, and where possible advances the realization of personal ambition.

Some factors remain constant, however. While every teacher is a unique individual with a particular personality, needs, motives and attitudes, he will share some common ground with his peers. As well as those aspects of the general situation which they construe similarly, there will be common ground among teachers performing similar roles or interacting with others performing similar roles. In an important sense what is in the teacher's interests will be determined by the roles being played, and this will be reflected in what constitutes a *problem* for him. It ought to be possible, therefore, to identify regularities in the accounts teachers give of their pastoral-care activities, and it is arguable that such patterns will reflect common problems faced by groups of teachers.

In analysing our field notes and transcripts of interviews we have found it useful to look at the sorts of things teachers choose to talk about, at the kinds of sentiments they express. In so far as these accounts reflect shared perceptions of situations and of the problems they pose for actors, it may be possible to identify a number of distinct perspectives, each with its own specific vocabulary of motive.[10] These generalizations are necessarily tentative as the work is not yet complete, but it does seem useful to try to identify paradigm cases of teachers who perceive problems in a particular way and articulate their positions in particular languages.

Teacher Accounts and Vocabularies of Motive

Although it is obvious that all accounts elicited in interviews are to some extent a function of the questions asked, we have been at some pains to formulate our questions in a way which allows the interviewee to determine the direction of the discussion where possible. The first step in analysing the material, therefore, has been to see what kinds of information the respondents have considered relevant and important to the questions asked. A preliminary analysis revealed that teachers have used the interviews to introduce a variety of topics which include the formal structure of the school, the welfare of the children, discipline, and curricular organization.

Some teachers have stressed the problem of discipline to the point where almost any question asked will be answered in terms of its implications for the teacher's handling of problems of classroom control. One teacher, for example, responded to questions about the House system and the Year system with statements like these:

> [The House System is] very important, if it is done properly. People in the House can keep tabs on truancy and inform the EWO, for example. A stink can be brought up very quickly because you teach them . . . The kids see the role of the Head of Year as purely discipline, but if a problem has been dealt with through the House, discipline may be there but it is more counselling . . .

When asked about the role of the Head of Year, she said:

> He was someone to send the child to when they were misbehaving in class. If it is purely disobedience then I would send them to the Head of Year, but if I knew there was something behind the disobedience then I would send them to the Head of House.

When asked whether she saw any divisions in the School, she described divisions between the Upper School and Lower School, and the House System, and then went on to say:

> I would like to see someone in overall charge of discipline. At the moment we have got X and Y (in one division) and W and Z (in the other division). The thing is Mr X will back you up but Mr W will say one thing to the teacher and quite another thing on the phone to parents; he never backs you up.

Asked about how she uses the weekly period set aside for a democratic form meeting to discuss issues of general concern, she said: 'If the form is noisy and I say "shut up, shut up", and they still don't, then I say: "get some work out" and we don't have a form period.'

A similar perspective is presented by another teacher, who described the House and Year systems as 'better than having just one dimension as in other schools I've taught in, as you have "two levers" on the child.' He saw no significant differences between the two systems, and his course of action in referring children indicated his disciplinary orientation: 'In individual cases the House tutor may be stronger than the Year tutor, so you go to the former. At least this arrangement gives you two bites at the cherry: if one doesn't pay off the other does.' Even the referral of children to the Counsellor was seen in these terms:

> I have tried to use the Counsellor twice over the last two terms. Once without any success at all, the other (when I was in dire need of him), he was away. One was two third-year boys I got annoyed with, and with reason. I had completely lost my temper and they called my bluff. I needed help. He came up and took them away. He later told me he wanted respect between the children and me, but we never got it. I asked for a written apology and only got a verbal one.

In the case of both these teachers, they have placed most weight on the problem of discipline. Although in the first example, the teacher mentioned the counselling dimension of the House system, it was questions of dealing with classroom control and receiving the appropriate

backing from the system which were foremost in her thinking. In the
second case, the respondent's perception of both the pastoral structure
and the role of the Counsellor are couched in terms of how to settle
matters of insubordination in a way that solves the problems of the
teacher; the problems of the pupils are not worthy of mention.

We suggest that these accounts are instances of a particular teacher-
language and reflect a particular teacher-perspective.[11] The concepts
of 'misbehaviour', 'disobedience' and of senior teachers being more
or less 'strong' and more or less reliable in 'backing you up' are indicative of what we might call the *teacher-centred language of control*.

A very different attitude can be found in the accounts of other
teachers, where the primary concern of the teacher seems to be the
welfare of the *children*. For example, one teacher thought there was
a strong philosophy in the school:

> The school caters for every need of the child right through. Although I am
> more on the academic side, I don't believe you can distinguish between
> academic and pastoral, although I have been told I should. The Junior
> House people and myself involve ourselves right from the early days of
> the children being in the school, but the form teachers are a bridge between
> the House staff and myself, to see that the children are looked after both
> pastorally and in their academic work.

Her attitude to record-keeping was equally insightful: 'Sometimes
something crops up in the fourth or fifth year because there are loop-
holes, for instance if a new teacher takes the class after the holidays.
We can find out the immediate problems from the new pupils' folders.
I look at these as an indication.'

Asked what weight she placed on Junior School reports, she replied
that she kept them by her as an indication, but always told her classes
that now they could make a completely fresh start:

> I don't like a stigma attached to a child and I don't like behavioural prob-
> lems in records. If a teacher insists on recording behavioural problems
> which can affect a child right through to career possibilities, I tell them
> to use a pencil so that it can be removed from the record later. I also
> don't like making a report on my class for the teacher who is going to take
> them on next. In fact up to now I have refused to do so.

On her relationship with the Counsellor, she said she is 'grateful for
his training in dealing with children, because I am always concerned
that I may be confusing a child or making the situation worse if I try
to deal with it.'

In these extracts, the prime motive being expressed is that of caring
for all aspects of the pupil's welfare. She rejected the division of children's problems into academic and pastoral in favour of a 'whole child'
approach, and was concerned that the problems of discipline for
teachers are not attributed for ever to a child through the labelling
processes of record-keeping. On this she has taken a firm stand in
refusing to meet the demands of other staff. Unlike the teachers in the
previous examples, she saw the value of the Counsellor, not in helping

her resolve her own problems, but in having an ability to help children without confusing them or exacerbating the situation, an ability which she fears she may not have herself and which leads to caution in her own efforts.

The interpretation of issues in terms of how they constitute problems for the children is echoed by other teachers. In a discussion about the sorts of problems she might discuss with parents, a form tutor gave the following examples:

> For example, how long a kid may sit at home worrying about his homework before he actually picks up a pen and does it. A child may sit for three or four hours. Once I know about this I can slant his homework in such a way as to help him over it . . .

> I have a girl who was a battered baby . . . she is very much a 'loner'. She has a bowel problem as well which makes her unpopular with the other children . . . every time she had a PE period she would run away. When I asked her why all she would say was 'I hate this school'. I got some of the girls together and talked about how we needed to convince her that we liked her. The girls co-operated in this. Now she doesn't run away . . . Now she thinks she likes the school.

For this teacher what was at first glance a problem of discipline or academic progress — the child who fails to do homework adequately, or the child who skips PE — was perceived as a *personal* problem for the child. The solution in both cases was adaptation *by* the teacher to the needs of the child; in the first case by appropriately tailoring homework, and in the second case by meeting a problem of peer-group acceptance with a peer-group strategy.

For both these teachers the child's welfare was the main consideration in their approach to teaching, and we might call this the *child-centred perspective*. Its expression is in terms like identifying a child as 'worrying' or being 'a loner', and places emphasis on the child's emotional response to school and what it offers: 'I hate school', for example, is accepted as admissible evidence in analysing and resolving the child's problem. Together with the concepts of labelling theory (whether implicit or explicit) we have here the bones of a truly child-centred language.

Other teachers displayed a similar concern for the welfare of the child, but with a rather different emphasis. Whereas the preceding quotations exemplify the expression of concern for pupils as human beings with problems of a personal nature, the following highlight a concern for the child as a pupil *qua* pupil — i.e. as one who is being educated. Thus, speaking of the integrated studies programme offered by the school, which makes extensive use of 'Key' lessons and work cards, one teacher observed:

> I disagree with X [a previous member of staff] who did not read enough education . . . one hour-long 'Key' lesson is not really as educational as X thought. Ten to twelve minutes *doing* something which is immediately followed up by the kids doing it would be more educational. The 'Key' lesson loses its impact (even films have no impact due to children's exposure

to television), and often isn't followed up for days . . . the work card
system can lead to wholesale copying of work from books. Added to this
is the fact that kids are so geared to following up the 'Key' lesson via the
work cards that a teacher who attempts to discuss the work with a kid may
be an 'intrusion' that is resented.

In talking about the general philosophy of the school he argued that

> We mustn't put so much emphasis on, for example, spelling or tables, that
> creativity is neglected, but the opposite can also be the case. A person who
> reaches a certain age unable to spell, regardless of his creative ability in
> what he writes, will be laughed at by others for the mistakes it includes.

Further, he recognized the importance of organizing the work according
to the internal logic of the learning process: 'Some subjects require
sequential learning, for example, some parts of Maths you cannot do
unless you have done other parts.' Finally, the learning process itself
must be appreciated in terms of its implications for the learner:

> For confidence children need to succeed and if you ask a child to make
> something, and it doesn't fit, for example, the joints make it wobble,
> the child knows he has failed and loses confidence; whereas if the design
> is what you are interested in, converting the design into a reality may or
> may not succeed, but the design may still have been good, and the children
> learn skills in this way as well.

What this teacher has introduced into the discussion is a philosophy of
education in which the structuring and imparting of knowledge has to
be geared to the cognitive processes of learning itself. The emphasis on
the 'confidence' of the child in his ability in any subject, and the stress
on striking a balance between instruction in necessary skills and opportunities for developing creativity are indicative of the pupil-centred
language in which such teachers make their practices accountable. It is
also indicative of a teacher perspective which might termed *pupil-
centred* as distinct from the child-centred perspective discussed earlier.

Yet other teachers have chosen to describe the pastoral-care arrangements of the school in terms of their efficiency as a bureaucratic
structure. Such accounts suggest that the efficacy of the system is
perceived in terms of its success in coping with problems confronting
teachers in their administrative role. A senior member of staff expressed
doubts about the merit of existing arrangements on the ground that

> vast, complicated hierarchies do not make for clarity. The whole thing
> seems incredibly complex to me . . . it's incredibly complicated. Some
> people seem to believe that the more complicated a system is, the better
> it is. Whether you do it vertically or horizontally, it needs to be clear-cut.

Commenting on the Faculty structure of the school, he expressed
similar sentiments, describing the difference in size and responsibility
of the existing faculties, mentioning that over one-third of the work of
the school came under one umbrella. 'This made Faculty structure
unwieldy. These divisions were due partly to the personalities and to

the degree of power in the past. I would favour a rationalized system of four or five large Faculties.' His is a plea for a rationalized bureaucracy based on a sound division of labour and clear rules of procedure. He did not object to structures as such, provided they were not ambiguous and ill-defined, or established on non-rational grounds:

> The trouble with all these structures is their tendency to get established on accidental personality and historical bases, and then to be perpetuated, however illogical subsequent events may have made them. Resistance to tidying them up is enormous but this can occasionally be overcome.

The prescription and definition of institutional roles is itself the subject of a document issued to all staff in September, and this displays a similar concern with administrative efficacy. It is organized under the headings:

A. Organization
B. Form Tutor's role — Registers
                       — Registration
                       — Dinners
                       — Rough Books
C. Teachers' 'free dinners', and Duties
D. Letters to Parents
E. Pigeon Holes
F. School Forum
G. Discipline   — emergencies
                        — detention
                        — tasks
                        — caning
H. Referrals to Counsellor
I. Office Duty

Although it is arguable that clarification of these matters is necessary for the school to discharge its duties as both an imparter of knowledge and a caring agency, the whole tone of the document is administrative and organizational. Thus, although 'pastoral care' is mentioned twice under 'Form Tutor's Role', it is not defined or discussed in any way; most of the space under this heading is devoted to administrative procedures such as the approved method of registering different sorts of absence and the issue of rough books. The problems to which this document is a response are those of the administrator. Like the accounts of the senior teacher, the document is basically about 'running a tight ship'. Its emphasis on clear definitions of duties and responsibilities, rules of procedure and the efficiency of the system are all part of an *administrator-centred language*.

One further perspective may be identified, and that is the attitude of teachers who see themselves primarily as teachers of a *subject* rather than as teachers of children or even of pupils. One teacher, for example, answered most questions in terms of curricular and academic considerations. She readily conceived of children in terms of their academic ability, for example the 'bright' and the 'dull', and saw the House system as no more than 'a way of grouping people'. She cited

'O' and 'A' level results as evidence of the effectiveness of the Faculty in which she taught. Even her relationship with her Head of House (formally designated a *pastoral* position) was described in terms of their common interest in the subject they taught. No consideration of the learning processes themselves is displayed in her account of her work. The sentiments she expressed were those of an authority whose interest is almost exclusively in teaching a particular subject on the curriculum. Hers is the language of the *subject-centred teacher*.

The analysis so far suggests that any conception of pastoral care as simple or unproblematic is native, to say the least. In the context of interviews which teachers *know* to be concerned with pastoral care, the structures and processes they discuss are interpreted in very different ways, and these differences indicate the variety of problems that teachers face as they go about their daily tasks. Depending upon which facet of the teacher's role is uppermost in their minds, and which facet they find most difficult to cope with, teachers choose to discuss very different issues, and to discuss the same issue in very different ways. In terms of their vocabularies of motive we have identified a number of perspectives, each expressed in a distinct language:

  a teacher-centred language of control
  a subject-centred language
  a child-centred language
  a pupil-centred language
  an administrator-centred language.

Obviously these categories are ones which we have produced in our attempts to make sense of teachers' accounts — after all, in seeking to understand reality the researcher makes an *interpretation* of the data, and thus produces his *own* account — and it is arguable that other categories could be devised. None the less, as the examples above show, there is ample evidence that these perspectives are not merely theoretical constructs but have some substance in fact. It seems to us that they have considerable explanatory potential for further analyses of pastoral care.

Rhetoric, Role-negotiation and the Presentation of Self

In Sections 2 and 3 we argued that two important factors affecting the actions of an individual are the maintenance of an appropriate self-image and the negotiation of a public image. Negotiating a successful public image is obviously important for the maintenance of a successful image of oneself, and requires some adjustment of one's actions according to the particular role and expectations of those with whom one interacts.

As noted earlier, Keddie has argued that the accounts teachers give in the educationist context are suspect.[12] To use Goffman's concept, the 'front' which the teacher presents is designed in such a context to meet the expectations of another educationist. It can therefore be argued that the accounts we have analysed above are not indicative of the 'real' sentiments of the teachers concerned. This is, of course, a problem, but the nature and diversity of responses we have received suggests that, to some extent at least, teachers are not merely playing an educationist role but are talking about problems of real moment in their lives. None the less the general point has to be taken, and it seems to us that the idea that language may be used in this rhetorical fashion is quite helpful in comparing what teachers say to us with what they say to each other in a different context. In addition, as Sharp and Green have argued,[13] the rhetorical use of a language (in their case that of the child-centred ideology of the Plowden Report[14]) can play a powerful role in maintaining a good self-image (and/or a good public image) by squaring actual behaviour with the philosophy one openly espouses. Moreover, bearing in mind our model of the teacher as rationally pursuing certain goals and attempting to gain the co-operation and approval of others as he does so, it is conceivable that teachers may adopt a particular perspective and employ a particular language, not because they believe in it, but because it wins the support of significant others and enhances (or protects) their status in the school. Finally, if problems of discipline, instruction and administration are as important to teachers as their accounts suggest, it is quite possible that much of what masquerades as pastoral-care provision is really concerned with resolving quite different problems altogether. In short, is it not possible that the 'official' account a school gives of its pastoral arrangements is largely rhetorical?

Something like this certainly seems to be the case in one meeting we observed of senior and medium-ranking staff with pastoral responsibilities. In the light of their responsibilities the agenda might have been expected to be comprised of issues directly concerned with child welfare. However, even the most charitable reading of the field notes made at that meeting leaves little doubt that the real issues being dealt with were administrative procedures, and the assertion and defence of individuals' status.

The first item on the agenda was a lengthy discussion of a form required by the County. Although this form had clear welfare implications the discussion was totally concerned with how the paper-work should be handled. A senior member of staff (P) sought the co-operation of those present in implementing a particular scheme for collecting and recording the necessary information, and the following interaction occurred:[15]

M Will a copy be sent home, and a copy kept in the House file?
N Mr O [headmaster] is keen that fifth-formers should have a report sent home . . .
P (interrupting): *I'll* continue with this if you don't mind Mr N . . . I'll keep a copy for reference.

Someone asks: Can't the forms be duplicated?
P thinks not; the fifth-year teachers will be 'up the creek' if we ask them to look after more pieces of paper.
Q [a fifth-form teacher and House Head] says he wouldn't object.
P says: It was a difficult meeting last week with the fifth-form teachers. They threw the other form out. It has to be done soon, he says, and N and Q agree, as there is a Parents' Evening coming up and the reports will be needed for then.
M thinks he should have a copy of the form.
N says: Yes, and it would also be very useful to us to have a copy when they come into the sixth form.
P says photo-copying it would be very expensive.
R [a Head of School] asks: Why not just use carbons?
P says the form tutors won't wear it. If we want to do that we'll have to put it to the form tutors and see what they say.
R's reaction suggests that if he had any say in it form tutors would do what they were told.
Chairman: What is the House Heads' reaction to what P was originally suggesting — the whole idea of the reports and then transferring the information to the other form?
(There is no objection to this.)
M suggests an alternative — that the Heads of House, if they want to, should make the duplicate.
P says this would be too much for the Heads of House ... he says that the copies in his office would, of course, be open to any House teacher who wanted to look.

Now there is no discussion here of the educational or welfare benefits which might be expected to accrue from one system of form-filling or another. Rather, there is a preoccupation with the practicalities of doing, including the administrative problem *par excellence*: finding a system which will actually be implemented by those lower down. What position people take up on the issue of the duplication and storage of material is not, however, administrator-centred. Its orientation lies in the status of individuals with empires to protect and interests to advance. Thus P, having advocated a particular scheme, is set against any alternatives which others suggest. Significantly, the language he adopts to discredit other suggestions is that of the administrator: he appeals to others with arguments which he knows will find favour with them — it's too expensive and the troops won't wear it. R, realizing that administrative considerations will carry the day, counters both arguments — it need *not* be expensive, and the troops had *better* wear it!

P is also interesting because of the concern he shows for his status throughout. The attempt by another (senior) member of staff to enter the discussion at an early stage is quickly squashed: '*I'll* continue with this if you don't mind ...', and the fact that this issue comes within his jurisdiction and not the other's is made clear to all. This also seems to be at the root of his concern over where the records should be kept. His arguments against *any* method of duplication may actually stem from a fear that, should *other* members of staff have their own copies of the form his monopoly over the documentation, storage and communication of such information will be lost. Here his interests are incompatible with those of M, who as a Head of House is equally anxious to establish that this issue falls within the jurisdiction of House staff. He clearly wants the form in the House folders and counters P's objections with the suggestion that it be left to the House Heads to make a copy if they want. But P isn't having this, and it is he who has the last word: in effect, if you want the information it's always available . . . but you have to come to *me* to get it! Thus he withstands a number of challenges to his status, all of which have derived from attempts to define the situation in ways which would enhance the status of the challengers. But, on this day at least, he carries all before him.

Subsequent items on the agenda are no more 'pastoral' than this. There is a discussion of Fire Drills and the 'signing-out' book for children going home ill, and though both are obviously connected with the welfare of the children, in both cases it is the procedural questions only which are dealt with. A discussion of who should be responsible for ensuring that registers are marked when teachers are away is equally administrative in tone. In short, a meeting of 'pastoral' staff turns out to be much more informative about both the problems of administrators and the personal ambitions and aspirations of members than it does about the welfare of the children whose individual care is their especial responsibility. How much more of the 'official' picture of pastoral care in this school is also rhetorical?

At least some other parts of the system are characterized by this disjunction between words and deeds. As most teachers admit, their duties as form tutors are rarely adequately discharged, partly because there just isn't time, and partly because the constraints imposed on the time-table by (among other things) a massive integrated studies programme make it impossible for many teachers to teach the forms they register. 'I don't have time to get to know them well enough for them to bring their problems to me' is a popular refrain, and many teachers approve of the school Counsellor precisely because he has the time to do what they are supposed to do as form tutors. The reality of the Friday morning form meeting period is equally remote from what is supposed to happen. Most teachers admit that they no longer try to create the democratic forum which is scheduled for this time, and the uses it is actually put to are many and varied. Many justify this in terms of the size of the class and the inability of young children to accept the self-discipline which committee procedures require.

These facts remind us that the teacher is not by any means the free agent he might like to be. Class sizes, the time-table and so on are all external constraints which seriously limit the courses of action open to him. The pastoral-care system, the role structure and the status hierarchy of the school are themselves part of the framework within which the teacher has to function, and for some teachers at least these seriously inhibit their attempts to care for children in the way they would like. We have already noted how one teacher rejected the official definition of a separate pastoral system (Houses) and a separate academic system (Years) on the grounds that the two are bound up with each other. Her account is couched in the language of the child-centred teacher and places a premium on the personal welfare of children, but her position is defined as responsible for *academic* concerns only. For her, the structure simply gets in the way. She has to *make* space for herself within the system by working on an informal level and, where possible, redefining her role accordingly.

Many teachers stressed the importance of informal interaction for the provision of pastoral care. Formal arrangements such as regular scheduled meetings with the Counsellor, and the designation of Heads of House and Heads of Year, seem less important in the day-to-day processes than the informal liaison and consultation which takes place in the staffroom or where teachers happen to be working together in other aspects of their role. To some extent teachers simply ignore the formal structure: they by-pass some roles, take short cuts to the person they think can most help, or else by private treaty sort it out for themselves. Some subject departments prefer to deal with problems of behaviour and adjustment *within* the department, and very little use is made of either the pastoral heads or the Counsellor.

However, it would be wrong to think that the formal structure inhibits every teacher. On the contrary, there is ample evidence that teachers *like* the existence of the structure, even when they are critical of it. Thus, although many teachers express dissatisfaction with the House/Year system, few of them would like to see it go. This is not to say they would not welcome some alternative structure. More often than not, their complaint is about the ambiguity and lack of clarity of the present system, and they go on to argue for a tighter system with a more rigid definition of roles. In short, they actually want their actions to be more closely prescribed than at present. Whereas for some teachers an ill-defined system allows freedom of action, which is important to them, for others the insecurity and uncertainty of the situation is most unwelcome. The problem of not knowing exactly who to go to, or in what order to consult others about an issue, is for them debilitating, and their performance as form tutors or housemasters suffers as a result.

This is not unconnected with considerations of status and prestige of the kind we saw at work in the meeting described above. Teachers readily talk about 'overlap', 'duplication of work', and 'treading on people's toes' as dangers inherent in an ill-defined structure, but this is a worry primarily because the teacher is afraid of 'doing the wrong thing'. Remembering what we said earlier about self-image and public image, many teachers fear incurring the wrath of others by going to the wrong person, and others crave a clearer definition of responsibilities in order to establish the boundaries of personal 'empires'. For them a clear-cut and well-defined pastoral-care structure is probably a necessary pre-condition of adequate role-performance and an adequate self-image to boot. To put it another way, teachers need to know where they stand, and it is arguable that formal pastoral structures may actually perform this latent function: it is perhaps not so much that the structure causes pastoral care to be provided, but rather that it improves the chances that it will, by giving teachers that sense of identity and security without which no facet of their role could be adequately performed.

The importance of informal structures, of the self-image of teachers, and of the ubiquitous problem of discipline in teachers' perceptions of their situation, is clearly recognized by the Counsellor in the school we are studying. He also provides an excellent example of the negotiation of a difficult role in which winning the confidence of both members of staff and pupils is crucial. It is arguable that his success as a Counsellor lies largely in his ability to 'be all things to all men' in such a way that he appears as a threat to no one and as a boon to most. In this we suspect that adoption of appropriate languages for the persons he deals with plays a part, although we haven't been able to check this to date. Be that as it may, other factors have certainly been at work.

Firstly, his position in the school is formally defined as quite separate from any of the hierarchies of status and responsibility. As he put it, he is only answerable to the Head but feels responsible to everyone. Problems of the 'pecking order' do not therefore arise, and staff are free to define his position as they like. Thus House staff see him as 'an addition to the pastoral-care system and not as a separate agent'. Other staff are inclined to accept him as 'one of them' and therefore someone to be trusted on the grounds of his many years of experience as a teacher before becoming a Counsellor, while senior teachers can assure themselves of their equality with him since he was formerly the head of a school himself. Secondly, he consciously attempts to win the confidence and co-operation of staff by mixing with them socially. Remembering the importance teachers place on informal contacts and the fear of the unknown which previous Counsellors created by 'keeping to themselves', this Counsellor makes a point of going regularly into the staffrooms at coffee-time and mixing with teachers on an informal basis. The distinction between formal and informal structures is brought out again in the fact that, despite his formal position outside the structure, teachers perceive him to be both an integral part of the pastoral team, a link between its members *and* an external support to them.

Where children are concerned, he attributes some of his success to the fact that he has no teaching time-table and does not have to switch roles — he can be the sympathetic listener at all times. When confronted with the possibility of doing some teaching he expressed concern that the children are used to 'being free and easy' with him and don't quite know how to respond to him in a teaching situation where he is in authority and has to maintain discipline. By only wearing one hat, children know he can be approached at any time and know *how* to approach him.

His management of the problem of confidentiality is indicative of a very careful and sensitive appreciation of what would constitute a threat for either a teacher or pupil. Teachers are convinced that he feeds them as much information as is necessary and does not withhold information to which they feel entitled, while children are confident that he is not 'on the teachers' side'. As one teacher said: 'Both parents and children will say things to him which they wouldn't say to a teacher, so he can give us some idea of the best way to deal with the child. He is an important link between the teacher and the pupil.' His use of one-to-one counselling in the privacy of his office, alongside regular meetings with House staff and his approachability in the staff-room, have allowed him to combine confidentiality with teachers' confidence that he is doing nothing behind their backs.

However, to some extent these strategies could only work as well as they have because of the foundations he has laid in interpersonal relations. His personal warmth and approachability, and his willingness to take on any problem that arises, have won the respect of virtually all members of staff. The fact that he works hard, mixes with them, and displays a real concern for others sets the scene for the ready acceptance of his avowals of confidentiality to the pupils and his professional responsibility to his peers.

Some Implications

The picture that emerges from this discussion is not one which inspires much confidence in the conventional wisdom of pastoral care. There is little evidence, in our work at least, that the institutionalization of pastoral-care roles necessarily leads directly to a greater concern for pupil welfare. Indeed, teachers seem more likely to perceive such roles in terms of their resolution of problems of teacher-control and administrative procedure. The variety of attitudes teachers display, and the distinctive languages they use in accounting for their actions, suggest that the very idea of a 'school' having a caring ethos is an unwarranted reification. Teachers' perceptions in this area are as varied as are the many facets of the teacher's role itself, and in the final analysis it is perhaps on the level of the teacher as a *person* with a particular personality, a particular self-image, and a host of ambitions, aspirations and hang-ups, that much of what goes on in schools has to be understood.

Our early suspicions that much of what is said and written about pastoral care is merely rhetorical seem vindicated. But this is not to say that teachers do not care or that pupil problems go unrecognized and unresolved. On the contrary, there have always been caring teachers, and no doubt there always will be. But as some of our examples demonstrate clearly enough, they are at least as likely to do their caring *despite* the system as because of it. And here the personal qualities of the teacher, and his or her ability to make space within the system, assume supreme importance. Why else does one Counsellor succeed where others have failed *within the same system*? The point to grasp is that it is not enough to think that because you have institutionalized 'pastoral care', children will be cared for. On the contrary, a structure which is poorly planned, inadequately defined or over-complex is quite as likely to be counter-productive.

The value or otherwise of institutionalizing pastoral care seems to depend very much on having the right people to work it. Some teachers will function adequately in almost any structure, and some would achieve as much as individuals if there were no structure at all. But *some* sort of structure is essential for those teachers for whom security, identity and 'knowing where you are' is of crucial importance. It is here, it seems to us, that pastoral-care structures may play an important part in providing points of anchorage for teachers in one important aspect of their role.

A second latent function may also be discerned: that is, that the concept of pastoral care (however inapt the term), and the creation of pastoral systems, is a reminder to all teachers that they have not discharged their obligations to their children unless they are more than mere instructors. The task which now awaits us is to galvanize that awareness into action by so organizing our schools and so training their teachers that these responsibilities are shouldered in more than name. In this it is clear that the sort of analysis we are engaged in has some important insights to offer.

The lessons for the eduational decision-makers should be clear enough. Planned provision for all aspects of the welfare of children in our schools should start, not with the woolly prescriptions of educationists, but with a realistic assessment of how teachers and children perceive the world of schooling and their place within it. Only through an appreciation of the tense relationship between the person and his role, between the subjective actor and the constraints of the objective structure within which he works out his destiny, is the potential for such provision likely to be realized.

References

1 This research is being undertaken by the Pastoral Care Research Unit in the Faculty of Education, Arts and Humanities, Chelmer Institute of Higher Education. A research grant from the SSRC and financial support from the Faculty are gratefully acknowledged.

2 M. Weber, *The Theory of Social and Economic Organization* (Free Press, Glencoe, 1964), p. 88.

3 This concept is developed in G. H. Mead, *Mind, Self and Society* (Chicago University Press, 1934), and refers to others whose response and approval

are accorded importance by the actor in the formulation of his actions. For example, parents are the first 'significant others' for most children. From all these significant others a 'generalized other' is developed.

4 The notion of 'typification' is developed by Schutz in various publications. For an overview of his thinking see A. Schutz and T. Luckmann, *The Structures of the Life-World* (Heinemann, London, 1974).

5 E. Goffman, *The Presentation of Self in Everyday Life* (Doubleday-Anchor, New York, 1959).

6 C. Fletcher, *The Person in the Sight of Sociology* (Routledge & Kegan Paul, London, 1975).

7 E. Goffman, *Stigma* (Prentice-Hall, New Jersey, 1963).

8 N. Keddie, 'Classroom Knowledge', in M. F. D. Young (ed.) *Knowledge and Control* (Collier-Macmillan, London, 1971).

9 As Fletcher points out, dichotomistic explanations nearly always are! See op. cit. (note 6), Ch. 2, especially pp. 18-19.

10 This concept is found in C. Wright Mills, 'Situated Actions and Vocabularies of Motive', in *Power, Politics and People* ed. I. L. Horowitz (Oxford University Press, London, 1967). Mills argues that motives may be considered as typical vocabularies through which actors vocalize and impute motives to themselves and others. The teacher-languages identified below are examples of such vocabularies.

11 For a discussion of pupil- and teacher-perspectives see D. H. Hargreaves, *Interpersonal Relations and Education* (Routledge & Kegan Paul, London, 1972).

12 op. cit. (note 8).

13 R. Sharp and A. Green, *Education and Social Control* (Routledge & Kegan Paul, London, 1975).

14 *Children and Their Primary Schools* Vol. I (HMSO, 1967).

15 To protect the anonymity of individuals, all actors are referred to as 'he'.

Conclusion

In this conclusion we wish to do three things: firstly, to draw together a number of themes which underlie the chapters of this book; secondly, to discuss a variety of suggestions contained within the chapters as to how the practice of pastoral care within the secondary school might be improved; thirdly, to consider 'grey areas' which continue to exist in discussions about pastoral care and which will require further attention in future studies.

Underlying Themes

Perhaps the most widely shared theme among contributors to this book is that the *status quo* of pastoral care in many schools has been characterized by a well-intentioned but insufficiently considered approach to meeting the welfare needs of children; that, furthermore, many teachers, and especially those with pastoral-care responsibilities, are uneasily aware of the limitations of existing provisions within their own and other schools. Such teachers are also well aware of the fact that much of the available literature on pastoral care is not of immediate relevance to the actual situations they encounter. All too often it deals with general principles and organizational patterns rather than confronting the problems they, as teachers, are actually struggling to overcome. In short, many teachers are unhappy about their existing practices but have become increasingly doubtful if much real help is to be expected from the sort of accounts which now represent the 'orthodox' view of pastoral care.

How has this gap between analysis and prescription on the one hand the practice on the other developed, and what are its characteristic features? To answer this question it is necessary to look back at the historic development of pastoral-care provision within the secondary school and to describe the emergence of a prevailing orthodoxy which has come to dominate the literature of pastoral care in recent times.

During the course of this century schools have become the focus of much welfare effort, partly at least as a response to powerful humanitarian imperatives. This effort, particularly in the case of the comprehensive school, has culminated in the setting up of elaborate systems of pastoral care. In no real sense anticipating such developments, a dominant conception of pastoral care has gradually emerged. It is this which we have depicted as 'the conventional wisdom'.* For a time pastoral-care developments appealed to and were justified in the terms of that wisdom. However, it has gradually become apparent to some theorists and many practitioners that the conventional wisdom presents a partially or even seriously distorted view of the realities of pastoral care in the secondary school. Much of the first section of this book is concerned, either explicitly or implicitly, with a critique of that wisdom from a variety of theoretical perspectives — philosophical, historical, and sociological. In the course of that critique it is suggested that pastoral care is a much more complex and problematic activity than the simplistic, child-centred notions of the conventional wisdom would allow. Further, to the extent that the conventional wisdom offers a narrowly prescriptive conception of pastoral care, concerned only with its manifest functions, it will be of limited practical value to chalk-face practitioners struggling with the day-to-day reality of the situations and pressures they actually face. This is not to suggest that the limitations of the conventional wisdom are entirely practical or empirical. It can also be argued that its conceptual and behavioural assumptions are more doubtful than its devotees are commonly prepared to admit. The interesting question remains: why has such a view of pastoral care continued to be so influential in the face of increasingly destructive criticism of the conceptual foundations and growing doubts of the empirical validity of the sort of child-centred approach which it seems to assume? There are a number of possible answers to this question. Firstly it is arguable that such a concept of pastoral care is now essentially employed in the ways in which schools publicly describe and legitimate their activities rather than as a guide to what they actually do. Certainly it must be admitted that its optimistic, child-centred, consensual and unproblematic depiction of school life presents a very attractive picture. Secondly it should also be recognized that schools have lacked realistic alternative perspectives worked out in any detail against which to evaluate their existing caring activities and to guide their practical future endeavours.

Though it was never either our wish or hope to offer a comprehensive alternative orthodoxy of pastoral care in opposition to that of the 'conventional wisdom', we did hope to suggest ways in which practitioners might evaluate their own activities more realistically and perhaps even to make a number of suggestions as to how things might be improved. In this context sections B and C of this book can be viewed as a debate between those who believe that schools have merely failed to develop, or have insufficiently considered the implications of, certain of their pastoral-care practices, and those who hold that in some respects schools have been badly misguided and have seriously misconceived the relationship between care and education on an altogether more fundamental level. Basically, what is at issue is whether

*See Chapter 1.

the shortcomings of existing pastoral-care practices spring from a failure to put into effect existing policies, or whether those policies themselves are located in fundamental misconceptions of the nature of pastoral care itself.

Pastoral care as inadequately developed and insufficiently considered
Perhaps the great majority of those who have reservations about pastoral care and its organization in the secondary school take this kind of view. Although they may trace the 'problems' of institutionalized pastoral care to apparently very different factors (and may accordingly point to very different 'solutions') they do seem to share a belief that in its essentials schools have got things more or less right. Not that existing systems and practices do not have limitations, but these can be corrected by supplementing and strengthening what exists rather than by fundamentally rethinking or reshaping them. Such analysis reveals a number of weaknesses and suggests a variety of ways in which existing practice might be improved. It is worth noting three of the areas of weakness which are discussed. (An analysis of the solutions which are offered is left mainly to the next section.)

(i) Inadequate or inappropriate use of the 'expert'
This argument has various aspects, some of which are not easily reconcilable. Firstly it is held that some of the failings of existing pastoral-care systems are due to the fact that teachers encounter children who have problems which are beyond the training and capacity of the ordinary teacher to deal with. There are at least two unsatisfactory solutions to this kind of situation. Either the teacher tries to deal with such problems unaided (and often does so inadequately) or else he ignores the problem as being beyond his capacity and hopes that it will eventually be resolved of its own accord. Neither kind of response will do. In such a situation what is needed is somebody with appropriate skill, experience and training to whom the teacher may turn (a school counsellor, home–school liaison officer, or the like). In short what is needed is an *expert*. This issue will be considered in greater detail in the next section. What does need emphasizing here is that in such a conception, the expert is seen as strengthening and supplementing existing systems rather than in any fundamental sense replacing or even significantly reshaping them.

(ii) Inadequacies in the role of the tutor and the pastoral head of department
The contribution made by teachers as tutors or as heads of pastoral-care departments is often said to be crucial if pastoral-care systems are to operate effectively. However, for many such teachers statements of this kind represent little more than empty rhetoric or pious moralizing. They are given little guidance as to what is expected of them and face conflicting demands as to what they should be doing. Furthermore

they are often allocated few resources to carry out their responsibilities and given little opportunity to develop the skills and knowledge which they require. However, in spite of all this it can be argued that the correction of such failings would not require drastic change.

(iii) Inadequacies in the role of 'teams' and 'groups'

All too often pastoral care in the secondary school is thought of as being an activity which is almost exclusively carried out by teachers operating as individuals and in isolation from their colleagues. Of course quite often the most effective form of care does take place in a trans-action between an individual teacher and an individual pupil, but there are occasions and types of situations where co-operative activity between groups of teachers might well be more appropriate. There are also situations in which the personal and social needs of children can be more effectively met when they are organized in long-standing, mutually supportive groupings. In this kind of analysis the ideal pastoral-care environment is conceived of as being a team of teachers taking a collective responsibility for a defined group of children in such a way that both individual and corporate care is facilitated. The relatively large size and comparatively loosely organized character of most existing house and year systems, whatever their other advantages, are not conducive to such corporate caring. However, it should be admitted that it is a fine distinction whether the implementation of such schemes would represent an addition to existing practice or a fundamental reworking of it.

Pastoral care as fundamentally misconceived.

Some critiques of pastoral-care practice within the secondary school point to the existence of flaws of a more fundamental kind than those considered above. For example, it has been argued that in some schools a number of radically different, sometimes conflicting, activities are lumped together and made the responsibility of the hard-pressed pastoral care staff. That, furthermore, some of these activities seem to have little to do with care at all except in the most obscure sense and a great deal more to do with control, discipline, containment and administration. In such a context 'caring' becomes something of a residual activity which 'pastoral care' staff perform as and when they can find the time. Another criticism, more fashionable if rather less fundamental than the last, suggests that many of the limitations of existing pastoral-care systems in schools can be traced to a miscon-ceived attempt to separate a school's learning from its caring functions — usually referred to as the 'academic/pastoral split'. This issue is con-sidered in a number of papers and is the unifying theme of Section C. While the papers in this section do share certain ideas they also contain very significant differences of emphasis and advice as to the changes that need to be made.

They all share the view that schools should be primarily concerned with creating opportunities for children to learn worthwhile things in the most effective way possible. If this view is correct it follows that the pastoral endeavour in schools must not be seen in isolation from their essential instructional functions. But in some schools these two endeavours are seen as separate — or worse. For example, elaborate pastoral-care systems which many schools have set up in recent times have absorbed resources which would have been better employed in the creation of more effective teaching strategies, particularly as all too often *the* major function of such systems seems to have been to mask deficiencies in the instructional activities of the school. The logic of such an argument is obvious. Scarce resources of teacher time and energy would be much better employed in improving the learning environment than in swelling the burgeoning bureaucracies of pastoral care which have mushroomed in recent years. In short, the most effective method which schools can use to improve the quality of their care is to devote considerably greater effort to facilitating learning. This account also stresses that the creation of effective learning environments for children is a potent form of caring in itself and one which would diminish the need for other forms of pastoral care.

Other accounts emphasize the learning implications of effective pastoral-care systems. Ideas like 'the pastoral curriculum' (Marland) and 'the social education and careers curriculum' (Watts and Fawcett) draw attention to the demands which various aspects of pastoral care might make on a school's curriculum. Such arguments serve to underline the artificiality of rigid attempts to divorce a school's pastoral from its academic functions. The implications of this kind of analysis are driven home forcefully by Buckley. In the context of a radical critique of 'the pupil—teacher contract' he argues that decisions about the curriculum of schools and their internal organizational structures and processes should be determined by considerations which view 'caring' and 'learning' as two aspects of the same endeavour. This will only be achieved, it is argued, where the same small team of teachers working together ('the teaching team') has the responsibility for making and carrying out both academic and pastoral decisions for and with a particular group of children ('the learning group'). While, on the face of it, such an arrangement bears a superficial resemblance to other kinds of 'team' solution its implementation would entail a change which would be, for most schools, far more radical. Being more radical it would also be more difficult to achieve. However, as with many of the papers, much less attention is given to the ways in which particular 'solutions' might be successfully implemented than to what changes are necessary, and why. We shall return to this point later. For the present let us consider who has the better of the debate as between those who believe that existing practice is essentially sound and those who advocate more fundamental changes. In the final analysis this is a decision which every reader must make for himself. Our hope is that the reader will have been convinced that the sorts of questions which have been raised in the course of this debate will be relevant to his own situation and that they are worth asking. Can the same be said of the sorts of solutions which have been offered?

Programmes for change

Although most of the chapters have been concerned primarily with an analysis and critique of the theoretical foundations, conceptual assumptions and actual practices of pastoral care in the secondary schools of today, as we have seen, they inevitably contain suggestions as to how things might be improved in the future. No two papers suggest exactly the same changes, and they range over a wide area, having among other things structural, conceptual, curricular, role and training implications for schools. Some of the suggestions are peculiar to particular writers, but a surprising number of broadly similar proposals are offered in common even where the analyses from which they are derived are very different. No attempt will be made to pick out every suggestion that has been made; rather, discussion will concentrate on the seven main types of solutions into which the bulk of proposals may be divided.

(i) The need for effective evaluation and analysis of existing practice

Teachers are not especially reluctant to reflect critically and carefully on their activities and attitudes. However, what they are being asked to do by a number of contributors is to take seriously the possibility that much of what they do in schools under the guise of pastoral care may, in fact, not be about care at all. Of course schools may well have to discipline, control, administer and perform many other similar kinds of activity, but are these things really the business of pastoral-care staff? In any case, if these sorts of activity really are the main functions of institutionalized pastoral-care systems, it would be much less confusing if this were made clear. It is hard to see how existing practice can be improved if the reality of that practice is not analysed and acknowledged. If teachers are to improve what they do they must start from what they really are doing rather than what they say they do or even what they would like to be doing. What is needed is for teachers to undertake an analysis of what pastoral care actually means for them and to assess realistically the existing practices of the schools in which they work. Such an analysis must surely precede any serious attempt to improve upon existing practice. This may not be a solutions as such, but it is necessary conditon of any effective solution which does not rely to an inordinate extent on serendipity.

(ii) Ending the pastoral/academic split

A number of contributors believe that no real improvement can be expected from any solution which assumes or continues to perpetuate this disastrous split in the activities of schools. It would probably be true to conclude that discussions on this issue are less concerned with offering particular, positive, practical solutions to the problems that schools face than with denying the validity of proposals and practices which are seen as being based on an unacceptable premise. However, one elaborate solution based on teacher teams and learning 'groups' has been worked out in some detail (by Buckley), as has a proposal for a 'pastoral curriculum' (by Marland). It has also been suggested that schools should reduce their commitment of resources to 'formal pastoral-care systems' and employ the surpluses so created on improving their 'learning systems' (Williamson).

(iii) Pastoral care and the curriculum

If the splitting of a school's academic from its pastoral responsibilities represents an unhealthy development, what are the alternatives? Two seem obvious: firstly, to create structures and develop roles in which teachers combine an academic with a pastoral responsibility; secondly, as a number of papers suggest, to keep the pastoral need in mind when making decisions hitherto considered to be essentially academic in character. In particular it is important to be clear about the curriculum implications of effective pastoral care. It is in this context that suggestions about a 'social education and careers curriculum', and rather more radically a 'pastoral curriculum', should be considered. Both seek to reunite caring and learning, and both do so by stressing the learning implications of effective care as a problem for curriculum planning.

(iv) Team and group solutions

The development of new kinds of teams of teachers and team approaches on the one hand (see Buckley, Marland, Craft) and of groups of children and group approaches on the other (see Button, Hamblin) is probably the category of solution that would command the most widespread support among our contributors. However, the very fact that both those who see a need for dramatic change in the process and organization of pastoral care and those who would be content with more marginal innovations can appeal to what is apparently the same kind of solution, suggests that it must be capable of widely differing interpretations. The sheer variety of suggestions and their very different assumptions about the efficacy of existing school practice might make the discussion especially relevant to teachers who wish to re-examine their own corporate activities and who are uncertain as to how they might proceed.

(v) Developing the role of the Tutor and of senior pastoral-care staff

That pastoral-care staff are often given far too much to do and too little time and support to do it with is a common enough complaint among such teachers. So, sadly, is the claim that being a tutor seems to mean very little indeed even when a great deal of time is allocated to it. However, limitations of time and resources and lack of adequate guidance as to what is expected of them as not the only problems of role which pastoral-care teachers face. They are too often starved of information and by-passed by more senior staff. They are, too, rarely given the opportunity, still less the encouragement, to develop greater levels of expertise in appropriate skills, for example those of guidance and counselling. Among other things, proposed solutions point to the need to clarify and strengthen the position of pastoral-care staff, the need to encourage such staff to develop necessary skills, and perhaps most of all the need to distinguish clearly and realistically what should and what should not be expected of them. In this context one revealing indication of the lack of seriousness with which the role of pastoral-care staff is taken is the small part which training for 'tutorship' plays in most initial teacher-training courses and the paucity of in-service courses concerned specifically with this aspect of the teacher's role.

(vi) Developing the role of the expert

A number of the proposals (see Watts and Fawcett, Milner, Craft) are concerned with the role of the expert in the pastoral-care context. The term 'expert' is usually taken to mean someone who is acknowledged as having special skills, knowledge and experience which have been gained as a result of an appropriate form of professional training. The contribution of a variety of different kinds of 'experts' are canvassed, ranging from school counsellors and home—school liaison officers to be located within the school to social workers and education welfare officers not located in the school but centring upon it. The sort of role envisaged for such experts varies from being an integral part of the pastoral-care system to being an appendage or supplement to it. Perhaps the key problem with regard to the use of the expert within the school lies in his relationship with 'non-expert' pastoral-care practitioners. Specifically, how does one make the optimum use of the very few experts located in schools when the bulk of pastoral-care activity for the foreseeable future is likely to remain in the hands of a very much larger number of non-experts? Given this situation, let us consider two possible roles for the expert. The first is widely canvassed and is the basis of much existing practice. In this, the expert is perceived as a resource upon whom teachers may call when they encounter problems which are beyond their abilities to deal with — essentially as a crisis agent of the last resort and as such outside the 'normal' pastoral-care system. The second, though less widely canvassed, is one which many experts find attractive. It is based on an argument about how a few experts can have the maximum possible beneficial effect on a school's pastoral-care system considered as a whole. Given that there are few experts and many non-expert staff it could be that the greatest contribution the former can make is to assist the latter to raise their level of awareness and skill rather than to exclusively employ their expertise to contain the most intractable of a school's care problems. It is possible that teachers will take a great deal of convincing before they accept this training role as a proper or even necessary activity for the expert.

(vii) Pastoral care and the welfare network

The caring activities of schools do not take place in a vacuum. As Craft shows, they are at the focus of a number of welfare networks based in and around the school. To be effective such networks need to be co-ordinated as a whole and in particular integrated with the pastoral-care systems of schools. In fact it can be argued that many of the limitations of existing pastoral-care systems *within* schools can also be traced to inadequacies of co-ordination and articulation. Given this specification of 'the problem' a number of possible answers are suggested. Problems of co-ordination can, at least in part, be overcome by the appointment of a clearly designed co-ordinator or co-ordinators. Craft suggests that this would be an appropriate role for school counsellors to peform, though there are indications that this kind of solution has by no means always been all that successful in practice. If articulation of the welfare effort, both in and around the school, is to be improved, suitable teams, involving both internal and external care agents, will need to be set up and clear channels of communication and referral will need to be established between groups responsible for various aspects of the welfare effort.

Up to this point we have attempted to offer a limited analysis of the sorts of issues which contributors have raised and to summarize the main kinds of improvements which they suggest. It remains only for us to point to some issues which should perhaps have received rather more attention than they have.

Some Grey Areas

Pastoral care and the 'needs' of children

Many of the papers (and much of the literature on pastoral care) are based explicitly or implicitly on ideas about the needs of children. However, considering how crucial the notion of 'need' is to the concept of 'education' in general and to that of 'pastoral care' in particular, it is curious that it has not been analysed at greater length. To some extent this omission can be explained by the hegemony which the 'child-centred' view has established over public accounts of what education should be. We are ourselves (as clearly also are most of our contributors) broadly sympathetic to that view. However we also feel, along with writers like Bernstein, Dearden, Peters,[1] Sharpe and Green[2] and White,[3] that it might be timely, even essential, to take another and rather more critical look at child-centred ideologies and to clarify what assumptions about 'child development', 'learning' and 'learning processes' they make. It would also be timely to attempt to establish the extent to which 'child-centred' ideologies do actually inform the activities of teachers, as opposed to offering a handy rhetoric with which to justify their practices — a point which the papers in Section D make clear.

There is one further omission in the general literature of pastoral care. Given that the needs of children are seen as a crucial factor both in justifying the organization for pastoral care and in determining its character, it is curious how little direct attempt has been made to get at the ways in which children perceive their own educational and welfare needs. We do know of people who have begun to look at how children perceive and construct ideas about their welfare needs (for example John Bazalgette of the Grubb Institute[4]), but little has, as yet, been published on this subject. In so far as pastoral care is said to be based on the needs of children it is, as yet, based almost entirely on the ways in which teachers perceive those needs. Perhaps such teacher perception will (even should) always be the determining influence in making decisions about how the needs of children should be met, but surely the views of children should also be considered.

The problem of organizational change

It is the *raison d'être* of this book that existing practices can and should be improved, and as we have seen, numerous solutions to the problem of improving those practices are advanced. Some of these 'solutions' would have far-reaching consequences for the ways in which schools operate — others are rather more modest in scale. Whether modest or fundamental, these would necessitate changes in existing processes, organizational patterns and, in some cases, even major changes in attitudes among teachers. While the proposals are worked out in some detail, much less attention is devoted to the problem of how the changes which they necessitate can be successfully accomplished. It is possible that the difficulties of achieving successful organizational change have been underestimated. In particular the sort of resistance such solutions may encounter from teachers and others who may have a strong commitment to existing practice must be recognized. To illustrate the problems likely to be encountered let us consider the sort of resistance which the two most widely canvassed 'solutions' might meet.

(a) Team approaches

In advocating new kinds of teams and team strategies, insufficient attention is given to the opposition such proposals are likely to provoke from those who perceive themselves as members of existing 'teams' (e.g. House staff). For the more senior members of such teams the changes may involve a loss of status, and for the more junior they will necessitate changes in work patterns to which they have become accustomed and in which they will suddenly discover virtues they had been unaware of in the past. Furthermore, many team approaches also appear to ignore the essentially hierarchic nature of most schools and the attachment of many teachers to existing patterns of authority and responsibility. Team solutions seem to assume that teachers will easily be able to set aside status considerations and act as groups of equals, even though the bureaucratic and hierarchic patterns in which they normally work ensure and emphasize that they are not equal. Of course, just because labour is stratified and differentiated this does not necessarily mean that co-operation is impossible between individuals at different levels. Neither, however, should it be assumed that to have established the 'need' for such co-operation is to have ensured that it will occur.

(b) Curriculum approaches
Some of the proposals entail new demands upon, or even whole new ways of looking at, the school curriculum. However logical and plausible are ideas like the 'pastoral' or the 'careers' curriculum, their implementation will involve, in many schools, difficult negotiations with hostile and well-entrenched groups who (not unreasonably) regard such proposals as damaging to their interests. In short, such curriculum proposals, whatever their other merits, appear to underestimate or even ignore the powers and motives of existing subject and other groups to protect 'their' area of the curriculum. We would not wish to conclude that just because organizational change is difficult to achieve it should not be attempted; rather, we would wish to emphasize that successful innovation has to be carefully prepared and planned for. Too many proposals for change seem to make unwarranted assumptions about the malleability of human beings, or seem to rely to an inordinate extent on the disinterestedness and general good will of teachers.

Social reality, the school and pastoral care
Lastly, it is all too easy to forget or ignore the social reality of the situation in which schools are located. Issues concerned with the hierarchic relationship of teachers to their pupils and of schools to the children in their care have to be seen as a reality. Talk about pastoral care, personal guidance and the like has to be seen in the context of schools as purveyors of packages of knowledge that lead to particular outcomes in a society which is prestructured and which is very largely beyond the ability of schools to affect. Some things are beyond the powers of schools to control and, as such, represent limitations and constraints on what schools can do. For example, talk of a pastoral curriculum will seem for some people a non-starter because of the demands of the academic curriculum, buttressed by the imperatives of public examinations, underwritten by the requirements of society for a specified kind of 'acceptable' selection process.

Furthermore, just as too many 'solutions' ignore the realities of power in the individual school, so also do they give too little consideration to similar realities in the society as a whole. In an important sense things happen because they are in the interests of groups and individuals and because such groups have the power to ensure that what they want does come about. We might all be on a fool's errand in trying to improve what happens in schools if at some stage we do not take account of such considerations.

A final thought

Much of what is written in this book is critical of aspects of what goes on under the guise of 'pastoral care' in schools. However, the extent and character of such criticism should not be misunderstood or exaggerated. No one who knows about what schools were like a hundred, or even fifty years ago, can fail to notice the great changes for the better which have taken place. Even in the recent past, rigid discipline backed by the regular resort to punishment (much of it physical) reflected an attitude among teachers in particular and society in general that the personal and welfare needs of children were no part of the responsibility of schools, or if they were, that such needs were seen as those of savages to be civilized. It is, in short, hard to believe that schools have not become more caring, humane and convivial places than they were. Part, at least, of the credit for such a beneficial change must surely be due to the emphasis which schools have given to pastoral care. If the exact meaning of the term continues to be elusive, and if its special contribution to improving the lot of children remains somewhat obscure, there seems little reason to doubt that without pastoral care schools would be grimmer and unhappier places. However, there also seems little reason to doubt that vestiges of those unhappier times continue to exist in some schools, and that even schools with effective pastoral-care systems and practices can be improved.

Our schools have much we can be proud of. But they are by no means perfect. In pastoral care, as in other facets of schooling, the rhetoric of the Great Debate and the fetish of fashion must be replaced with critical and reasoned analyses of existing strengths and weaknesses.

References

1 in R. S. Peters (ed.), *Perspectives on Plowden* (Routledge & Kegan Paul, London, 1969).
2 op. cit.
3 J. P. White, *Towards a Compulsory Curriculum* (Routledge & Kegan Paul, London, 1973).
4 J. Bazalgette, 'The Pupil, The Tutor and the School', paper presented to Organization in Schools Course on Pastoral Care, Churchill College, Cambridge, July 1978.

Suggested reading

The definitive statement on Pastoral Care is M. Marland, *Pastoral Care*, (Heinemann, 1974) in the Heinemann Organization in Schools Series. Two other volumes in this series provide a good starting point for discussion and further reading. They are: K. Blackburn, *The Tutor* (1975), and P. E. Daunt, *Comprehensive Values* (1975).

For connections between care in schools and other welfare institutions, see: M. Craft, J. Raynor, and L. Cohen, (eds.), *Linking Home and School* (3rd edition, Harper and Row, 1980).

A sound programme for the systematic planning of pastoral care in schools is provided in: D. Hamblin, *The Teacher and Pastoral Care* (Blackwell, 1978). The companion volume *The Teacher and Counselling* (Blackwell, 1974), though more specialized, is also to be recommended. For an interesting approach to working with small groups, see L. Button, *Developmental Group Work with Adolescents* (Hodder and Stoughton Unibooks, 1974). Numerous articles on many aspects of guidance and counselling can be found in the *British Journal of Guidance and Counselling*, edited by P. P. Daws, D. H. Hamblin, B. Hopson and A. G. Watts. For a comprehensive account of guidance and counselling in education in the light of the evolution of attitudes to social welfare, see P. M. Hughes, *Guidance and Counselling in Schools* (Pergamon, 1971).

Some connections between pastoral care and the organization of schooling are investigated in E. Richardson, *The Teacher, The School and the Task of Management* (Heinemann, 1973), and a variety of pastoral structures are described and assessed in: B. M. Moore, *Guidance in Comprehensive Schools* (NFER, Slough, 1970).

For those especially interested in careers guidance, see J. Hayes and B. Hopson, *Careers Guidance: The Role of the School in Vocational Development*, (Heinemann, 1971).

Some recent papers on various aspects of pastoral care are to be found in H. J. Blackham (ed.), *Education for Personal Autonomy*, (Bedford Square Press, 1978).

Notes on Contributors

Ron Best is Senior Lecturer in Education and a member of the Pastoral Care Research Unit, Faculty of Education, Arts and Humanities, Chelmer Institute of Higher Education. He is joint author of several articles on pastoral care.

Keith Blackburn is Deputy Head of Altwood School, Maidenhead, and author of *The Tutor* (Heinemann, London, 1974).

John Buckley is Deputy Director of the North West Educational Management Centre and was formerly Head of Castle Manor School, Suffolk.

Leslie Button is Senior Lecturer at the University College of Swansea, where he leads the Action Research Project into Developmental Group Work in Schools. His published works include *Developmental Group Work with Adolescents* (London U.P., 1975) and *Discovery and Experience* (Oxford U.P., 1969/70).

Peter Corbishley is a Research Officer at the London University Institute of Education. His research findings are reported in *Mixed Ability Teaching in the Secondary School* (edited by B. Davies and R. Cave, Ward Lock, London, 1977).

Maurice Craft is Professor and Head of the Department of Advanced Studies in Education at Goldsmiths' College, University of London. He has contributed articles to books on Careers Guidance, Education, and Social Work, and is editor of *Guidance and Counselling in British Schools* (Arnold, 1974) and *Linking Home and School* (Harper and Row, London, 3rd Edition, 1980). From 1970 to 1972 he was a Consultant to Devon County Council on guidance and counselling in comprehensive schools.

Sean Dooley is Senior Lecturer in the Philosophy of Education in the Faculty of Education, Arts and Humanities, Chelmer Institute of Higher Education.

John Evans is engaged on research into Mixed-Ability Teaching for His Ph.D. at London University Institute of Education.

Beryl Fawcett is a Senior Fellow of the National Institute for Careers Education and Counselling at Cambridge.

Douglas Hamblin is Senior Lecturer in the Department of Education, University College of Swansea, where he is responsible for advanced courses in Pastoral Care, Guidance and Counselling. He has published numerous articles and is the author of *The Teacher and Counselling*

Blackwell, Oxford, 1974) and *The Teacher and Pastoral Care* (Blackwell, 1978).

Patrick Hughes is Senior Lecturer in Education at the University of Reading, where he is in charge of training courses for Guidance personnel and Careers Officers. He is the author of *Guidance and Counselling in Schools: A Reponse to Change* (Pergamon, Oxford, 1971).

Colin Jarvis is Principal Lecturer in Education and a member of the Pastoral Care Research Unit, Faculty of Education, Arts and Humanities, Chelmer Institute of Higher Education. He is joint author of several articles on pastoral care.

Michael Marland is Headmaster of North Westminster Area Community School and General Editor of the Heinemann Organization in Schools Series. He is the author of numerous books including *Language Across the Curriculum* (Heinemann, London, 1977), *Pastoral Care* (Heinemann, London, 1974) and *The Craft of the Classroom* Heinemann, London, 1975).

Patricia Milner is tutor to Counselling courses at South West London College. She is the author of *Counselling in Education* (Dent, London, 1974).

Diane Oddy is Research Assistant in the Pastoral Care Research Unit, Faculty of Education, Arts and Humanities, Chelmer Institute of Higher Education.

Peter Ribbins is a Lecturer in the Department of Social and Administrative Studies in Education, University of Birmingham, and an associate member of the Pastoral Care Research Unit, Chelmer Institute of Higher Education. He is joint author of several publications on pastoral care and the organization of schooling.

H. J. F. Taylor is Area Educational Psychologist in Hertfordshire County Psychological Service. He is the author of *School Counselling* (Macmillan, London, 1971).

Mike Taylor is Tutor to the Essex County Language and Reading Centre at Chelmer Institute of Higher Education.

A. G. Watts is a Senior Fellow and Executive Director of the National Institute for Careers Education and Counselling. He is author of *Diversity and Choice in Higher Education* (Routledge and Kegan Paul, London, 1972) and *Schools, Careers and Community* (with Bill Law, Church Information Office, 1977), and an Editor of the *British Journal of Guidance and Counselling*.

Derek Williamson is a Housemaster at Highgate Wood School in the London Borough of Haringey.

Index

able child, 172, 173
academic/pastoral: division, 58, 67,
    82, 107, 126–7, 149–50, 182,
    190, 209, 214, 216, 219, 274–5,
    277; integration, x, 108, 149–50,
    155–6, 189, 192–3, 202–203,
    220, 258, 277
action research, 64, 67, 75, 76
Adelman, C., 93
administration, 167, 262–5, 274
adolescence, 38, 39, 66–7, 70, 75,
    101, 185, 202, 203, 228, 241
'The advantages of bureaucracy'
    (Musgrove), 175
aggression, 81, 84, 97–9, 100–1
Albemarle Report, 39
alienation, 11, 13, 78
Assessment of Performance Unit, x
Association of Directors of Social
    Services, 36, 42
Australia, 46
authority, 19–21, 71, 77, 99, 100,
    125, 138, 186, 195, 202, 216, 218
autonomy: personal, 3, 18, 19, 22–3,
    24, 27, 30, 58, 102, 107, 125;
    of school, ix, x, xi–xii
Avon Teachers' Centre, 169

Bandura, A., 101
Barnes, D., 241
Baron, R., 92
Bazalgette, J., 163, 280
Becker, H.S., 13
behaviour modification, 81, 82–4,
    92–3, 101, 103, 140–2
Bennett, N., x
Bennett, S.J., xii, 7
Bernstein, B., 177, 238, 279
Best, R.E., 30, 46
Blackburn, K., 53
Blackburn Curriculum Development
    Centre, 169
Blau, P.M., 175
Bowlby, J., 136
Boyson, Rhodes, 201

British Association for Counselling, 26
British Association of Social Workers
    (BASW), 35, 42, 43
Britton, J., 226, 234
Broadbent, D.E., 142
Brophy, J., 90
Broughton High School, 159
Buber, M., 184
Buckley, J., 275
Bullock Report, x, 225
bullying, 97
bureaucracy, 174–6, 220, 260–1
Button, L., 57, 60, 114, 165, 169
buzz-group discussion, 63, 67

Callaghan, James, ix, x
Campbell, R., 121–2
careers: adviser, 7, 8, 127; conventions,
    127; curriculum, 277, 281; depart-
    ment, 113, 115–16, 188; education,
    25, 54, 55, 108–17, 118–19, 151–
    2, 159–60, 163, 165, 166, 201, 220,
    275; guidance, 57, 108, 109, 110,
    151–2, 202; officer, 35, 39, 40, 41,
    44, 45, 109, 116, 127; teachers, 8,
    34, 35, 39, 40, 41, 43, 57, 109,
    113–14, 116, 123, 129, 220
Careers Research and Advisory Centre,
    179
Careers Service, 29, 109, 114; see also
    Youth Employment Service
case conferences, 44, 45, 129
casework model, 72–4, 165–6
Cave, R.G., xi, 33
CSE, ix–x, 13, 113, 164, 180
Chance, J., 85, 94
Cheshire, 35
chief education officers, 34
Children in Distress, 57
child-centred: education, 3, 27–8, 58,
    259–60; perspective, 109–10, 139,
    259, 272, 279–80
child guidance clinic, 28, 33, 124
child guidance service, 34, 35, 41, 44,
    45, 129